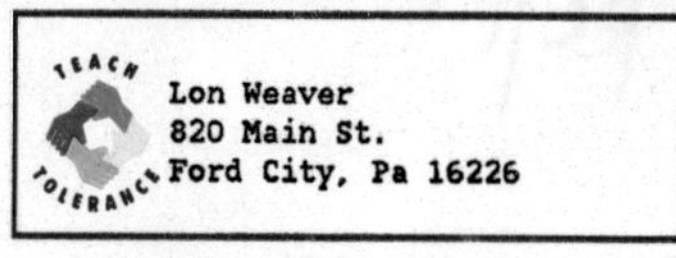
TEACH
TOLERANCE
Lon Weaver
820 Main St.
Ford City, Pa 16226

D1562717

THE RELIGION OF INDIA

MAX WEBER

THE RELIGION OF INDIA

THE SOCIOLOGY OF HINDUISM AND BUDDHISM

TRANSLATED AND EDITED BY

HANS H. GERTH AND DON MARTINDALE

Munshiram Manoharlal
Publishers Pvt Ltd

ISBN 81-215-0571-2
This edition 1996
Originally published in 1958 by The Free Press

Printed and published by Munshiram Manoharlal Publishers Pvt. Ltd.,
Post Box 5715, 54 Rani Jhansi Road, New Delhi 110 055.

PREFATORY NOTE

Max Weber's early twentieth-century study of the religions and civilization of India is a great pioneering adventure in the sociology of ancient India. Weber's insight and analysis—especially his application of the sociological perspective to the work of classical Indologists and the religious texts available to him—were to add much to the store of the social scientist. Later, historians and archaeologists were to confirm a surprising number of Weber's theories.

The central concern of this and other of Weber's studies of countries we today describe as "developing" was with the obstacles to industrialization and modernization. Weber anticipated by several decades a problem that has come to occupy the post-World War II world. Why had these countries failed to display the full consequences of those rationalizing tendencies which, to Weber's mind, had so powerful an affinity with the scientific-technical transformation of the West? He isolated religious institutions and the key social strata which mediate them to the wider society as crucial for the original formation of social-psychological orientations to the practical concerns of life and, hence, for receptivity or resistance to industrialization.

H.H.G.
D.M.

CONTENTS

CONTENTS

PART I

THE HINDU SOCIAL SYSTEM

CHAPTER I
INDIA AND HINDUISM

1. The General Place of Hinduism[1]

INDIA, in contrast to China, has been, and remains, a land of villages and of the most inviolable organization by birth. But at the same time it was a land of trade, foreign, particularly with the Occident, as well as domestic. Trade and credit usury appeared in India from ancient Babylonian times. In the northwest Indian commerce was under constant perceptible Hellenic influence. At an early period the Jews settled in the South. Zarathustrians from Persia immigrated to the Northwest, constituting a stratum wholly devoted to wholesale trade. Into this situation came the influence of Islam and the rationalistic enlightenment of the great mogul Akbar. Under the great moguls, and also repeatedly before them, all or almost all of India for generations was formed into one political unit. Such periods of unity were interrupted, however, by long periods of disintegration with the country divided into numerous, constantly warring political dominions.

Princely methods of warfare, politics, and finance were rationalized, made subject to literary and, in the case of politics, even quite Machiavellian theorizing. Knightly combat and the disciplined army equipped by the prince appeared. While, as is occasionally maintained, use of artillery did not develop here for the first time, it appeared early. State creditors, tax farming, state contracting, trade and communication monopolies, etc., developed in the fashion characteristic of occidental patrimonial logic. For centuries urban development in India paralleled that of the Occident at many points. The contemporary rational number system, the technical basis of all "calculability," is of Indian origin. The "positional" number system has existed for an undetermined time. The zero was invented and used sometime after the fifth or sixth century A.D. Arithmetic and algebra are considered to have been independently developed in India. For negative magnitudes the term "debts" (Ksaya) was used. In contrast to the Chinese, the Indians cultivated rational science (including mathematics and grammar). They developed numerous philosophic schools and religious sects of almost all possible sociological types. For the most part the schools and sects developed out of the basic need for rational consistency which was expressed in the most varied spheres of life. For long periods tolerance toward religious and philosophic doctrines was almost absolute; at least it was infinitely greater than anywhere in the Occident until most recent times.

Indian justice developed numerous forms which could have served capitalistic purposes as easily and well as corresponding institutions in our own medieval law. The autonomy of the merchant stratum in law-making was at least equivalent to that of our own medieval merchants. Indian handicrafts and occupational specialization were highly developed. From the standpoint of possible capitalistic development, the acquisitiveness of Indians of all strata left little to be desired and nowhere is to be found so little antichrematism and such high evaluation of wealth. Yet modern capitalism did not develop indigenously before or during the English rule. It was taken over as a finished artifact without autonomous beginnings. Here we shall inquire as to the manner in which Indian religion, as one factor among many, may have prevented capitalistic development (in the occidental sense).

The national form of Indian religion is Hinduism. The term "Hindu" was first used under the foreign domination of the Mohammedans to mean unconverted native Indians. Only in recent literature have the Indians themselves begun to designate their religious affiliation as Hinduism. It is the official designation of the English census for the religious complex also described in Germany as "Brahmanism." The term "Brahmanism" refers to the fact that a definite type of priest, the Brahman, was the leader of the religion. It is known that the Brahmans constituted a caste and that, in general, the institution of the castes—a system of particularly rigid and exclusive hereditary estates—played and continue to play a role in the social life of India.

Also, the names of the four main castes of classical Indian learning as represented in the *Laws of Manu* are known: Brahmans (priest); Kshatriyas (knights); Vaishyas (free commoners); Shudras (serfs).*

The general public is quite unfamiliar with the details of the castes with the possible exception of vague ideas about the transmigration of souls. These ideas are not false, they merely require clarification in terms of the abundant sources and literature.

Under the heading "religion" the tables of the *Census of India* for 1911 list, in round numbers, 217½ million people as "Hindus," i.e., 69.39 per cent of the population. Among the imported faiths there are: Mussulmen (66-2/3 million or 21.26 per cent); Christians, Jews, Zoroastrians, and "Animists" (10.29 million or 3.28 per cent). The following non-Hindu religions are listed as native to India: Sikhs[2] (around three million or 0.86 per cent); Jains (1.2 million or 0.40 per cent); Buddhists (10.7 million or 3.42 per cent). However, all but a third of a million of the Buddhists reside in Burma (which since early times was almost nine-tenths Buddhistic); the remainder live in the bordering territories of Tibet (hence not on classically Indian but Mongolian territory), partly in outlying Indian territories, partly in central Asia.

To be sure, the census figures by decades cannot be compared without reservations. The percentage of Hindus since 1881 decreased from 74.32 per cent to 69.39 per cent; Islam rose from 19.74 per cent to 21.22 per cent; Christians, from 0.73 per cent to 1.24 per cent; and, finally, Animists, from 2.59 per cent to 3.28 per cent. This last figure, and also part of the percentage shifts, rests not only upon the considerable numbers of children of the uncultured animistic tribes but to a large extent upon differences in census enumeration. A further small part of the proportional decrease of Hindus is to be accounted for by the extension of the census to Burma, which resulted in a considerable increase in counted Buddhists. For the rest, the relative decline of the Hindu is partially to be attributed to differential birth and mortality rates. The relatively low social status and correspondingly low standard of living of the Hindu masses has, to some extent, religious causes. Child marriage, female infanti-

* Translator's note: The spelling of caste names follows Jawaharlal Nehru's *The Discovery of India* (New York: John Day, 1946).

cide, the prohibition of the remarriage of widows, led to the reduction in the number of children and the high mortality of women of the upper castes; nutritional difficulties due to food taboos during bad harvest have been important among the lower strata.

Another small part of the decrease of Hindus is to be ascribed to single conversions to Islamism and Christianity, the converts being mainly from the lower castes for the betterment of their social situation. Formal conversions to Hinduism do not officially exist; according to the theory of Hinduism, they are impossible. This leads us forthwith to a consideration of important peculiarities of Hinduism.

A "sect" in the sociological sense of the word is an exclusive association of religious virtuosos or of especially qualified religious persons, recruited through individual admission after establishment of qualification. By contrast a "church," as a universalistic establishment for the salvation of the masses raises the claim, like the "state," that everyone, at least each child of a member, must belong by birth. It demands sacramental acts and, possibly, proof of acquaintance with its holy learning as a precondition of its membership rights, but establishes as a duty the observance of the sacraments and the discharge of those obligations which are a condition of active membership rights. The consequence of this is that when the church reaches its full development and has power, it coerces opponents to conform according to the principle *coge intrare*. The individual is normally "born" into the church, single conversions and admissions occurring only until the time the church has attained its principal goal--the unification of all men in the universal church. (Hinduism has some of the properties of a church conjoined to sect-like exclusiveness.)

One belongs to a strictly birth-religion, like Hinduism, merely by being born to Hindu parents. However, Hinduism is "exclusive" in the sense that in no other way can the individual enter its community, at least the circle of those considered fully qualified religiously. Hinduism does not wish to encompass mankind. No matter what his belief or way of life, anyone not born a Hindu remains an outsider, a barbarian to whom the sacred values of Hinduism are in principle denied.

Like most generalizations about Hinduism this is true only with qualifications. Quite apart from the sporadic relaxation of the exclusiveness of the upper castes, as reported by the Census, there were important processes in some of the lower castes. Some of these castes not only recruit excommunicated former members of other castes but occasionally do so quite indiscriminately. For example, the impure caste of the Bhangi of Bombay Province is partially made up of *outcastes* from higher castes. However, the Bhangi of the "United Provinces" were recruited by admitting voluntary applicants, and hence were often identified, as Blunt does in the Census Report of 1911, with the Tshandala, the lowest unclean caste of the ancient law books. Several other castes, in principle, allow individuals to affiliate.

A great number of outcastes belong to the Vaishnabs, a sect-caste which to this day offers a haven to rebels against Brahmanical rule. Furthermore, imperfectly Hinduized tribes and tribal castes burdened with residues of tribal descent often receive individual affiliates. Most lenient are the very low-ranking pariah tribes of mat- and basket-weavers.

In general, the more completely Hinduized in the classical pattern, the more exclusive the caste. And genuine old Hindu castes hold that individual affiliation with a caste is impossible. Hence Ketkar[3] goes too far in constructing the facts above into the generalization that Hinduism "leaves it" to the various castes whether or not to accept strangers and that no caste can lay down the law for another. Formally, each caste formulates its own principles, but in a typical Hindu caste the affiliating individual would forego all sib ties. In fact, rules, prerequisites, and forms of individual recruitment are nonexistent. Where individual affiliation takes place it is indicative of an absence rather than the existence of rules. In the systematic Hinduization of a region, at least according to ancient theory, the Hinduized barbarians could at best join the lowliest unclean caste of the Tshandala.

Occasionally, for instance in the *Manu-Bhashya,* II, 23, the question is raised as to when a conquered barbarian territory becomes suitable for sacrifice, i.e., "ritually pure"; the answer given is that it is ritually pure only when the king establishes the four castes and reduces the barbarians to Tshandala. Obviously, the other castes (including Shudra castes) can develop in a given place only by the immigration of Hindus of those castes. Vanamali Chakravanti[4] maintains that the numerous Tshandala of the South Eastern regions originated from such immigration. In any case the barbarian must, as it were, work up from the ranks (*von der Pike auf*) and can advance only by way of metempsychosis. That is not to say that the barbarian will always be considered socially inferior to the accepted impure caste. His social status depends upon his style of life.

The Census Report of 1901 states that tribes outside the caste system enjoy greater esteem than do the lower castes of impure village artisans precisely because they are not "conquered" subjects. If they were to affiliate with castes they would be received by the pure castes. This is obviously similar to the relative social estimation of Indians and Negroes in the United States. The higher esteem of the Indians is in the last analysis due to the fact that "they didn't submit to slavery." Therefore the American gentleman permits intermarriage and commensalism with Indians but never with Negroes. In areas where the caste system has not been shattered, a non-Hindu, a European, for instance, can find only members of impure castes for domestic service; the domestic servant of the ritually pure Hindu castes without exception belongs to and must belong to pure castes.

Thus, with some qualifications the principle holds that anyone not born a Hindu remains an outsider. And although, as has been indicated, there are "open-door castes" they are unclean. Ecclesiastical institutions of universal grace employ excommunication for certain sacreligious offences, but only to the extent that the banned person foregoes churchly means of grace while remaining subject to ecclesiastical jurisdiction and sanction.

Hinduism, however, is exclusive—like a sect. For certain religious offences a person is forever excluded from the community. A Brahman caste, for instance, cancelled the re-admission of members after their forced conversion to Islamism. It did this despite their absolution by penance and purification when it became known that the applicants had been compelled to eat beef.

This case is comparable to that of the heroic sects of early Christendom, including the Montanists, who (because of Matthew, 10, 33), in contrast to the corporate church organization, deemed absolutely irreparable the participation of Christians in emperor worship. It was, for this very reason, that the Romans had made emperor worship compulsory during the time of the Diocletian persecutions.

Insofar as individual recruitment was possible, at least the expelled Brahmans might have found a haven among one of the unclean castes of beef-eaters. But a man who has knowingly killed a cow could not possibly be accepted as a fellow-Hindu. To put it more precisely: the castes suspected, with good reason, of coöperating in cattle poisoning practices (especially the currier castes) are an abomination for every Hindu, even though these castes are officially correct.

2. *Diffusion Patterns of Hinduism*

HINDU propaganda in the grand manner occurred in the past. It is still of considerable importance. In the course of about eight hundred years the present Hindu system has spread from a small region in Northern India to an area comprising over 200 million people. This missionary propagation was accomplished in opposition to "animistic" folk belief and in conflict with highly developed salvation religions. The system is still expanding from census to census.

Ordinarily, the propagation of Hinduism occurs in approximately the following way. The ruling stratum of an "animistic" tribal territory begins to imitate specific Hindu customs in something like the following order: abstention from meat, particularly beef; the absolute refusal to butcher cows; total abstinence from intoxicating drinks. To these certain other specific purification practices of good Hindu castes may be added. The ruling stratum gives up marriage practices that may deviate from Hindu custom and organizes itself into exogamous sibs, forbidding the marriage of their daughters to men of socially inferior strata. The Brahmans, by the way, are often very tolerant with regard to marital customs. During the Hinduization of many a small region, for instance, existing matrilineal lines were left in peace. Moreover, some castes maintaining high standards have survivals of totemic organization, as will be shown. The same tolerance is shown for alcohol and food other than beef. In this respect individual members of genteel castes such as the Vishnuites and the Shivaists often differ more markedly than do the castes. The assumption of additional Hindu customs follows rapidly: restrictions are placed upon contact and table community; widows are forced into celibacy; daughters are given into marriage before puberty without being asked; the dead are cremated rather than buried; ancestral death sacrifices (*sraddha*) are arranged; and native deities are rebaptized with the names of Hindu gods and goddesses. Finally, tribal priests are eliminated and some Brahman is requested to provide and take charge of ritual concerns and thereby also to convince himself and provide testimony to the fact that they—the rulers of the tribe—were of ancient, only temporarily forgotten, knightly (Kshatriya) blood. Or, under favorable circumstances, the tribal priests borrow the Brahman's way of life, acquire some knowledge of the Vedas, and maintain that they are themselves Brahmans of some special Veda school and members of an ancient well-known Brahman sib (*gotra*) going back to such and such sage (*Rishi*). Presumably it had only been forgotten that they had immigrated from an ancient Hindu region centuries ago. Now they seek to establish relations with recognized Indian Brahmans.

It is not always easy to find true Brahmans ready to accept such spurious propositions, and neither in the past nor nowadays would a high-caste Brahman accept them. However, numerous Brahman subcastes were and are still to be found. Some of recognized Brahman-quality are considered socially degraded because they serve lower castes, perhaps meat-eaters and wine-drinkers. They were and are ready to accept such propositions. Pedigree, and the required origin-myth, possibly reaching back to epic or pre-epic times, are borrowed or simply invented, documented, and witnessed, permitting the claim to the rank of Rajput (royal relationship, the present-day term for Kshatriya).

Fleet[5] proved the frequent falsification of princely pedigrees in Southern India as early as the ninth century. Surviving irregularities in conduct are then eliminated, and a scanty Vedic education is required of the knights and of the stratum to be considered twice-born free men (Vaishyas). Assimilation is completed with the ceremony of girdling and binding themselves with holy ties. The ritual rights and duties of the various occupations are regulated in Hindu manner.

This accomplished, the ruling stratum seeks social intercourse on equal footing with equivalent strata in ancient Hindu territory. When possible they seek to attain intermarriage and commensalism with its Rajput sibs, acceptance of food cooked in water from Brahmans, admission of their own Brahmans to old Brahmanical schools and cloisters. But this is extremely difficult and as a rule does not initially succeed. A true, or today presumably true, Brahman or Rajput will listen sympathetically and with good humor to the origin legend of such an upstart Rajput stratum, if, for example, an interested European relates it. No true Brahman or Rajput would dream of treating the new fellows as his peers.

Alas, time and wealth make a difference. Large doweries to Rajputs who marry their daughters, and other means of exerting social pressure, are employed and there comes a time—today often relatively quickly—when the manner of origin is forgotten and social acceptance is completed. A certain residue of rank degradation usually remains the lasting burden of the parvenu.

There, in substance, is the typical way in which Hinduism has been extensively propagated in new territories since its full development.

This extensive propaganda was paralleled by an intensive propaganda which followed similar principles wherever Hinduism held sway.

As a social phenomenon "guest peoples"* existed everywhere within the Hindu community. They are to be found to this day. Contemporary remnants still evident among us are the gypsies, a typical ancient Indian guest people which, in contrast to others, has wandered outside of India. In earlier times similar phenomena occurred on a far larger scale in India. There, as elsewhere, the guest people does not primarily appear as an

---

* Weber's terms "guest" and "pariah" peoples refers to a series of groups in diverse constellations. The groups seem to be marked by the following typological extremes. (1) Peoples who as a result of invasion and conquest are expropriated from their lands by immigrant caste groups and reduced to economic dependence on the conqueror. From the standpoint of the conquerors such peoples are "guests" even though they are older settlers than the conquerors. As soon as the caste system is established the newcomers may begin to assimilate the "barbarians" (the original settlers) by assigning them to the lowest of the castes. (2) Peoples who have lost their home lands completely and turned into itinerant artisans and, like the Gypsies, live a dispersed migratory dependent existence.

Obviously both of these groups find themselves in situations which have come to be described as "marginal" by Stonequist. *Contemporary Social Theory* Ed. by Harry E. Barnes, Howard Becker, and Frances B. Becker, New York: D. Appleton Century, 1940, pp. 35 ff.

On occasion, following general usage, we employ the term "marginal trading peoples" for trading "guests." Weber's frequent comparative references to the Jains, the "Jews of the far East" and to the Jews of the occidental Middle Ages seems evidence for the soundness of this procedure.

absolutely homeless wandering people. More frequently the guest peoples are of tribes which still possess village settlements of their own, but dispose of the product of their household or tribal industry interlocally; or of tribes where the members may periodically lease their services interlocally as harvesters, day laborers, repair men, hired helpers; or, finally, of tribes which may traditionally monopolize interlocal trade in a special product.

The increase in population of wood and mountain barbarian tribes on one hand, and the increasing demand for labor in the developing culture areas on the other created, with increasing wealth, numerous lower or unclean services. When the local resident population declined to take them over, these occupations fell into the hands of alien workers of foreign origin who were permanently lodged in urban areas but retained their tribal affiliations. Guest industry became highly developed in a form resembling that of specialized communities. Certain highly skilled trades are found in the hands of men native to the region, but such men were viewed as outsiders by village peoples. They did not live in the village but on the outskirts—in German, on the *Wurth;* they shared no part in the rights of the villagers, but rather formed into interlocal organizations of their own which answered for them and had jurisdiction over them. In the village they had only guest rights, partially under religious, partially under princely guarantee. Such phenomena are also found outside of India.

Frequently, the representatives of a guest industry are excluded from intermarriage and commensalism, and therefore are held to be ritually "impure." When such ritual barriers against a guest people exist, we shall, for our present purposes, use the expression *pariah people.* As far as the Hindus are concerned, the term would be quite incorrect. The Pulyian or Parayan (pariah) caste of Southern India by no means represents the lowest stratum or a stratum of outcastes, as Abbe Raynal believes. A caste of ancient weavers (and today also farmhands), first mentioned in inscriptions of the eleventh century, they did not rank high socially and had to live outside the village, but they had, and have, fixed caste privileges. The leather-workers (Chamar) and streetsweepers ranked lower. And lower still are castes like the Doms and others who mainly represent the dregs of the castes.

We use the term pariah here in the usual European sense, much in the way the term Kadi is used in Kadi-justice. The term pariah people in this special sense should not be taken to refer to any tribe of workers considered by a local community "strange," "barbaric," or "magically impure" unless they are at the same time wholly or predominantly a guest people.

The purest form of this type is found when the people in question have totally lost their residential anchorage and hence are completely occupied economically in meeting demands of other settled peoples—the gypsies, for instance, or, in another manner, the Jews of the Middle Ages.

The fluid transition from the guest industry of settled tribes to a pariah people of this pure type is accomplished through numerous transitional steps. In Hindu territory a ritualistic barrier was, and is, established against all tribes not affiliated with the Hindu association. All such unaffiliated tribes are magically defiled. In every village may be found certain indispensable guest workers—for example, workers with cowhides and leather—who, despite their indispensability for a millenium have been absolutely impure. Their very presence may infect the air of a room and so defile food in it that it must be thrown away to prevent evil enchantment. According to his caste, ritualistic infection by a man of impure caste may even destroy the sexual potency of a Brahman. Hence they stand entirely outside the Hindu association. No Hindu temple is open to them.

The power of such circumstances is alone great enough to force a long series of transitional adjustments toward full integration into the social order. First, there were and are numerous degrees of segregation. While impure guest workers have been excluded since ancient times from the village association, they are not thereby made outlaws. The village owes them a definite compensation for their services and reserves for them a monopoly in their respective vocations. Moreover, their regulated ritualistic rights and duties by their very gradations denote a positively defined legal position. Even when Brahmans and members of other high castes may have to avoid contact with them or even their very presence, the positive religious rules of Hinduism are decisive for the nature of these relations. Above all, a violation of these norms by the impure guest worker results not only in the measures taken by the Brahmans or village community, but also, under certain circumstances, by his own community. Besides, it is a source of magical disadvantage in this world, and reduction of salvation chances in the next.

One must ascribe membership in the Hindu community to those impure guest workers and pariah peoples who adhere to such norms and regulations despite their essentially underprivileged status position. Indubitably, they have been considered members for centuries, inasmuch as they do not represent barbarian tribes but impure castes in Hindu classification.

Quite different is the case of those tribes, whose guest position is defined by traditional rules, applying to those trafficking with alien overseas traders. Such tribes have neither positive nor negative religious rank, but are considered to be simply impure barbarians. They recognize no religious duties of a Hindu sort. They not only have their own deities but, what is more important, their own priests; although both of these situations occur also among Hindu castes, the "barbarians" simply ignore the institutions of Hinduism. Such tribes are as little Hindu as the Christians and Mussulmen.

There are, however, various transitional stages on the way to Hinduization. As Blunt observes in the Census report, a considerable section of the people listed in the census as "Animists" consider themselves Hindus. However, some of the people listed in the Census as impure castes are under certain circumstances inclined to reject all relation to Hinduism, particularly to the Brahmans. In fighting for the significance of their national culture today, the representatives of Hinduism seek to define Hinduism as broadly as possible. They claim as a Hindu anyone who passes one of the possible tests of Hinduism defined by census authority, hence also a Jain, Sikh, or Animist. In extending their definition of Hinduism, the Hindus are met halfway by the tendency toward Hinduization among these outsiders.

This tendency among guest tribes living among Hindus takes roughly the following form: its guest workers readily begin to claim and accept certain services from those Brahmans who regularly serve impure castes, e.g., the casting of the horoscope for marriage dates and similar family activities, while continuing to call upon their own priests for other services. If such guest workers take up trades of Hindu castes, usually impure, they must conform to prescriptions applied elsewhere to that trade in order to avoid too sharp resistance. The more they approach the pure type of a pariah people—i.e., the more they lose their stability in a closed tribal territory, or the less important this becomes—the more their social situation depends upon the norms their Hindu environment establishes, the more likely they are to adjust their ritualistic conduct to it, and the more they borrow typical Hindu customs and find themselves in the end essentially in the position of a (usually impure) Hindu caste.

The sole caste designation by pariah peoples monopolizing ancient crafts or trades is the old tribal name. Sometimes when the tribe forms an additional endogamous caste division of an old Hindu caste the tribal name is continued beside the caste name. This tribal name is then the last residue of their origin.

Most varied transitional states of Hinduization, i.e., the transformation of tribes into castes, are to be found. Sometimes assimilation takes a mixed form, partially extensive, partially intensive propaganda; sometimes subdivisions of a tribe are received as a guest people by several castes, while the remaining subdivisions continue to exist without losing their form of tribal organization. The Ahir represent a mixed Hinduized tribe originally of shepherds and herdsmen. In Bombay Province even today (1911) some castes have subcastes of Ahirs in addition to their usual ones. Thus the Brahmans in Khandesh have the Sonars, the Lohars, and the Koli. There, as elsewhere, the Ahir carpenters, goldsmiths, and blacksmiths do not intermarry with the professionally identical non-Ahir castes, whereas Ahir carpenters and Ahir blacksmiths, though of different castes, often do intermarry. Moreover, Ahirs who remained herdsmen often are totemically organized like a tribe, and not by sibs like a caste. On the other hand, in some castes the Ahir have disappeared completely as subcastes or have never existed as subcastes. (An inscription[6] mentions a prince of Iodhpur who had chased the tribe of the Ahir out of a village and established the caste order at the place.) We shall not pursue this typology—enough has been given to indicate how fluid are the boundaries of Hinduism.

Usually the propaganda advances in the form of a slow-moving recruitment of whole associations into the Hindu community. In principle, at least, it cannot be otherwise, since individuals can never affiliate directly with that community except as members of another association, a caste; and since affiliation always takes place in terms of the fiction that the respective association had been a caste of yore, somewhat similar to a Catholic dogma which is never newly enacted like a modern law, but is rather "found" and "defined" as having always been valid. It is in this way that the hereditary character of Hindu religion is revealed.

What were, and are, the motives working for the reception? The Brahmans, serving as intermediaries, primarily have material interest in opportunities for expanding income, ranging from service fees for the casting of horoscopes to prebends and the gifts due to house and sacrificial priests. Rich gifts of cattle, money, jewelry, and, above all, land and land rent (pepper-rent) were the compensations for Brahmans who provided the necessary "proofs" of genteel descent for the Hinduized ruling stratum of an area undergoing assimilation.

And what were the motives of the group desiring assimilation? The "tribes" which would be transformed into "castes," particularly their ruling stratum, assume an enslaving yoke of rituals hardly duplicated elsewhere in the world. They surrendered pleasures—for instance, alcohol, which is relinquished in general only with great reluctance. What, then, was the reason?

Legitimation by a recognized religion has always been decisive for an alliance between politically and socially dominant classes and the priesthood. Integration into the Hindu community provided such religious legitimation for the ruling stratum. It not only endowed the ruling stratum of the barbarians with recognized rank in the cultural world of Hinduism, but, through their transformation into castes, secured their superiority over the subject classes with an efficiency unsurpassed by any other religion. In the distant past, the services of the Brahmans were not, as a rule, sought primarily and exclusively by nobles; nor were the nobles always the only stratum seeking Hinduization, as assumed above in accordance with nineteenth-century conditions. On occasion the nobles were probably direct opponents of the Brahmans.

In ancient times it was the kings, rather, who took the lead in the struggle for Hinduization. As the Slavic princes of the East called into their lands German priests, knights, merchants, and peasants, so the kings of the East Ganges Plain and of Southern India from the Tamils to the southern tip called upon Brahmans trained in writing and administration. Their services were enlisted to assist the prince in the formal organization, in the Hindu manner, of his patrimonial bureaucratic rule and status structure and to consecrate the prince as a legitimate Raja or Maharaja in the sense of the Hindu Dharmashastras, Brahmanas, and Puranas. Telling documents of land-grants issued sometimes simultaneously to dozens, even hundreds of obviously immigrant Brahmans, are found dispersed throughout India.

Similar to the legitimation interest of the ruling groups are the interests lying back of the voluntary acceptance of Hindu rites by pariah peoples who, by this means, only acquire the humiliating situation of an impure caste. Yet, from the standpoint of Hinduism, they are impure anyway, and obliged by restrictions to keep their place. Hence it is advantageous to secure a monopoly over their work opportunities by recognizing them as a legitimate "caste," however underprivileged, rather than an alien people. Also by borrowing organizations peculiar to Hinduism (e.g., the caste *panchayat,* to be discussed later) the assumption of caste status can be given practical significance.

These caste organizations, like quasi-trade unions, facilitate the legitimate defense of both internal and external interests of the lower castes. To be sure, substitutes might well be found for these organizations. Perhaps, too, in the past, religious hopes were frequently an important factor in the Hinduization of such pariah peoples, for, as we shall see, Hinduism holds out hopes to the socially oppressed strata. The peculiarities of the religious promise which Hinduism offers to underprivileged classes help explain their relatively minor resistance in view of what one would expect of the abysmal distance Hinduism establishes between social strata.

Certainly there are, and were, rebellions against the Hindu order rising from the impure castes. Certain specifically proletarian prophecies hostile to the Brahmans will be discussed in Part II. There are today a number of communities which expressly deny all Brahmanical authority. If, in any external respects, such communities behave as castes, official Hindu and the former British census authorities are inclined to treat them as castes, in spite of the dubious status of the communities or their will in the matter. Rebellions by lower castes undoubtedly occurred. The question is: Why were there not more of them, and, more important, why did the great, historically significant, religious revolutions against the Hindu order stem from altogether different, relatively privileged strata and retain their roots in these?

The approximately correct view may be formulated provisionally: the internalization of the Hindu order by underprivileged strata, guest and pariah tribes, represents the adjustment of socially weak strata to the given caste order—the legitimation of their social and economic situation. However, the struggle for or against acceptance of Hinduism for entire territories generally was led by the rulers or ruling strata. In any case, the strongest motive for the assimilation of Hinduism was undoubtedly the desire for legitimation.

Hinduism was an almost irresistible social force. For centuries two salvation religions expressly hostile to the Brahmans–Jainism and to a greater extent, Buddhism—have contended with Hinduism throughout the Indian culture area. In no way universally predominant, they were officially established confessions. They have been completely defeated through the restoration of Hinduism—so completely that in 1911 the Jains comprised only .40 per cent of the population (in 1891 they were still .49 per cent, in 1901, .45 per cent and, indeed, most of these remained only in a few cities of west India.

That the decrease is due exclusively to the greater mortality of the urban population, as stated in the Census of 1911, may well be questioned. During 1881-91 there was a relative increase from .45 to .49. On the whole, the urban Jains have a lower mortality rate than have the urban Hindus. Of the ancient national Buddhist church, only in Orissa, does a community (of around 2,000 persons) remain. Other Buddhists enumerated elsewhere in India are immigrants.

Truly sanguine persecutions of these heterodoxies were indeed not lacking during the Hindu restoration, but they obviously do not account for the unusually quick victory of Hinduism. Favorable political circumstances contributed to the victory. Decisive, however, was the fact that Hinduism could provide an incomparable religious support for the legitimation interest of the ruling strata as determined by the social conditions of India. The salvation religions, as we shall see, were unable to supply such support. A further striking phenomenon is in agreement with this.

We have observed the momentum of the caste system in its diffusion through the assimilation of tribes. Once established, the assimilative power of Hinduism is so great that it tends even to integrate social forms considered beyond its religious borders.

Thus religious movements of expressly anti-Brahmanical and anti-caste character, that is, contrary to one of the fundamentals of Hinduism, have been in all essentials returned to caste order.

The process is not hard to explain. When a principled anti-caste sect recruits former members of various Hindu castes and tears them from the context of their former ritualistic duties, the caste responds by excommunicating all the sect's proselytes. Unless the sect is able to abolish the caste system altogether instead of simply tearing away some of its members, it becomes, from the standpoint of the caste system, a quasi-guest folk, a kind of confessional guest community in an ambiguous position in the prevailing Hindu order. Further definition of the situation by the remaining Hindus depends upon the style of life elaborated in the new community. If the sect permitted a way of life Hinduism considers ritually defiling (beef consumption), the Hindus treat it as a pariah people, and if this condition continues long enough, as an impure caste. We have already noted the fluidity of such transitions. If ritualistic defilement is not indicated, in time (particularly if the activities of the sect members are of a ritualistic nature—and such is usually the case), the sect may take its place among the surrounding castes as one with special ritualistic duties.

The sect developing into a caste needs only to be interested in securing its social rank over and against other castes. There is no obstacle to this; indeed, there are Hindu castes which repudiate the Brahmans for their own priests. In the course of time the sect can be recognized either as a single caste (sect-caste) or as a caste with subcastes of different social rank. This last occurs when the sect members are socially quite heterogeneous. Finally, development can follow the pattern described as tribal assimilation to the Hindu order. The upper strata of the sect become priests, landlords, merchants seeking recognition as Brahmans, Kshatriyas, and Vaishyas, but the remaining plebs become one or more Shudra castes—in order to share the social and economic privileges of the upper castes of their Hindu surroundings.

At the present time the ancient sect of the Lingayat is going through this development. Originally, in the Middle Ages, it represented a type of particularly sharp and principled "protestant" reaction to the Brahmans and the caste order. From census to census it has come to conform more and more to the

Hindu order, and it now demands the registration of its members according to the four classical Hindu castes. For some time the Lingayat sect has undergone a characteristic process of status differentiation suggestive of the gentility claimed by the descendants of the Mayflower Pilgrims in New England. The descendants of the first converts considered themselves more genteel and highly privileged than the latter proselytes.

The members of the Jain congregations, which today frequently intermarry with certain (merchant) castes, are occasionally considered Hindus by Hinduists.

Buddhism, in principle, had not infringed upon the caste order. Its monks, as we shall see, were and are thought to be out-and-out heretics, and they themselves claim to be non-Hindus. That did not, however, prevent isolated Buddhistic communities on the North Indian border from acquiring a peculiar caste stratification after the monasteries had become secularized into prebends.

Islam, too, succumbed in India to the engulfing tendency toward caste formation. In this case, caste formation could be linked to the typical status stratification of classical Islam. The actual or alleged descendants of the prophet and certain families religiously ranking close to his sib (the Sayyid or Sherif) had privileged status. Likewise, status stratification developed after indiscriminate propaganda had been halted for financial reasons and the ancient privilege exempting old believers from taxation had been denied to new converts, thus posing one group against the other. In India, this meant the setting of the Middle Eastern and Persian immigrants against Indian proselytes. Finally, and appropriate to the feudal character of ancient Islamic society, the sibs of the landlords stood opposed to the sibless peasants and, above all, to the craftsmen. These differences with their respective variations determined the form Islamic castes developed in India.

We are not here concerned with the fact that numerous Hindu castes worship Islamic saints alongside Hindu deities, that mixed formations like the sect of the Sikhs developed, and that Indian Islam also borrowed numerous Hindu rituals. What interests us here is the assimilative power of the Hindu life order due to its legitimation of social rank and, not to be forgotten, possible related economic advantages.

The central significance of the Hindu social order is expressed primarily in the interrelation of the doctrinal and ritualistic-ethical aspects of the religion.

3. *Hindu Doctrine and Ritual*

LIKE Confucianism, Hinduism knows the dualism of "doctrine" and "ritualistic duty." A distinction is made in Hindu terminology[7] between *Dharma* and *Mata.* Mata refers to metaphysical theology. To Christian doctrine (*Kristi-mata*), for example, belong such ideas as the following: that all (and only) men have "souls"; that a supramundane being created the world and all souls out of nothing; that each soul lives but once on the earth and is nevertheless immortal; that after life on earth, the soul must spend its eternal life in heaven or hell; that God produced through a virgin a God-incarnate son whose deeds and accomplishments are significant for man's salvation.

That schism occurs in the interpretation of special elements of Christian doctrine is no surprise to the Hindu. He is familiar with such differences through the sharp doctrinal cleavages of his philosophic schools and sects. Among the Brahmans, some Vishnu and Shiva sects would not even utter the names of each other's Gods.

Again, a Hindu is not disturbed by the fact that there are certain teachings one must accept to be a Christian—(although some Hindus may deny it, the same phenomena appears in Hinduism)—while other controversial teachings may be freely discussed in one and the same church of as strict doctrinal authority as the Catholic.

Precisely this freedom of opinion obtains in Hinduism to an exceptional degree—so much so that the concept of "dogma" is entirely lacking. Without becoming a non-Hindu, a Hindu could accept highly important and most characteristic doctrines which every denominational Christian would consider exclusively his own. For example, he could accept the whole Christology and its elaborations, which, in fact, deeply influenced the development of Vishnuite Krishna mythology. Also, the Hindu could accept the doctrine of justification through faith, a belief which also existed in Hinduism among the Bhagavat sects long before Christ.

More important from the Hindu standpoint are other elements, or rather pre-suppositions of Christian teaching, which for the Hindus, make it a doctrine of barbarians (*mlechha-mata*) as it was for Hellenic man. These differences could also cause Christology and the doctrine of justification to change their meaning radically when taken into Hinduism. First, it would be necessary to renounce the claim of Christian doctrines to universal validity. In Hinduism a teaching may be orthodox without being bindingly valid, a situation illustrated in the doctrinal differences in the interpretation of the Last Supper by the Reformed Church and the Lutherans when they united in an evangelical established church. And, indeed, the doctrinal fluidity of Hinduism is not incidental but, rather, the central issue of "religion" as we conceive it. According to Christian concepts, the promise of transcendant values is the primary reason for belonging to a "religion." Moreover, in raising the issue of transcendant ends is posed the problem of the "path of salvation" (*marga*), the means by which the holy object is attainable by men.

Disregarding the sacred, but "this-worldly" values represented by Hinduism, and considering it as a unit, Hinduism offers a choice of three apparently exclusive holy ends in the beyond. (1) Rebirth to a new temporary life on earth in circumstances at least as fortunate as the present ones; or, what, in contrast to the Christian, is for the Hindu in the same category, rebirth in a paradise (a) in the world of God (*salokya*), or (b) near to God (*samipya*), or (c) as an apotheosized God (*sarupya*). Rebirth in paradise occurs with the same provisions as earthly rebirth; it is for a limited time followed by another rebirth. (2) A second possible holy object is unlimited admission to the blissful presence of a supramundane God (Vishnu), hence immortality of the individual soul in one of the three forms listed above. (3) The third holy object is the cessation of individual existence and (a) mergence of the soul in the all-one (*sayujya*), or (b) submergence in *nirvana;* the nature of this latter state is in part variously explained and in part left obscure.

All three forms of the sacred ends are orthodox, although the third (to be precise: 3a) is specifically Brahmanical. It is preferred by the most distinguished Brahman sect of the Smartras. Indeed, by these circles the immortality doctrine is regarded as "unclassical" though not anti-Hindu, somewhat as the Taoistic doctrine is by the Confucians and the Pietist doctrine of grace by classical Lutherans. At any rate, the classical Hindu has a choice between the first and third goals of holy endeavor.

According to which teaching the Hindu follows, the paths leading to each of the three sacred ends differ radically. Asceticism, contemplation, works considered ritualistically pure, good works in the sense of social accomplishment (particularly professional virtues), enthusiastic faith (*bhakti*), are cumulative, alternative, or exclusive means to holy ends, according to the end sought. Nor is the view lacking in classical literature (the Mahabharata) that the individual secures for himself the kind of sacred value epitomized by the deity in whom he has faith and with whom he seeks refuge. Thus, the conception that "to you may happen, as you believed" is taken in its most daring sense.

Broader religious tolerance than this in a single religion is hardly conceivable. In truth, it may well be concluded that Hinduism is simply not a "religion" in our sense of the word. This is exactly what some of its representatives (Ketkar among others) emphatically affirm. What the Occidental conceives as "religion" is closer to the Hindu concept *sampradaya*. By this the Hindu understands communities into which one is not born—hence "open-door castes"—but to which one belongs by virtue of common religious aspiration and common sacred paths. Hindu scholars call such communities *theophratries*. Among the *theophratries* in India are Jainism, Buddhism, some of the revivals of Vishnu faith in a redeemer, and the Shiva sect of Lingayat, all of which, insofar as they retain their essential beliefs and practices, were and are considered absolutely heretical. This is the case even though Buddhism, for example, does not doubt the existence and power of Hindu gods and the theophratric Vishnu sect; and the Lingayat worships each one of the great gods of the Hindu triad (Brahman, Vishnu, Shiva). These communities are, furthermore, regarded as heretical, even though, at least from our standpoint and for the most part from that of Hinduism, there is no basic difference between their particular sacred values and paths and those of orthodox Hinduism. At least they are far less divergent than the widely different paths of salvation admittedly orthodox. In contrast to Hinduism all these theophratries receive individuals into their fellowships. But even this is not decisively heretical.

Nor does affiliation with a sect bring about excommunication. As indicated by the later parts of the epics and *puranas*, from its beginning specific Hindu religiosity has accepted the appearance of sects as completely normal. In fact, the truly devout

Hindu is not merely a Hindu but a member of a Hindu sect as well. And it may even happen that while the father is a Shivaist the son may be a Vishnuist.[8] In practice, this means that one of them was instructed by the *directeur de l'ame* (the *guru*) of the Shiva sect, the other by one of the Vishnu sect. After completion of his instruction one was received into sect membership by being informed of the sect's *mantra*, i.e., its slogan-like prayer-formula. He bears the symbols of the sect (forehead marking, etc.), frequents its temples, and, finally, prays exclusively and directly to Vishnu or Shiva, as the case may be, or to one of their incarnations. (He considers the other two deities of the triad as mere aspects of his own God.) He observes both the general rites of his caste and the special rites of his sect, as is orthodox Hindu practice.

In contrast to the orthodox sects, the heresy of the theophratries consists in the fact that they tear the individual away from his ritualistic duties, hence from the duties of the caste of his birth, and thus ignore or destroy his *dharma*. When this occurs the Hindu loses caste. And since only through caste can one belong to the Hindu community, he is lost to it. *Dharma*, that is, ritualistic duty, is the central criterion of Hinduism.

Hinduism is primarily ritualism, a fact implied when modern authors state that *mata* (doctrine) and *marga* (holy end) are transitory and "ephemeral"—they mean freely elected—while *dharma* is "eternal"—that is, unconditionally valid.

The first question a Hindu asks of a strange religion is not what is its teaching (*mata*) but its *dharma*. The Christian *dharma* of a Protestant is, for the Hindu, something positive in baptism, communion, church attendance, rest on Sunday and other Christian festivals, the table prayer. These observances would be acceptable to the members of all good Hindu castes with the exception of communion. When administered in either of its forms communion requires the drinking of alcohol, and compulsory table community with noncaste fellow-Christians. Moreover, the negative aspects of the Christian *dharma*—that, for example, it permits Christians to eat meat, particularly beef, and drink hard liquor—stamp it as the *dharma* of impure barbarians (*mlechha dharma*).

What, then, is the content of *dharma* to a Hindu? We learn that *dharma* differs according to social position and, since it is subject to "evolution," which is not absolutely closed and completed, *dharma* depends upon the caste into which the individual is born. With the split of old into new castes *dharma* is specialized. Through the advance of knowledge *dharma* can be further developed.

The conservative circles of Hinduism would, of course, accept this characterization unreservedly only for the remote past—that age (in India the Kali-age) of prophetic inspiration which every priest-controlled religion (including Judaism, Christianity, and Islamism) must consider as ended in order to secure itself against innovation. In any case, *dharma* can be developed, like the divine commandments of a denominational religion, by "finding" thus far unknown, but eternally valid consequences and truths. This "discovery" comes about primarily through the adjudication and binding preceptual responses of competent authorities. The Brahmans find such authorities in the Castris and Pandits–scholars in sacred law, educated in Brahmanical schools and Brahmanical institutions of higher learning, the holy seat of Shringeri (for the South) or Shri Sankaraharya of Sankeshwar (for the North and Northwest). Among the authorities were Brahmanical monastic superiors whose position may be roughly compared to that of the superiors of the Carragheen (southern Ireland) monasteries in the time of their organization.

The other castes were subject to the jurisdiction of their caste institutions which, formerly more than today, depended in problematical cases upon the verdict of the Brahmans. *Dharma* depends first on sacred tradition, the adjudication, the literary and rationally developed learning of the Brahmans. Just as in Islamism, Judaism, and early Christianity, there is no "infallible" doctrinal authority of definite priestly office because the Brahmans represent no hierarchy of officials. The everyday *dharma* of the caste derives its content, in large measure, from the distant past with its taboos, magical norms, and witchcraft. Hindu *dharma*, however, is more extensively and in practice more significantly an exclusive product of the priesthood and its literature than the present-day ritualistic commandments of the Catholic Church. This fact has had important consequences for Hinduism.

4. The Place of the Vedas

OFFICIALLY, Hinduism, like the other book religions, has a holy book—the Vedas. Here we wish to understand by Vedas only the collections of hymns, prayers, formulae. In a broader sense all "sacred" Hindu books, including the Brahmans and Upanishads and the Transitional Sutras, are counted among the Vedas. One of the few essentially binding duties of Hindu "faith" is not—at least not directly—to dispute their authority. In the traditional view, any sect which, like the Jains and Buddhists, does not recognize their authority cannot be a Hindu sect. While at present this is not universally held, it is without question the normal view. But what does recognition of the authority of the Vedas—this collection of songs and hymns, ritualistic and magical formulas of varying age (some 600 years old, some 2,000)—what, in fact, does it mean?

The major constituent parts of the Vedas (rooted in the specialized functions of the Vedic priests during sacrifice) were originally orally transmitted. After their transcription by different schools of Brahmans they continued in accordance with ancient correct practice to be withheld, from non-Brahman readers, as the Bible is withheld from the laity in the Catholic Church. Brahmans were able to impart knowledge of only certain sections of the Vedas, and that only to laymen of the highest castes.

This secrecy was not due solely to the monopolization of magical formulae, a practice originally characteristic of all priests. Such secrecy had even more compelling objective reasons than those applying to the Vulgata after the strengthened position of the Brahmans made magical monopolization superfluous. One is tempted to think of the Occident. The New Testament contained passages of an ethical substance which first had to be explained away by priestly interpretation (and thus in part turned into their exact opposite) before they were suitable for the purposes of a mass church in general and a priestly organization in particular. This was no problem for the Vedas, for they do not contain a rational "ethic." The ethical world of the Vedas is simply that of all heroic ages, as expressed by singers dependent upon gifts from kings and heroes—singers who did not fail to emphasize their own powers and the powers of the gods they might magically influence.

The tenacity with which the Vedas retained this primitive character is to be explained by the fact that the hymns and particularly the prayer-formulae were believed to be magically proven and they were, therefore, sacredotally stereotyped. This preserved them from the kind of expurgation to which equivalent ancient Chinese literature was subjected by Confucius (and perhaps others) and the historical and cosmological Hebraic literature by the priesthood.

In consequence, the Vedas contain nothing about the divine and human affairs fundamental to Hinduism. The three great gods of Hinduism, even their names, are hardly mentioned. The Vedas have nothing to say about the specific character the Hindu gods acquired later. The gods of the Vedas are functional and hero gods, externally similar to those of Homer. The Vedic hero is a castle-dwelling, charioteering warrior-king with a war band of Homeric type and with a similar accompaniment of predominantly cattle-breeding yeomen.

The great Vedic gods, especially the two greatest in their opposed characteristics are Indra and Varuna. Indra, the god of the thunderstorm, was (like Jahveh) a passionately active war and hero god, and, thereby god of the irrational fate of heroes. Varuna was the wise, omniscient, functional god of eternal order, particularly legal order. Both these gods have almost disappeared from Hinduism. No cults are built around them. They lead a purely historical life by grace of Vedic scholars. We could hardly expect more, however, considering the instability of the numerous Hindu deities and considering the practice which Max Müller called "henotheism," i.e., the practice, used even by the ancient singers, of referring to the god appealed to as the mightiest or only god in order to win his favor.

The Vedas rather defy the *dharma* of Hinduism. To a Christian, the official recognition of the Vedas might appear to be a "formal principle" of Hinduism in the manner of the Protestant recognition of the Bible—always with the reservation that it is at least not absolutely indispensable. With similar reservations the sacredness of the cow, and hence the absolute prohibition against killing cows, if anything, might be considered among the ritualistic "substantive principles" of Hinduism forming part of universal Hindu *dharma*. Whoever does not accept them as binding is not a Hindu.

The worship of the cow (and to a less degree the veneration of cattle generally) had extensive economic and ritualistic implications. Even today rational animal husbandry fails because, in principle, the animals must not die an unnatural death and hence are fed although their use value is long gone. (The ritualistically illegal poisoning of cattle by outcastes provides some remedy.) Cow manure and cow urine are believed to be purifying. To this day a correct Hindu who has dined with a European will disinfect himself (and perhaps fumigate his residence) by use of cow manure. No correct Hindu will bypass a urinating cow without putting his hand into the stream and wetting his forehead, garments, etc. with it as does the Catholic with holy water. During a poor harvest heroic economy serves first to provide fodder for the cow.

A beef-eater is either barbarian or low caste. The source of these Hindu conceptions is of no concern to us here; the point is the Vedas supply no evidence for such attitudes toward cattle and take beef-consumption for granted. In their attempt to explain this, Hindu "modernists" maintain that the contemporary (Kali) age is so wicked that the liberty of the golden age in this respect could no longer be granted. Moreover, if we look beyond the ritualistic prescriptions to the structured core of Hindu ideas, we fail to discover in the Vedas a single trace of such fundamental conceptions as the transmigration of souls and the derived *karma*-doctrine (of compensation). These ideas can only be interpretively read into some ambiguous and undatable passages of the Vedas.

Vedic religion knows only of a Hades, Yama's realm, and a Heaven of the Gods essentially comparable to the "kingdom of the fathers" in Homeric and Germanic antiquity. Neither the special heaven of the Brahmans nor the somewhat Christian or Olympian heaven of Vishnu or Shiva are to be found in the Vedas not to mention the "wheel" of rebirths and *nirvana*. Vedic religion affirms not only life and its values in the sense in which the later mass religion of Hinduism became life-affirmative in contrast to virtuoso-religion, but it addressed itself to things of this world as did similar religions which grew out of half-charismatic, half-feudal warrior and booty communities.

Obviously, the Vedas might possibly yield information concerning the pre-history of Hinduism, but they are not a source of insight into its content and its earliest historical forms. The Veda is a sacred book for Hinduism in about the way Deuteronomy is for Christianity. To acknowledge the authority of the Vedas, as demanded of the Hindu, means *fides implicita* in a more fundamental sense than that of the Catholic Church, and precisely because no savior is mentioned whose revelation could have substituted new law for old.

In practice, this means simply the acknowledgment of the authority of Hindu tradition resting on the Veda and the continued interpretation of its world image; it means acknowledgment of the rank station of its leaders, the Brahmans. The Vedas contain only incipient and preliminary steps of the later development and classic form of Hinduism.

5. *The Brahmans and the Castes*

IN CLASSICAL Hindu times as well as today, the position of the Brahman can be understood only in connection with caste; without an understanding of this it is quite impossible to understand Hinduism. Perhaps the most important gap in the ancient Veda is its lack of any reference to caste. The Veda refers to the four later caste names in only one place, which is considered a very late passage; nowhere does it refer to the substantive content of the caste order with the meaning it later assumed and which is characteristic only of Hinduism.[9]

Caste, that is, the ritual rights and duties it gives and imposes, and the position of the Brahmans, is the fundamental institution of Hinduism. Before everything else, without caste there is no Hindu. But the position of the Hindu with regard to the authority of the Brahman may vary extraordinarily, from unconditional submission to the contesting of his authority. Some castes do contest the authority of the Brahman, but in practice, this means merely that the Brahman is disdainfully rejected as a priest, that his judgment in controversial questions of ritual is not recognized as authoritative, and that his advice is never sought. Upon first sight, this seems to contradict the fact that "castes" and "Brahmans" belong together in Hinduism. But as a matter of fact, if the caste is absolutely essential for each Hindu, the reverse, at least nowadays, does not hold, namely, that every caste be a Hindu caste. There are also castes among the Mohammedans of India, taken over from the Hindus. And castes are also found among the Buddhists. Even the Indian Christians have not quite been able to withhold themselves from practical recognition of the castes. These non-Hindu castes have lacked the tremendous emphasis that the Hindu doctrine of salvation placed upon the caste, as we shall see later, and they have lacked a further characteristic, namely, the determination of the social rank of the castes by the social distance from other Hindu castes, and therewith, ultimately, from the Brahman. This is decisive for the connection between Hindu castes and the Brahman; however intensely a Hindu caste may reject him as a priest, as a doctrinal and ritual authority, and in every other respect, the objective situation remains inescapable; in the last analysis, a rank position is determined by the nature of its positive or negative relation to the Brahman.

"Caste" is, and remains essentially social rank, and the central position of the Brahmans in Hinduism rests primarily upon the fact that social rank is determined with reference to Brahmans. In order to understand this, we shall turn to the present condition of the Hindu castes, as described in the excellent scientific Census Reports. We shall also consider briefly the classical theories of caste contained in the ancient books of law and other sources.

Today the Hindu caste order is profoundly shaken. Especially in the district of Calcutta, old Europe's major gateway to India, many norms have practically lost their force. The railroads, the taverns, the changing occupational stratification, the concentration of labor through imported industry, colleges, etc., have all contributed their part. The "commuters to London," that is, those who studied in Europe and maintained voluntary social intercourse with Europeans, were outcasts up to the last generation; but more and more this pattern is disappearing. And it has been impossible to introduce caste coaches on the railroads in the fashion of the American railroad cars or station waiting rooms which segregate "white" from "colored" in the southern states. All caste relations have been shaken, and the stratum of intellectuals bred by the English are here, as elsewhere, bearers of a specific nationalism. They will greatly strengthen this slow and irresistible process. For the time being, however, the caste structure still stands quite firmly.

First we must ask: with what concepts shall we define a "caste"? (The term is of Portuguese derivation. The ancient Indian name is *varna*, "color.") Let us ask it in the negative: What is not a caste? Or, what traits of other associations, really or apparently related to caste, are lacking in caste? What, for instance, is the difference between caste and tribe?

6. Caste and Tribe

AS LONG as a tribe has not become wholly a guest or a pariah people, it usually has a fixed tribal territory. A genuine caste never has a fixed territory. To a very considerable extent, the caste members live in the country, segregated in villages. Usually in each village there is, or was, only one caste with full title to the soil. But dependent village artisans and laborers also live with this caste. In any case, the caste does not form a local, territorial, corporate body, for this would contradict its nature. A tribe is, or at least originally was, bound together by obligatory blood revenge, mediated directly or indirectly through the sib. A caste never has anything to do with such blood revenge.

Originally, a tribe normally comprised many, often almost all, of the possible pursuits necessary for the gaining of subsistence. A caste may comprise people who follow very different pursuits; at least this is the case today, and for certain upper castes this has been the case since very early times. Yet so long as the caste has not lost its character, the kinds of pursuits admissible without loss of caste are always, in some way, quite strictly limited. Even today "caste" and "way of earning a living" are so firmly linked that often a change of occupation is correlated with a division of caste. This is not the case for a "tribe."

Normally a tribe comprises people of every social rank. A caste may well be divided into subcastes with extraordinarily different social ranks. Today this is usually the case; one caste frequently contains several hundred subcastes. In such cases, these subcastes may be related to one another exactly, or almost exactly, as are different castes. If this is the case, the subcastes, in reality, are castes; the caste name common to all of them has merely historical significance, or almost so, and serves to support the social pretensions of degraded subcastes towards third castes. Hence, by its very nature, caste is inseparably bound up with social ranks within a larger community.

It is decisive for a tribe that it is originally and normally a political association. The tribe is either an independent association, as is always originally the case, or the association is part of a tribal league; or, it may constitute a *phyle*, that is, part of a political association commissioned with certain political tasks and having certain rights: franchise, holding quotas of the political offices, and the right of assuming its share or turn of political, fiscal, and liturgical obligations. A caste is never a political association, even if political associations in individual cases have burdened castes with liturgies, as may have happened repeatedly during the Indian Middle Ages (Bengal). In this case, castes are in the same position as merchant and craft guilds, sibs, and all sorts of associations. By its very nature the caste is always a purely social and possibly occupational association, which forms part of and stands within a social community. But the caste is not necessarily, and by no means regularly, an association forming part of only one political association; rather it may reach beyond, or it may fall short of, the boundaries of any one political association. There are castes diffused over all of India. Of the present Hindu castes (the chief ones), one may say that twenty-five are diffused throughout most of the regions of India. These castes comprise about 88 million Hindus out of the total of 217 million. Among them we find the ancient priest, warrior, and merchant castes: the Brahmans (14.60 million); Rajputs (9.43 million); Baniya (3.00 or only 1.12 million–according to whether or not one includes the split subcastes); Cayasts (ancient caste of official scribes 2.17 million); as well as ancient tribal castes like the Ahirs (9.50 million); Jats (6.98 million); or the great, unclean, occupational castes like the Chamar, the leather workers (11.50 million); the Shudra caste of the Teli, the oil pressers (4.27 million); the genteel trade caste of the goldsmiths, the Sonar (1.26 million); the ancient castes of village artisans, the Kumhar (potters) (3.42 million) and Lohar (blacksmiths) (2.07 million); the lower peasant caste of the Koli (cooli, derived from *kul*, clan, meaning something like "kin"–*Gevatter*) (3.17 million); and other individual castes of varying origin. The great differences in caste names as well as several distinctions of social rank which, in the individual provinces, derive from castes obviously equal in descent, make direct comparisons extremely difficult. Yet today, each of the subcastes and also most of the small castes exist only in their respective small districts. Political division has often strongly influenced the caste order of individual areas, but precisely the most important castes have remained interstate in scope.

With regard to the substance of its social norms, a tribe usually differs from a caste in that the exogamy of the totem or of the villages co-exist with the exogamy of the sibs. Endogamy has existed only under certain conditions, but by no means always, for the tribe as a whole. Rules of endogamy, however, always form the essential basis of a caste. Dietary rules and rules of commensality are always characteristic of the caste but are by no means characteristic of the tribe.

We have already observed that when a tribe loses its foothold in its territory it becomes a guest or a pariah people. It may then approximate caste to the point of being actually indistinguishable from it. The Banjaras, for instance, are partly organized as castes in the Central Provinces. In Mysore, however, they are organized as an (Animist) tribe. In both cases they make their living in the same way. Similar instances frequently occur. The differences that remain will be discussed when we determine the positive characteristics of caste. In contrast to the tribe, a caste is usually related intimately to special ways of earning a living, on the one hand, and, on the other, to social rank. Now the question arises, how is caste related to the occupational associations (merchant and craft guilds) and how is it related to status groups? Let us begin with the former.

7. *Caste and Guild*

GUILDS of merchants, and of traders who figured as merchants by selling their own produce, as well as craft guilds, existed in India during the period of the development of cities and especially during the period in which the great salvation religions originated. As we shall see, the salvation religions and the guilds were related. The guilds usually emerged within the cities, but occasionally they emerged outside; survivals of these are still in existence. During the period of the flowering of the cities, the position of the guilds was quite comparable to that occupied by guilds in the cities of the medieval Occident.

The guild association (the *mahajan*, literally, the same as *popolo grasso*) faced the prince on one hand and, on the other, the economically dependent artisans. These relations were about the same as those of the great guilds of literati and of merchants with the lower craft-guilds (*popolo minuto*) of the Occident. In the same way, associations of lower craft guilds existed in India (the *panch*). Moreover, the liturgical guild of Egyptian and late Roman character was perhaps not entirely lacking in the emerging patrimonial states of India. The uniqueness of the development of India lay in the fact that these beginnings of guild organization in the cities led neither to the city autonomy of the Occidental type nor, after the development of the great patrimonial states, to a social and economic organization of the territories corresponding to the "territorial economy"[10] of the Occident. Rather, the Hindu caste system, whose beginnings certainly preceded these organizations, became paramount. In part, this caste system entirely displaced the other organizations; in part, it crippled them; it prevented them from attaining any considerable importance. The "spirit" of this caste system, however, was totally different from that of the merchant and craft guilds.

The merchant and craft guilds of the Occident cultivated religious interests as did the castes. In connection with these interests, questions of social rank also played a considerable role among guilds. Which rank order the guilds should follow, during processions, for instance, was a question occasionally fought over more stubbornly than questions of economic interest. Furthermore, in a "closed" guild, that is, one with a numerically fixed quota of income opportunities, the position of the master was hereditary. There were also quasi-guild associations and associations derived from guilds in which the right to membership was acquired in hereditary succession. In late Antiquity, membership in the liturgical guilds was even a compulsory and hereditary obligation in the way of a *glebae adscriptio,* which bound the peasant to the soil. Finally, in the medieval Occident there were "opprobrious" trades, which were religiously déclassé; these correspond to the "unclean" castes of India. The fundamental difference, however, between occupational associations and caste is not affected by these circumstances.

First, that which is partly an exception and partly an occasional consequence for the occupational association is truly fundamental for the caste; the magical distance between castes in their mutual relationships.

In 1901 in the "United Provinces" roughly ten million people (out of a total of about forty million) belonged to castes with which physical contact is ritually polluting. In the Madras Presidency, roughly thirteen million people (out of about fifty-two million) could infect others even without direct contact if they approached within a certain, though varying, distance. The merchant and craft guilds of the Middle Ages acknowledged no ritual barriers whatsoever between the individual guilds and artisans, apart from the aforementioned small stratum of people engaged in opprobrious trades. Pariah peoples and pariah workers (for example, the knacker and hangman), by virtue of their special positions, come close sociologically to the unclean castes of India. And there were factual barriers restricting the connubium between differently esteemed occupations, but there were no ritual barriers, such as are absolutely essential for caste. Within the circle of the "honorable" people, ritual barriers to commensalism were completely absent; but such barriers belong to the basis of caste differences.

Furthermore, caste is essentially hereditary. This hereditary character was not, and is not, merely the result of monopolizing and restricting the earning opportunities to a definite maximum quota, as was the case among the absolutely closed guilds of the Occident, which at no time were numerically predominant. Such quota restriction existed, and still exists in part, among the occupational castes of India; but restriction is strongest not in the cities but in the villages, where a quota restriction of opportunities, insofar as it has existed, has had no connection with a guild organization and no need for it. As we shall see, the typical Indian village artisans have been the hereditary "tied cottagers" of the village.

The most important castes, although not all castes, have guaranteed the individual member a certain subsistence, as was the case among our master craftsmen. But not all castes have monopolized a whole trade as the guild at least strove to do. The guild of the Occident, at least during the Middle Ages, was regularly based upon the apprentice's free choice of a master and thus it made possible the transition of the children to occupations other than those of their parents, a circumstance which never occurs in the caste system. This difference is fundamental. Whereas the closure of the guilds toward the outside became stricter with diminishing income opportunities, among the castes the reverse was often observed, namely, they maintained their ritually required way of life, and hence their inherited trade, most easily when income opportunities were plentiful.

Another difference between guild and caste is of even greater importance. The occupational associations of the medieval Occident were often engaged in violent struggles among themselves, but at the same time they evidenced a tendency towards fraternization. The *mercanzia* and the *popolo* in Italy, and the "citizenry" in the north, were regularly, organizations of occupational associations. The *capitano del popolo* in the south and, frequently, though not always, the Bürgermeister in the north were heads of oath-bound organizations of the occupational associations, at least according to their original and specific meaning. Such organizations seized political power, either legally or illegally. Irrespective of their legal forms, the late medieval city *in fact* rested upon the fraternization of its productive citizenry. This was at least the case where the political form of the medieval city contained its most important sociological characteristics.

As a rule the fraternization of the citizenry was carried through by the fraternization of the guilds, just as the ancient *polis* in its innermost being rested upon the fraternization of military associations and sibs. Note that the base was "fraternization." It was not of secondary importance that every foundation of the occidental city, in antiquity and the Middle Ages, went hand in hand with the establishment of a cultic community of the citizens. Furthermore, it is of significance that the common meal of the *prytanes*, the drinking rooms of the merchant and craft guilds, and their common processions to the church played such a great role in the official documents of the occidental cities, and that the medieval citizens had, at least in the Lord's Supper, commensalism with one another in the most festive form. Fraternization at all times presupposes commensalism; it does not have to be actually practiced in everyday life, but it must be ritually possible. The caste order precluded this.

Complete fraternization of castes has been and is impossible because it is one of the constitutive principles of the castes that there should be at least ritually inviolable barriers against complete commensalism among different castes. As with all sociological phenomena, the contrast here is not an absolute one, nor are transitions lacking, yet it is a contrast which in essential features has been historically decisive.

The commensalism existing between castes really only confirms the rule. For instance, there is commensalism between certain Rajput and Brahman subcastes which rests upon the fact that the latter have of yore been the family priests of the former. If the member of a low caste merely looks at the meal of a Brahman, it ritually defiles the Brahman. When the last great famine caused the British administration to open public soup kitchens accessible to everyone, the tally of patrons showed that impoverished people of all castes had in their need visited the kitchens, although it was of course strictly and ritually taboo to eat in this manner in the sight of people not belonging to one's caste. A separate lower caste (the Kallars) has arisen in Bengal among people who had infracted the ritual and dietary laws during the famine of 1866, and in consequence been excommunicated. Within this caste, in turn, the minority separate themselves as a subcaste from the majority. The former maintaining a price ratio of six seers for the rupee, separated themselves from those maintaining a price ratio of ten seers for the rupee.

At the time of the famine the strict castes were not satisfied with the possibility of cleansing magical defilement by ritual penance. Yet under threat of excommunicating the participants, they did succeed in securing employment only of high-caste cooks; the hands of these cooks were considered ritually clean by all the castes concerned. Furthermore, they made certain that often a sort of symbolic *chambre séparée* was created for each caste by means of chalk lines drawn around the tables and similar devices. Apart from the fact that in the face of starvation even strong magical powers fail to carry weight, every strictly ritualist religion, such as the Indian, Hebrew, and Roman, is able to open ritualistic back doors for extreme situations.

Yet, it is a long way from this situation to a possible commensalism and fraternization as they are known in the Occident. To be sure, during the rise of the kingdoms, we find that the king invited the various castes, the Shudra included, to his table. They were seated, however, at least according to the classic conception, in separate rooms; and the fact that a caste that claimed to belong to the Vaishya was seated among the Sudra in the Vellala Charita occasioned a famous (semi-legendary) conflict, which we shall have to discuss later.

Let us now consider the Occident. In his letter to the Galatians (11:12,13ff.) Paul reproaches Peter for having eaten in Antioch with the gentiles and for having withdrawn and separated himself afterwards, under the influence of the Jerusalemites. "And the other Jews dissembled likewise with him." That the reproach of dissimulation made to this very Apostle has not been effaced shows perhaps just as clearly as does the occurrence itself the tremendous importance this event had for the early Christians. Indeed, this shattering of the ritual barriers against commensalism meant a destruction of the voluntary ghetto, which in its effects is far more incisive than any compulsory ghetto. It meant to destroy the situation of Jewry as a pariah people, a situation that was ritually imposed upon this people.

For the Christians it meant the origin of Christian "freedom," which Paul celebrated triumphantly again and again; for this freedom meant the universalism of Paul's mission, which cut across nations and status groups. The elimination of all ritual barriers of birth for the community of the eucharists, as realized in Antioch, was, in connection with the religious pre-conditions, the hour of conception for the occidental "citizenry." This is the case even though its birth occurred more than a thousand years later in the revolutionary *conjurationes* of the medieval cities. For without commensalism—in Christian terms, without the Lord's Supper—no oathbound fraternity and no medieval urban citizenry would have been possible.

India's caste order formed an obstacle to this, which was unsurmountable, at least by its own forces. For the castes are not governed only by this eternal ritual division. A nabob of Bankura, upon the request of a Chandala, wished to compel the Karnakar (metal workers) caste to eat with the Chandala. According to the legend of the origin of the Mahmudpurias, this request caused part of this caste to flee to Mahmudpura and to constitute itself as a separate subcaste with higher social claims. Even if there are no antagonisms of economic interests, a profound estrangement usually exists between the castes, and often deadly jealousy and hostility as well, precisely because the castes are completely oriented towards social rank. This orientation stands in contrast to the occupational associations of the Occident. Whatever part questions of etiquette and rank have played among these associations, and often it has been quite considerable, such questions could never have gained the religiously anchored significance which they have had for the Hindu.

The consequences of this difference have been of considerable political importance. By its solidarity, the association of Indian guilds, the *mahajan,* was a force which the princes had to take very much into account. It was said: "The prince must recognize what the guilds do to the people, whether it is merciful or cruel." The guilds acquired privileges from the princes for loans of money, which is reminiscent of our medieval conditions. The *shreshti* (elders) of the guilds belonged to the mightiest notables and ranked equally with the warrior and the priest nobility of their time. In the areas and at the time that these conditions prevailed, the power of the castes was undeveloped and partly hindered and shaken by the religions of salvation, which were hostile to the Brahmans. The later turn in favor of the monopoly rule of the caste system not only increased the power of the Brahmans but also that of the princes, and it broke the power of the guilds. For the castes excluded every solidarity and every politically powerful fraternization of the citizenry and of the trades. If the prince observed the ritual traditions and the social pretensions based upon them, which existed among those castes most important for him, he could not only play off the castes against one another—which he did—but he had nothing whatever to fear from them, especially if the Brahmans stood by his side. Accordingly, it is not difficult even at this point to guess the political interests which had a hand in the game during the transformation to monopoly rule of the caste system. This shift steered India's social structure—which for a time apparently stood close to the threshold of European urban development—into a course that led far away from any possibility of such development. In these world-historical differences the fundamentally important contrast between "caste" and "guild," or any other "occupational association," is strikingly revealed.

If the caste differs fundamentally from the guild and from any other kind of merely occupational association, and if the core of the caste system is connected with social rank, how then is the caste related to the status group, which finds its genuine expression in social rank?

8. *Caste and Status Group*

WHAT is a "status group?" "Classes" are groups of people who, from the standpoint of specific interests, have the same economic position. Ownership or nonownership of material goods, or possession of definite skills constitutes a class situation. "Status," however, is a quality of social honor or a lack of it, and is in the main conditioned as well as expressed through a specific style of life. Social honor can adhere directly to a class situation, and it is also, indeed most of the time, determined by the average class situation of the status-group members. This, however, is not necessarily the case. Status membership, in turn, influences class situation in that the style of life required by status groups makes them prefer special kinds of property or gainful pursuits and reject others. A status group can be closed (status by descent) or it can be open.*

A caste is doubtless a closed status group. All the obligations

---

* It is incorrect to think of the "occupational status group" as an alternative. The "style of life," not the "occupation," is always decisive. This style may require a certain profession (for instance, military service), but the nature of the occupational service resulting from the claims of a style of life always remain decisive (for instance, military service as a knight rather than as a mercenary). (*Eds.*)

and barriers that membership in a status group entails also exist in a caste, in which they are intensified to the utmost degree. The Occident has known legally closed "estates," in the sense that intermarriage with nonmembers of the group was lacking. But, as a rule, this bar against connubium held only to the extent that marriages contracted in spite of the rule constituted *mésalliances,* with the consequence that children of the "left-handed" marriage would follow the status of the lower partner.

Europe still acknowledges such status barriers for the high nobility. America acknowledges them between whites and Negroes (including all mixed bloods) in the southern states of the union. But in America these barriers imply that marriage is absolutely and legally inadmissible, quite apart from the fact that such intermarriage would result in social boycott.

Among the Hindu castes at the present time, not only intermarriage between castes but even intermarriage between subcastes is usually absolutely shunned. Already in the books of law mixed bloods from different castes belong to a lower caste than either of the parents, and in no case do they belong to the three higher ("twice-born") castes. A different state of affairs, however, prevailed in earlier days and still exists today for the most important castes. Today one occasionally encounters full connubium among subcastes of the same caste, as well as among castes of equal social standing. According to Gait's general report for 1911,[11] this was the case for the equally genteel castes of the Baidya and Kayastha in Bengal, the Kanet and the Khas in the Punjab, and, sporadically, among the Brahmans and Rajputs, and the Sonars, Nais, and the Kanets (women). Enriched Maratha peasants may avail themselves of Moratha women for a sufficient dowry.

In earlier times this was undoubtedly more often the case. Above all, originally connubium was obviously not absolutely excluded, but rather hypergamy was the rule. Among the Rajputs in Punjab, hypergamy often still exists to such an extent that even Chamar girls are purchased. Intermarriage between a girl of higher caste and a lower-caste man was considered an offense against the status honor of the girl's family. However, to own a wife of lower caste was not considered an offense, and her children were not considered degraded, or at least only partially so. According to the law of inheritance, which is certainly the product of a later period, the children had to take second place in inheritance (just as in Israel the sentence that the "children of the servant"—and of the foreign woman—"should not inherit in Israel" has been the law of a later period, as is the case everywhere else).

The interest of upper-class men in the legality of polygamy, which they could afford economically, continued to exist, even when the acute shortage of women among the invading warriors had ended. Such shortages have everywhere compelled conquerors to marry girls of subject populations. The result in India was, however, that the lower-caste girls had a large marriage market, and the lower the caste stood the larger was their marriage market; whereas the marriage market for girls of the highest castes was restricted to their own caste. Moreover, by virtue of the competition of the lower-caste girls, this restricted marriage market was by no means monopolistically guaranteed to upper-caste girls. And this caused the women in the lower castes, by virtue of the general demand for women, to bring high prices as brides. It was in part as a consequence of this dearth of women, that polyandry originated. The formation of marriage cartels among villages or among special associations, Golis, as frequently found, for instance, among the Vania (merchant) castes in Gujarat and also among peasant castes, is a counter-measure against the hypergamy of the wealthy and the city people, which raised the price of brides for the middle classes and for the rural population. If in India[12] the whole village—the unclean castes included—consider themselves to be interrelated, that is, if the new marriage partner is addressed by all as "son-in-law" and the older generation is addressed by all as "uncle," it is evident that this has nothing whatsoever to do with derivation from a "primitive group marriage"; this is indeed as little true in India as elsewhere.

Among the upper castes, however, the sale of girls to a bridegroom of rank was difficult, and the more difficult it became, the more was failure to marry considered a disgrace for both the girl and her parents. The bridegroom had to be bought by the parents with incredibly high dowries, and his enlistment (through professional matchmakers) became the parents' most important worry. Even during the infancy of the girl it was a sorrow for the parents. Finally, it was considered an outright "sin" for a girl to reach puberty without being married. This has led to grotesque results: for example, the marriage practice of the Kulin Brahmans, which enjoys a certain fame. The Kulin Brahmans are much in demand as bridegrooms; they have made a business of marrying *in absentia,* upon request and for money, girls who thus escape the ignominy of maidenhood. The girls, however, remain with their families and see the bridegroom only if business or other reasons accidentally bring him to a place where he has one (or several) such "wives" in residence. Then he shows his marriage contract to the father-in-law and uses the father's house as a "cheap hotel." In addition, without any costs, he has the enjoyment of the girl, for she is considered his "legitimate" wife.

Elsewhere infanticide is usually a result of restricted opportunities for subsistence among poor populations. But in India female infanticide was instituted precisely by the upper castes. This occurred especially among the Rajputs. Despite the severe English laws of 1829, as late as 1869, in twenty-two villages of Rajputana there were twenty-three girls and 284 boys. In an 1836 count, in some Rajput areas, not one single live girl of over one year of age was found in a population of 10,000 souls! Infanticide existed alongside child marriage. Child marriage has determined, first, the fact that in India some girls five to ten years old are already widowed and that they remain widowed for life. This is connected with widow celibacy, an institution which, in India as elsewhere, was added to widow suicide. Widow suicide was derived from the custom of chivalry: the burial of his personal belongings, especially his women, with the dead lord. Secondly, marriages of immature girls has brought about a high mortality rate in childbed.

All of this makes it clear that in the field of connubium, caste intensifies "status" principles in an extreme manner. Today hypergamy exists as a general caste rule only within the same caste, and even there it is a specialty of the Rajput caste and of some others that stand close to the Rajput socially, or to their ancient tribal territory. This is the case, for instance, with such castes as the Bhat, Khatri, Karwar, Gujar, and Jat. However, the rule is strict endogamy of the caste and of the subcaste; in the case of the latter, this rule is, in the main, broken only by marriage cartels.

The norms of commensalism are similar to those of connubium: a status group has no social intercourse with social inferiors. In the southern states of America, social intercourse between a white and a Negro would result in the boycott of the former. As a status group, caste enhances and transposes this social closure into the sphere of religion, or rather of magic. The ancient concepts of taboo and their social applications were indeed widely diffused in India's geographical environs and may well have contributed materials to this process. To these taboos were added borrowed totemic ritualism and, finally, notions of the magical impurity of certain activities, such as have existed everywhere with widely varying content and intensity.

The Hindu dietary rules are not simple in nature and by no means do they concern merely the questions (1) what may be eaten, and (2) who may eat together at the same table. These two points are covered by strict rules, which are chiefly restricted to members of the same caste. The dietary rules concern, above all, the further questions: (3) Out of whose hand may one take food of a certain kind? For genteel houses this means above all: Whom may one use for a cook? And a further question is: (4) Whose mere glance upon the food is to be excluded? With (3) there is a difference to be noted between food and drink, according to whether water, and food cooked in water (*kachcha*) is concerned, or food cooked in melted butter (*pakka*). *Kachcha* is far more exclusive. The question with whom one may smoke is closely connected with norms of commensality in the narrower sense. Originally, one smoked out of the same pipe, which was passed around; therefore, smoking together was dependent upon the degree of ritual purity of the partner. All these rules, however, belong in one and the same category of a far broader set of norms, all of which are status characteristics of ritual caste rank.

The social rank positions of all castes depend upon the question of from whom the highest castes accept *kachcha* and *pakka* and with whom they dine and smoke. Among the Hindu castes the Brahmans are always at the top in such connections. But the following questions are equal in importance to these, and closely connected with them: Does a Brahman undertake the religious services of the members of a caste? And possibly: to which of the very differently evaluated subcastes does the Brahman belong? Just as the Brahman is the last, though not the only authority in determining, by his behavior in questions of commensalism, the rank of a caste, so likewise does he determine questions of services. The barber of a ritually clean caste unconditionally serves only certain castes. He may shave and care for the "manicure" of others, but not for their "pedicure." And he does not serve some castes at all. Other wage workers, especially laundrymen, behave in a similar manner. Usually, although with some exceptions, commensality is attached to the caste; connubium is almost always attached to the subcaste; whereas usually, although with exceptions, the services by priests and wageworkers are attached to commensality.

The discussion above may suffice to demonstrate the extraordinary complexity of the rank relations of the caste system. It may also show the factors by which the caste differs from an ordinary status order. The caste order is oriented religiously and ritually to a degree not even partially attained elsewhere. If the expression "church" was not inapplicable to Hinduism, one could perhaps speak of a rank order of church estates.

9. *The Social Rank Order of the Castes in General*

WHEN the Census of India (1901) attempted to list by rank contemporary Hindu castes in the presidencies—two to three thousand or even more, according to the method of counting used—certain groups of castes were established which are distinguishable from one another according to the following criteria:

First come the Brahmans, and following them, a series of castes which, claim rightly or wrongly, to belong to the two other "twice-born" castes of classical theory: the Kshatriya and the Vaishya. In order to signify this, they claim the right to wear the "holy belt." This is a right which some of them have only recently rediscovered and which, in the view of the Brahman castes, who are seniors in rank, would certainly belong only to some members of the twice-born castes. But as soon as the right of a caste to wear the holy belt is acknowledged, this caste is unconditionally recognized as being absolutely ritually "clean." From such a caste the high-caste Brahmans accept food of every kind.

Throughout the system, a third group of castes follow. They are counted among the Satsudra, the "clean Shudra" of classical doctrine. In Northern and Central India they are the Jalacharaniya, that is, castes who may give water to a Brahman and from whose *lota* (water bottle) the Brahman accepts water.

Close to them are castes, in Northern and Central India, whose water a Brahman would not always accept (that is, acceptance or nonacceptance would possibly depend on the Brahman's rank) or whose water he would never accept (Jalabyabaharya). The high-caste barber does not serve them unconditionally (no pedicure), and the laundryman does not wash their laundry. But they are not considered absolutely "unclean" ritually. They are the Shudra in the usual sense in which the classical teachings refer to them. Finally, there are castes who are considered unclean. All temples are closed to them, and no Brahman and no barber will serve them. They must live outside the village district, and they infect either by touch or, in Southern India, even by their presence at a distance (up to sixty-four feet with the Paraiyans). All these restrictions are related to those castes which, according to the classical doctrine, originated from ritually forbidden sexual intercourse between members of different castes.

Even though this grouping of castes is not equally true throughout India (indeed there are striking exceptions), nevertheless, on the whole, it can be quite well sustained. Within these groupings one could proceed with further gradations of caste rank, but such gradations would present extremely varied characteristics: among the upper castes the criterion would be the correctness of life practices with regard to sib organization, endogamy, child marriage, widow celibacy, cremation of the dead, ancestral sacrifice, foods and drinks, and social intercourse with unclean castes. Among the lower caste one would have to differentiate according to the rank of the Brahmans who are still ready to serve them or who will no longer do so, and according to whether or not castes other than Brahmans accept water from them. In all these cases, it is by no means rare that castes of lower rank raise stricter demands than castes who otherwise are considered to have a higher standing. The extraordinary variety of such rules of rank order forbids here any closer treatment. The acceptance or avoidance of meat, at least of beef, is decisive for caste rank, and is therefore a symptom of it, but an uncertain one. The kinds of occupation and income, which entail the most far-reaching consequences for connubium, commensalism, and ritual rank, are decisive in the case of all castes. We shall speak of this later.

In addition to all these criteria, we find a mass of individual traits. Thus, for instance, the Makishya Kaibarthas (in Bengal) increasingly reject community with the Chasi Kalibarthas because the latter personally sell their (agricultural) products in the market, which the Makishya do not do. Other castes are considered *déclassé* because their women participate in selling in the stores; generally, the coöperation of women in economic pursuits is considered specifically plebeian. The social and work structure of agriculture is strongly determined by the fact that certain acts are considered absolutely degrading. Often caste rank determines whether or not one uses oxen and horses or other draft and pack animals in gainful work; it determines which animals he uses and how many (for example, the number of oxen employed by the oil pressers is thus determined).

Yet, even if we took them all into account, we could not establish a list of castes according to rank because rank differs absolutely from place to place, because only some of the castes are universally diffused, and because a great many castes, being only locally represented, have no interlocal rank order which could be determined. Furthermore, great rank differences appear between subcastes of a single caste, especially among the upper castes, but also among some of the middle castes. One would often have to place individual subcastes far behind another caste, which otherwise would be evaluated as lower.

In general, the problem arose (for the census workers): Which unit should really be considered a caste? Within one and the same caste, that is, a group considered to be a caste in Hindu tradition, there is neither necessarily connubium nor always full commensalism. Connubium is the case with only a few castes, and even with them there are reservations. The subcaste is the predominantly endogamous unit, and in some castes there are several hundred subcastes. The subcastes are either purely local castes (diffused over districts of varying size), and/or they constitute associations which are delimited and especially designated according to actual or alleged descent, former or present kind of occupational pursuit, or other differences in style of life. They consider themselves as parts of the caste and in addition to their own names carry the name of the caste; they may be legitimated in this by a division of the caste, or by reception into the caste, or simply by usurpation of rank. Only the subcastes actually carry on a life of unified regulation, and they alone are organized—insofar as a caste organization exists. Caste itself often designates merely a social claim raised by these closed associations. Often, but not always, the caste is the womb of the subcaste; and on rare occasions the caste is characterized by certain organizations common to all subcastes. More frequently, the caste has certain characteristics of life conduct traditionally common to all subcastes.

Nevertheless, as a rule the unity of caste exists side by side with the unity of subcastes. There are sanctions against marriage and commensalism outside the caste which are stronger than those imposed upon members of different subcastes within the same caste. Also, just as new subcastes form themselves easily, the barriers between them may be more unstable; whereas the barriers between communities once recognized as castes are maintained with extraordinary perseverance.

It is perhaps impossible to determine the rank order of the castes; it is contested and subject to change. An attempt was made in 1901 by the British census to settle this rank order once and for all. It was not repeated; the excitement and discontent that resulted was out of all proportion to the intended result. The attempt to classify the castes set off a signal for competitive demands by the castes for social rank and the procurement of historical "proofs" to support their claims. It led to remonstrances and protests of all kinds and called forth a considerable, and partly instructive literature.

Castes of questionable rank sought to exploit the census for stabilizing their position and used the census authorities, as one census expert put it, as a kind of herald's office. Amazing claims of new rank were made. The Bengal Tshandal, for instance, the lowest caste alleged to stem from a mixture of Brahman women with Shudra men (actually a Hinduized guest people from Bengal), rebaptized themselves Namashudra and sought to trace their descent to a pure caste and "prove" their Brahman blood.

Quite apart from such cases, however, were various former professional soldier and robber castes, which since the pacification of the land had led quiet lives as land-tilling castes. Now they seized the opportunity to pose as Kshatriyas. Nonrecognized "Brahmans" (ancient tribal priests) buttressed their claims for recognition. All castes in any way engaged in trade sought recognition as Vaishyas. Animistic tribes demanded registration as castes and with as high rank as possible. Certain sects sought re-integration into the Hindu community.

Such agitation over the question of rank as the census occasioned had not occurred previously. But the past was in no way free from revolutions of rank order.

Who arbitrated such rank contests? And who made decisions on matters related to rank? It was stated above that, in general, the Brahmans to this day, are theoretically, the final authorities on questions of rank. Official banquets requiring the attendance of Brahmans always necessitated correct decisions about rank questions. The Brahmans in the past, as now, were in no position to settle the problems alone. As far as we can determine, in the period before the foreign conquests rank questions were always decided by the king or his official advisor on ritualistic matters. Such a chief of protocol was either a Brahman or an official who, as a rule, sought the legal advice of a Brahman. We know, however, of many cases in which Indian kings personally degraded single castes in due form or expelled individuals, including Brahmans from their castes. The person concerned often experienced this as an unjust infringement upon his well-established rights. Degraded castes often continued to contest such decisions for centuries; the Brahmans, however, usually took it.

Moreover, the king advised by Brahmans who had immigrated at his request, had authority to make decisions concerning the original or renewed ordering of caste ranks throughout large territories as, for instance, East-Bengal under the Sena-dynasty. The king was able, too, to make decisions about single caste duties. Under the last great all-Indian rule of the Mahrattas at the turn of the eighteenth century, the legal opinions of Brahmans about questions of single caste duties were submitted to the Peshwa, a descendant of a Brahman family, who obviously gave his *exequatur* after substantive discussion of the controversial issues. The abolition of this support of the Brahmans by the secular arm today—except in the remaining Hindu vassal states where residues survive—is said to have caused the diminished compliance with the decisions of the Brahmans. In short, religious and secular power cooperated in the interest of the legitimate order.

The position of the king allowed him to select the most pliable of the Brahmans. Under the circumstances, not the king's power, but that of the Brahmans and the castes, is astounding. Brahmanical and caste power resulted from the inviolability of all sacred law which was believed to ward off evil enchantment. In problematic caste situations Indian kings followed the unconditional and magically sanctioned principle "Prerogative breaks the common law"; the caste, on the other hand, was sustained only by its economic importance. The royal judge was bound by the traditional customs of the single caste; jury members for the particular caste had to be admitted to court trials, and castes were brought before the royal judge only by organs of the single caste which normally had jurisdiction over caste affairs. Even today single caste organs settle caste problems: they excommunicate, impose fines or amends, settle disputes, and, in relative independence, develop through their judicial practices the norms for newly emerging legal questions. We cannot, therefore, avoid a survey of the problems of caste jurisdiction, practice, and organization.

With this in mind, it is necessary to examine the principles which determine the structure and boundary lines of the various caste types, a question hitherto touched only tangentially.

10. Caste and Sib

THERE remains to be examined still another important peculiarity of Indian society which is intimately interrelated with the caste system. Not only the formation of castes but the heightened significance of the sib belongs to the fundamental traits of Indian society. The Hindu social order, to a larger extent than anywhere else in the world, is organized in terms of the principle of *clan charisma.* "Charisma" means that an extraordinary, at least not generally available, quality adheres to a person. Originally charisma was thought of as a magical quality. "Clan charisma" means that this extraordinary quality adheres to sib members per se and not, as originally, to a single person.

We are familiar with residues of this sociologically important phenomenon of clan charisma particularly in the hereditary "divine right of kings" of our dynasties. To a lesser degree the legend of the "blue blood" of a nobility, whatever its specific origin, belongs to the same sociological type. Clan charisma is one of the ways personal charisma may be "routinized," (i.e., made a part of everyday social experience).

In contrast to the hereditary chieftain in times of peace who, among some tribes, could also be a woman, the warrior king and his men were heroes whose successes had proven their purely personal and magical qualities. The authority of the war leader, like that of the sorcerer, rested upon strictly personal charisma. The successor also originally claimed his rank by virtue of personal charisma. (The problem, of course, is that more than one "successor" may raise such claims.) The unavoidable demand for law and order in the question of successorship forces the followers to consider different possibilities: either the designation of the qualified successor by the leader; or the selection of a new leader by his disciples, followers, or officials. The progressive regulation of these originally spontaneous and nonprocedural questions may lead to the development of elective bodies of officials in the manner of "princes," "electors," and "cardinals."

In India a suggestive belief won out: that charisma is a quality attached to the sib per se, that the qualified successor or successors should be sought within the sib. This led to the *inheritance* of charisma, which orginally had nothing to do with heredity. The wider the spheres to which magical belief applied, the more consistently developed such beliefs became, the wider, in turn, the possible field of application of clan charisma. Not only heroic and magico-cultic abilities, but any form of authority, came to be viewed as determined and bound by clan charisma. Special talents, not only artistic but craft talent as well, fell within the sphere of clan charisma.

In India the development of the principle of clan charisma far surpassed what is usual elsewhere in the world. This did not occur all at once; clan charisma was in conflict with ancient genuine charismatism which continued to uphold only the personal endowment of the single individual, as well as with the pedagogy of status cultivation.

Even in the Indian Middle Ages, many formalities in the apprenticeship to and practice of handicraft show strong traces of the principle of personal charisma. These are evident in the magical elements of the novitiate and the assumption by the apprentice of journeyman status. However, since, originally, occupational differentiation was largely interethnic and the practitioners of many trades were members of pariah tribes, there were strong forces for the development of charismatic clan magic.

The strongest expression of clan charisma was in the sphere of authority. In India the hereditary transmission of authority, i.e., on the basis of family ties, was normal. The further back one traces the more universal the institution of the hereditary village-headship is found to be. Merchant and craft guilds and castes had hereditary elders; anything else was normally out of the question. So self-evident was priestly, royal, and knightly office charisma that free appointment of successors to office by patrimonial rulers, like the free choice of urban occupations, occurred only during upheavals of the tradition or at the frontiers of social organization before the social order was stabilized.

The exceptional quality of the sib was (note!) realized "in principle." Not only could knightly or priestly sibs prove to be barren of magical qualities and thus lose them as an individual does, but a *homo novus* could prove his possession of charisma and thereby legitimatize his sib as charismatic. Thus, charismatic clan authority could be quite unstable in the single case.

In the study of W. Hopkins of present-day Ahmadbad, the Nayar Sheth—the counterpart of the medieval Lord Mayor of the Occident—was the elder of the richest Jain family of the city. He and the Vishnuite Sheth of the clother's guild, who was also hereditary, jointly determined public opinion on all social, i.e., ritualistic and proprietary questions of the city. The other hereditary Sheths were less influential beyond their guilds and castes. However, at the time Hopkins made his study a rich manufacturer outside all guilds had successfully entered the competition.

If a son was notoriously unfit his influence waned—be it the son of a craft, guild or caste elder or the son of a priest mystagogue or artist. His prestige was channelized either to a more adequate member of the particular sib or to a member (usually the elder) of the next richest sib. Not new wealth alone, but great wealth combined with personal charisma legitimatized its possessor and his sib in social situations where status conditions were still or once again fluid. Although in single cases charismatic clan authority was quite unstable, everyday life always forced compliance with sib authority once it was established. The sib always reaped the benefits of individually established charisma.

The economic effects of sib integration through magical and animistic beliefs in China was described in a previous work.* In China the charismatic glorification of the sib, countered by

---

* Cf. Max Weber, *The Religion of China,* Trans. by H. H. Gerth, (Glencoe: The Free Press, 1951), Chapter VII and VIII.

the examination system of patrimonial dominion, had economic consequences similar to those in India. In India, the caste organization and extensive caste autonomy and the autonomy of the guild, which was still greater because it was ritually unfettered, placed the development of commercial law almost completely in the hands of the respective interest groups. The unusual importance of trade in India would lead one to believe that a rational law of trade, trading companies, and enterprise might well have developed.

However, if one looks at the legal literature of the Indian Middle Ages one is astonished by its poverty. While partially formalistic, Indian justice and the law of evidence were basically irrational and magical. Much of it was formless in principle, because of hierocratic influence. Ritually relevant questions could only be decided by ordeals. In other questions the general moral code, unique elements of the particular case, tradition (particularly), and a few supplementary royal edicts were employed as legal sources.

Yet, in contrast to China, a formal trial procedure developed with regulated summons (*in jus vocatio*, under the Mahratts summons were served by clerks of the court). The debt-liability of heirs existed but was limited after generations. However, the collection of debts, although debt bondage was known, remained somewhat in the magical stage or in that of a modified billet system. At least as a norm, joint liability of partners was lacking. In general, the right of association appeared only late in Indian development and then only in connection with the right of religious fraternities. The law of corporations remained inconsequential. All sorts of corporations and joint property relationships received mixed treatment. There was a ruling on profit sharing which, incidentally, extended also to artisans coöperating under a foreman, hence in an *ergasterion*.[13] Above all, however, the principle, recognized also in China, that one should grant unconditional credit and pawn objects only among personally close members of the phratry, among relatives and friends, held also in India. Debts under other circumstances were recognized only under provision of guarantors or witnessed promissory notes.[14]

The details of later legal practice, to be sure, were adequate to implement trading needs but they hardly promoted trade on its own. The quite considerable capitalistic development which occurred in the face of such legal conditions can be explained only in terms of the power of guilds. They knew how to pursue their interests by use of boycott, force, and expert arbitration. However, in general, under conditions such as those described, the sib fetters of credit relationships had to remain the normal state of affairs.

The principle of clan charisma also had far-reaching consequences outside the field of commercial law. Because we are prone to think of occidental feudalism, primarily as a system of socio-economic ties, we are apt to overlook its peculiar origins and their significance.

Under the compelling military needs of the time of its origin, the feudal relationship made a free contract among sib strangers basic for the faith-bound relation between the lord and his vassals. Increasingly feudal lords developed the in-group feeling of a unitary status group. They developed eventually into the closed hereditary estate of chivalrous knights. We must not forget that this grew on the basis of sib estrangement among men who viewed themselves not as sib, clan, phratry, or tribe members but merely as status peers.

Indian development took quite a different turn. It is true that individual enfeoffment of retainers and officials with land or political rights occurred. Historically, this is clearly discernible. But it did not give the ruling stratum its stamp, and feudal status formation did not rest on land grants. Rather, as Baden-Powell[15] has correctly emphasized, the character of Indian developments was derived from the sib, clan, phratry, and tribe.

Before continuing we shall have to clarify our terminology. The Irish term "clan" is ambiguous. In our terminology the typical organization of warrior communities consists of: (1) the tribe or a collectivity of "phratries"—in our terminology, primarily always associations of (originally, magically) trained warriors; (2) the sib, i.e., charismatically outstanding agnatic descendants of charismatic chieftains. The plain warrior did not necessarily have a "sib" but belonged to a "family" or a totemic (or quasi-totemic) association besides his phratry and possibly unitary age group.

A gens of overlords, however, had no totem; it had emancipated itself from it. The more the ruling tribes of India developed into a ruling class the more survivals of the totem (*devaks*) vanished and "sibs" emerged (or better, continued to exist). A blurring of charismatic clan differences occurred when the phratry began to develop "we-feeling" on the ground of common descent, rather than of joint defense, and hence became a quasi-sib.

In India the charismatic head of the phratry distributed conquered land; manorial prerogatives among fellow-sib members; open fields among the ordinary men of the phratry. The conquering classes must be conceived of as a circle of phratries and sibs of lords dispersing over the conquered territory under the rule of the tribe.

Prerogatives were enfeoffed by the head of the phratry (*raja*) or where one existed by the tribal king (*maharaja*) only, as a rule, to his agnates. It was not a freely contracted trusteeship. Fellow-sib members claimed this grant as a birthright. Each conquest produced, in the first place, new office fiefs for the sib of the king and its subsibs. Conquest was, therefore, the *dharma* of the king.

However different some details of the Indian from its occidental counterpart, the ascendency of the secular overlords and their estates had similar basis. No matter how often individual charismatic upstarts and their freely recruited followings shattered the firm structure of the sibs, the social process always resumed its firm course of charismatic clan organization of tribes, phratries, and sibs. Among the Aryans the ancient sacrificial priests, even at the time of the early Vedas, had become a distinguished priestly nobility. The various sibs of the priestly nobility divided according to hereditary function and appropriate clan charisma into hereditary "schools." Given the primacy of magical charisma claimed by the clans, they and their heirs—the Brahmans—became the primary propagators of this principle through Hindu society.

It is clear that the magical charisma of the clans contributed greatly to the establishment of the firm structure of caste estrangement, actually containing it *in nuce*. On the other hand, the caste order served greatly to stabilize the sib. All strata which raised claims to distinction were forced to become stratified on the pattern of the ruling castes. The exogamous kinship order was based on the sib. Social situation, ritual duty, way of life and occupational position in the end were determined by the charismatic clan principle which extended to all positions of authority. As clan charisma supported the caste so the caste, in turn, supported the charisma of the sib.

CHAPTER II

THE MAIN GROUPING OF THE CASTES

MODERN social science long considered the four castes of classical learning to be mere literary constructions. This view is no longer maintained, and our preceding discussions showed its assumptions to be far too sweeping.

Even today the usual classification of castes under the four old classes determines the stereotyped greeting of the Brahman. No wonder that present-day castes strive to be classified in terms of the Brahmans. The significance of the four ancient castes is confirmed by the inscriptions on monuments, which frequently refer to them. Of course, it is important to remember that the authors of the inscriptions were quite as much under the spell of the literary tradition as the modern representatives of a caste claiming Kshatriya or Vaishya rank. But the very nature of the phenomena we are dealing with confirms the assumption that the statements in the law books refer to a serious—be it ever so stereotyped—picture of historical social reality, and are not simply constructions out of nothing.

The two lower so-called "castes" of the law books were perhaps never castes at all in the present-day sense of the term, but, even in classical times, were rank-classes of castes. Originally they were simply status groups. An occasional passage of the literature observes: "The Vaishya and Shudra were there before the Brahmans and Kshatriyas ever existed." The Vaishyas were the ancient freemen who were surpassed by the noble sibs—the noble sibs being war nobles, hence chieftains, and later knightly gentes and partially, also, priestly nobles as found elsewhere. The status inferiors of the freemen were "helots" (Shudras).

The symbolic combat[1] between an Arya and a Shudra, a phase of the Gravamayana-festival, is comparable to similar significant ceremonies in Sparta. In fact, this opposition is much sharper than the one between both upper castes and the Vaishyas.

The Brahmans and Kshatriyas engaged in certain, prescribed, exclusive activities which implemented their styles of life as status groups: for the Brahmans—sacrifice, study of the Vedas, receipt of gifts (particularly land grants), and asceticism; for the Kshatriyas—political rule, knightly feats of valor. The occupations of a Vaishaya—tillage and trade and, particularly, the lending of money at interest—were considered by both upper castes as unbecoming to their rank and station. However, in time of need, when it proved impossible to earn one's living conventionally, it was temporarily permissible, with some reservations, to take up the occupations of a Vaishya.

In contrast to this, the way of life of the Shudra signified "menial service." The correct Brahman cannot join the modern army, for he would have to obey superiors from a lower caste or of barbarian descent. The classical sources subsume occupations under "menial service" for other castes in a far more explicit and literal sense than anywhere else. This is to be explained by the characteristically Indian organization of the primeval village crafts. As briefly indicated above, workers who were enumerated, in English terminology, as members of an "establishment" were actually kinds of cottagers—not serfs of individual employers but village helots to whom were leased small hereditary holdings. In Dekkan, under the Mahrattas, two typical categories of such village servants were to be found: the Baruh Balowtay, comprising the ancient typical crafts of carpenter, blacksmith, cobbler, potter, barber, washerman, bard, astrologer, leather-worker, watchman, effigy cleaner, *mullah* (in pure Hindu villages, the butchers of sacrificial sheep); and the Baruh Alowtay, comprising the later crafts of the gold and coppersmith, blacksmith, water carrier, janitor of the village gate, and courier, gardener, oil presser and a number of religious clerks. Not all positions were actually filled.[2] The composition of these village servants was not typical throughout. In Bombay Province the Mahars were found among them. Formerly, they were peasants, then, as expert boundary surveyors, they were degraded to village servants and settled on outlying plots. Nowadays they frequently become chauffeurs despite conservative protests. As a rule the village compensated them for their services, not by payment for single services, but by a fixed share of the harvest yields or wages in kind. The kinds of artisans who belonged to this group varied in different regions, but in the main they are typical for all India to this day.

If we examine the Indian castes in terms of occupational composition, we find that rarely does a Brahman or Rajput, no matter how deeply degraded, ever take up one of the ancient crafts. Rajput peasants, however, are quite frequent; in fact, the majority of their caste are peasants. But, even today, the Rajput who does his own ploughing is degraded, in contrast to the absentee owner. Hence, increasing profits through overseas export, among other things, permitted a rapid increase of landlordism. Other castes which claim Kshatriya rank usually demand precedence over "rusticated" Rajputs. The ancient characteristic rejection of the trader, and the tradition of court service led the Rajputs to prefer even the lowest forms of domestic service, (held to be ritually pure), rather than engaging in a craft. From the other side of the status hierarchy there is a great demand for high-caste domestics; such persons must be ritually pure and capable in order to serve the lord and lady physically, particularly to serve water to them.

1. The Brahmans

To some extent the same circumstance determines certain monopolies of the present-day Brahman caste, particularly the employment of almost exclusively Brahman cooks in high-caste houses. For the rest, the Brahmans were and are infiltrating occupations, particularly administrative posts which demand writing skill and education—just as the clerics of our Middle Ages. In the South, the Brahmans have maintained a monopoly of administrative positions into modern times. Ritualistic obligations made it difficult for the Brahmans to enter the medical profession, and they are but sparsely represented in the field of engineering.

All of this is quite in agreement with the Indian tradition of dividing the castes into four types. The law books mirror other features of prescribed life styles of the upper castes which bear the stamp of authenticity and, in part, of great antiquity. The law books hold a man to be degraded unless he acquires the holy belt before an affixed and prescribed age limit. Furthermore, they recognize typical patterns of conduct for different age levels—which actually held only for the highest caste, the Brahmans.

The Brahmans have never been a tribe although more than half of them live in the upper Ganges Valley—their home base—and in Bengal. Originally, the Brahmans were magicians who developed into a hierocratic caste of cultured men. They had to undergo a course of instruction which even in classical times consisted only in learning the sacred (magical) formulae and ritualistic practices, and in the mechanical rote-learning of the orally transmitted Vedas under the tutelage of a freely chosen Brahmanical teacher who recited the classical works word for word. This kind of preparation, externally a purely literary schooling of priests, contained vestiges of ancient magical asceticism, which permit us to recognize the origin of the Brahmans out of the primeval magicians.

The general stages in the development of the Brahmans into a caste is clear, but not its causes. Obviously, the priesthood of the Vedic period was not a closed hereditary status group even though the clan charisma of certain priestly sibs was established in the eyes of the people alongside the personal charisma of the ancient magician. Among the functionally specialized priests the *hotar* or fire priest, played the chief role in cult practices. The historical ascendancy of the Brahmans seems to have several reasons. Perhaps the older assumption holds—that the increasingly stereotyped cult practices and magical formulae made the master of sacrificial ceremonies, that is, the Brahman, more and more the decisive leader. The main cause, however, may have been the increasing significance of family priests of nobles and princes as opposed to those administering the community sacrifice.[8] This would suggest, if this modern assumption is correct, the diminishing importance of the military association in contrast to that of the prince and his vassals. The magicians had invaded the circles of ancient priestly nobles and, finally, had taken over their legacy.

The ascent of the Brahmans from magical "family chaplaincy" explains why the development of priestly "office" remained quite alien to the Hindu priesthood. Their position represents a specialized development from the universally diffused guild organization as of magicians and their development into a hereditary caste with ever-rising status claims. At the same time, the development was a triumph of "knowledge" (or magically effective formulae) over the merely empirical "craft" of the ancient priests. At any rate, the very power of the Brahmans is connected with the increasing significance of magic in all spheres of life.

The school of the Atharava Veda,[4] with its collection of specifically magical formulae, demanded that the princely house chaplains be taken always from their midst. Astrology and other specific forms of Brahmanical knowledge originated in this school. There are sufficient indications in the law books to prove that magic did not triumph in all spheres of life without a struggle. It was consummated only during the course of the Brahmans' ascent to power. A king's triumph in battle, as well as other successes in life were thought to depend upon successful sorcery. Failure was ascribed to the family priest or to the actor's own ritual offenses.

Since the knowledge of the Brahmans was secret, the monopoly of education by their own progeny resulted automatically. Thus, alongside educational qualification for the priesthood there appeared qualification by birth. The *decapaya* (a part of the sacrifice) required geneological proof that the ancestors of the officiating priests had been soma drinkers for ten generations. Presumably their merits were meditated upon during the sacrifice.

Only in obscure residua did the old conception survive which based Brahman quality upon personal charisma. The novice (*bramacarin*—student Brahman) was still subjected to the severe regulation of life characteristic of magical asceticism. Particularly, sexual and economic asceticism were required. According to ancient conceptions the novice had to live chastely and by mendicancy. The teacher, by magical means, "made" a Brahman out of the disciple—originally irrespective of his descent. The decisive source of power of the full Brahman was his learning of the Vedas, a learning which was viewed as peculiarly charismatic. A Brahman reproached because he was born of a Shudra woman answered his opponent by proposing a fire ordeal to decide who had the greater Vedic knowledge.[5] After completing his education and the appropriate ceremonies, the Brahman was expected to establish a household, become a *grishastha.* He now became an active Brahman—if he engaged at all in professional work and did not remain a rentier or take up one of the permissible emergency pursuits.

Brahmanical activities consisted of sacrifice and instruction. Brahmans were economically bound so rigidly and visibly by etiquette that they could not use their personal services to earn their livelihoods in the manner of a vocation. The Brahman accepted only gifts (*dakshina*), not pay. The giving of gifts for the use of their services was, of course, a ritualistic duty. Sacrifice without gifts brought evil enchantment; moreover, his magical power enabled the Brahman to avenge severely the denial of gifts by curses or intentional ritualistic errors in the performance of the sacrifice, bringing misfortune to the lord of the sacrifice. Righteous vengeance was actually developed into a methodical procedure. The minimum value of gifts was stipulated and unfair competition among Brahmans prohibited. It was permissible, and under certain conditions prescribed for the Brahman to inquire in advance as to the size of the intended gift. Their tremendous magical power permitted the Brahmans—in A. Weber's expression—"true orgies of covetousness." We are reminded of the well-known passage in Goethe's *Faust* (concerning the stomach of the church) when we read the principle that nothing can harm the Brahman's belly. It has, however, only ritualistic significance. A Brahman could atone by simple means for any or almost any offense against dietary ritual.[6]

The social and economic privileges of the Brahmans were unsurpassed by those of any other priesthood. Even the excrement of a Brahman could have religious meaning as a divination means. The principle of *ajucyata*—forbidding the oppression of a Brahman—included, among other things, that a judge must never adjudicate in favor of a non-Brahman against a Brahman; the *arca* (respect) due to a Brahman or at least the Brahman's claim to respect was higher than a king's.

The peculiarities of the Brahmans as a religious status group will be discussed below (see Part II). Here we are concerned only with the economic advantages that accompanied the specific caste claims for *danam*, gifts. The classical form of compensation on the part of distinguished lords consisted in land grants, cattle, rents dependent on land or tax yields, money, jewelry, and precious objects in that order. At least according to Brahmanical theory the right to receive land grants was a monopoly of the Brahman caste and its most important economic privilege. The innumerable inscriptions concerning prebendal foundations (the majority of all preserved Indian inscriptions) prove that actually the typical, full-caste Brahman of the Indian Middle Ages was a hereditary prebendary.

The typical, and originally the highest station of the Brahman, however, was and remained *purohita* (house chaplain) of one or several princes.[7] Thus, he was the spiritual director of the prince in personal and political affairs. Upon this position the "bread of Brahmanhood," as it was called, depended. From it was derived the political and social power of the caste. A king without a *purohita* could hardly be a full king; similarly, a Brahman without a king could hardly be a full Brahman. To this day, the power of the Brahman rests more upon his position as father confessor, and his indispensability for the many family ceremonies of a distinguished household than upon the almost negligible caste organization per se.

In their role as house priests, the Brahmans imposed upon ambitious castes certain features of the social order (sib and marriage system). This did not result from any decision by some authoritative organ of their caste. Economically the place of the Brahmanical house priest was somewhat similar to that of our "house physician." It was a principle that one should not, without need, exchange a priest once he had been used—according to ancient sources, at least not within the same year. This is matched by the protection of the *jajmani* (patronage) relation against the competition of other Brahmans through strict etiquette. This is similar to the behavior of our house physicians who commonly adhere to such formalities in the interest of their status situation, and to the damage of the patient. This voluntary patronage relation substitutes for the dioceses of a hierarchically organized church. Thus, the total position of the Brahman has remained similar to that of the ancient sorcerer and medicine man.

When the Brahman sees the son of his son, he is expected to retire from the household and become a forest dweller. As a forest dweller, he is able through ascetic exercises to achieve the miraculous power of a magician and the power to enchant deities and men. Thus he concludes his life as an apotheosized "superman." This caste duty, too, a caste duty which today is essentially theoretical, is a survival of the magicians' organization by age classes.

As a rule, distinguished Brahmans never become permanent employees of a congregation or parish. Hindu religion has no "congregation." Moreover, high-caste Brahmans never become the hired priests of Hindu sects or village associations. Brahmans often serve as Vishnu priests, and also perform lowly services in temples—for instance, in well-paid positions of the Vallabhakhari sect and with the Gujarat-Yajurvedis. But when they do they always incur some degradation. As we shall see later, the relation between Hindu sect members and priests or mystagogues is very different from that of an occidental sect with its employed *ministry*. No high-caste Brahman is or was gladly the "servant" of a community like a Shudra. Even to accept a position as temple priest could, under certain conditions, strongly degrade him. These facts are partially correlated with the social peculiarity of Brahmanhood as a sorcerers' caste, partially with the feudal structure of Indian society, and partially, however, with the position held by priests in tribes and village communities before Hinduization.

The cult practitioner belonged, in general, simply to the hereditary "establishment" of the village—like the *mullah* and all sorts of present-day temple servants.[8] The single pariah tribes which gradually turned into Hindu castes not only had deities of their own, en masse, but also their own priests who became caste gods and caste priests. The artisan castes, who were interspersed among other castes, have with great stubbornness continued to insist on exclusive service by members of their own caste in opposition to the Brahmans. The Kammalars, for example, may serve in place of many others which the census reports discover in present-day India. These skilled metal-wood- and stone-workers claim to stem from the artisan god Visvakarma. Upon the call of kings they dispersed widely to Burma, Ceylon, Java and claimed the ranks of priests and also that of newly arrived itinerant Brahmans. As magical artisans as well, they obviously served other castes as *gurus*, ministering to the individual: "The Kamalar is everybody's *guru*."[9] Tribal castes, living in separate villages, regularly retained their traditional priests. The Brahmans won influence over these tribal priests essentially through their superior education, particularly their astrological learning which was beyond the competition of village and caste priests.

To the Brahmans, of course, such priests were completely degraded, insofar as they accepted their existence at all—self-evidently for all impure castes and objectionable in the case of pure castes. Occasionally, as we saw, tribal priests serving ruling sibs won recognition as Brahmans, though usually as socially declassed Brahmans. It is not our purpose here to pursue the extensive social differentiation of Brahmans which resulted from this, and from the declassing of Brahmans serving despised castes.[10] Nor shall we examine the caste rank of the numerous Brahmans, today the majority, who have changed their callings. Our concern is only the close connection between the special position of the Brahmans and that of the kings and noble castes, the Kshatriyas.

2. *The Kshatriyas*

THE ancient Indian warlord of the Vedas is *primus inter pares* among the *maghavan* who suggest somewhat the nobles of *Phocaea.* In classical times these gentes were replaced by the Kshatriya caste which later substantially disappeared.

In the oldest sources we discern the dawn beginnings of military organization in India. We find castle-dwelling kings of the Homeric type with their sibs and followings (king's men). The universally diffused charismatic heroism in the manner of the Nordic Berserks and the Israelite Moshuahs, the charismatic "Degen" of charismatic warrior chieftains—all these belonged to the past and only traces of them survived in epic times.

The ancient, universally diffused organization of warriors as a brotherhood of young men, the systematic, magical hero-asceticism of boys, the stages in the warrior novitiate, initiation of the *ephebes* into the phratry of bachelors living in collective economy with captured girls in long houses, the retirement of ex-service (militia) men into marriage and domesticity, the reservations made for elders (in Japan, *inkyo*) unable to serve—all these have vanished. Indeed, vestiges survive of the ancient charismatic warrior probation and of the principle that a man disqualified for the armed forces remains a "woman," i.e., deprived of political rights. They survive in the highly important *upanayana* ceremonies (ancient initiation rites) which the boys of a "twice-born" caste—thus far Shudras (like women)—had to undergo before securing membership status. But the ceremony itself, completed at a very early age, was a vestige comparable to our "confirmation."

The Kshatriya of classical literature lacked the special character of our medieval knighthood. Their social position rested on sib and clan charisma and not on a feudal hierarchy. This was true even before the crystallization of caste forms. The

Kshatriyas were and remained kings, subkings, and in the lowest stratum, village notables with special economic privileges.

Classical sources ascribe to the Kshatriyas the function of "protecting" the population politically and militarily. The king not furnishing protection for his subjects from thieves and robbers is held liable for damages done to them. According to the sources, each officer, including the tax-farmer of later kingdoms, had the same duty of protection and eventual restitution for any damages done to a certain district. (The size of the district varied with the size of its central community.) So far, this caste duty grew out of experience. Indeed, it contained, as some further evidence indicates, vestiges of the ancient conception of the charismatic role of the king. The king defeated in battle was responsible for the sins of his subjects as well as his own. The king who spoke false justice was magically burdened with the sins of the intentionally or accidentally injured party—a more stringent analogy to the conception underlying the *Urteilschelte* in Germanic law. That king is good whose subjects are prosperous and experience no famine. Famine was always a sign of magical offense or the charismatic insufficiency of the ruler. In case of need, the king does penance. The people may and should get rid of a king found permanently divested of his charisma.

Out of these charismatic conceptions in the great kingdoms of the Indian Middle Ages there easily developed the theory of patriarchal "welfare" and "protection." However, it was eclipsed by the transformation of hero-charisma into "vocational" duty of an estate of knights.

Warfare is the *dharma* of the Kshatriyas in classical and medieval sources. Except for the intermissions brought by the universal monarchies, war was as ever-present in India as between the ancient city-states. Only when a king had conquered all others was he entitled to the great horse sacrifice which brought the fortunate, officiating Brahmans 100,000 cattle. This occurred with approximately the frequency with which the Janus temple in Rome was closed. The celebration is historically ascertained.

That a king should ever fail to consider the subjugation of his neighbors by force or fraud remained inconceivable to secular and religious Hindu literature. When the founder of the Mahratt empire failed to conduct war for one year, the neighboring lords considered it a sure indication that he was mortally ill. In the Kshatriya's militaristic code, death in bed was not only considered dishonorable but a sin against caste *dharma.* When a Kshatriya felt his powers weaken he was expected to seek death in battle.

According to legend the old Kshatriyas were wiped off the face of the earth, vengeance for their enmity toward the Brahmans. There is certainly a grain of truth in this as in the legend of the struggle of Vicvamithras against Vaishtha. The ancient Kshatriyas, about the time of Buddha (sixth century B.C.), were a highly educated estate of urban- and castle-dwelling nobles, comparable, in this regard, to the knighthood of Provence in the early Middle Ages. They were later displaced by the Rajputs. The Rajputs, partly stemming from what is today Rajputana and Southern Oudh, rose in about the eighth century to overlordship and spread through the kingdoms as a typical warrior stratum. Many are illiterate to this day. They correspond to later tribes who enter the caste order by way of service to the great kings as paid knights or mercenaries.[11] The Rajputs formed by far the most distinguished tribe among those supplying mercenaries and were most completely Hinduized in the manner of the Kshatriyas.

The ancient Kshatriyas gentes rivaled the Brahmans in education and were, as we shall see, the supporters of anti-Brahmanical salvation religions (such as Buddhism). The Rajputs, on the other hand, had to submit to the superior Brahmanical education and, in common with patrimonial kinship, supported the Hindu restoration. The peculiar, unclassical segregation of the Rajputs into exogamous subdivisions indicates their derivation from a tribe of mercenary knights. No family tree extends further back than the fifth century and 90 per cent are settled in North India, especially the Northwest.

The political feudalism which prevailed in Rajputana until modern times corresponded very closely to the type reported in classical times. The Raja had the best land as a desmene (Persian, Khalsa). The vassals enfeoffed with prerogatives also received land grants. They had to render knightly pay escheatage. The Raja had the right (1) to tax part of the harvest yield; (2) to dispose of wasteland—which was important for it involved rights to timber, deforestation, and hereditary property rights for payment of a woodcutting tax and the assumption of rent obligations payable in lump sums; (3) to mining, treasure-seeking, and other similar regalia; and (4) to collect fines for punishments. All these economic rights could, in part, also be enfeoffed.

As a rule, in India, in accordance with the universal principle of clan charisma, only sib and clan members of the ruling clan tended to be enfeoffed; the system was not based upon a personal relation of trust between sib strangers. In early times enfeoffment did not comprise seignorial but only economic and personal rights of political origin. The Kshatriyas were royal sibs, not feudal landlords.

In the Dravidic states the king, in each village, had a royal hide (*majha*) which was paralleled by the tax-exempt priestly hide* (*pahoor*). As his power increased the king installed his representative, *mahta,* beside or in place of the old village chieftain (*munda*). The charismatically privileged (*dhuinhar*) families which supplied these village chiefs had tax-free land, while the other land lots (*khunt*) had become taxable and were considered "the king's land."[12] The conquerors essentially retained this arrangement and generally feudalized it. In the Middle Ages elements of a truly feudal structure are to be found in most parts of India, particularly in the west—often in quite occidental form. The Rajas had coats of arms.[13] There were enfeoffments with knightly ceremonies.[14] But the law books knew no true seignorial rights in the villages. These were a product, not of feudalization, but of later prebendalization of political authority.

Many times under the great kings high military command posts were combined with territorial fiefs, which were turned into hereditary economic rights.[15] After the death of a vassal in combat his position as leader of the respective troops was given to someone else. The incumbent received several villages as hereditary fief of fallowland. So, too, with high political posts.[16] Among the great political fief-holders, royal descent or relationship[17] was the rule, not, however, without exception.[18] The prerogatives of princes like those of vassals were considered alienable to a large degree.[19] Constant feuds occurred over large areas of India. Particularly in the South epitaphs, typically, are for knights who fell in battle against cattle-thieves, and therefore entered heaven.[20]

What was the characteristic derivation of those elements of

---

* We read *Priesterhufe* rather than *Priesterstufe.* (*Eds.*)

the Rajput caste most representative of older traditions? The question can best be answered by pointing to the political overlords such as petty princes, enfeoffed knights, office nobles, or landlords with political rights and duties. These nobles were never pure scribes, but an estate of politico-military fief-holders of quite a different type, especially including military prebendaries to be discussed presently. The changes in Indian organization and administration, particularly military, are bound up in this.

The army of the epics and of the oldest historical sources (Megasthenes and Arrian) is similar, though at a more advanced stage than the Homeric army. Heroes (*curah*) with their followings (*arugah*) are the champions, duelling frequently. The leaders of army divisions are not "officers" or "strategists" but particularly good warriors qualified through charismatic heroism. The army was indeed organized for battle; however, combat took place without order. The heroes rushed to attack the most worthy opponents. In the epics the death of the leader automatically signified the defeat of his army.

Alongside the king's followings, there were those warriors (such as the office nobles of kings) who could not equip themselves with weapons and chariots, and as well paid warriors of the prince also in peacetime received their wages from the prince. If such paid warriors died, their widows remained in the care of the king. According to Arrian, these warriors, who provided their own weapons, ranked below the nobles and priests but were separated from the peasants.

In addition to organization by phratries, as found in Homer, there appeared already purely tactical divisions of 10, 100, 1,000. Elephants and chariots were in typical numerical relation to cavalry and infantry. The armed forces were soon rationally organized, staffed by officers, and supplied and equipped increasingly out of kingly magazines. The army soon lost all traces of a people's militia or a knights' summons.

Kingly administration became patrimonial and bureaucratic. On the one hand, it developed a regulated hierarchical order of officials with local and functional competences and appeals; on the other hand, however, administrative and court offices were not kept separate and the jurisdictional spheres of a bewildering manifold of offices were fluid, indeterminate, irrational, and subject to chance influences.[21]

As shown by inscriptions, an elaborate filing system developed as early as the first dynasty of great kings (that of the Maurya, third and fourth centuries B.C.).[22] As is well known from its innumerable edicts, in the administration of the great Buddhist king Ashoka, an incredible love of writing developed.[23] In a fashion characteristic of patrimonial bureaucracies, the regents of state territories were relatives. The Arthasastra ("political science") of the Kautaliya, edited by Chanaukya,[24] and ascribed to a minister of the great Maurya king, Chandragupta, supplements this picture. Comprehensive statistics were to form the basis of administrations. All inhabitants were to be registered by caste, sib, calling, possessions, and income. The inhabitants were to be required to have passports and were to be controlled throughout their entire lives. For fiscal authorities the greatest danger to the state, next to subversion, was thought to be impairment of the "will to work"; therefore, theatres and musical bands in the country, alcohol trade and inns everywhere were to be restricted. And the spies of the administration were to report upon the most intimate private life of the subjects.

The king engaged in trade, and his administration, by means of market police, controlled prices. The Raja still retains trading monopolies: for saffron in Kashmir, precious stones in South India, horses in the West, weapons and fine textiles in the East, elephants throughout India. In contrast to the conditions presupposed by the Jatskas, price controls were an element of royal political finance. Furthermore, all conceivable tax sources were exploited—from taxes on mistresses whom the king kept for the needs of travelling merchants to money fines on burgers whom the king, according to the author's advice, would entice to commit punishable offenses by means of agent provocateurs.

In contrast to Buddhist and other pious sectarian kings, Hindu kings confined the interests of administration essentially to two objectives: the raising of manpower for the army and tax collection. Particularly under the Moguls, the administration increasingly sought to secure both objectives by means of stipulation of taxes in lump sums and prebendalization. A military prebendary assumed the obligation of forming a definite contingent. For this purpose, they were leased the respective tax yields for soldier's pay, rations, and other necessities. This led to the establishment of *Jagir*-prebends which were obviously modeled after the ancient temple and Brahmanical prebends. When invested with the right of disposition of wasteland, the Jagirdar easily turned into a landlord even though the origin of the right was politico-military. There were military fiefs similar to the Roman military border fief, the Ghahata. Even after 1000 A.D. officials derived their livelihoods essentially from the royal magazines,[25] and the money economy made headway in public finance by fits and starts and, as in the Middle East, with the assistance of private capital.

The king gathered his taxes by farming out their collection or leasing them as a prebend for payment of fixed lump sums. The tax farmers developed into a class of landlords known as Zamindari (Bengal) and Talukdari (particularly in Oudh). They became true landlords only when the British administration held them liable for the tax assessment, treating them for this reason as "proprietors." If one examines the list of their claims under the Mogul rule, their rights originally derive from the custom of holding the guarantors of military and financial contributions of the district responsible for the rest of the administration, including the administration of justice, the cost of which they had to advance.

Also in the occidental state at the beginning of modern times there appeared tax farming and the commissioning of entrepreneurs with army recruitment—entrepreneurs to whom finance had largely to be entrusted. In India, however, under the great kingdoms those central institutions failed to develop which in the West allowed the princes gradually to take back military and financial administration into their own hands. The Mahrattas were the only ones to re-introduce, in principle, an independent fiscal economy and precisely for this reason their administrative technique was superior to that of the Moguls. The rule of the Mahrattas was simply, at least in intent, that of a national dynasty while the foreign dominions remained more completely dependent upon middlemen. The Mahrattas, therefore, used the Brahman caste for all administrative purposes, including the military; in other regimes, in general, the lower castes of scribes competed with the Brahmans. Islam especially utilized castes of scribes in opposition to the Brahmans.

This phase of Indian administrative history led to the development of various prebends en masse. Above all, it led to the emergence of a stratum of landlords which developed out of tax farming and military prebendalization. The tax farmers and military prebendaries had to assume the administrative costs of their districts and to guarantee all military and financial contributions. If successful, these landlords had a free hand and little fear of intervention by central power. Their copyholds were as good as completely *"mediatized"* (annexed, appropriated).

A peculiar Indian development occurred in the elaboration of a whole series of graduated rents based upon the tax duties of the peasants and payable out of the produce of the land. Above the peasant proper, the actual cultivator of the land, was one or, as a rule, a community of land renters who as proprietors of the land were held liable by the authorities for the tax levy. However, between these proprietors and the authorities there was usually a middleman—the Zamindar or Talukdar—who laid claim either to a share of the rent (in the Northeast often 10 per cent of the tax levy) or to seignorial rights.

The Northeast pattern resulted from the restriction of profits for this category of middleman tax farmers to a 10 per cent quota of all tax income. This kind of regulation is also found in the Middle East.

To complicate matters, at times a new type of infeuded middleman developed beside the old, and these were invested by "birth" with rights to rent. Or again, there appeared landlords whose rights were based on the fact that they "bought" the village by assuming the obligation of paying tax arrears. Furthermore, hereditary village chiefs sometimes advanced rent claims which gave them a kind of landlord character.

Since the eighteenth century the Mahrattas regime systematically carried out the quota allocation of tax yields to single prebendaries which had precedence over the state which retained the rest. In a fashion similar to the infeudation policy of the Normans, they made certain that no prebendary received his income solely from his own bailiwick, but obtained at least part of his income from others.

The special character of the social strata, resting on this economic basis, was determined by its origin and nature. The occidental *seigneurie,* like the oriental Indian, developed through the disintegration of the central authority of the patrimonial state power—the disintegration of the Carolingian Empire in the Occident, the disintegration of the power of the Caliphs[26] and the Maharadja or Great Moguls in India. In the Carolingian

Empire, however, the new stratum developed on the basis of a rural subsistence economy. Through oath-bound vassalage, patterned after the war following, this stratum of lords was joined to the king and interposed itself between the freemen and the king. Feudal relations were also to be found in India, but they were not decisive for the formation either of a nobility or landlordism.

In India, as in the Orient generally, a characteristic seigniory developed rather out of tax farming and the military and tax prebends of a far more bureaucratic state. The oriental seigniory therefore remained in essence, a "prebend" and did not become a "fief"; not feudalization, but prebendalization of the patrimonial state occurred. The comparable, though undeveloped, occidental parallel is not the medieval fief but the purchase of offices and prebends during the papal seicento or during the days of the French *Noblesse de Robe*. The Indian Rajas, occasionally, also sold tax and political prebends of all kinds. Not only were the historical stages of Indian and European developments different, but a purely military factor is important for the explanation of the different development of East and West. In Europe the horseman was technically the paramount force of feudalism. In India, in spite of their numbers, horsemen were relatively less significant and efficient than the foot soldiers who held a primary role in the armies from Alexander to the Moguls.

The chancery formalities of the Great Mogul states, so far as they are known, are similar to those of the Turkish type and their models, the Caliphate and the Sassanid administrations.* Even before the foreign dominations an extraordinary rationalization of tax collection had led to the penetration of clerical techniques into every phase of political administration. The village scribe, who everywhere had a place alongside the village chief, was the lowest but none the less an important authority in this bureaucracy of scribes. The prebends of the scribes were contested by Brahmans and others, by distinguished and *parvenu* castes alike. The Mahrattas rule was characterized by a consistent dualism of *deshmukh* (district official) and *patel* (village mayor), both the *deshpandya* and the *kulkurmu* (village calculators) who stood beside them were usually Brahmans.

---

* **Caliph was the title of Mohammed's theocratic successors. The Sassanids, a dynasty of Persian kings, ruled from 226 to 641 A.D. (*Eds.*)**

The content of the concept *Kshatriya* is unclear. Does it mean "the families of petty kings" or "knighthood"? This, too, must be explained in terms of the political structure of India with its vascillation between fragmentation into innumerable petty kingdoms—originally simple chieftainships—and centralization into patrimonial empires. In military affairs these opposed tendencies may be traced back to epic times for even then, beside the combat of heroes, is to be found the beginnings of a disciplined army. Even at the time of Alexander's invasion this disciplined army was not self-equipped but equipped and supplied out of the king's magazines. The dualism between self-equipped warriors and disciplined soldiers separated from ownership of the means of warfare—one of the most important historical contrasts—persisted and did not even completely disappear under the rule of the Moguls.

The social prestige of self-equipped knights was always different from that of soldiers equipped by the king or a recruiting officer. However, the hiring of mercenaries from all sorts of half-barbarian tribes and the enfeoffment of the more deserving with land and prerogatives since the time of the Rajputs must have made status differences fluid.

Similarly, the vascillation of social structure and political organization created a fluid situation. When the tendency toward feudalization was ascendant the king, as usual, made use of old distinguished secular or priestly nobles; when the tendency toward patrimonialism was ascendant the king appointed lower-class upstarts to positions of political power.

The strength of the noble elements deriving from the ancient chieftainship and war following among the present day Rajputs cannot be ascertained.[27] Certainly it is not great. During epochs when patrimonial bureaucratic tendencies were ascendant, tax farmers and office prebendaries were admitted and became landlords added en masse to the ranks of the old nobility. Furthermore, soldiers of fortune and mercenaries, often after a number of generations, laid claim to recognition as Kshatriyas as do, even today, a number of half-Hinduized peasant tribes which once provided these soldiers. Since the end of mercenary warfare and the pacification of India the peasant tribes have had to gain their livelihoods through peaceful pursuits.

Certain tribes in the past had built up large empires through conquest. Since the disintegration of these empires and their conquest by the British they have fallen into a peculiar interstitial situation between "tribe" and "caste." To these in particular belong the Mahratta, a tribe native to the northwest coast. The tribal name (*Maharatha*—great warrior) is to be found in inscriptions before our chronology. Hiuen Tsang extols their chivalrous method of warfare in his travel descriptions. Even at that time they fought rank-and-file although a residue of heroic ecstasy appears in the intoxicatory incitement of men and elephants before the battle.

Under Islamic rule this stratum's castle fiefs and service as soldier knights were continued, and, eventually, they rose in revolt against the Great Moguls, establishing during the eighteenth century the last national Hindu regime in India. The "nobles" (*assal*) i.e., former warriors, claimed Kshatriya rank and a mixture with Rajput families had clearly taken place. Ritualistic and sib organizations were established in essentially Hindu manner, good (*deshashth*) Brahmans served as their priests. However, their tribal origin is betrayed in vestiges of the totemic (*devak-*) organization. The peasants (*kunbi—Mahratta*) are segregated by status barriers.

The noble rank of such alien tribes of knights was questioned and the claim advanced by tribal soldiers of fortune that they were Kshatriyas was never recognized. The status order of the South Indian Tamils[28] at the time of the beginning of our chronology and their Hinduization was as follows: only the immigrant Brahmans were designated as "twice-born" (for they alone wore the holy belt); they were followed by Tamil priests (*Arivars,* ascetics) and noble landlords, the *Ulavars,* the "lords of the waters" (irrigation) from whose ranks kings and political vassals were recruited; following these were various castes of cattle-breeders and artisans; finally, as fifth estate, the *Padaiachia,* soldiers. Each stratum was segregated from the others. Later Brahmanical classification placed the traders above the *Vellalars* (the old *Ulavars*) who in the meantime had become "rusticated." Naturally, here, as elsewhere, the Brahmans refused to class professional soldiers, provisioned by the king, as "twice-born" castes.

The Khati may illustrate the fate of such ancient "warrior" tribes (actually often robbers and cattle-thieves). They possessed strong castles in Sindh. Since their expulsion they have settled in Ahmadabad, taking up occupations as landlords

(*Talukdari*) and peasants. They are sun worshipers, though utilizing Brahmans as priests, with a centralized organization. Like old plebeian tribes of professional soldiers they are relatively unstable in occupational pursuits. The Khatris of Bombay originally were a warrior caste claiming Kshatriya rank. Even today they claim the right to the holy belt but have become cotton-weavers. The old soldier and robber tribe of the Halepaika of Bombay since the fall of the Dravidian Empire have become distillers of palm oil.

The position of nonmilitary office-holders remained problematical. Pure tax farmers, Zamindari, were recruited from various castes by the moguls and secured no special caste rank of their own. Some of the old office prebendaries fared better, insofar as lower-ranking people at all obtained rank equivalent to the Brahmans or Rajputs. The type of administration determined which groups were able to advance. Finally, of course, the rank and status ascent of the quite unmilitary bureaucratic scribes of the great kingdoms is contested to this very day.

The patrimonial origin of the officialdom is expressed in the name *Amatya* (originally meaning "house companion"). Indian kings, at least, seem not to have employed unfree officials, as was done in the Middle East. The status pride of such free officials was expressed in the assumption that the official holds his position "through friendly agreement with his king and lord," a formula found in an inscription for the empire of the western Chalukya Dynasty of the twelfth to thirteenth centuries.[29] The bulk of the officials, however, belonged to the *britya*, including harem watchmen and poor soldier mercenaries.

In the course of time only the social rank of the official's claims of origin was changed. Patrimonialism broke the old monopoly of offices by the knighthood. The great kings, first of the Maurya —later of the Gupta—Dynasty (the first since the fourth century B.C., the second since the fourth century A.D.) ruled the land by means of officials drawn from the Shudra castes. Brahmanical literature attributes this to the opening of the Kali-epoch. It corresponds, however, to the nature of patrimonial states everywhere and particularly to oriental patriarchalism.

Surely the old Kshatriya caste had considered enfeoffment with political power its special monopoly. The caste was not able to retain its monopoly, however, and indeed it helped work the decomposition of the caste. The patrimonial state utilized as officials not only Brahmans but scribes of other castes. Without binding itself to any single status group, the state bestowed prebends, including tax-collection, on civil (*bürgerliche*) tax farmers, army recruitment on *condottieri.* In the form of the Jagirdar, Talukdar, and Zamindar the state created tax prebendiares of all sorts and endowed them with political power. The state freed itself from dependence on any single stratum. In fact the kings themselves were often merely fortunate *parvenus.* Monarchs appeared who described themselves as the sprouts of Brahman's feet (hence as Shudras).

According to strict theory not even royal descent could make a nobleman out of a Shudra. Recently the Rajbansi caste in Bengal excommunicated a member because he had given his daughter in marriage to a member of a caste of cooks who had a Raja ancestor.

As a rule political authority is a preponderant advantage in the competition for rank. Hence today unmilitary office nobles compete for caste rank with the Rajputs and military nobles generally. This is particularly true of the great caste of scribes as, for example, the purely bureaucratic Kayasth in Bengal and the semi-bureaucratic military prebendaries, the Prabhu—a small group only found in Bombay. The Prabhu were once a military class enfeoffed since the rule of the Gupta with local administrative duties (tax-collection, documents and records, military administration). They have retained their position for a very long time.

In Bengal there were only a few rural Rajput families. Only one of the well-known families appears to belong to them without doubt. Since the Sena dynasty the territory of Bengal has been organized in patrimonial bureaucratic fashion. The Kayasth—a caste of scribes also appearing in other regions—were still viewed as pure Shudras in the Vellala Charita (sixteenth century). Now the Kayasth in Bengal claim to be Kshatriyas of a higher rank than the Rajputs.

The occupational composition of these castes of officials with literary education differs greatly from that of the Rajputs and other old soldier castes, who show an especially high rate of illiteracy. At present very few Rajputs are found in modern political and private-economic administration in which Brahmans and scribes play an important role. The same holds for advocacy, the press, and the "learned" professions.

In Calcutta 30 per cent of the Kayasths are clerks. The Brahmans and Kayastha vie for first place among the clerks, lawyers, doctors, journalists, and engineers. In Bombay Province 74 per cent of the Rajputs and 92 per cent of the Mahrattas are engaged in agriculture, but only 2 per cent and 3/10 of 1 per cent respectively are to be found in political administration, and 8/10 of 1 per cent and 2/100 of 1 per cent respectively in the learned professions. That is about the same percentage as the despised peasant caste of the Kuli in Gujarat. There, seven per cent of the Brahmans and 27 per cent of the Prabhus are engaged in administration and 22 and 18 per cent respectively in the learned professions. Recruits for administration and the learned professions are also drawn from the trading caste of the Lohars with 5-8/10 per cent and 27 per cent respectively. Only rarely does a Rajput become a shopkeeper, a Mahratta almost never. To this day the Mahratta caste stands for love of feudal pomp and leisure.

The caste rank of the Kayasth is constantly and passionately contested, particularly by the old Bengal doctors' caste, the Baidya, which claims higher rank because it practices the full Upanayam ceremony and feels entitled to read the Vedas. The Kayasth, for their part, insist that the Baidya surreptitiously obtained the right to wear the holy belt only a hundred years ago through the help of bribed Brahmans. Both parties may well be historically right. The Kayasth undoubtedly were Shudras. On the other hand, despite the great age of medicine as a special science in India, the physician's castes, at best, could have had Vaishya rank like other castes of the old guild association (*mahajan*). Today the Baidyas and similar castes in other regions often claim higher rank than the Rajputs because the Rajputs do not consider it absolutely degrading under certain circumstances to lay a hand on the plough. The Baidya can back their own rank claims by pointing to the fact that the Sena Dynasty developed out of their caste.

All in all, the present castes recognized as having more or less undisputed Kshatriya rank are quite mixed in character and bear the traces of the historical changes which Hinduism has undergone politically since the rise of clerical administration. Even more problematic was and is the situation of the third caste of classical teaching, the Vaishya.

3. *The Vaishyas*

AS THEY appear in classical learning the Vaishyas suggest somewhat our stratum of free commoners. Viewed negatively, i.e., in contrast to the higher castes, the Vaishyas lacked the ritualistic, social, and economic privileges of a priestly and lay nobility. Viewed from below, in contrast to the Shudra, the most important privilege of the Vaishyas—though it is never expressly mentioned—was their right to own land, a right clearly denied to the Shudras. In the Vedas the word *vica* is used in the sense of "people," "subjects" (of the ruler).

In classical sources the Vaishya is, first, a peasant. Even in the law books, however, the loaning of money for interest, and trade are recognized as permissible occupations for this class. Furthermore, it is noteworthy that in classical times a rigid social distinction was drawn between animal husbandry and tillage. Only the former is a permissible emergency occupation for a Brahman. This agrees with ancient, widely-held views. Almost everywhere animal husbandry was man's work; primitive tillage was woman's or slave's work.

In post-classical times and at present the conception of the Vaishya as a "peasant" has completely vanished. Even in early historical times trade was held to be the true occupation of the Vaishya, Vaishya and *vanik* (trader) being considered identical. A caste claiming Vaishya rank today seeks to prove that it always was a trader caste.

The removal of the peasantry from status equality with urban propertied and income groups probably was determined by a number of factors. Feudalization was doubtless the first, patrimonial fiscalization and prebendalization the second. Even in classical times the Vaishya were held to exist in order to be "consumed" by the higher estates. In the Middle Ages the Vaishya was of interest to the higher estates only as a taxpayer.

Medieval India was a land of villages. The size of a kingdom was stated in terms of the numbers of its villages, that is to say, tax units. In later times they were stated in *lakhs*—rent units based upon tax assessment. The land tax was and remains the absolutely decisive source of finance and the most important object of enfeoffment and prebend formation.

In classical times the king was called the "taker of the sixth part," for one-sixth of the harvest, the ancient traditional land tax, was considered reasonable. Actually the tax had been raised to that level and—contrary to old doctrine—reached such heights that the theory developed ascribing land monopoly to the king. In Bengal and some South Indian conquest territories this probably approached reality.

We owe to B. H. Baden-Powell the comprehensive investigation of the Indian village. As sources for his investigation he utilized the British tax assessment. For the rest, the inscriptions on monuments and literary sources, throw only scanty light on the past of the Indian peasant. However, since the time of the Mogul rule, and often earlier, fiscal interest was decisive for the position of the peasants with respect to others. Since that time the (primarily administrative) issue has been: Who is to assume the tax liability?

When each field is separately assessed and each village landowner is liable for the tax on his property the village is a *Ryotvari* or *Raiyatvari* village. In this case there is no landlord. Instead, the ancient clan charismatic village head (*patel*) is considered to be a government official invested with great authority; and he gathers the taxes. In central India the patel holds the tax-free and inheritable Watan land as a kind of hereditary fief, as a village may. The *patel* lives in a centrally located, often fortified residence. A village *"mark"* (tract of land) beyond the cultivated acreage does not exist today; this land belongs to the state, which alone can grant the right of settlement on it.

Conditions are different when a circle of owners has joint liability to the state for the tax levy payable as a lump sum (*jama*). Such a circle of proprietors often has a *panchayat* as a representative organ and is authorized to issue administrative decrees concerning the villagers and the village *mark*, the wasteland. The *panchayat* leases for rent the fields of the village to peasants, village craftsmen, and village traders. At its own discretion the *panchayat* partitions the wasteland and separates and distributes "Sir" land (desmesne land) from the village *mark* among the respective participants and the village community as a whole and possibly permits temporary leases of the latter. In such a village there is no *patel* with a paramount position based on charismatic prerogatives; rather a *lambardar* (administrator) may represent the common interests of the villagers against the fiscal authorities. Land allotments and corresponding tax obligations may be distributed among the participants as hereditary quotas (*patti*). Hence such villages are called *patti-*

dari, or according to other standards (particularly the individual owner's ability to pay), *bhaiachara* villages.

Baden-Powell rightly assumes that *pattidari* villages developed out of landlord's estate. *Zamindari* villages are owned by single lords and are often found today. Even the Kautaliya Arthacastra cited above, contains the advice to mortgage the wasteland to an available guarantor of the tax levy. The authenticity of the statement is assured for the Raja's economic charges—though not his strictly political rights—were divisible and inscriptions frequently report donations of villages at definite quotas (*vritti*) to a plurality of Brahmans.

Baden-Powell,[30] however, assumes the same origin for the *bhaichara* villages, except that the quotas presumably have disappeared. This assumption is not convincing, however, for to this day tax assessments may lead to the deliberate transmutation of *raiyatvari*[31] villages into *bhaiachara* villages with joint tax liability and jurisdiction over the village *mark*.

We owe to Baden-Powell the sharp distinctions between different types of modern village communities. Moreover, he brought into clear focus the retention of the sib and phratry (he says "clan") as the basis of the land leases of the overlords. He also called attention to the significance of land surpluses in early times for the structure of the village. The following propositions of Baden-Powell suggest analogy to other Asiatic areas and will be retained: (1) Completely collective tillage (agrarian communism) of villages was not the primeval structure of rural India. In any case it was not of importance for the later structure of agrarian society. (2) The tribe (and possibly its subdivision, the military association of the phratry) considered itself to be possessor of the occupied territory and repulsed attacks on it. (3) The ancient Indian village did not have a village "common"—at least not necessarily—and rights to the "common" were not integral to the peasant's holdings in the European sense. This resulted from the abundance of land and the persistence of phratry organization. (4) Seignorial prerogatives based on a feudal structure, similar or equivalent to that of the Occident, have hardly played a role in the structure of agrarian India. The social structure of agrarian India, rather, was determined, on the one hand, by the sib and phratry (clan) community of conquerors, and on the other, by the leases of tax prebends. (5) Clearing of the land, on the one hand, and conquest, on the other, constituted the most ancient titles to landholding.

The present-day stratum of land cultivators are called *upri*, "occupants" in official language. Concretely, they are the people who plough the land and pay the rents to the partners of the *pattidari* and *bhaichara* community. Since the British reform laws, they now stand with respect to property relations in a situation analogous to that of Irish tenants since Gladstone's agrarian reforms. Obviously this was not their original situation.

Classical literature, particularly the law books, but also the *Jatakas* and the authors of their time,[32] know neither the lord's manor nor the present-day "joint village." Land purchase and semi-tenancy, not on village land, however, are to be found. *Allmende* (pasture land) and village herdsmen are found in North India. Originally the right of preemption of village associates in contrast to outsiders is unquestioned. South Indian villages sometimes join together to form a new community unit.[33] Village communities sometimes receive grants from the king,[34] and sometimes they act collectively, for example, as donators with their *panch* representing the community.[35] From these facts it is clear that there existed a primary "village community" independent of tax liabilities; it had to exist wherever settlements of conquerors faced the conquered.

The Indian field system could not consist of scattered holdings lying in different fields in the manner of the German system. To be sure, the *pattis* are often dispersed because of differential soil qualities (rotation of plots occurs sporadically) but on the whole the scattered plots are large and do not represent calculable blocks of comparable size. Landholding was determined by the number of ploughs a man owned and hence the land he had to work. Since, initially, there was an abundance of available land, calculation was unnecessary. Water, however, was an economic good, for irrigation purposes and, as Baden-Powell emphasized, anyone who would have taken liberties with it would have met resistance. There were redistributions of land in order to equalize livelihoods. As a result of increasing tax pressure, phenomena similar to those found in Russia occurred. Tax assessment determined the right (and possibly the duty) to land.

Strong, secondary community relations always developed where fertility was based on irrigation. Water shares were doubtlessly apportioned according to costs. Such irrigation projects, however, could serve as the basis for extensive economic differentiation. To be sure, lake reserves of water and their implements were often established as foundations.

More often, however, rich entrepreneurs individually or jointly constructed them, supplying water for rent. This was the origin of the "water lords" of South India.

An even more important source of property privilege was the "*watan* land,"[36] the land of the village chief, priest, accountant, and at times other village servants. Such land was hereditary and later became alienable. Above all, these officials either enjoyed tax freedom or paid only fixed taxes in contrast to the harvest shares of peasants which, in practice, (though not in theory) could be increased. Under the rule of the Maharattas office prebendaries sought, at least in their own villages, to take the *watan* land into their own hands, no matter from what sources they drew their income. It became a point of honor for the socially dominant strata to retain this office prebend in the family. Indeed, the higher the tax-load mounted the more desirable *watan* land became. It was, therefore, much sought-after as a pure investment opportunity by the highest strata of society.

The ancient epics of North India were familiar with the service prebend. Such service prebends varied in size, in terms of the rank of office, from rents of lots to the rents of entire cities. Obviously, the old patrimonial monarchy had sought to prevent *watan* land from turning into hereditary property rights and, in particular, into land-holdings. Later the Maharattas attempted but by no means fully succeeded in preventing the same thing in the South.

Initially, the special quality of *watan* land derived from its role in the status situation of the village chief. More exactly it was land possessed by the charismatically endowed sib of the village chieftain in return for service. There were a considerable number of similar titles attached to the status qualities of the owner. In particular, the complete monopolization of Aryan village lands by the conquerors and the dispossession of the conquered must have established differences, the development of which can no longer be assessed. We do, however, have confirming evidence of titles to land, "the right of Brahman prebends," and especially frequent inscriptions from the Indian Middle Ages stating a right to land possession known as *bhumichchida* which doubtlessly indicates an hereditary landholding exempt from arbitrary tax raises. These derived from the status position of the entitled sib and its clan charisma.

Generally the members of the privileged associations ("joint villages") of rent-receiving landlords claim their partnership as a birth right (*mirasi* is translated by Baden-Powell as "birth right") derived from membership in a charismatic (princely) clan. In fact, all land bearing an hereditary title and (possible) fixed rent is technically called "*miras.*" The "*mirasi*" quality of possessions was primarily determined by the hereditary status of the sib and later the caste. However, such landlords formed classes which, even when they did the managing themselves, refused as long as possible to lay hand to the plough, thus to avoid the ritualist degradation that occasionally occurred among impoverished Rajputs and other distinguished landowners. In the records of the Indian Middle Ages "village inhabitants" (as an estate obviously not declassed) appear as witnesses, donators, or "rural people" alongside the royal sib, the officials, and urban traders. In such cases we cannot be certain whether the reference is to landlords, genuine peasants, or some middle group. It is most probable[37] that as a rule they were landlords. While generally excellent in their presentation of the various castes, the census reports are unclear on this point. Naturally, the differences among the rural strata are at present quite fluid. Two groups of villagers obviously have best maintained their place as "independent" peasants (in the German sense):* the Khumbi in the West and North and the Vellalar in the South. The first appeared primarily in areas where the structure of rural society was basically determined by military rather than financial differentiation—usually the separation of knights and professional soldiers from peasants. As is usual in such cases, social differentiation was essentially less rigid.[38]

The Vellalar, however, represent the old class (previously mentioned) of freemen (landlords) who were "rusticated" under patrimonialism and the domination of the soldier army, and who were degraded in caste rank after the consummation of the Hindu system. From both castes are recruited the most efficient and businesslike cultivators of India; the Khunbis in particular appear quite receptive to modern economic methods; for example, they are inclined to invest their savings in factories and securities.

* "Self-employed" persons; in this case, owner-operators. (*Eds.*)

In general, among the relatively high-ranking rural castes are to be found a number of Hinduized tribes, such as the Jat, Gujar, Koch. Some, extremes of settled landowners, derive from castes of former professional soldiers; the scattered remainders represent nonnoble landlords who are considered relatively distinguished.

To some extent, in times of continuous feuds the free peasants through commendation could become village tenants, invested with political power. Occasionally, also, this occurred through indebtedness or simply through acute or chronic acts of violence.[39] However, the great mass of Indian peasants were not declassed for such reasons. Rather, the financial system of the great kingdoms reduced them to mere subjects for rent squeeze. They could not receive consideration as members of "twice-born" castes.

Multitudes of more or less completely Hinduized native tribes are to be found among the peasants; ritual reasons alone prevent their reception as Vaishya. In one inscription [40] a prince of the region of Iodhpur boasts of having chased out the *Ahir,* and established the *mahajan*—that is, the Brahmans, *prakriti* (which the translator would like to interpret to mean Kshatriya), and the Vaishya. Generally, and except where ritual impurity was involved, Hinduized tribes were viewed as "pure Shudras." The Vellallar, however, were never believed to belong to the Shudra.

In short, the caste-fate of the peasants bore traces of the social changes which resulted from the fiscalism of the bureaucratic state. A series of conditions, in part quite general, in part specifically Indian, coöperated to bring this about.

The loss of social class by the common freemen in the occidental Middle Ages was connected with their separation from the circle of the militarily trained, and hence from full-fledged membership in the warrior community which developed into professional knights. Economically, this development was caused by the increase in population, which, in coöperation with general culture conditions, led to intensified husbandry. Intensive agriculture required increasingly the competence of the freeman who lived off his family's labor. Thus he became economically less and less expendable and pacifistic. In contrast to the freeman of Tacitus' report, the mass of freemen had to take to the plough. In the Occident ploughmanship did not declass men to the same degree as in historical India, as the Roman Cincinnatus legend (a propaganda legend) and Nordic examples indicate.

For India certain social factors reinforced those normally tending to down-grade the peasant. In all the world including the ancient Occident, the development of the cities and the civil classes has led to the social depredation of the *pisang* (peasants).[41] For the *pisang* did not participate in the conventions of cultured urban society, and militarily and economically he could not keep abreast of its development. The same opposition of urban and rural people (*pasira* and *janapada*) is evinced in Indian sources of all kinds. In this connection, however, the special circumstances in India must be taken into account.

As we shall see,* Indian urban development facilitated the emergence of the principle of *ahimsa* which is observed by the pacifist salvation religions, by Buddhism, and most strictly by Jainism. With the development of the principle of *ahimsa,* the peasant, who in plowing destroys worms and insects, was not only declassed but ritually degraded. The peasant was reduced to even lower status than he had had in Jewry and (ancient and medieval) Christendom; and some traces of this status remained after the disappearance or curtailment of the urban salvation religions.

Animal husbandry, as it was a bloody business, sank deeply in social estimation. The cultivation of a number of special crops —vegetables, tobacco, beets, and others—was held to be degrading and indeed defiling for various ritualistic reasons. Finally, the increasing emphasis on literary culture and learning as the supreme religious and status qualification in place of magical charisma led to the social oppression of the peasant—a phenomenon which appears as well in Judaic Palestine and in medieval Christendom (for example, in Thomas Aquinas).

Often it goes unnoticed that in Christendom the peasant has come to his present position of honor and esteem only since the development of rationalism and scepticism among the bourgeois classes has turned the churches, for support of their power, to the traditionalist instincts of the peasants.

In ancient times peasant peoples gave precedence to animal husbandry in the vocational rank order. This was followed by tillage. Trade and especially money-lending[42] was everywhere suspect and scorned. Later, however, trade was considered far superior. Trade came to be rated higher, if for no other reason

* Part II, particularly the section on the Jains. (*Eds.*)

than that animal husbandry necessitated operations such as castration.

This is a radical reversal of the rank order of Vedic times. In the Vedas the merchant (*pani*) appears only as a wanderer, as a rule from strange tribes, haggling by day, stealing by night, collecting his riches in secret hordes, hated by God because he acts the miser against gods (in sacrifice) and men, especially holy singers and priests. Therefore, the "godless treasures" of the merchant stand in contrast to the wealth of the nobles who fill the hands of singers and priests. "*Ari*," the rich, the mighty, has, therefore, an evil and a good meaning, as Pischel and Geldner have observed.[43] He is the most sought-after, hated, and envied of men; one cannot be alone with him peacefully; he is fat and haughty, especially when he fails to pay singers and priests other than his own. He should give, and give again; when he does, he is the "darling of gods" and men. But the merchant simply does not do this.

At any rate, even the Athararvaveda[44] contains a prayer for the increase of the money which the merchant takes to market in order to make more money. All primitive religion honors wealth. Indeed, Indra is considered the god of the merchants and the Rigveda permits wealth to gain Heaven.[45] Wealth gives even the Shudra influence, for the priest accepts their money.

The odium of trade disappeared completely in the time of the city development. Monied wealth and trade remain the typical qualifications of the Vaishya in the Indian Middle Ages and, at present. However, the Vaishya have undergone many a crisis in their caste rank. As in the Occident during the time of the power of the guilds and the blossoming of the cities, a caste such as that of the goldsmiths was highly esteemed. In some territories even today goldsmiths hold first place and almost parallel the rank of Brahmans. It is noteworthy that North Indian sources considered them the typical guild of profligate charlatans.[46]

Similarly, some other Bengal trader castes, which in the time of the establishment of the great kingdoms served as moneylenders of princes were ranked as Vaishyas at the zenith of their power, and later as degraded Shudra castes. According to reports, this resulted from conflicts with the Sena kings, especially with Vallala Sena. Modern claimants for rank elevation usually blame him for having overthrown the old caste ranks.

The evidence is convincing that the patrimonial bureaucratic dominion brought about changes here as in the case of the noble castes. The present-day caste order in Bengal bears traces of a catastrophy. In other territories there is evidence of a decay or stagnation in the development of bourgeois power which often blurred the boundary lines between the Vaishya and Shudra.

The present-day trading castes of high rank are only in part ancient urban merchant castes. In part they grew out of the monopolistic trade organizations which the patrimonial prince called into being; and not every trader caste is necessarily a caste of high rank. Some of them, indeed, are impure and probably developed out of pariah tribes which monopolized the respective trade. Once again administrative history is mirrored in caste relations.

Money economy developed in India at about the time of the rise of Hellenism in occidental trade. Overseas and caravan trade with Babylon and later with Egypt existed far earlier. In India, as in Babylon, the procurement of coined money, that is, money in some way signed, later stamped, or molded metal blocks of a certain weight, remained at first a private affair of the great trader families with a trusted coinage.[47]

Silver, the contemporary metal of India's currency was not produced in India. Gold, which the great kings of the early centuries used for coins, was produced in but small amounts. The treasures of precious metal came from trade with the West and can be estimated by the booty figures of the Mohammedans. Such treasures served essentially hoarding purposes, although it is perhaps no mere accident that one of the periods of flowering guild power or a renaissance of guild power during the second century A.D. coincided with the great influx of money from the Roman Empire and the coinage of *aurii* coins of the Roman type. The rulers of the Maurya Dynasty, including Ashoka, did not as yet mint coins of their own. The influx of precious metals from Greece and Rome stimulated the great kings of the first century A.D. to do so while the old private coins and *ersatz* coinage long remained in circulation.

In India, as in Babylon, the lack of a state coinage did not hinder the rise of capitalist trade and political capitalism. From around the seventh century B.C. for almost a thousand year period capitalism developed and expanded. The market appeared and became the administrative center. In times as late as the rule of the Maharattas, villages without markets (*mouza*) were linked for purposes of administration to the *kusha,* the market towns (a kind of *metrokomia* in the sense of late Antiquity). The cities lost their initial character as mere princely fortifications (*pura, nagara*). They acquired—particularly on the sea coasts—a section which in its structure was related to the ancient seat of the prince and in its form, as the *mercato* in Italy, (the economic market, the place where buying and selling occurred was related) to the *piazza* (*del campo della signoria*), the place where, on public summons, the militia was reviewed and tournaments held. Evidence of these functions is clearly retained, in present-day Siena, in the layout of dual squares, before and behind the *palazzo publicco,* and in the dualism of castle (*kasbah*) and market (*bazaar*) in Islamic cities. A description of the Tamil city of Kaviripaddinam, from the period shortly before our chronology, may serve as illustration.

Located in the trading city are most of the bazaars, workshops, and homes of the *yavana* (occidental) merchants. Located in the royal city are the luxury crafts: the Brahmans, doctors, astrologers, bards, actors, musicians, flower-decorators, pearl-string-makers, and absentee landlords. Between the two city districts extends the market place. The Tamil kings kept Roman mercenaries.[48]

Rich nobles moved into the cities to consume their rents. According to one chronicle only the owners of one *kror* equaling 100 *lakhas* (the measuring unit for the great prebends according to their number of villages and rents) were permitted to dwell in the city.[49] There now appeared the possibility of accumulation of wealth through trade as well as rent.

Caravan trade was typically organized by caravan leaders and the guilds (*creni,* later called *gana*) rivaled the knighthood and priesthood in power. The king became financially dependent on the guilds with no means of controlling them other than playing them off against one another or bribery. Even in the epics[50] the king, after a defeat, expresses his concern about them (excepting his relatives and the priests). In several cities a gentile-charismatic chief appears at the head of the guilds, a chief representing the interests of the citizenry before the king. The elders of the guild (*marksherren*) stand at his side as an advisory body. This was, for example, the case in Ahmadhabad. Now the three genteel estates were those of the secular and priestly noble and the trader. They were often considered peers, they often intermarried, they had concourse with princes on equal footing.

The merchants financed the wars of the princes and had them mortgage or lease prerogatives to them as individuals or to their guild. And like the "commune" in the Occident, especially in France, the sworn brotherhood of the ruling estates also in India[51] encroached upon the land. The intellectual aristocracy of the priests, the knightly nobles, and the bourgeoise plutocracy competed for social influence. Even rich artisans, i.e., those who participated in trade, trafficked with the prince. Some of the artisans, at least, had apparently free choice of occupation. It was a time in which people of all classes, even the Shudra, were able to obtain political power.

The rising patrimonial prince with his disciplined army and officialdom was increasingly embarrassed by the power of the guilds and his financial dependence on them. We learn that a *vanik* (trader) denied a war loan to a king with the comment that the *dharma* of princes was not to conduct war, but to protect peace and peaceful prosperity of the citizens. He added, however, that the loan could perhaps be given anyway if the king were able to provide a suitable castle as security. There is described, furthermore, the great rage the king discharged at a banquet when the trader castes refused to take their place among the Shudras where the lord chamberlain had referred them and they left under protest. When these events were communicated by the officials to the king, he degraded these castes below the Shudras. Whether or not the actual events of the account of the Vellala Charita[52] are true, they obviously indicate typical states of tension.

The antagonism between princely officials and bourgeois plutocrats was natural. The Kautaliya Arthasastra supplies evidence for this in the damnation of the goldsmiths who may partly have controlled ancient private coinage, and who were, partly, money-lenders to princes. Added to their weaknesses in numbers certain peculiarly Indian conditions had fateful consequences for the bourgeoisie in their struggle against the patrimonial prince: first, was the absolute pacifism of the salvation religions, Jainism and Buddhism, which were propagated, roughly, at the same time as the development of the cities. (The possible causal interrelationship between urbanism and the salvation religions and its significance will be discussed below.) Second, there was the undeveloped but established caste system. Both these factors blocked the development of the military power of the citizenry; pacifism blocked it in principle and the castes in practice, by hindering the establishment of a *polis* or *commune* in the European sense.

Under such circumstances the army of Hoplites of the ancient *polis* could not develop. Impossible, too, were the summons of the guilds and the armies of condottieri of the medieval occidental city, both of which led in military technique. For example, the army of the Florentines was the first in Europe, so far as we can tell, to utilize firearms. To be sure, Megasthenes knew self-governing cities.[53] Vaicali at the time was a free city; a council of 5000, that is to say all those who could contribute an elephant, governed through a *uparaya* (viceroy).[54] While the epics tell of kingless lands it held them to be unclassical—usually one should not live in them.[55] This view agrees with the interest situation of the priest who is economically and socially dependent on the king. The beginnings of status privileges are to be found. The ancient assemblies (*samiti* and *sabha*) of the people were indeed either assemblies of armies or from early times—as in the epics—legal assemblies in which speakers on the law qualified by their charisma, or by their position as elders in interpreting the law. Without these elders the epics did not recognize the assemblies as lawful *sabhas*.[56]

In the epics the king sought council from his relatives and friends. At the time, the nobles, (actually the top officials), occasionally formed a royal council. In South India considerable restrictions of royal prerogatives continued into the Middle Ages. There were representative assemblies with rights similar to those of our estates. In the cities, according to the epics, city elders[57] and citizens (*paurah*)[58*] are to be found alongside the priests who, with the increasing administration of scribes, gain greater prominence as officials. In the later parts of the epics the priests are found almost alone as advisors of the king.

By now the city had become "a place where learned priests[59] are located," somewhat in the manner of the early medieval *civitas* as the place of a bishop. The king derived a certain quota

---

* *From Max Weber,* p. 256 f. Where Weber stresses discipline rather than *firearms* as decisive. (*Eds.*)

of his officials for urban administration from the Vaishya caste when they were rich, and from the Shudra caste when they were virtuous (these obviously served as the collectors of liturgies or taxes from the guild).[60]

Now it is always the royal officials who do the administrative work. As far as is known, a republican city administration in the occidental manner has nowhere been developed in a lasting and typical form, regardless of how clearly beginnings have pointed in this direction. In most Indian cities, the king and his staff always have remained dominant no matter what consideration they might have made in the single case to the power of the guilds. As a rule, guild power remained pure money power, not backed by an independent military organization. Hence it collapsed as soon as the princes found it expedient to depend upon priests and officials.

In India, too, the power of capital was great wherever numerous petty princes sought its support. In the long run, as everywhere else, however, capital could not retain independent power against the great kingdoms.

The Brahmans and the kings played off the intrinsically superior caste organization against the guilds. The caste could punish recalcitrant members with excommunication; as we know, sacredotal means of coercion were of paramount significance for the economic history of our Middle Ages, too. A guild might attempt to secure observance of its rules; for example, restraint of competition among its members belonging to different castes. Ultimately, in such cases, the guilds could do so only by requesting that the castes employ their sanctions or by calling on the king.[61] After the defeat of guild power the kings often commissioned traders as royal merchants with extensive monopolies in mercantilist interest, investing them with high rank in a fashion quite similar to that of modern occidental history.

However, the ancient independence of the guilds, and their role as representative of the citizenry against the king was gone. At any rate, they were hardly to be found throughout India. Under the dominion of the Mahrattas the market was an administrative center, but each market by itself; hence in cities having several markets, the various city districts with their markets were separately organized, like rural market places (*kuscha*). There is nothing comparable to true self-government in the occidental manner. In some parts of India, particularly in the South during the Middle Ages, certain social privileges and monopolies continued to exist as survivals of the ancient position of the guild and of privileged royal merchants. We do not know the content and privileges in single cases and they gradually dissolved into purely titular prerogatives.

Tamil kings granted the rights of *aujuvannam* and *manigranam* in one city to strangers and merchants, in one case to a Jew.[62] The substance of the rights cannot, it seems, be ascertained. The first one, the "five caste right" may perhaps signify membership in a *mahajan* corporation of artisans in North Indian manner as well as a trading monopoly with respect to the five crafts. These "five crafts" are undoubtedly those practiced by the five legendary sons of the craftsman's god Visvakarma: iron, wood, copper, brass, stone, gold, and silver work which we shall discuss below.

In a second case certain trades are expressly designated as subordinate to the privileged ones and the recipient of the grant is designated as "Lord of the City." It is mentioned that a commission monopoly (putting out system?) and tax exemption be included in his privilege. For the rest certain revenues and honorific rights are connected with these positions such as the right to festive garments, sedans, umbrellas, lamps, music, etc.

The rise and fall of many commercial strata in the monopolistic system of the patrimonial princes is still evident in the position of contemporary Indian trader castes. The caste of the Lamani or Vanjani, also known as Banjari in the Bombay Presidency, are for example, a migratory guest tribe, who at one time controlled the salt and corn trade in the western Hindu states and who followed the armies as reported during the sixteenth century. Perhaps they represent a background element of the present-day Vania (Bania) caste.

Traces of the ancient guild organization and also of the *mahajan*, the guild brotherhood, survive in parts of the Gujarats.[63] In fact, the name *mahajan*, meaning *popolo grasso* (big people), was by no means restricted to the guilds. Rather, the inscriptions show that, originally, nobles (generally the Brahmans in the country and under certain conditions the members of other twice-born castes) were referred to as *mahajan*. During the guild epochs, however, and in the guild cities the term referred to members of the guilds; in various regions of western and central North India, there are trader sub-castes which to this day claim the designation *mahajan* for themselves.

Some castes belong to the ancient trading estate of the Vaniks, and maintain their old rank position to this day except for certain sects such as the Jains, organized and monopolizing trade as a quasi-caste. (It will be discussed later.) Among the former belong particularly the Bhaniya who are widely diffused especially in West India. On the whole they are correct Hindus (vegetarians and teetotallers), wearing the holy belt, while in Bengal, the territory of the strictest patrimonial bureaucratic organization due to the activities of the Sena kings, the ancient trader castes of the Gandhabaniks and Subarnabaniks have since descended to low rank.

The Bhaniya, to be sure, have changed their ritual sufficiency to facilitate distant journeys which, as we shall see, are suspect to Hinduism. The degree of adaptability to modern conditions varies among the trading castes,, depending upon the extent to which their caste rules permit them to set up branch establishments and travel in order to visit patrons. The Bhaniya especially are relatively unrestricted in these respects and hence "more modern" than other castes.

The economically ascending castes of liquor traders are for ritualistic reasons almost never admitted as peers by the ancient trader castes. Details are out of place here. The foregoing indicates how extensively the present-day Vaishya castes bear the traces of India's historical fate and political make-up, especially the fate of its citizenry.

A further residue of ancient feudal times is found in the present, relatively favorable caste rank of such occupational castes as the bards, (of the widely diffused caste of the Bhats), astrologers, genealogists, posters of horoscopes, who were formerly indispensable for every princely court and distinguished family and who are today indispensable as well for broad strata of low anti-Brahmanical castes. They belong in most cases to the twice-born and rank often before the Vaishya class. The high rank of the previously mentioned intellectual aristocracy of the Baidya (physicians), too, hangs together with their relation to distinguished houses.

Quite a few castes which formerly were and still are artisans claim Vaishya rank. Personal appearance in the market by respectable castes was held to be degrading and occasionally led to caste schism. Such artisans as claim caste rank do so when they work up their own raw materials and offer their product for sale, which usually yields them the polite address of *vanik* (merchant). This brings us to the boundaries of the Shudra castes, castes which were the pillars of Indian industry.[64]

4. The Shudras

AMONG the industrial castes two groups were outstanding. First we must consider a socially, i.e., ritualistically degraded caste which was able neither to give water to Brahmans nor employ them as house priests. Since all castes of the South can accept water only from their respective members, only the latter criterion applies there. In addition to its very different elements the Shudra class comprises primarily the ancient village crafts, hence artisans and workers who have no full right to the land. Such workers and artisans receive garden land, wages in kind or money, and their work from times of early settlement has been an indispensable supplement to the household economy of the peasants.

The peers of these workers and artisans were and are the remaining village servants whose local composition varied widely from place to place, often including the village priests. It is quite probable that they constituted the historical nucleus of the ancient Shudra class which had no right to village lands. As a rule the interlocal trades, such as the large, ancient weaver castes, hold an equivalent position. Of equivalent rank are the tailors, most of the potters, part of the peddler trades, the liquor dealers and oil pressers, and, finally, the numerous castes of farmhands and small holders. The caste rank of the potters varies widely depending on whether they work at the disk or use the form, or use oxen or the always-degrading donkey. In large territories, where these village outsiders were sufficiently numerous, they formed at times a separate community with a special *patel* provided by the most important trade, for example, the carpenters.[65]

Ranking just above this ritualistically degraded stratum is another, substantially less degraded stratum which is considered to be "pure." In addition to the whole series of peasant castes, which vary in rank in the different regions which contain the mass of this class, there is typically to be found in this stratum a qualitatively important category of castes, the so-called *Nabasakh*—or *Nine-part-group*. The Nine-part-group obviously forms the kernel of the so-called *Sat-Shudra* (pure Shudra).

The occupations of this group are urban industries and trades: betel, perfume, and oil vending, pastry-making, gardening, and at times the making of pottery. An equal or superior position is occupied by the gold and silversmiths, lacquer-workers, masons, carpenters, silk-decorators, and a series of similarly specifically luxury or city occupations. Other castes occasionally belong to this group as a result of historical vicissitudes.[66] Similarly, there are Shudra castes of domestic servants of varying types which are held to be "pure."

These classifications were in no way systematized. At times practical necessity played a role in the elevation of an occupation. A man rendering personal service, who is forced, while caring for the patron's person, to touch him—a butler or barber, for example—could hardly be assigned to an impure caste. For the rest, the view may be correct that artisans who first appeared with the development of the city were not village bondsmen and hence from the beginning were social superiors to these menials and therefore also ritually privileged.[67] The industries which participated in urban retail trade were in a socially more favorable situation because of their personally independent economic position. Moreover, during the flowering of the cities they often organized into guilds while castes such as the weavers here, as in the Occident, were employed by the guilds for wages and placed under strong pressure. Thus the economic structure of the ancient city economy, or, better, the beginnings of one as it existed in India, casts its shadow into the very present. In any case, urban economy must have had great significance for the development of the Shudra class. In ancient literature[68] the idea may be found that the city in general was the settlement of Shudras, of craftsmen. However, urban economy per se, and the later establishment of individual crafts on its soil does not suffice to explain the rank differences between the various occupations.

The law books[69] enjoin the Shudra to dutiful "service." Only when he could find no service was he permitted to become an independent trader or craftsman. The sentence allows but one conclusion if any: slaves and bondsmen of the overlord, unless exploitable in his *oikos*, received in return for taxes (*apophora, obrok, leibzins*) permission for independent work on their own account in a manner similar to that of occidental and oriental Antiquity, of the Middle Ages, and of Russia prior to the abolition of serfdom. Direct evidence for this appears to be lacking. Contemporary vestiges of similar conditions, however, are to be found. There is, for example, a small caste of "slaves" in Northwestern India. These are domestic servants who outside their duties in the households have been permitted by their masters freely to pursue their trades. Also the insignificance, of compulsory slave labor in Indian industry, agrees with this. In any case the sources clearly indicate: (1) that bondsmen artisans appear alongside (2) the especially important and characteristically Indian village artisans, and (3) urban guild artisans. None of these, however, seems to represent the true archetype of the Shudra.

Four types of craftsman appear in the Indian economic order from the epics until the Middle Ages and in part until the present. These are:

(1) Helots of single villages settled on the village outskirts (*Wurth*) received a fixed wage in kind or some land. The work of these artisans almost always takes the form of strict wage labor, that is to say, the patron furnishes all materials (helot handicrafts).

(2) Artisans settled in separate, self-governing villages of their own.[70] There they offered for sale their services or wares made from their own raw materials or they sold their products personally or through traders in distant markets, or, finally, they worked at the places of their patrons (tribal handicraft).

(3) Artisans who were settled by a king, prince, temple, or landlord on their lands. Such artisans could be either bond or free men but were in any case subject to servitude. They supplied the lord's demand for goods (either *oikos* or liturgical handicraft). The latter may in part be combined with price labor. Since the rise of patrimonialism liturgical crafts are represented primarily by defense workers, by ship-builders and armorers who, reportedly, were often forbidden to work for private patrons. Blacksmiths and similar craftsmen, too, were subject to especially strict controls. (They are the crafts which in the early Roman state formed the *centuria fabrum.*)

(4) Independent artisans who settle in definite streets of the city and as price workers or wage workers offer their wares or their services in a bazaar (bazaar handicraft). A considerable part of the group probably were not permanent urban residents but represent an offshoot of the second category. Even at present,

we learn from Bombay, that the artisan, when aged or sufficiently prosperous, often retires from the city to his village. At any rate, this category does not represent a primary type, nor does the third. The princes, especially the rich ones of the trading cities of South India and Ceylon, recruited artisans from afar for the construction of palaces and temples. The princes settled such imported artisans with land in return for their service to the courts as construction workers and artist craftsmen. Their legal status varies. Alongside such purely liturgical artisans, compensated by service benefices and payment in kinds, there are to be found contractually free or tariffed wage workers who came of their own accord. The size of the land prebends of the Ceylonese royal craftsmen depended upon the nature of their services. Legally the craftsman was free to retire at any time from his service and to renounce his prebend.

The first category, helot handicraft, may frequently have been derived from the second group through the summoning of craftsmen from pariah tribes who had worked as itinerant journeymen at their patrons' places and then settling them in the village. The age of helot handicraft actually cannot be stated, for the early sources permit no clear insight into the situation of artisans. It is highly probable, however, that the development of helot handicraft soon followed the establishment of permanent settlements. In all probability the true primary form of such labor is that of tribal handicraft.

In the primary form of tribal handicraft, a tribe or tribal division settled in a village, producing for increasingly distant markets. Possibly, too, members of the tribe migrated into the neighborhood of princes and courts, there developing new, closed handicraft villages. We have reports of such handicraft villages precisely in nearby places.

The journeyman of the king arrived like the Brahmans at the call of a prince and permitted themselves to be settled in his territory. These royal artisans enjoyed a high degree of personal security. Under the Maurya Dynasty anyone who did severe bodily injury to an artisan had to face capital punishment. The relatively high rank of the Tanti weaver caste in Bengal as compared with the rank of weavers in other regions may possibly be explained by their origin from a royal Bengal craft. Apparently (and understandably) such royal handicraftsmen maintained on the whole the most distinguished rank among the artisans. Particularly in the great epoch of building which followed the introduction of stone construction in India (third century B.C.) there must have been an increased demand for them, especially for the newly developed craftsworkers, stonecutters, and masons. Until the time of King Ashoka (third century B.C.) the ancient city of Pataliputra had wooden walls. Only under King Ashoka was the city fortified by brick walls. At the same time stone houses were built. The Indian Great Kings, too, established their bureaucracy, at least in part, as a construction bureaucracy. Thus, the increased demand must have elevated the position of such craftsmen and benefited the situation of their helpers and the decoration workers.

A similar rise in importance for the craftsmen involved must have been accomplished by the subsequent imports of precious metals from the Occident. An important illustration is found in the Kammalar artisans of South India and the nearby Islands. The rank order of the occupations is as follows: (1) iron workers, (2) wood workers, (3) copper and bronze workers, (4) stone and (5) precious metal and jewel workers—the five-caste craftsmen,[71] (Panchvala) as they are named in Mysore. They worship Visvakarma as an ancestral lord and vocational god and have—as noted earlier—their own priests. They claim high rank, at times even Brahmanical descent.[72]

The great and persisting schism in the South between the castes of the "right" and "left hands" resulted from their insurrection against the Brahmans. In any case their rank was in general higher than that of the craftsmen of ancient local trades as, for example, the potters and weavers. In Malabar they were considered impure, probably because they were schismatics. Yet social rank and likewise economic power position resulted often from very particular conditions. Such rifts as develop may in fact cut through one and the same caste. The Sutars in Bombay in their role as village carpenters are village servants. Their urban caste members became ship-builders and claimed to be Brahmans. When denied admittance as Brahmans, they developed priests of their own and discontinued commensalism with the village carpenters. Quite apart from special urban conditions, circumstances may place a premium upon the services of the helot artisans. When irregular services or services beyond those which are customary are demanded of the helot artisan, such as repairs out of season, he is favored by his monopoly position. The village smith especially seems often to have raised considerable pretensions in India as elsewhere.

Literary sources and inscriptions on monuments show the considerable scope of the princely *oikos* and liturgical handicraft.[73] Royal (and similarly temple) artisans represented high quality labor among the Indian artistic crafts. Secure in their prebends they could afford the "time" to manufacture artistic products. Commarasvamy mentions without further references a vase in Delhi which was produced by three generations of a family of royal artisans. Almost always princely officials, and with the great kings, ministerial committees for industry developed; these offices could hardly have served any other purpose than to supervise the work of these artisans.[74]

The substitution of money taxes for *corvées* is consistent with the character of administrative development; it brought these artisans into line with other trades of the royal cities which were subject to tax and license obligations. Tax payment was viewed as a compensation for trade monopolies[75] which were almost always guaranteed to some extent to settled artisans. On the other hand, there is found within the princely *oikos* the development of the *ergasterion*[76] as we know it from later occidental antiquity, especially from Egypt, as well as from the Byzantine and Middle-Eastern Middle Ages. Where royal grants of artisans to temples or Brahmans, or knightly vassals occur we may generally interpret the documents as referring to *oikos* or liturgical artisans.[77] Though not probable it is quite possible that as the king increasingly claimed the right to land and free disposition of the subjects' economic services, he may also have farmed out helot artisans or even tribal artisans.

In the time of guild power urban artisans to some extent shared the guild's prosperity. Where organized craft guilds often charged high initiation fees (varying according to the respective craft they might amount to several hundred dollars, a small fortune in India at the time). Like merchant guilds, price worker guilds developed hereditary membership; they imposed fines and controlled with these sanctions the nature of the work (holidays, work time), and established, above all, guarantees for the quality of the wares. As indicated, however, many craftsmen were dependent on the traders and their putting-out system. The self-government of artisans with the development of patrimonialism shared the fate of the guilds opposite the advancing caste organization and the power of royal bureaucracy. In the cities as seats of princes royal guild masters appeared early. Without question, the king in his financial interest, controlled the crafts with increasing severity. The fiscal interests of the king may well have contributed to the stabilization of the caste order. It is necessary to assume, of course, that many guilds turned directly into castes (or subcastes) or as divisions of pariah tribes were not separate from them in the first place.

Artisan castes, at least the upper crust of the artisan-artists, had a fixed system of apprenticeship. The father, grand uncle, elder brother took their places as teaching masters and after the completion of apprenticeship, as house masters to whom all wage earnings had to be surrendered. Apprenticeship under a strange master of the caste is found. It followed rigid traditional norms and involved reception into the house community, with corresponding submission to the master. In theory, an apprentice had to acquire basic technology as prescribed by the Silpa Castra, a product of priestly scholarship. Therefore, stone-cutters were at times held to be a caste of literati and had the title *acarya* (teacher, master). The occidental parallel to this vacillating position is that of the "architect" at the time of the construction of Gothic domes, a problem treated by Hasack.

In general, the tools of the Indian artisan were technically so simple that many of them were self-made. Among some handicrafts the tools were worshipped as quasi-fetishes and the caste often honors them even at present in the Dasahra-festival. Alongside other traditional traits, this stereotyping of tools was one of the strongest handicaps to all technical development. The parallel in the fine arts was the stereotyping of models and the rejection of all designing after nature. Among some building crafts, particularly among handicrafts working with sacred objects, elements of technical procedure (e.g., painting the eye of a sacred picture) assumed the character of a magically relevant ceremony which had to follow definite rules. Any change of technique required often—with usually negative results—the consulting of an oracle, as the potters once found in the goddess Bhagavati.

It is difficult to determine in detail how long strict caste closure of various royal and urban handicrafts has existed in various territories. Several handicrafts may work closely together. Thus Colonel Hendley found a combination of wood, stone, and metal work in North Jaipur.[78] But as a rule it is accompanied by strict guarantee of hereditary patronage.

The lowest caste stratum was considered to be absolutely defiling and contaminating. First, this stratum comprised a number of trades which are almost always despised because they involve physically dirty work: street-cleaning and others. Furthermore, this stratum comprised services which Hinduism had to consider ritually impure: tanning, leather work, and some industries in the hands of itinerant guest workers. However, it would be a great mistake to believe that the three industrial strata distinguished by us, that is, original urban or royal artisans, original village artisans, original guest workers, approximately fit the three-caste framework of the Sat-shudra, ordinary Shudra, and impure castes, if anyone disregards special, ritualistically determined exceptions (as for example, the leather trades).

Quite apart from ritually determined (direct or indirect) exceptions from that rule, caste organization presents far too colorful and irrational a picture. A great many, at first puzzling cases can only be classified in terms of their concrete historical development. For many others, general reasons for the ascent or descent of a caste or subcaste can be stated. This depends upon the conditions determining the origin, developments, or change of castes and subcastes. With this, we complete our survey of the empirical caste order and resume the discussion of general conditions.

CHAPTER III
CASTE FORMS AND SCHISMS

1. Caste Criteria

THE British census experts rightly distinguish two basic types of castes: tribal and professional. Our previous discussion of the former may now be supplemented. In all probability a multitude of castes developed historically from Hinduized tribal and guest peoples. It is principally these which make the picture of the caste rank order so irrational. For, other things being equal, a tribe which at the time of its Hinduization was settled on its own land achieved and maintained higher rank than pure pariah tribes which have been Hinduized. Moreover, a tribe which supplied mercenaries and soldiers of fortune fared still better. How then are we to recognize "tribal castes"?

A tribal caste is often identifiable by the form of its name. Yet, in the course of Hinduization quite a few tribes have assumed professional names. There are other criteria: subcastes frequently state a common ancestor; true upper castes usually have ancestral subcaste figures. There are frequently survivals of totem organization. Former tribal deities may be retained and, above all, tribal priests may serve as caste priests. Finally, members may be recruited from definite territories. Both the last named criteria are important only when taken in combination with one or other of the preceding criteria, for there are professional castes with strictly local recruitment and their own priests.

The endogamy of a tribal caste is often the less strict the closer it is to tribal status; it is also less exclusive toward caste outsiders. Generally pure-professional castes are most inflexible in these respects, which proves that ritualistic caste exclusiveness, though partly determined thereby, is no mere religious projection of ethnic strangeness.

The tribal caste is most clearly recognizable when one or several of a plurality of castes of the same profession retain a tribal name in addition to the usual professional caste name. The extent to which the castes were originally tribal castes is not determinable. The lowest castes may indeed have developed largely out of guest and pariah tribes. However, this is certainly not true of all of them. Relatively few of the more esteemed handicrafts, particularly the free and liturgical crafts of the cities and the ancient merchant castes, could have had this origin. Probably most of them developed out of economic specialization—from the differentiation of properties and skills. The peculiarity of Indian development which requires explanation is this: Why did it result in caste formation?

Apart from the reception of tribes caste formation could be modified only by caste schism.

2. *Caste Schism*

CASTE schism is always expressed by the complete or partial denial of connubium and commensalism. This may, in the first place, result from residential mobility of caste members. Migrant members were suspect of having offended against ritual caste duties. At very least, their correctness could not be controlled. The nomadism of cattle-breeders contributed to their loss of rank. Inasmuch as only Indian land, and that only insofar as proper caste order is established on it, can be holy land, strict orthodoxy views as doubtful any change of residence even within India since it takes the immigrant into a different ritualistic environment.

Only in cases of absolute necessity was travel considered correct. Internal migration in India, therefore, even at present, is far below what might be expected in view of the great transformation of economic conditions. More than nine-tenths of the people live in their native districts. As a rule only ancient village exogamy leads to settlement in another village. Permanent settlement of caste members in other places regularly results in the split up into new subcastes, for the residentially stable members refuse to consider the descendants of migrants as their peers.

As the Hindu system spread eastward from the upper Ganges, new subcastes of the old were formed which, other things being equal, ranked below those of the west.

A second reason for caste schism was the renunciation by some members of various former ritual duties or, the reverse of this, the assumption by some of new ritual duties. Both the renunciation of old rituals or the assumption of new ones could have a variety of causes. (1) Membership in a sect could absolve some ritual prescriptions or impose new ones. This is not very frequent. (2) Differentiation within a caste could lead the propertied members to assume the ritual obligations of higher castes, or to claim higher rank than formerly. To realize such aspirations one had first to break away from intermarriage and commensalism with former caste members. Today simple property differentiation quite often is made the occasion for splitting the community. (3) Occupational changes could lead to schism. According to rigid traditionalistic observance, not only change of occupation but a mere change of work technique may be sufficient reason for the followers of tradition to consider the community as broken. While such consequences do not always occur in fact, it is, perhaps, the most frequent and, in practice, the most important occasion for caste schism. Finally, (4) the disintegration of the ritualistic tradition among some of the members may lead the orthodox ones to cancel communal relations with them.

Today new castes may originate also from ritually illicit intercaste cohabitation. As is known, classical theory explained all impure castes in terms of caste mixture—the explanation, of course, is quite unhistorical. Still, there are some instances of caste origin from caste mixture, hence from concubinage.

Finally, schisms may simply result from the failure to settle all sorts of internal disputes. This is strongly disapproved of as a reason for caste fission and is usually concealed by alleging ritual offences on the part of the opponent.

Of greatest interest to us are the economic reasons for caste and subcaste origin: property differentiation, occupational mobility, technological change. We may be certain that property differentiation—occupational mobility was legitimate only by way of emergency pursuits—resulted in caste schism far less frequently under the national dynasties than it does at present. For the Brahmans, whose power then was incomparably greater, upheld the caste order as established and habitual. If the stability of the caste order could not hinder property differentiation, it could at least block technological change and occupational mobility, which from the point of view of caste were objectionable and ritually dangerous. Today, the very fact that new skills and techniques actually lead to the formation of new castes or subcastes strongly handicaps innovation. It sustains tradition no matter how often the all-powerful development of imported capitalism overrides it.

All historical signs indicate that the truly strict caste order was originally based on the professional castes. This is indicated in the first place by the geographical distribution of tribal and professional castes. To be sure, one can rarely ascertain whether any given caste originated out of ethnic or gentile charismatic professional differences. In Bengal, for instance, the ancient caste of blacksmiths, the Lohars, are a typical professional caste which undoubtedly is ethnically heterogeneous. Yet in the later conquest territories of East Bengal and the South, castes which can be proven to have been originally tribal castes decidedly outnumber and overshadow professional castes. On the other hand, on the classical soil of North Central India, castes traceable (or presumably so) to original gentile charismatic occupational classes without ethnic differences are more frequent.[1] Besides, professional castes, particularly those of industry, are the very pillars of rigid caste segregation and tradition—alongside pure peasant castes, for which a rigid traditionalism goes without saying. The rigid traditionalism of these professional castes is expressed in their still tenacious attachment to their customary pursuits—they are second in this only to a few very ancient pariah tribes. In the traditionless environs of metropolitan Calcutta, among the Hindu castes more than 80 per cent of the laundrymen followed their traditional pursuits, as did more than 50 per cent of the Hindu castes of fishermen, street-cleaners, basket-weavers, pastry cooks, domestic servants, and even goldsmiths. However, only 30 per cent of the scribes (Kayastha) were clerks, and only 13 per cent of the Brahmans were priests, teachers, pandits, and cooks.[2] As a consequence of European competition only 6 per cent of the old weaver castes (Tanti) were engaged in their trade.

As one would expect, the devastating competition of European and now Indian capitalist industry has completely eliminated quite a number of professions or at least their handicraft basis. Where this is not the case, the ratio of professional caste members who continue their traditional pursuits despite basic transformation of the economy still remains extraordinarily high. The majority of the workers for specifically "modern" job opportunities, particularly big industry, are recruited, not from the ancient industrial castes, but predominantly from rural migrants, declassed and pariah castes, and declassed members of certain higher castes.

Modern capitalist businessmen (if at all Indian) and commercial and administrative employees are largely recruited from certain ancient trader castes. Quite understandably, furthermore, in view of the nature and educational prerequisites of modern office work recruitment also occurs from literati castes which earlier had a wider occupational choice than the industrial castes.[3] In Bombay Province the most important castes engaged in administrative pursuits appear in the following order: Prabu (ancient caste of officials) 27 per cent of the caste members; Mahars (village officials) 10 per cent; Brahmans 7.1 per cent; Lohana (genteel traders) 5.8 per cent; Bhatia (traders) 4.7 per cent; Vania (members of the great ancient trading caste) 2.3 per cent; Rajputs, 2 per cent; all other castes had less than 1 per cent of their members in administration.

Economically, the traditionalism of the professional castes rests not only upon a mutual segregation of the various branches of production, but also, and today very often, upon the protection of the livelihood of caste members against mutual competition. The artisan belonging to the ancient "village staff" who was settled on garden land or who received a fixed income was absolutely protected in this respect. However, the principle of patronage protection, the guarantee of the *jajmani* relation, went much further and still is strictly enforced by numerous occupational castes. We learned of the principle in connection with the Brahmans, and the meaning of the word *jajmani* ("sacrifice giver") suggests that the concept originated in the conditions of the Brahman caste. It could, perhaps, best be rendered by "personal diocese." The status etiquette of the Brahmans secures their dioceses among some other castes. They are by the caste organization and indeed—as always in India—hereditary (clan charismatic).

The Chamar hereditarily receives the dead cattle from certain families and supplies them with leather for shoes and other needs; meanwhile his wife serves the same circle of patrons as midwife. The beggar castes have definite begging districts somewhat like our chimney-sweeps (however, these are hereditary). The Nai serves his hereditary patron as barber, manicurist, pedicurist, bather, and dentist. The last two pursuits are virtually degrading. The Bhangi is street-cleaner for a definite district. According to reports some castes, e.g., the Dom (domestics and beggars) and the Bhangi, have alienable patronage which often formed part of dowries.[4] Where the institution exists today, trespassing on another's patronage rights still constitutes a ground for excommunication from the caste.

However, not only do the ancient occupational castes sustain a rigid traditionalism, but also, in general, they uphold the strictest ritualistic caste exclusiveness. Nowhere are endogamy and the exclusion of commensualism more rigidly observed than by the occupational castes, and this is by no means true only of the interrelation of high with low castes. Impure castes shun infectious contact with nonmembers as rigidly as high castes. This may be taken as conclusive proof of the fact that mutual exclusiveness was predominantly caused, not by social, but by ritualistic factors based on the quality of many of these castes as ancient guest or pariah people. Especially "correct" Hindu communities are to be found precisely among the old industrial castes and in part among the impure castes.

The extreme caste traditionalism of many industrial and indeed lower castes (apart from an important religious ground to be examined later) is determined by their frequently strict caste, or as a rule subcaste, organization. (Normally this organization supports caste discipline; more will be said later on this subject.)

The caste organization suggests the ancient village community with its hereditary headman and its council of sib or family heads. In fact, the existence of a village *panchayat* is today denied with great vehemence.[5] Allegedly there are only caste-*panchayats* and among these the *panchayats* of peasants belonging to one caste and settled in a village. In terms of the material available in continental Europe, indeed the issue can only be whether the *panchayats* of numerous villages representing the village members ("full peasants") have their origin in the caste or were somehow modelled after early village institutions.[6] (The latter appears most probable.)

The position of the village chief was never absolutely hereditary, but only gentile charismatic. An unfit village head could under certain conditions be deposed; the successor, however, was usually chosen from the same family. As already noted, this principle of clan charisma pervaded all Indian organization from the political association to the guild. Strict primogeniture of rules only later became sacred law. As a rule the guild leaders and elders (*shreshthi*) were and remained hereditarily charismatic. This was also true for the caste, at least for the leader, *sar panch*, and often also for the members of the *panchayat*.

Originally, all economic or official functions served the "community," and in the Indian villages were always incumbent upon hereditarily settled workers who were paid in kind. This may have helped to conserve and diffuse this arrangement which, as documented by inscriptions, is to be found elsewhere, for example, among Mid-Eastern artisans in Hellenic times. A contributing factor was possibly a royal investiture of men responsible for the various industries and their services at the time of the great Hindu patrimonial kingdoms. But the ancient, principle of clan charisma remained the decisive underpinning of the Brahman.

The idea of electing the leaders in our present-day sense was indeed nowhere originally basic to religious and (decidedly less so), then, to political organization. What to us may appear as an election always was the dutiful recognition or acclamation of a man endowed with personal or gentile charisma. The old position of the "elders" in the reformed presbyterial constitutions was still charismatic. The constitution of our "synodal constitutions" in contrast developed out of the modern concept of representation. In India, too, the recent repeated meetings of the *sabhas* (caste assemblies of all members or at least of all heads of families) is of modern origin. Today, for example, they not only make decisions about the sending of students to Japan, but also about changes in important social customs; for example, the lifting of the ban on the remarriage of widows, a question which earlier could not have been decided by voted resolutions but only by the judgment of the Brahmans.

As a rule, the dioceses of the *panchayat* represent delimited local areas. Interlocal interest associations or cartels for the discharge of definite business appear within the castes. Survivals of guilds as divisions of castes or as caste leagues are to be found. Likewise there are guild residues which comprise caste outsiders. In exceptional cases there may be found a central organization of entire castes which is considered superordinate to the *panchayat*. This occurs for the most part in territories which for a long time formed unitary political realms. In contrast, local caste schism is greatest where no political unity existed for long periods.

3. *Caste Discipline*

WHAT is the jurisdiction of the *panchayat* or its corresponding organ? It is highly variable. Occupational issues in no way form the center of gravity; at present the caste or subcaste does not function primarily as a guild or trade union. Most issues involve questions of ritual. Among the issues adjudged by the *panchayat* are, in order, adultery and other offences against intersexual ritualistic etiquette and atonement for other ritualist offences of the members including especially the offence against the rules of intermarriage and commensalism or against purity and dietary laws. Problems such as these always played an important role in the decisions of the *panchayat*, because tolerance of magical offenders by the caste could draw evil magic upon the whole caste.

However, professional problems play a very significant role among some ancient and traditionally stable middle and lower castes. In the first place, the caste is self-evidently concerned with all shifts of members to ritually degrading or suspect pursuits, be they new professions or new techniques. According to the circumstances, this may in practice have far-reaching implications. But there are also nonritualistic caste problems such as the violation of *jajmani* rights by a caste member or infringement by outcastes or strange castes upon the caste's economic monopoly. Furthermore, other caste rights may be violated by caste outsiders. It is precisely the ancient and traditionalistic castes which intervene most vigorously in economic affairs, which suggests that this aspect of the caste order probably had far wider significance in earlier times.

The assumption by many industrial and lower castes of the functions of a guild or trade union is explained by the typical interest situation of handicraftsmen and skilled workers. This, in turn, explained the frequent and quite intense caste loyalty of the lower castes. Nonpayment of debts, divisions of wealth and bagatelle trials are not unusual among members today. However, occasionally castes seek to hinder members from bearing witness against one another. Most questions, however, are of a ritualistic nature, and occasionally they concern fairly important issues. The power of the *panchayats* and *sabhas* has been growing in the field of ritual. In truth this is a characteristic phase of a slowly progressive emancipation movement from the power of the Brahmans which finds expression in these apparently archaic caste affairs. This preoccupation is the Hindu equivalent of the striving for "congregational autonomy" in the Occident.

Against outsiders the sanction of the caste is boycott; against members its sanctions are the imposition of money fines, judgments of ritualistic expiation, and in case of obstinacy and grave cases of the violation of caste norms, excommunication (*bahishkara*). Today this last does not mean excommunication from Hinduism, but only from the single caste. To be sure, this may have wide ramifications. Anyone, for example, who continues to accept the services of the excommunicated caste member may be boycotted.

Today most *panchayats* (and other equivalent organs) make decisions without consulting the *castris* and *pandits,* such consultation being considered optional. Of course, some castes, including the lower ones, still appeal to one or other of the holy seats (the monasteries in Sankeshwar or Shringeri). According to ancient Hindu conceptions autonomous legal enactments by a caste was out of the question. Holy right always can only be revealed or recognized anew, as having existed of yore. However, the present-day lack of a Hindu political authority and the resulting weakened position of the Brahmans, has permitted occasionally independent legal enactments as a due and correct form of recognizing the law. As in the case of usurpation of caste rank the abolition of the political and patrimonial church state structure of the old kingdoms here clearly worked tangibly and distinctly in the direction of a slow disintegration of caste tradition.

The less thoroughly tribal castes are Hinduized the more features of ancient tribal organization are substituted for those of the typical caste. We shall not examine these here in detail.

Finally, the high castes, especially the Brahmans and Rajputs, often lack all unified durable organization in their subcastes as well as the main caste. As far as we can determine, this has always been true. In urgent cases such as gross ritualistic offences of a member the heads of the *maths* (monasteries) are called together; more recently, also, assemblies of the respective caste division are called. Unquestionably, the Brahmans, and their *castris* and *pandits*, their schools and monasteries, the acknowledged centers of sacred study and the ancient, famous, holy seats generally, know how to preserve their authority. However the Vedic schools, the philosophic schools, the sects, and ascetic orders have long been in competition with one another. Furthermore, the ancient distinguished Brahman clans have been opposed, on the one side, to those who have gradually usurped the rights of Brahmans, and on the other, to those strata and subcastes which were degraded to Brahmans of lesser rights. All these antagonisms produced deep internal tensions. They inhibit ingroup relations, the strong "we-feeling" based on status consciousness toward the outside.

Among the Rajputs the great influence of Brahmanical house priests (*purohita*) in maintaining ritualistic correctness substituted for the lack of caste organs. Some of the subcastes always have had strong organizations and their status feeling is fairly strong. Even the great diversity of occupational pursuits of the two castes remains on the whole well within the limits of ritualist correctness. The emergency occupations mentioned by Manu indicated how very old they are.

The pure castes of scribes are best understood as products of the patrimonial Indian kingdoms. Their historical influence extends into the present. In contrast to the ancient social and feudal aristocracies these castes of scribes have high pretensions to caste rank but incomparably less status pride. This is quite understandable, and made clear by their present occupational composition. Among the trader castes residues of the ancient guilds have survived. For the rest, their organization today seems less strict under the native princes who often exploit the economic and particularly the urban castes, but, as well, the pariah peoples for liturgical duties and corresponding monopoly rights.

With this we may conclude this sketch which, despite its lengthy treatment of the caste system, must unavoidably remain very incomplete.

4. *Caste and Traditionalism*

WE ARE now in a position to enquire into the effects of the caste system on the economy. These effects were essentially negative and must rather be inferred than inductively assessed. Hence we can but phrase a few generalizations. Our sole point is that this order by its nature is completely traditionalistic and anti-rational in its effects. The basis for this, however, must not be sought in the wrong place.

Karl Marx has characterized the peculiar position of the artisan in the Indian village—his dependence upon fixed payment in kind instead of upon production for the market—as the reason for the specific "stability" of the Asiatic peoples. In this, Marx was correct.

In addition to the ancient village artisan, however, there was the merchant and also the urban artisan; and the latter either worked for the market or was economically dependent upon merchant guilds, as in the Occident. India has always been predominantly a country of villages. Yet the beginnings of cities were also modest in the Occident, especially inland, and the position of the urban market in India was regulated by the princes in many ways "mercantilistically"—in a sense similar to the territorial states at the beginnings of modern times. In any case, insofar as social stratification is concerned, not only the position of the village artisan but also the caste order as a whole must be viewed as the bearer of stability. One must not think of this effect too directly. One might believe, for instance, that the ritual caste antagonisms had made impossible the development of "large-scale enterprises" with a division of labor in the same workshop, and might consider this to be decisive. But such is not the case.

The law of caste has proved just as elastic in the face of the necessities of the concentration of labor in workshops as it did in the face of a need for concentration of labor and service in the noble household. All domestic servants required by the upper castes were ritually clean, as we have seen. The principle, "the artisan's hand is always clean in his occupation,"[7] is a similar concession to the necessity of being allowed to have fixtures made or repair work done, personal services, or other work accomplished by wage workers or by itinerants not belonging to the household. Likewise, the workshop[8] (*ergasterion*) was recognized as "clean." Hence no ritual factor would have stood in the way of jointly using different castes in the same large workroom, just as the ban upon interest during the Middle Ages, as such, hindered little the development of industrial capital, which did not even emerge in the form of investment for fixed interest. The core of the obstacle did not lie in such particular difficulties, which every one of the great religious systems in its way has placed, or has seemed to place, in the way of the modern economy. The core of the obstruction was rather imbedded in the "spirit" of the whole system. In modern times it has not always been easy, but eventually it has been possible to employ Indian caste labor in modern factories. And even earlier it was possible to exploit the labor of Indian artisans capitalistically in the forms usual elsewhere in colonial areas, after the finished mechanism of modern capitalism once could be imported from Europe. Even if all this has come about, it must still be considered extremely unlikely that the modern organization of industrial capitalism would ever have *originated* on the basis of the caste system. A ritual law in which every change of occupation, every change in work technique, may result in ritual degradation is certainly not capable of giving birth to economic and technical revolutions from within itself, or even of facilitating the first germination of capitalism in its midst.

The artisan's traditionalism, great in itself, was necessarily heightened to the extreme by the caste order. Commercial capital, in its attempts to organize industrial labor on the basis of the putting-out system, had to face an essentially stronger resistance in India than in the Occident. The traders themselves in their ritual seclusion remained in the shackles of the typical oriental merchant class, which by itself has never created a modern capitalist organization of labor. This situation is as if none but different guest peoples, like the Jews, ritually exclusive toward one another and toward third parties, were to follow their trades in one economic area. Some of the great Hinduist merchant castes, particularly, for instance, the Vania, have been called the "Jews of India," and, in this negative sense, rightly so. They were, in part, virtuosi in unscrupulous profiteering.

Nowadays a considerable tempo in the accumulation of wealth is singularly evident among castes which were formerly considered socially degraded or unclean and which therefore were especially little burdened with (in our sense) "ethical" expectations addressed to themselves. In the accumulation of wealth, such castes compete with others which formerly monopolized the positions of scribes, officials, or collectors of farmedout taxes, as well as similar opportunities for politically determined earnings typical of patrimonial states. Some of the capitalist entrepreneurs also derive from the merchant castes. But in capitalist enterprise they could keep up with the castes of literati only to the extent to which they acquired the "education" nowadays necessary—as has been occasionally noticed above.[9] The training for trade is among them in part so intense—as far as the reports allow for insight—that their specific "gift" for trading must by no means rest upon any "natural disposition."[10] That ancient castes with strong occupational mobility often drift into occupations whose demands on "natural disposition" form the greatest psychological contrast imaginable to the previous mode of activity, but which stand close to one another through the common usefulness of certain forms of knowledge and aptitudes acquired through training, speaks against imputations of "natural disposition." Thus, the frequent shift, mentioned above, from the ancient caste of surveyors—whose members naturally know the roads particularly well—to the occupation of chauffeur may be referred to among many similar examples. However, in spite of the adaptability of some of the castes we have no indication that by themselves they could have created the rational enterprise of modern capitalism.

Finally, modern capitalism undoubtedly would never have originated from the circles of the completely traditionalist Indian trades. The Hindu artisan, is nevertheless, famous for his extreme industry; he is considered to be essentially more industrious than the Indian artisan of Islamic faith. And, on the whole, the Hindu caste organization has often developed a very great intensity of work and of property accumulation within the ancient occupational castes. The intensity of work holds more for handicraft and for individual ancient agricultural castes. By the way, the Kunbis (for instance, those in South India) achieve a considerable accumulation of wealth, and nowadays, as a matter of fact, it takes modern forms.

Modern industrial capitalism, in particular the factory, made its entry into India under the British administration and with direct and strong incentives. But, comparatively speaking, how small is the scale and how great the difficulties. After several hundred years of English domination there are today only about 980,000 factory workers, that is, about one-third of 1 per cent of the population.[11] In addition, the recruitment of labor is difficult, even in those manufacturing industries with the highest wages. (In Calcutta, labor often has to be recruited from the outside. In one near-by village, hardly one-ninth of the people speak the native language of Bengal.) Only the most recent acts for the protection of labor have made factory work somewhat more popular. Female labor is found only here and there, and then it is recruited from among the most despised castes, although there are textile industries where women can accomplish twice as much as men.

Indian factory labor shows exactly those traditionalist traits which also characterized labor in Europe during the early period of capitalism. The workers want to earn some money quickly in order to establish themselves independently. An increase in wage rate does not mean for them an incentive for more work or for a higher standard of living, but the reverse. They then take longer holidays because they can afford to do so, or their wives decorate themselves with ornaments. To stay away from work as one pleases is recognized as a matter of course, and the worker retires with his meagre savings to his home town as soon as possible.[12] He is simply a mere casual laborer. "Discipline" in the European sense is an unknown idea to him. Hence, despite a fourfold cheaper wage, competition with Europe is maintained easily only in the textile industry, as two-and-a-half times as many workers and far more supervision are required. One advantage for the entrepreneurs is that the caste division of the workers has so far made any trade union organization and any real "strike" impossible. As we have noticed, the work in the workshop is "clean" and is performed jointly. (Only separate drinking cups at the well are necessary, at least one for the Hindus and one for the Islamites, and in sleeping quarters only men of the same caste sleep together. A fraternization of labor, however, has (so far) been as little possible as a *conjuratio* (sworn confederation) of the citizens.[13]

Unfortunately, there are but scanty materials concerning the participation by castes in modern capitalist business—at least, only a few detailed descriptions are available to the outside student.

Apparently in Calcutta modern "skilled" labor is mainly recruited from the castes of the Kaivartha (an old tribal caste of peasants and fishermen), the Kayasth (scribes), and Tanti (an old weaver caste). Unskilled handworkers, so-called coolie workers, also are recruited from the castes of the Kaivartha and Kayasth as well as from the despised castes of the Goala (an old pariah tribe of dairy men), and the Chamar, the large unclean caste of leather workers of Bengal. Today the lowest castes deprived of their traditional pursuits are here and elsewhere most strongly represented among the coolies.

Millhands proper come primarily from four castes: the Tanti (weavers), Kaivartha (peasants and fishermen), Chamar (leather workers), and Kayasth (scribes).

In contrast to this 45 per cent of the Chatri (allegedly Kshatriya, actually an ancient tribe of professional soldiers) are peasants, peons, and domestics; almost none is found in public service or industry.

The textile industry of the province of Bombay employs 63 per cent of the weavers' castes, 11.7 per cent of the Bhatia (an old marginal trading people), 9.8 per cent of the Vani (genteel traders), 3.8 per cent of the Rajputs, over 1 per cent of the Prabhu (officials), and Mahan (village officials), fewer of the remaining castes. The traders and last mentioned castes primarily represent the entrepreneurs (or proprietors in the case of the Rajputs). In Bombay Province, commerce (exclusive of food industries) engages the following percentages of the castes: Brahmans, 3.2 per cent; Vania (an old caste of aristocratic traders), 24.85 per cent; Bathia (an old marginal trading people, 7 per cent; Rajputs and Mahratta, practically none; Prahbu (officials), 9.3 per cent; Lohana (an old distinguished trading caste in Sindh), 6 per cent; weavers, Koli (small holders), Kunbi (peasants), Mahar (village officials), practically none; Pandhari (palm juice distillers), 2 per cent; considerable fractions of the old traders' castes today are employed in the food industries (probably mainly in retail trade). Thus, 4 per cent of the Vania; 61.3 per cent of the Bhatia, 22.8 per cent of the Lohana are so employed. Of all other castes only a few and practically none of the genteel castes are employed in the food industry.

Gait in the general Report of the 1911 Census states the following with reference to the income of the main castes (from sources other than office, pension, and securities–Part IV of the

Income Tax Act) and the reports from census superintendents: In Bengal there were around 23,000 persons assessed for income tax from gainful employment. The Mohammedans with twenty-four million or 51.7 per cent of the people had only 3,177 persons taxable for income from gainful occupation, hence somewhat over one-eighth of the total. The single Kayasth caste (of scribes) had almost as many and, indeed, some from enterprises, some from professions. Next in importance were the Brahmans constituting 50 per cent of those assessed and drawing their income from profits. The Shahar (119,000 persons) a small subcaste of the Sunri, monopolizing the liquor traffic, were almost equal in representation to the Brahmans. They represented the highest percentage of taxable persons. Beside them only the oil pressers and trader castes of the Teli had over 1,000 taxable persons; all other castes had less. The report found it surprising that the ancient trader castes of the Gandhabaniks and Subarnabaniks, which, judging by the names, were originally spice and precious metal traders were represented only by 500 taxable persons; however, in terms of proportional numbers (from 100,000 and 120,000 persons) this is still stronger representation than the Teli-caste (one and a half million).

The trading caste of the Shaha is of low Shudra rank: the Brahmans do not always accept water from its members. Shahas take to modern profit opportunities with fewer scruples than do the Teli (who in Bengal rank equal to the Nabasakh group) and the castes of the Gandhabaniks and Subarnabaniks which probably have a justified claim to former Vaishya rank. This is quite plausible but also indicative of the traditionalistic spirit of true ancient Hinduism.

In contrast to the Islamites of Bengal, the superior adaptability of appropriate Hindu castes to the rational pursuit of profit is apparent. The relative inferiority of the Islamites in these respects appears in all other provinces. The Islamic Sheik caste has big taxpayers (particularly in Punjab) essentially among the large landlords, like the Rajputs, Babhans (a distinguished landlord and corn wholesaler caste), and frequently also the Brahmans and the Khatri standing near the Rajputs. In Bombay Province rentiers were most strongly represented among the castes of the Brahmans, Prabhu (officials), Mahar (village officials), Lohana (traders).

In Bihar among those taxable for capitalistic income are primarily the Agarvals (a subcaste of the Kewat, an ancient trader caste). Among the taxable classes, the Kalvan and Sunri (ancient castes of palm juice distillers) and the Teli (oil pressers) quantitatively rank equal with the distinguished castes of Brahmans and Babhans. Among them these seven castes obtain one-half of their taxable income from trade.

In the upper Ganges Valley (United Provinces), the ancient territory of classical Hinduism, in Punjab and in the South the wealthiest people are usually the ancient trader castes of the Baniyas, deriving their income from trade. In the Northwest the Khatris (an ancient, distinguished, internationally famous caste of traders and scribes) play a significant role as rent-receiving landlords alongside the Brahmans. Furthermore they outdistance all other castes in income from industry. However, the Kayasth (in the upper Ganges Valley) draw a disproportionately high share of income from professions.

The partial employment of tremendous native wealth as investment capital in modern business was of relatively minor importance for a long time. In the jute industry it is lacking almost completely. "Bad experiences" not only with entrepreneurs and *associes,* but also with foremen was back of this. Even now, for example, in the Indian jute industry only the overseer—but almost no other technical or commercial functionary—is of Indian descent (the latter are mainly Scotchmen).[14] Furthermore, the Jute industry with an average of 3,420 employees per plant[15] is the most highly developed large industry in India.

Differential pecuniary acquisitiveness, favors bestowed upon literati, and, above all, upon traders who are, from the Hindu standpoint ethnically less principled (liquor dealers), and the strong preference of Hindu wealth for commercial investment is obvious in comparison with Islamite wealth. This is in agreement with the often noted industriousness of the more traditionalistic Hindu artisan as compared with the Islamite craftsman. Both phenomena are co-determined by the system of Hindu caste duties. We shall now turn to this important point.

5. The Religious Promise of the Caste System

AS NOTED earlier, Hinduism is unusually tolerant of doctrine (*mata*) while placing greatest emphasis on ritual duties (*dharma*). Nevertheless, Hinduism has certain dogmas—to be discussed presently—if by dogma one means credal truths whose denial is considered heretical and places the group if not the individual outside the Hindu community.

Hinduism recognizes first of all a number of official systems of doctrine. We shall discuss them briefly later in a survey of the salvation religions of the intellectual strata. Here we are interested only in the fact that heterodox doctrines do exist. Two are particularly mentioned in the literature: the philosophy of the materialists and that of the Bauddhas (Buddhists).

What, specifically, makes Buddhism heterodox? Certainly not the rejection of Brahmanical authority since this is found also among Hindu castes. The admission of all castes to salvation is also found among the Hindus. The recruitment by Buddhism of monks from all castes might have turned it into a ritually impure sect-caste. The rejection of the Vedas and Hindu ritual as without value for salvation, however, was a greater gravamen. The Buddhists established their own *dharma* which in parts was more severe than that of the Brahmans. And they are reproached not only for their ritualistic castelessness but also for their heretical teaching, regardless of whether this was the true reason for denying them recognition as Hindus.

What was the heresy of the Buddhists and what does it have in common with the heresy of the materialists in opposition to the teaching of the orthodox schools? The Buddhists, like the materialists, denied the existence of the soul, at least, as a unity of the "I." (For the time being we use the term "soul" in a quite provisional and undifferentiated way, hence without regard to the fact that Hindu philosophy developed several metaphysical conceptions of the nature of the soul.) The denial of the belief in a soul had for the Buddhists—and, indeed, at the decisive point to be mentioned presently—an almost purely theoretical significance. Yet the decisive (theoretical) impulse (for the development of the heresy) was apparently located here. For Hindu philosophy and all that one can designate as "religion" of the Hindu beyond pure ritualism depends on the belief in the soul.

All Hindus accept two basic principles: the *samsara* belief in the transmigration of souls and the related *karman* doctrine of compensation. These alone are the truly "dogmatic" doctrines of all Hinduism, and in their very interrelatedness they represent the unique Hindu theodicy of the existing social, that is to say, caste system.

The belief in the transmigration of souls (*samsara*) grew directly out of universally diffused representations of the fate of the spirit after death. It appears elsewhere in the world, for example, in Hellenic antiquity. In India the fauna and coexistence of different colored races may have facilitated the origin of the idea. It is quite probable that the "army of monkeys" which, according to the *Ramayana,* appeared in South India, was in fact an army of dark Dravidians. Rightly or wrongly it appears that apes and men were thought to be alike and that this idea suggested South India, the seat of black peoples, who looked like apes to the Aryans.

Originally, the departed soul was as little viewed as "immortal" in India as elsewhere. The death sacrifice was intended to put the souls at rest and allay their envy and wrath against the fortunate living. The residence of the "fathers" remained problematical. According to the Brahmanas they faced death by starvation without sacrifice. Sacrifice, therefore, was considered to be the primary merit. Occasionally, also, one wished the gods a long life and increasingly the assumption appears that the existence of neither gods nor men is eternal in the next world.[16]

When the Brahmans began to speculate about their fate, there gradually appeared the teaching of a "second death" leading the dying spirit or god into another existence. The idea that this existence was also on earth was joined to the concept of "animal souls" which probably existed in India as elsewhere. With this the basic elements of the teaching were given.

The connecting of the doctrine of transmigration of souls with that of compensation for good and evil deeds in the form of a more or less honorable rebirth is not exclusively Indian, but is found elsewhere, for example, among the Hellenes. However, two principles are characteristic of Brahman rationalism which determined the pervasive significance of the doctrinal turn: (1) it was believed that each single ethically relevant act has inevitable consequences for the fate of the actor, hence that no consequence can be lost; the doctrine of *karma;* (2) the idea of compensation was linked to the individual's social fate in the societal organization and thereby to the caste order. All (ritual or ethical) merits and faults of the individual formed a sort of ledger of accounts; the balance irrefutably determined the fate of the soul at rebirth, and this in exact proportion to the surplus of one or other side of the ledger.

In India, belief in destiny, astrology, and horoscope-casting were widely diffused for a long time. On closer inspection it seems that the horoscope might well indicate man's fate, but that *karma* determined the good or evil significance of the constellation for the individual. There could be no "eternal" reward or punishment for the individual; such, indeed, would be entirely out of proportion to finite doings. One can stay in heaven or hell only for a finite period.

In general, both heaven and hell play a secondary role in Indian thought. Originally, heaven for the Hindus was probably only a Brahman and warrior heaven. Moreover, hell could be avoided by the blackest sinner through the most convenient purely ritualistic means—the speaking of a certain formula in the hour of death, even when this was spoken by others (even unknowingly and by the enemy).

There was however no sort of ritual means and in general no (inner-worldly) deed which would allow one to escape rebirth and second death. The universal representation that sickness, infirmity, poverty—in short all that was feared in life—resulted from one's own conscious or unconscious, magically relevant failings was here elaborated into the view that man's fate was his own doing. Appearances all too clearly contributed the idea that ethical compensation comes to each life here and now. The idea of metempsychosis had been developed; close at hand was the conception that merits and failings of past lives determine present life and those of the present life determine one's fate in future lives on earth. This conception was evidently developed by the Brahmans at first as an esoteric doctrine. That man was bound in an endless sequence of ever new lives and deaths and he determines his own fate solely by his deeds—this was the most consistent form of the *karma* doctrine.

To be sure, the sources, particularly inscriptions on monuments, indicate that this was not always consistently maintained. The traditional death sacrifice insofar as it aimed at influencing the dead contradicted this. As in Christendom we find prayers, sacrifices, donations, and construction of buildings in order to raise the merits and improve the future fate of one's ancestors. However, such residues of different conceptions did not alter the fact that the individual was continuously and primarily concerned with the question of how to improve his fate of rebirth. The inscription indeed shows this. One brings sacrifices and establishes foundations to be reborn into similarly good or better circumstances; for example, to be born again with the same wife or same children; princes wish to reappear in the future in a similar respectable position on earth. And here is to be found the decisive interrelation with the caste order.

The very caste situation of the individual is not accidental. In India the idea of the "accident of birth" so critical of society is almost completely absent. The idea of "acident of birth" is common to traditionalistic Confucians and occidental social reformists. The Indian views the individual as born into the caste merited by conduct in a prior life. The individual Hindu is actually believed to have used or failed to use "foresight" in the choice of his caste, though not of his "parents" as the German joke has it. An orthodox Hindu confronted with the deplorable situation of a member of an impure caste would only think that he has a great many sins to redeem from his prior existence. (Blunt, in the Census Report of 1911, reports an expression of distinguished Hindus to this effect, with reference to the Chamar.) The reverse of this is that a member of an impure caste thinks primarily of how to better his future social opportunities at rebirth by leading an exemplary life according to caste ritual. In this life there is no escape from the caste, at least, no way to move up in the caste order. The inescapable on-rolling *karma* causality is in harmony with the eternity of the world, of life, and, above all, the caste order.

No true Hindu doctrine knows of a "last day." Widely diffused doctrines maintain that there are epochs in which the world, like the Germanic *Götterdämmerung,* returns to chaos, but only to begin another cycle. The gods are as little immortal as men. Indeed, some teachings maintain that a god such as Indra, for example, is but a name for changing and exchangeable personalities. An especially virtuous man may, indeed, be reborn as a god such as Indra. The fact that the devout individual Hindu usually did not realize the grandiose presuppositions of *karma* doctrine as a whole is irrelevant for their practical effect which is our concern.

Karma doctrine transformed the world into a strictly rational, ethically-determined cosmos; it represents the most consistent theodicy ever produced by history. The devout Hindu was accursed to remain in a structure which made sense only in this intellectual context; its consequences burdened his conduct. The *Communist Manifesto* concludes with the phrase "they (the proletariat) have nothing to lose but their chains, they have a world to win." The same holds for the pious Hindu of low castes. He too can "win the world," even the heavenly world; he can become a Kashtriya, a Brahman, he can gain Heaven and become a god–only not in this life, but in the life of the future after rebirth into the same world pattern.

Order and rank of the castes is eternal (according to doctrine) as the course of the stars and the difference between animal species and the human race. To overthrow them would be senseless. Rebirth can drag man down into the life of a "worm in the intestine of a dog," but, according to his conduct, it might raise and place him into the womb of a queen and Brahman's daughter. Absolute prerequisites, however, were strict fulfillment of caste obligations in this present life, the shunning of ritually sacrilegious yearning for renouncing caste. The commandment "let every man abide in the same calling"—eschatologically motivated in early Christendom—and lasting devotion to one's calling were anchored in the Hindu promise of rebirth and more firmly than in any other "organicist" social ethic. For Hinduism did not join occupational stability to teachings of the moral nature of the person's vocational stability and humble modesty, as do patriarchal forms of Christendom, but to the individual's very personal interest in salvation.

Hinduism is characterized by a dread of the magical evil of innovation. Even today the Indian jute peasant can hardly be moved to fertilize the land because it is "against custom."[17] In addition to this Hinduism places its supreme premium upon caste loyalty. The salvation doctrine of Hinduism promises rebirth as a king, noble, etc., according to present caste rank to the artisan who in his work abides by prescribed traditions, never demands overpay, never deceives as to quality. In the often cited principle of classical teaching: "It is better to fulfill one's (caste) duty even without reward than someone else's no matter how excellently, for therein always lies danger." The neglect of one's caste duties out of high pretensions unfailingly is disadvantageous in the present or future life.

It is difficult to imagine more traditionalistic ideas of professional virtues than those of Hinduism. Estranged castes might stand beside one another with bitter hatred—for the idea that everybody had "deserved" his own fate, did not make the good fortune of the privileged more enjoyable to the underprivileged.

So long as the *karma* doctrine was unshaken, revolutionary ideas or progressivism were inconceivable. The lowest castes, furthermore, had the most to win through ritual correctness and were least tempted to innovations. Hinduism's particularly strong traditionalism finds its explanation also in the great promises which indeed were at stake for the lowly caste whenever the members deviated from their caste.

It was impossible to shatter traditionalism, based on caste ritualism anchored in *karma* doctrine, by rationalizing the economy. In this eternal caste world, the very gods in truth, constituted a mere caste—to be sure, superior to the Brahmans, but as we shall see later—inferior to the sorcerers who through asceticism were provided with magical power. Anyone who wished to emancipate himself from this world and the inescapable cycle of recurrent births and deaths had to leave it altogether—to set out for that unreal realm to which Hindu "salvation" leads. More will be said later about this Indian concept of salvation. We must first consider a different problem.

6. *Developmental Conditions of the Caste System*

PECULIAR to Hinduism is the combination of *karma* theodicy—to be found elsewhere—with the caste structure. Granted this the question is: from whence is this caste order, found nowhere or only incipiently elsewhere, and why, of all things, in India?

In view of the numerous disagreements among even the most distinguished Indologists and the reservation that accordingly only guesses are possible, some previous observations may be developed further. Obviously, mere occupational stratification per se could not give birth to such sharp segregations. The origin of the castes in liturgical guild organization is neither demonstrable nor probable. The great number of originally ethnic castes, moreover, indicates that occupational differentiation alone is not a sufficient explanation however great its contribution may have been. That ethnic factors alongside status and economic factors were important for the formation of castes is beyond doubt.

The attempt has been made more or less radically to simply equate caste stratification with racial differences. The eldest term for "status," (*varna*) means "color." Tradition often distinguishes the castes by typical skin color: Brahmans, white;

Kshatriyas, red; Vaishyas, yellow; Shudras, black. Anthropometric researches, especially those of Risley, have yielded typical degrees of anthropometric differences by caste. Hence correlation has been established. However, one should not assume that the caste order could be explained as a product of "race psychology"—by mysterious tendencies inherent in the "blood" or the "Indian soul." Nor can one assume that caste is the expression of antagonism of different racial types or produced by a "racial repulsion" inherent "in the blood," or of differential "gifts" and fitness for the various caste occupations inherent "in the blood."

Such notions also creep into the discussion of the North American Negro problems. With reference to the alleged "natural" antipathy of races it has been rightly pointed out that several million mixed bloods represent a sufficient refutation of this alleged "natural" strangeness. Indian blood is at least as strange if not more so, yet, every Yankee seeks to trace Indian blood in his pedigree. If the chieftain's daughter Pocohontas were responsible for the existence of all those Americans who wish to stem from her, she must have had as many children as August the Strong.

At best we can say that race or, better, the juxtaposition of racial differences and—this is sociologically decisive—of externally striking different racial types has been quite important for the development of the caste order in India.[18] But one must see this in proper causal interrelation.

Only the antagonism of the *Arya* and the *Dasyu* appears in the ancient Vedic period. The name *Arya* remains as a term for the distinguished, the "gentleman." The *Dasyu* was the dark colored enemy of the invading conqueror; his civilization, presumably at least, was on the same plane. The *Dasyu* had castles and a political organization. Like all peoples from China to Ireland the Aryan tribes then lived through their epic period of charioteering, castle-dwelling knights. This knighthood is technically called *Maghavan,* dispensers of gifts. The knights were named by singers and wizards dependent upon their gifts, praising the donator, deriding and attempting magically to damage the stingy. Among the Aryans these singers and wizards played a powerful and in time apparently increasingly important role. "We and the Maghavan," "our Maghavan" were phrases by which the sorcerers affixed themselves to the knights. Their magic was thought to contribute a great deal to victory. In the period of the Brahmanas and epics magic mounted in importance to unheard-of proportions.

Originally, the transition between the warrior and priestly (Rishi) gentes was free. In the epics, however, the king Visvamitha had to practice asceticism for thousands of years until the gods, in fear of his magical powers, endowed him with Brahman quality. The prayer of the Brahman procured victory for the king. Like a tower the Brahman overshadowed the king. He was not only a ritualistic "superman," but his power equalled that of the gods, and a king without a Brahman is simply said to be "without guidance" for guidance by the *purohita* was self-understood. Reality often contradicted these claims. In areas conquered by the knights during the early Middle Ages—of pre-Buddhistic times—the present-day Bihar, the knightly community (Kschatriya) did not think of recognizing the Brahmans as their peers.

At first the great patrimonial Hindu kingdoms used the Brahmans in support of their legitimation interest. Then the Islamic conquest smashed the politico-military power of the Kshatriya but sustained the Brahmans as an instrument of social control. The pretensions of the Brahmans in classical literature and the law books were then stereotyped.

There were a number of reasons for the channelization of priestly power into the caste system. Ethnic antagonism takes form with respect to contrasts of external bearing and way of life of various social groups. The most striking contrasts in external appearance simply happens to be different skin color. Although the conquerors replenished their insufficient supply of women by taking women from among the conquered, color differences still prevented a fusion in the manner of the Normans and Anglo-Saxons.

Distinguished families the world over make it their honor to admit only their peers for courting their daughters while the sons are left to their own devices in satisfying their sexual needs. Here and not in mythical "race instinct" or unknown differences of "racial traits" we reach the point at which color differences matter. Intermarriage with despised subjects never attained full social recognition. The mixture, at least from a sexual union, of upper-class daughters with sons of the lower stratum remained socially scorned. This stable barrier was reenforced by magical dread. It led to the elevation of the importance of birthright, of clan charisma, in all areas of life.

We noted that under the sway of animistic beliefs positions are usually linked to the possession of magical charisma, particularly power positions of a sacredotal and secular nature. But the artisan's craft in India soon tended to become clan charismatic, finally it became "hereditary." This phenomena–found elsewhere–nowhere appears so strongly as in India. This was the nucleus of the caste formation for those positions and professions. In conjunction with a number of external circumstances this led to the formation of true castes. Charismatic sibs and phratries occupied the conquered land, settled in villages, reduced the conquered to rent-payers or village artisans, agricultural or industrial workers, referred them to the outskirts and *Wurthen*, or into special helot and craftsman villages.

Soon, however, workers from industrial pariah tribes settled outside the villages. The conquerors retained the "right to the land" in a manner similar to the Spartans, as the right to assign a rent-yielding landlot (*kleros*).

In order to understand the process of caste formation one should constantly keep in mind the external resemblance of the situation of the Indian village artisan and of conquered tribes to the place of the helots in the Spartan state regardless of how great the difference was in other respects. The village-dwelling sibs of the conquerors and the conquered stood opposite one another as collectivities. Personal slavery lost importance in view of the fact that the subject (Shudra) indeed was a servant, but in principle, not a servant of a single individual, but of the community of the "twice-born."

The conqueror found some presumably quite considerable industrial development among the conquered people. These industries and the sale of products, however, did not develop into local specializations centered around the market and city, but, in reverse, transformed the economy from one of self-sufficient households to production for sale by way of interlocal and interethnic professional specialization. We know the equivalent in primitive form, for example, from von der Steinen's description of Brazil and other studies. The individual tribe, tribal division, or village as a special group engages in tribal industry for markets, producing a special export product, selling the accumulated surplus products of their domestic industry. This may be facilitated by the near location of raw materials, rivers and other means of communication, by the accidental acquisition of a skill and its subsequent hereditary and secret transmission. The trained specialists turn into journeymen and settle as guest workers temporarily, finally permanently in foreign communities. Such interethnic division of labor appears in very different continents and areas. Of course, considerable vestiges are to be found also in antiquity and the medieval Occident.

The continued predominance of interethnic specialization in India was due to the weak development of cities and urban markets. For centuries the markets were represented by princely castles and peasant villages. In their villages the conquerors preserved their sib cohesion even after they became completely rusticated. This was due to the "racial" antagonisms which provided effective support for clan charisma.

In its initial stages patrimonial fiscalism reinforced this development. Fiscal authorities found it convenient, on the one hand, to have dealings with only a single responsible taxpayer; on the other, to hold the full village associates jointly responsible for tax payments. Fiscal authorities turned first to the old conqueror villages, accepting a guarantee of the tax payment through the joint liability of all full village associates and leaving distribution and disposition over ploughland to their discretion. It is probable though not ascertainable that subject tribes engaging in special industrial activities had to pay tributes in lump sums—this would have stabilized the traditional structure of crafts.

All cities were fortresses of the realm. Guest workers settled in and around them and were placed liturgically, hence usually hereditarily, under a princely supervisor. The artisans consisted of bondsmen restricted to special occupations, leagues of guest workers sharing joint tax liability, or industrial tribes. The fiscal interest of the patrimonial administration in license fees and excise taxes led, indeed, as noted, to a sort of urban market policy similar to that of the Occident. The development of urban industries, particularly urban price work, stimulated the emergence of merchant and craft guilds and finally of guild confederations. These, however, comprised only small islands surrounded by an ocean of village artisan cotters, of tribal industries, of guest trades. By and large, industrial specialization was bound to the developing guest peoples. In the cities, however, racial and ethnic strangeness of guest artisans led to the segregation of the groups from one another and prevented the multitude of craftsmen from organizing in the manner of the occidental *popolo*. And, finally, nowhere did the fraternization of the citizens per se produce a highly developed military force in the manner of the *polis* of antiquity and the city of the south European medieval Occident. Instead, princely overlords directly stepped into the place of the knights, and they were religiously pacifistic due to the politically neutral character of Indian salvation religions.

With the overthrow of the guilds by the princes, incipient urban developments of occidental stamp were destroyed. Allying themselves with the Brahmans, the patrimonial princes, in accord with the continental nature of India, relied upon the rural organizations as sources for armies and taxes. In rural areas, however, division of labor by guest peoples and old village artisan cotters remained the main line of development. The cities brought only an increase in the number of trades and the establishment of rich merchant and price workers' guilds. In accordance with the *jajmani* principle, the Brahmans and village artisans established a quota regulation of subsistence opportunities and the hereditary appropriation of patronage. Once again the universally accepted principle of clan charisma supported developments. The princely grants of interlocal trade monopolies led in the same direction, for these too were unusually granted to marginal trading peoples. Sib and village exogamy, endogamy of guest tribes, the permanent, mutual segregation of guest peoples sanctioned by ritual and worship, never shattered by religious fraternities of autonomous citizenries ruling the country—all these gave the Brahmans the opportunity to stereotype religiously the given order in terms of ritualistic regulation.

The Brahmans' interest was to sustain their power position which grew out of their ancient monopoly of magical qualities, the means of coercion, and the requisite training and education. Princely prerogatives supplied the Brahmans with the means to suppress the heterodox salvation religions of the urban citizenry, the aspirations of the distinguished merchant and craft guilds. The guilds had often restrained or newly established non-Brahmanical tribal or professional priests who claimed Brahman rank. The Brahmans defined the autonomy of these associations as usurpation and suppressed them.

The importance of these urban developments is indicated in the very means used by the contemporary anti-Brahmanical, genteel bourgeois castes. First, they aim at abolishing participation in the official temple cult and at restricting themselves to the house-cult. This gives the individual opportunity to choose an agreeable Brahman, thereby, a powerful coercive weapon of the princes and Brahmans, (hence a sort of "interdict") the closing of the temple is voided. A second, more radical means of revolt against Brahmanical authority is to train priests from members of one's own caste and employ them in place of Brahmans. A third consists in the anti-Brahmanical tendency to settle caste affairs, including ritualistic ones, through the *panchayats,* or finally, to settle them in modern caste meetings instead of turning to a *pandit* or a *math* (monastery) for their solutions.

The development of a stratum of magicians into a charismatic estate is, indeed, not peculiar to India. Inscriptions from Hellenic antiquity (Milet) occasionally report a guild of holy dancers as an estate in power. However, there was no room on the soil of *polis* fraternization for the mutual and general religious and ritualistic estrangement of guest artisans and tribes.

Purely professional, hence freely recruited traders and craftsmen occurred only spottily in India and remained dependent on conformism with the ritualistic usages prevalent among the multitude. Such conformism was supported by ritualistic closure guaranteed to vocational associations, the legitimate monopolization of their subsistence opportunities. As in the Occident, patrimonial bureaucracy did not at first hinder, but rather promoted, the closure of trades and guilds. In the first place, the administrations policy was merely to substitute some interlocal association for purely local monopolies of the city economy. The second stage of occidental princely politics, however, namely, the alliance of the princes with capital in order to increase their power against the outside, was out of the question in India because of its continental character and the value of the land tax which could be raised *ad libidum.*

At the time of guild power the princes were financially quite dependent on them. However, the unmilitary urban stratum was in no position to resist princely power once the prince tired of what seemed to him an outrageous dependency and when he financed the costs of administration by substitution of tax liturgies for capitalistic tax farming. With the aid of the Brahmans, princely patrimonialism successfully mastered the guild citizenry which was at times powerful. Brahmanical theory served in an unequalled manner to tame the subjects religiously. Finally, the invasion and domination of foreign conquerors benefited the power monopoly of the Brahmans. The foreign conquerors divested the most important competitors of the Brahmans of all power because it conceived them to be politically dangerous. Thus the knighthood and the residue of urban guilds were reduced.

The power of the Brahmans, on the other hand, grew during the time of the conquerors. After a period of fanatical iconoclasm and Islamic propaganda, the conqueror resigned himself to accept the continued existence of Hindu culture. Indeed, priestly power under foreign domination always serves as a refuge for the conquered and as a tool of domestication for the foreign overlords.

With the increasing stabilization of economic conditions the ritually segregated guest and pariah tribes were more and more integrated into the expanding caste order which thus became the dominant system. For a thousand years, from the second century of our era to the beginning of Islamic rule, we find the caste system in an irresistible and ever-continued expansion, slowed down through the propaganda of Islamism. As a closed system, the caste order is a product of consistent Brahmanical thought and could never have come to power without the intensive influence of the Brahmans as house priests, respondents, father confessors, advisors in all life situations, and princely officials whose writing skill brought them into increasing demand with the rise of bureaucratic administration.

Ancient Indian conditions, however, provided the structural elements for the caste system: the interethnic specialization of labor, the development of innumerable guest and pariah peoples, the organization of village crafts on the basis of hereditary artisan cotters, the monopoly of internal trade by guest trades, the small extent of urban development, and the flow of occupational specialization into the channels of hereditary status segregation and monopolization of patronage. Likewise the secondary beginnings of liturgical and fiscal organization of occupations by the princes, and their strong interest in legitimacy and domestication of the subjects encouraged an alliance with the Brahmans and the joint preservation and stabilization by prince and Brahman of the established sacred order of Indian society.

All factors important for the development of the caste system operated singly elsewhere in the world. Only in India, however, did they operate conjointly under special Indian conditions: the conditions of a conquered territory within ineffable, sharp, "racial" antagonisms made socially visible by skin color. More strongly then anywhere else, magical as well as social rejection of communion with strangers was called forth. This helped preserve the charisma of distinguished sibs and established insurmountable barriers between strange ethnic subject tribes, guest and pariah peoples and their overlords even after definitive integration of guest and pariah peoples into the local economic community.

Individual acceptance for apprenticeship, participation in market deals, or citizenship—all these phenomena of the West either failed to develop in the first place or were crushed under the weight first of ethnic, later of caste fetters.

We repeat, however: this well-integrated, unique social system could not have originated or at least could not have conquered and lasted without the pervasive and all-powerful influence of the Brahmans. It must have existed as a finished idea long before it conquered even the greater part of North India. The combination of caste legitimacy with *karma* doctrine, thus with the specific Brahmanical theodicy—in its way a stroke of genius—plainly is the construction of rational ethical thought and not the product of any economic "conditions." Only the wedding of this thought product with the empirical social order through the promise of rebirth gave this order the irresistible power over thought and hope of members and furnished the fixed scheme for the religious and social integration of the various professional groups and pariah peoples.

Where the connection between the theodicy and social order is lacking, indeed—as in the case of Indian Islam—the caste order can be assimilated externally but it remains a *caput mortuum,* fit to stabilize status difference, to represent economic interests through the borrowed *panchayat,* and, above all, to adapt men to the constraint of the social environment; but it is devoid of the "spirit" which nourishes this order on its native soil. On

Islamic ground this order could not have emerged; nor does it exert marked influence over the "vocational ethic" similar to that of the Hindu professional castes. The Census Reports[19] plainly show that the Islamic castes lack some of the most important characteristics of the Hindu caste system, especially ritualistic defilement through commensalism with nonmembers—even though commensalism and social intercourse among different social strata may be avoided and rather rigidly so, as is often the case, after all, in Western society. Ritual defilement, however, must be lacking; the religious equality before Allah of all who profess the prophet precludes it. Endogamy, to be sure, exists but with far less intensity. Properly understood, the so-called Islamic castes are essentially status groups and not castes. Furthermore, the specific anchoring of the vocational ethic in caste is lacking; missing, too, is the authority of the Brahman.

The prestige of the Brahmans which was behind the developing caste system is in part purely magical and in part cultural—deriving from the fact that as a stratum the Brahmans represented a special quality and distinct cultivation. We have still to examine the peculiarity of Brahmanical education and its underlying conditions.

There is a further reason for examining the peculiarities of Brahmanical education. The caste system and *karma* doctrine place the individual within a clear circle of duties and offer him a well-rounded, metaphysically-satisfying conception of the world. However certain and unambiguous this ethically rational world order might present itself, the individual, once he raised the question of the "meaning" of his life in this compensatory mechanism, could experience it as dreadful.

The world and its cosmic social order was eternal and individual life but one of a series of the lives of the same soul. Such lives recur *ad infinitum:* therefore, any one in the last analysis is a matter of complete indifference. The Indian representation of life and the world prefers the image of an eternally rolling "wheel" of rebirths—which by the way, as Oldenberg has observed, also is to be found occasionally in Hellenic philosophy.

It is no accident that India has produced no historiography to speak of. The interest in historically unique forms of political and social relations was far too weak for a man contemplating life and its passage. It is sometimes maintained that alleged Indian "passivity" derives from a climatically determined "enervation." This belief is completely unfounded. India has been permanently involved in a state of ferocious warfare and unbridled lust of relentless conquest as no land on earth. However, to any thoughtful and reflective person, life destined to eternal repetition could readily appear completely senseless and unbearable.

It is important to realize that it was not primarily the dread of ever-new life on this earth which is after all so beautiful. Rather it was dread of the ever-new and ineluctable death. Ever and again the soul was enmeshed in the business of living and the heart enchained to things and, above all, to dear ones. Ever again it must be senselessly torn from them through rebirth to be entangled in unknown relations to face the same fate. Such repeated death was truly dreadful. One can hardly fail to feel this and to be moved by the pathos when reading between the lines of the inscriptions the preachings of Buddha and other redeemers.

All salvation religions of Hinduism are addressed to one common question: how can man escape from the wheel of rebirth and thereby ever new death? How is salvation possible from eternally new death and therefore salvation from life? In the following we shall consider the ways of life and their effects on conduct which issued from the answers to this question.

PART II

ORTHODOX AND HETERODOX HOLY TEACHING OF THE INDIAN INTELLECTUALS

CHAPTER IV

ANTI-ORGIASTIC AND RITUALISTIC CHARACTER OF BRAHMANICAL RELIGIOSITY

1. Brahmanical, Hellenistic and Confucian Intellectual Strata

THE FACT that the Brahmanical priestly stratum was a distinguished and cultivated nobility, later a class of genteel literati determined its religiosity. As in comparable cases, e.g., the Confucians, orgiastic and emotional ecstatic elements of ancient magical rites were not taken over, and for long periods were either completely suppressed or were permitted only as unofficial folk magic.

As V. Schroder has demonstrated, in individual instances residues of ancient orgiasticism are to be found in the Vedas.[1] Indra's drunkenness and dance, and the sword dance of the Maruts (corybantics) stem from the intoxication and ecstasy of heroes. Moreover, it is obvious that the great priestly soma-sacrifice was originally a cult-tempered intoxication orgy. The much-discussed dialogues of the Rigveda are presumably the slender residues of cult drama.[2]

However, the official ritual of the Vedas with all its hymns and formulae rest upon sacrifice and prayer and not on typical orgiastic technique—dance emotionality, sexual or alcoholic intoxication, meat orgiasticism—all of which were rather carefully eliminated.

Ritualistic copulation in the fields as a means of securing soil fertility and the lingam cult with its phallic hobgoblins, the *gandharvan,* are very ancient in India. But the Rigveda is mute with respect to them. Nor does the Rigveda know of the corporeal epiphany of deities and demons characteristic of the cult drama. Undoubtedly, even the genteel priestly singers of old

Vedic times,[3] and, indeed, the hereditary Brahmanical priesthood viewed it as somewhat vulgar, in part, however, as a dubious competition with their own wizardry which was based on ritualistic knowledge.

In the Vedas the ancient fertility god Rudra, with his orgiastic cults of sex and meat, has a diabolical character. Later he was worshipped as Shiva, one of the three great Hindu gods, on the one hand, as patron of the later classical Sanskrit *drama,* on the other, as god of the ubiquitous lingam cult. While in the Vedas Vishnu is a secondary figure, in the later triad he appears as Shiva's rival and is honored in pantomines as a great celestial and fertility god, as patron of the dance drama and erotic orgies of the Krishna-cult.

At the sacrifice, the laity was "denied the cup"—only the priest drank soma. The same held for sacrificial meat. While female deities were extremely important for ancient and modern Asiatic folk beliefs, in the Vedas they were completely eclipsed as fertility demons of primarily orgiastic sex cults. In the Atharva-Veda, containing a later canonization of materials probably as old as those of other Vedas, the magical character of dirges and hymns again appeared in place of the cult. This corresponds in part to the derivation of the materials from the private magical "curing of souls" as against the derivation of the materials of the other Vedas from sacrificial offerings on behalf of the body politic. The change is due in part to the increasing importance of sorcery. As the ancient warrior community was thrust into the background by princely power, the noble sacrificial priest of old was displaced by the princely court magician, the *purohita.*[4]

In details the Atharva-Veda is not completely cold toward figures of folk belief (for example, the *gandharvan*). But in it, too, ritual formulae, not orgiasticism and ecstasy, are magical implements. In the Yajurveda priestly sorcery has become paramount. Brahmanical literature ever inclined toward formalistic ritualism. Alongside the Brahman, as in China beside the official with his state cult, we find the house father (*grihastha*) performing important ritualistic duties; thoroughly regulated by the Grihya-sutra. The Dharma Sutras (law books) then drew all social relations of the individual into their compass. Thus, the whole of life became enmeshed in a net of ritualistic and ceremonial prescriptions. Punctilliously to observe them all became, at times, well-nigh impossible.

In contrast to the intellectuals of ancient Hellenic *polis*-culture with whom they must be compared,[5] (the Brahmans and the intellectual stratum under their influence) were bound by position to magic and ritual. The hereditarily-charismatic priest-nobles of ancient Greece (e.g., the *Butades*) were divested of all substantive influence through the development of the city and came to represent the stupidity of rural gentry (as especially the *eteobutades*) rather than any spiritual value. The Brahmans, by contrast, have always preserved their connection with sacrifice and magic in the service of the princes.

In all these respects the attitude constellation and conduct of the Brahmans compares with that of representatives of Confucian culture. In both we find a status group of genteel literati whose magical charisma rests on "knowledge." Such knowledge was magical and ritualistic in character, deposited in a holy literature, written in a holy language remote from that of everyday speech. In both appears the same pride in education and unshakable trust in this special knowledge as the cardinal virtue solely determining all good. Ignorance of this knowledge was the cardinal vice and source of all evil. They developed a similar "rationalism"–concerned with the rejection of all irrational forms of holy seeking.

Both Brahman and Mandarin rejected all types of orgiasticism. Just as the Confucian literati rejected the Taoistic magicians, so the Brahmans rejected all magicians, cult priests, and holy seekers. Their intelligence had not been cultivated by Vedic education and the Brahmans viewed them as unclassical, despicable, and worthy only of extermination. Of course, in neither case (Chinese or Indian) could the implied program be consummated. Though the Brahmans succeeded in preventing the development of a unified organization of unclassical priests, it was at the price, as we shall see, of permitting many hierarchies of mystagogues partly within their own stratum, and therewith a disintegration of unified holy learning into sect soteriologies.

This, and a series of important related differences from Chinese developments was bound up with the different social structures of the respective intellectual status groups. Both passed through developmental stages at times remarkably similar. In the end their external difference appears most sharply. In China the Mandarins form a stratum of officials and candidates for office; in India the Brahmans represent a status group of literati partly comprising princely chaplains, partly counsellors, theological teachers, and jurists, priests, and pastors. In both cases only a portion of the status group occupied the characteristic positions. As numerous Chinese literati without office prebends earned their bread partly in the offices of the Mandarins, partly in the employment of all sorts of societies, so the Brahmans were always employed in most varied positions, including situations of great trust with secular princes. We noted, however, that an actual career in office was not only atypical of the Brahman, but indeed, was contrary to type, while for the Mandarin it was held to be the one thing worthy of men. The typical prebends of the distinguished Brahmans were not state-paid salaries and profit opportunities from tax collections and extortion in patrimonial state offices but fixed land and tribute rent. Unlike the prebends of the Mandarins which were subject to recall and at best granted for a short term, the Brahman's rents were permanent grants for life or for several generations or forever to individuals or organizations (monasteries, schools).

The external situation of the Chinese and Indian intellectual strata appears externally most similar when one compares conditions of the period of the Warring States in China with those in India of about the time of the ancient Jatakas or again of the medieval expansion of Brahmanhood. At that time in India the Hindu intellectuals largely constituted a stratum of men educated in literature and philosophy and dedicated to speculation and discussion of ritualistic, philosophical, and scientific questions. In part they formed schools who were withdrawn in meditation, in part they wandered between princely and noble courts. Despite all schisms, in the last analysis the Brahmans considered themselves to be a unified group of cultural representatives. They were advisors to single princes and nobles in private and political questions, organizers of states on the basis of correct doctrine. This is quite similar to the literati of China in the time of Warring States. There always remained, however, an important difference.

The highest Brahman station in ancient times was that of court chaplain; later, and to the time of British rule the senior in rank and consulting jurist, that is, the Brahmanical chief *pandit,* was the first man of the land. The Chinese literati of all philosophical schools gathered around the imperial supreme *pontifex* who was their consecrated chief as the living vessal of the sacred tradition. According to the claims of the literati, this *pontifex maximus* was also the sole legitimate secular ruler, the *lord paramount* of all secular princely vassals of the Chinese "church-state."

Nothing equivalent existed in India. In this epoch of innumerable splinter states the literati faced a plurality of petty princes without a legitimate *lord paramount* from whom to derive their power. The concept of legitimacy was rather simply that the single prince was ritualistically correct when and to the extent to which his behavior, especially toward the Brahmans, conformed with the holy tradition. Otherwise he was held to be a "barbarian" just as the feudal princes of China were judged by the yardstick of their correctness as defined by the teaching of the literati. But no matter what power an Indian king might yield in matters of ritual he was never at the same time a priest.

Obviously this difference between Indian and Chinese history goes back to earliest and but hypothetically accessible times. Even the ancient Vedic literary tradition describes the dark-skinned opponents of the Aryans in contrast to themselves as "priestless" (*abrahmana*). With the Aryans, however, we meet the beginnings, along with the prince, of the independent priest, trained to perform sacrificial rites. In contrast, the oldest tradition of the Chinese knows nothing of independent priests standing beside a strictly secular prince. Among the Indians the role of the prince has apparently grown out of strictly secular politics, out of war expeditions of charismatic warrior chieftains, whereas in China it grew out of the role of supreme priest. It may well be impossible ever to advance even to hypothetical assumptions concerning the historical events explaining the establishment of this ever-important contrast between the unity or duality of political and priestly prerogatives. The same difference, indeed, is also found with quite "primitive" peoples and empires even in direct contiguity and otherwise identical culture and race. Originally it would seem to have been brought about by quite concrete, thus "accidental" circumstances which once established continue to influence developments.

The different configuration of political and theocratic power was highly consequential in every respect. First, externally, it was important for the social structure of the intellectual strata of both China and India. In the time of the Warring Kingdoms the Chinese literati were still, as a rule, recruited from the ancient, "great" charismatic families, though personal charisma of written knowledge was already so significant that parvenus increasingly appeared in ministerial positions. When the imperial *lord pontifex* again managed to unite the plenitude of secular prerogatives in his own person the monarch, as *supreme pontifex,* could, corresponding to his interest in power, link admission to office to the purely personal qualification of correct literary education. Thus he was able definitively to secure patrimonial rule against the feudal system. The literarily trained became primarily a bureaucratic stratum.

In India the opposition between gentile charisma and personal charisma was not completely settled even in historical times. However, it was always the learned priesthood, which defined the qualification of the novitiate. With the full assimilation of the Brahmans to the Vedic priest-nobility, the question of charisma was decided at least for official doctrine. By the time of the first universal monarchies, the independent priesthood had become so firmly established in its possession of spiritual authority as a charismatic guild, that is to say, as a "caste" with fixed educational prerequisites for office holding, that it could no longer be shaken.

In the Yajur-Veda this position (which appears first in the Atharva-Veda) of the Brahmans is visualized completed. "Brahman," meaning "prayer" in the Rigveda is now "holy power" and "holiness." The Brahmanas merely carried this further, we read: "The Brahmans who have learned the Vedas and teach them, are human gods."[6] No Hindu prince or great king was able to claim pontifical power and the later—Islamic—foreign rulers were disqualified for it from the first, and were far from raising such claims. The point of Cathapatha Brahmana, resting on these contrasts in social structure, are the respective "world views" of the Chinese and Indian intellectuals strata with their consequences for ethical conduct.

In China theocratic patrimonialism and a stratum of literati aspiring to public office was the appropriate basis for a social ethic of pure utilitarianism. The "welfare-state" idea, with a strong materialistic turn issued from the charismatic responsibility of the ruler for the external, meterologically-conditioned well-being of the subjects. Besides this, however, it followed from the place of the literati with its social philosophical interests and pride in education opposite the unlearned masses.

After all, philosophical men can do no better than strive for material welfare, and material position is also the best means for maintaining peace and order. Finally, the idea of the welfare state followed also from the rentier ideal of the very bureaucracy, the securing of fixed income as basic to the gentleman's way of life. The status opposition between the cultured and uncultured and reminiscences of liturgical provisions for needs led to ideas approaching "organic" theories of state and society. Naturally, such ideas suggest themselves to any political welfare organization. However, the levelling effects of Chinese patrimonial bureaucracy tended to restrict such notions.

Not the organic status group structure, but the patriarchal family provided the dominant image for social stratification. The patrimonial bureaucracy could recognize no other autonomous social force. The stronger and more independent the actual functioning organizations, particularly the guilds and guild-like societies and the sibs, the less could theory use them as a basis for an organic social structure. Theory simply bypassed them as mere factual data. Hence in China the "vocational" ideal type of organismic view of society existed only in beginnings and remained alien to the ruling stratum of genteel literati.

2. Dharma *and Absence of the Concept of Natural Law*

THINGS were quite different in India. Here the priesthood, holding its own beside the political rulers, had to take into account the sovereign world of political power. The priests recognized the autonomous rulers of this world simply because they had to. As we saw, the power relation between Brahmans and Kshatriyas was quite unstable for a long time. Even after the status superiority of the Brahmans was theoretically established, the prerogatives of the great kings, who had meanwhile risen to power, remained independent and essentially secular. Indeed, the duties of the kings as against the Brahmanical hierocracy, like those of any status group, were determined by their *dharma*, which formed part of Brahmanically regulated holy law. But this *dharma* differed for every status group, hence also for the kings. Though according to theory only the Brahmans could give authoritative interpretations, kingly *dharma* self-evidently represented a unique and independent type which was by no means identical with that of the Brahman.[7]

There was no universally valid ethic, but only a strict status compartmentalization of private and social ethic, disregarding the few absolute and general ritualistic prohibitions (particularly the killing of cows). This was of great moment. The doctrine of *karma* deduced from the principle of compensation for previous deeds of the world, not only explained the caste organization but the rank order of divine, human, and animal beings of all degrees. Hence it provided for the coexistence of different ethical codes for different status groups which not only differed widely but were often in sharp conflict. This presented no problem. In principle there could be a vocational *dharma* for prostitutes, robbers, and thieves as well as for Brahmans and kings. In fact, quite sincere attempts at drawing these extreme conclusions appeared. The struggle of man with man in all its forms was as little a problem as his struggle with animals and the gods, as was the existence of the positively ugly, stupid, and—from the standpoint of the *dharma* of a Brahman or other "twice-born"—positively objectionable. Men were not—as for classical Confucianism—in principle equal, but forever unequal. They were as unlike as man and animal. All men, however, had equal opportunities, but not in this life. Through rebirth they could either achieve heaven or descend to the animal kingdom or to hell.

The conception of an "original sin" was quite impossible in this world order, for no "absolute sin" could exist. There could only be a ritual offense against the particular *dharma* of the caste. In this world of eternal rank orders there was no place for a blissful original state of man and no blissful final kingdom. Thus there was no "natural" order of men and things in contrast to positive social order. There was no sort of "natural law." But there was, in theory at least, only holy, status-compartmentalized positive law in areas which remained unregulated as indifferent. There were positive statutes of princes, castes, guilds, sibs, and agreements of individuals. All the problems which the concept of "natural law" called into being in the Occident were completely lacking. There simply was no "natural" equality of man before any authority, least of all before a super-worldly god.

This is the negative side of the case. Most important, it excluded forever the rise of social criticism, of rationalistic speculation, and abstractions of natural law type,[8] and hindered the development of any sort of idea of "human rights." Animals and gods, at least, in consistent elaborations of doctrine, were only different, *karma*-conditioned incarnations of souls, thus common "rights" were obviously out of the question and could exist for these beings as little as common "duties." The concepts "state" and "citizen," even that of "subject" did not appear. Only status *dharma* was recognized—the rights and duties of kings and other castes to themselves and others.

As patron of the *rayat* (client), the Kshatriya had the ascribed *dharma* of "protection" essentially in the sense of defence against the outside. The Kshatriya was also responsible for the administration of justice and integrity of trade and related matters. Such ethical commandments were his *dharma.* For the rest it was the primary duty of the prince, as for others, but particularly for the prince, to support and further the Brahmans, especially by sustaining their authoritarian regulation of the social order according to holy right, not to tolerate attacks upon the Brahman's station. The struggle against anti-Brahman heterodoxy is clearly required and it did occur. But this in no way altered the place of the prince, and politics retained their autonomy in a peculiarly significant manner.

Chinese literature in the epoch of the contending princes recognized (at least in theory, however ineffectual it may have been in practice), the concept of "just" and "unjust" wars and an "international law" as an expression of common Chinese culture. The *imperial pontifex,* once in the position of autocrat, claimed dominion over the world including barbarians. He conducted only "just" wars. Any resistance against him was rebellion. If he succumbed, this was symptomatic of the loss of heavenly charisma and forfeiture of right to rule.

Things were similar for the Indian prince. When he was defeated or when his subjects were unfortunate for long, this was proof of magical offences or of charismatic deficiencies. Hence success of the king was decisive. But this had nothing to do with his "right," only with his personal fitness and particularly the magical power of his Brahman. The Brahman's sorcery rather than the king's ethical "right" procured kingly success, that is, if the Brahman knew his craft and was charismatically qualified. As in the Occident, in India the knightly conventions of epic Kshatriya times established certain status customs for the feud and breaches were held to be objectionable and unchivalrous. To be sure, Indian knightly combat probably was never practiced with such far-reaching courtesies as represented by the famous herald's call of the French knighthood to their opponents before the battle of Fontenoy: *"Messieure les Anglais, tirez les premiere."* On the whole the opposite prevailed. In the epics not only men, but even the gods (Krishna) with perfect equanimity waive the most elementary rules of knightly combat in order to win. And as in the Hellenic *polis* of classical times,[9] so the princes already in the epic of the Maurya epoch and more so in later times practiced as a matter of course the most naked "Macchiavellianism" without objections on ethical grounds.

The problem of a "political ethic" has never preoccupied Indian theory and in the absence of ethical universalism and natural right, it could hardly be otherwise. The *dharma* of the prince[10] was to conduct war for the sake of pure power per se. He had to destroy his neighbor by cunning and fraud and no matter what crafty, unknightly, and ruseful means, by surprise attack, when in distress through instigation of conspiracies among his subjects and bribing his trusted friends. He had to keep in check and tax his own subjects through spying agent provocateurs and a sophisticated cunning and suspicion. Here power politics (and to our mind quite unholy egotism of princes) were practiced for their own sake. All political theory was a completely oral technology of how to get and hold power. It went far beyond what was familiar and average practice for the *signores* of the early Italian Renaissance in these respects and was completely devoid of all "ideology" in our sense of the word.

3. Knowledge, Asceticism, and Mysticism in India

EXPEDIENCY obtains in all profane areas of life. It is typical of Hinduism, in contrast to the anti-professionalism of Confucianism, to do justice in their own terms to the informing spirit of most varied spheres of life and knowledge, promoting the development of special science. Thus it was that alongside important mathematical and grammatical contributions they developed especially a formal logic as the technology of rational proof (*hetu* with the derivative *hetuvadin,* the logician). A special philosophical school, Nyaya[11] (founded by Gotama) occupied itself with the technology of the syllogism and the

Vaisesika[12] school (recognized as orthodox) by applying these formal aids to cosmology arrived at the theory of atomism.

In Hellenic antiquity the further development of atomism after Democritus into a modern natural science was handicapped despite more extensive mathematical foundations. This was due largely to the socially-conditioned invasion and triumph of an exclusive interest in social criticism and social ethics after Socrates, which proved inimical to the development of natural science.

In India, in contrast, the socially anchored unshakability of certain metaphysical presuppositions pushed all philosophy in the direction of individual salvation-striving.[13] This served as a barrier to the development of special science as well as to a framing of the problem of thought in general. The resulting "organic" societal doctrine of Hinduism, in default of other standards, could elaborate the *dharma* of each profession solely out of the peculiarities of its technique. It thus produced only terminologies for special callings and spheres of life, from construction technique to logic as the technology of proof and disproof to the technology of eroticism.[14] The social theory of Hinduism, however, furnished no principles for an ethical universalism which would raise general demands for life in the world.

Such literature of India, as one can pose as parallel with the philosophical ethic of the West was—or, better, became—something quite different, namely, a metaphysically and cosmologically substructured technology of the means to achieve salvation from this world. This is the final, general anchorage point of all philosophical and theological interest in India. The orders of life and its *karma*-mechanism were eternal. A religious eschatology of the world was as little possible here as in Confucianism. Only a (practical) eschatology of single individuals could develop, based on the attempt to escape the *karma*-mechanism and wheel of rebirth.

The fact of these ideational developments as well as their form are correlated with social peculiarities of the Indian literati stratum, their vehicle. While the Brahmans, like the Mandarins, enhanced their status by their knowledge of the social order, there remained, nevertheless, this vast difference: the Chinese literati constituted a political bureaucracy which renounced magical techniques as the scorned arts of sorcerers while the Brahmans were by background and nature priests, i.e., magicians. This was the historical condition of the very different place asceticism and mysticism held for both.

Confucianism scorned magic as a parasitical humbug contrary to the distinguished man's sense of dignity. The mandarin rejected magic as completely useless and barbaric. In the period of free-office holding by the literati, in the time of the warring princes, anchoritism and the contemplation of philosophers blossomed. The effects were never completely eradicated from Confucianism. However, with the transformation into a certified statum of office prebendaries such nonutilitarian ways of life were increasingly rejected as unclassical. Reminiscences of mysticism accompanied Confucianism only as shadowy heterodox counter-images. Asceticism, moreover, disappeared almost completely. Finally, the few important orgiastic residues in folk religiosity in no way changed the eradication, on principle, of these irrational forces. In contrast, Brahmanhood was never able completely to shake off the historical relation to ancient magical asceticism out of which it had grown. The name of the novice (*bramacharin*) is derived from magical novitiate chastity and the stipulation of contemplative forest life, so to speak, a form of retirement for the aged (today appearing as a mitigation of the original custom which presumably signified the killing of the old), stems from the same source.[15] In classical sources[16] they are extended to the two other status groups of the "twice-born" but were originally characteristic only of magician asceticism. Both prescriptions (novitiate chastity and contemplative forest life) are today and have indeed long been obsolete. However, their place in classical literature remains. And, finally, contemplative mysticism as a type of gnosis remains the crown of the classical Brahmanical style of life, the goal of every well-educated Brahman though the number of those who actually pursue it was as small in the medieval past as today.

We must examine more closely the place of Brahmanical culture with respect to asceticism and mysticism and, as far as the context makes it indispensable, also certain related philosophical representations growing out of the culture. The Hindu salvation religions, including Buddhism, arose on the basis of such philosophic conceptions, partly in typical opposition to them, but, in any case, only in close relation with them.

Technically, Indian asceticism was the most rationally developed in the world. There is hardly an ascetic method not practiced with virtuosity in India and often rationalized into a theoretical technology. Often in India have some forms been pushed to their final—and to us, often grotesque—conclusions. The *urdhamukti-sadhu's,* downward suspension of the head and live burial (*samadh*) were still practiced in the nineteenth century. Alchemy appears at present.[17]

The origin of classical Indian asceticism was in the ancient practice of magician ecstasy with its various functions and with the usual purpose of achieving magical power. The ascetic aspired to power over the gods. He was able to force them; they feared him and did his bidding. To bring about something exceptional the god, too, practiced asceticism. Thus the supreme being of old philosophy had to make mighty ascetic efforts to give birth to the world. Ascetic magical potency (*tapas*) was conditioned through a sort of (hysterical) brooding intensity. With sufficient asceticism man could achieve anything, an idea still accepted as self-evident in classical Sanskrit drama.

The charismatic attainment of magical potency was highly personal and bound to no status group. Hence these magicians in earliest times were certainly not recruited only from official priestly or magician castes, as were the Brahmans. While this continued to be possible, it was difficult, and becoming more so, as the Brahmanhood turned into a status group of genteel experts, resting its claims on knowledge and genteel cultivation. The more this was the case the less was Brahmanhood able to encompass all forms of magical asceticism. Immanent rationalism of knowledge and culture, as usual, obstructed irrational, orgiastic-ecstatic asceticism; the status pride of cultured men resisted undignified demands of ecstatic therapeutic practices and the exhibition of neuropathic states. Thus Indian development took a course partially similar to that of magic in China. Some magical practices, the acute-pathological, emotionally ecstatic—in this sense "irrational"—were either explicitly rejected as unclassical and barbarian or actually not practiced within the status group and precluded by its way of life. As noted, this occurred widely, paralleling the development of similar forms among the Chinese literati. A stratum of genteel intellectuals, however, could take a quite different stand toward the forms of apathetic ecstasy (the developmental nuclei of contemplation) and all ascetic practices capable of rationalization.

They might be useful for mandarin state officials; not, however, for a priesthood. In fact, magical practices could not be completely withdrawn from them. The Brahmans received or, better, retained some elements of magical asceticism and ecstasy, for, in contrast to the mandarins, they were not a political officialdom but a magician caste. The magical elements retained were the more systematically rationalized the more the Brahmans turned into genteel literati. The Chinese literati, traditionally alien to all asceticism, could not accomplish this but had to permit magic to degenerate in the hands of tolerated or scorned professional magicians and the Taoists. The points of departure for both types of political development differed decisively and was also felt here. Brahmanical philosophy, in striking contrast to that of the Chinese, posed for itself central problems, which, both in manner posed as in form of answer, often could not be understood without consideration of the importance of rationalized asceticism and ecstasy for all basic elements of correct Brahmanical living.

The *bramacharin* (novice) was personally subordinate to the strict authority and household discipline of the teacher.[18] He was enjoined to chastity and mendicancy and his life was ascetically ordered throughout. Retirement to the forests (as *vanaprastha*) was thought to be the ideal way of life for the aging Brahman, leading finally to heart-searching in eternal silence as a hermit (the fourth *Asrama*) and the attainment of the qualification as a *yati* (an ascetic, inwardly free of the world).[19] Not only were these things present, but in a large measure the innerworldly life-conduct of the classical Brahmar himself as *grihastha* (householder) was ascetically regulated. Alongside the avoidance of plebeian forms of profitable pursuits, above all trade, usury, and personal tillage, stood numerous prescriptions which later appeared again in the world–denying Hindu salvation religions.

The intensification of vegetarianism and abstinence from alcohol clearly developed out of opposition to meat orgies; the very strong tabooing of adultery and the admonition to control the sexual impulse in general has similar anti-orgiastic roots. Anger and passion were here, as in China, taboo because of the belief in the denomical and diabolic origin of all emotions. The commandment of rigid cleanliness, especially in eating, stemmed from magical purity rules. The commandment of veracity and liberality and the prohibition against laying hands on other people's property, in the last analysis, were but a sharpening of the universally valid (for the possessors) basic features of the ancient neighborhood ethic.

One should not, naturally, exaggerate the ascetic elements in the worldly way of life of the Brahmans in historical times. With the introduction of occidental art forms the Russians in the seventeenth century protested that a saint should not be "fat as a German."[20] Indian art required the opposite. A *mahapurusha* must be fat because a visibily good nutritional state was considered a sign of richness and distinction. Above all the properties and elegance of the genteel cavalier must never be violated. Occasionally the practical every-day ethic of the Brahmans resembles that of the Confucians in this. In classical literature as well as in the Puranas[21] there are repeated recommendations that one say what is true and pleasing, not what is untrue and pleasing, but possibly also not what is true and unpleasing.

As the Brahmans, so all genteel intellectuals—also the Buddhist very expressly—emphasize the importance of being "Aryan." To this day the term "Aryan" (also in compounds) is used somewhat in the sense of the *kaloikagathoi,* of the "gentleman." Even in epic times it was an acknowledged principle that one was "Aryan" not through skin color but by education alone.[22] Typical of the Brahman was masculine rejection of woman in a sense similar to the Confucian, yet with an infusion of ascetic motives missing among the Confucians. Woman was representative of ancient sexual orgiasticism which was rejected as undignified and irrational, seriously disturbing holy mediation. Buddha allegedly said that another impulse of the strength of the sex drive would make salvation impossible.

The irrationality of women, however, was also later strongly emphasized by Brahmanical writers, far more presumably, than in the time of courtly salon-culture of the Kshatriya. The Vishnu-Purana,[23] for example, states that a man should not treat his wife without respect or patience. However, he should trust no important business to her and never completely trust her. All Indian authors agree that no wife can be assumed to be faithful to her husband for "ethical" reasons. Presumably each matron secretly envies the sophisticated *hetaira*—for which one could hardly blame her, given the privileged situation of the *hetaira* in the salon and the poetic glamour with which, in contrast to

China, sophisticated Indian eroticism, lyrics, and even drama hallowed her.[24]

Alongside the relatively "ascetic" features of the Brahman's regulated workaday life stands the rational method for the achievement of extraordinary holy states. Indeed, there was a school (Mimamsa, founded by Jaimini) held to be orthodox, which acknowledged ceremonial good work per se as the holy path. But this is not the case for classical Brahmanical teaching. In classical times the following was fundamental: ritual and other virtuous deeds alone could merely help improve rebirth chances but could not lead to salvation. This is always dependent on extraordinary behavior qualitatively extending over and beyond the duties in the world of the castes: namely, ascetic flight from the world and contemplation.

The development of such salvation doctrines signified essentially, as is to be expected of intellectuals, a rationalization and sublimation of the magical holy states. This proceeded in three directions: first, one strove increasingly for personal holy status, for "bliss" in this sense of the word, instead of for magical secret power useful to professional sorcery. Secondly, this state acquired a definitely formal character, and, indeed, as was to be expected, that of a gnosis, a sacred knowledge essentially though not exclusively, based on apathetic ecstasy, which corresponded best with the status characteristics of the literati stratum. All religious holy seeking on such a foundation had to take the form of mystical seeking of god, mystical possession of god, or, finally, mystical communion with the godhead. All three forms, preeminently however, the last named, actually appeared. The union with the godly came to the fore because the development of Brahmanical gnosis increasingly moved in the direction of depersonalizing the supreme godhead. This occurred partly in correspondence with the inherent tendency of all contemplative mysticism, partly because Brahmanical thought was moored to ritual and its inviolability, hence saw divine majesty in the eternal, unchangeable, impersonally lawful order of the world but not in the stages of its destiny. The earlier precursor of Brahma was originally the "Lord of Prayer," the functional deity of magical formulae. With the enhancement he rose to divine supremacy just as the earthly prayer masters, the Brahmans achieved highest status rank.

The rational interpretation of the world with respect to its natural social and ritual orders then was the third aspect of the rationalization process, which the Brahmanical intellectual stratum consummated in reworking the religio-magical material. Such a form of interpretation must have led to the emergence of ontological and cosmological speculation, to the rational arguments *re* holy paths and goals. In China, as indicated, this was not absent, but far less important. In India such speculation actually provided the distinguishing stamp to the religiosity.

In speculative areas, however, the Brahmans were never, at least for long, without competition. Beside the Brahmanical sacrificial and prayer cult appeared popular individual ecstatic magic and orgiasticism. Certainly the specific unclassical, emotional-irrational forms of holy states never disappeared. Later and into the present they appeared ever anew in mass revivals. Similarly the holy seeking of genteel laity stood alongside that of genteel Brahmans. The heterodox salvation religions, certainly Buddhism, found support precisely in their beginnings in genteel lay circles. How far the same holds for the development of classical Indian philosophy is controversial among Indologists and can hardly be ascertained. Emphasis has been laid on the fact that classical literature contains repeated instances of Brahmans instructed by wise kings in basic philosophic questions. That the ancient knighthood was well educated in literature, that the classical Kshatriya, before the appearance of the great kingdoms, had participated in philosophical thought is beyond all doubt. In India discussion of natural and religious philosophy reached a high point around the beginning of the seventh century B.C.[25] During this time cultured laymen appear among the most important participants in the controversies. Certainly the Brahmans never played a secondary role in this.

Even in Vedic times priestly power was quite strong.[26] It did not decline but increased. Periodically and locally it may have been thrust into the background and, at times, may have been confined to certain territories in North India as during domination of the salvation religions when it was, perhaps, restricted to Kashmir. But the priestly tradition has never been uprooted. Above all, the priest rather than a changing political organization carried Indian culture. As in the Homeric age in early times the Rishi and holy bards wandered through the territories of Aryan castle kings, bearing the unity of religious and poetic culture. Similarly in the time of the city- and castle-dwelling Kshatriya knighthood, the Brahmans were cultured representatives of the transformed and widened cultural orbit of North India. This is quite equivalent to the Chinese literati in the time of Warring Princes. Initially Brahmanical knowledge could not maintain this. Later it rather supplemented the education of knightly youth with elements of Vedic knowledge. It thus gained an unmistakably strong influence over the lay mind.

Despite all sharp antagonisms of the philosophical schools which first emerged, the Brahmans preserved their status cohesion throughout the individual Indian states. As Hellenic gymnastic-musical education, and only this, distinguished Hellene from barbarian, so Vedic-Brahmanical education qualified the civilized man, corresponding to the presuppositions of classical Indian literature. An *imperial pontifex,* found in China as symbol of cultural unity, and in Islam and the Christian Middle Ages, was lacking in India as in classical Greece. Both were cultural communities only by virtue of social organization (caste here, the *polis* there) and by virtue of the education of their intellectual strata.

In contrast to Greek development, in India the homogeneity of the intellectuals was assured by the Brahmans. For the rest, Brahmans and laymen, as representatives of the philosophy, stood alongside one another, like the monks and secular clergy and, with the beginnings of humanism, increasingly also cultured lay persons in the Occident. As the epics still plainly show, lay circles were not alone and perhaps not even pre-eminently responsible for the decomposition of the ancient unbroken Brahmanical religious philosophy. The sceptics (*tarkavadins*) with whom the Mahabharata deals as with godless babblers and covetous sophists, peddling their antiBrahmanical wisdom all over the country, correspond actually to the Hellenic sophists of classical times. They were in fact wandering ascetic teachers stemming from a Brahmanical school (Nyaya) which as such was recognized as orthodox and developed the syllogism, rational logic, and dialectical art as a special learning.

4. *Sramana and Brahmanical Asceticism*

THE Brahmans were as little able to maintain the monopoly of personal mystic holy seeking as that of philosophy and science.

They certainly claimed it. This was because mystical holy seekers, especially the anchorites, in India as elsewhere, were considered to be possessors of holy charisma and even revered as saints and wonder workers, giving them a power the Brahmans wished to monopolize for themselves. Until the present, official theory wished to recognize as full *sramana* or *samana* (hermit) among *sadhu* (monks)[27] only the *sannyasi* in the early sense of the word,[28] that is, those who transferred out of the Brahmanical caste to the life of the monk. Orthodox teaching always rigorously reaffirmed this Brahmanical monopoly, most sharply, of course, against the lower strata.

In the Ramayana an ascetic of great miraculous powers has his head cut off by heroes because he is a Shudra and has nevertheless dared to assume these superhuman capabilities. This very passage indicates, however, that even according to orthodox learning in the time of the epics the Shudra was capable of achieving magical powers through asceticism. And the monopolistic claim never given up officially, was never completely effective in practice.[29]

Indeed, it cannot even be fully ascertained whether the later organization of the actual monasteries (*math*) were first undertaken by Brahmanical *sramana* or only introduced in imitation of heterodox institutions. The first possibility cannot be excluded, as the Brahmanical hermit upon achieving the quality of *yati* (full-ascetic) always appeared (1) as teacher and (2) as magical helper in time of need, gathering scholars and lay admirers around him. However, it is questionable how far one can rightly speak of monks and cloisters in pre-Buddhistic times. In addition to the old ascetic, early tradition, indeed, recognizes the hermit and isolated professional ascetic. Likewise, for otherwise the establishment of certain teachings would not have been possible, it certainly knew, the "school" as a community, later called "*parishad.*"

According to late Hinduistic rules, the school should comprise twenty-one trained Brahmans; in earlier times, however,[30] it often had but three to five. In one account[31] the disciples go on strike against their Brahman who wishes to take on more students. At the time that could have no longer been the rule; yet it indicates how far Brahmanhood of preBuddhistic times still was from engaging in mass propaganda. Philosophical speculation and science was developed by the hermits and secular priests with their personal pupils, partially by the formally organized schools. The later cloister (*math*) was, as a systematically diffused mass phenomenon, first found in the time of competing sects and professional monkdom. Nevertheless, the transition from the philosophical school to the monastery was fluid, considering the ancient asceticism of the novices (*bramacharin*), at least if the teaching tradition adopted a boarding-school type of education which could be very old.

The school or quasi-monastic organization was secured by foundations and primarily provided opportunities for the Brahmans to devote themselves to learning without having to secure a livelihood. Also, where later, prebends were appropriated, the (hereditary) allotment to the ancient school or group of monastic prebendaries was frequently prerequisite to being a caste or subcaste member of full Brahmanhood: that is to say, to that stratum of Brahmans qualified for performing rites—correspondingly for accepting *dakshina* (fiefs and foundation grants). Other Brahmans were held to be lay persons and did not enjoy these all-important privileges of full caste members.[31]

The form of the later normal monastic organization as well as the kind of monkdom in general appears also to suggest as the historical point of departure a formally free school community of teachers and pupils with that following among the laity who through support and gifts to the community sought to win advantages for itself now and in the hereafter.[32] Apparently the systematic organization into communities with fixed rules was still lacking. Purely personal relations formed the basis of cohesiveness, so far as such was present. Ancient Buddhism itself shows, indeed, traces of this patriarchal structure, as we shall see. The bonds of piety which bound such a holy teacher and spiritual advisor, the *guru* or *gosain*[33] to his students and clients, was in Hindu ethics so extraordinarily strong, that these relations could have and must have been basic to almost all religious organizations.

Each *guru* enjoyed an authority over his students superior to that of the father.[34] If he lived as a *sramana* the *guru* was an object of worship by the laity (hagiolatry). For, according to undoubted doctrines, right knowledge supplied magical power. The Brahman's curse was fulfilled if he had proper knowledge of the Veda and, given the case, he preferred to test it by a fire ordeal. The holy gnosis enabled him to perform miracles.

Famous wonder-working *gurus* may well have bequested to their descendants their dignity as teachers by virtue or gentile charisma, or they may have designated their successors. Election, determination, and acclamation of the qualified charismatic leaders by the disciples served only as an expedient. At least in the time of the Upanishads, it was assumed that only a *guru* could impart proper wisdom. Hence quite a few identifiable founders of philosophical schools and sects have left behind them hierocratic dynasties, which often for centuries elaborated the founders' learning and technique of gnosis. To this day innumerable (usually small) monasteries and quasi-monastic[35] communities in India are to be found which, so far as they maintain organizational interrelations, primarily followed the system of branch establishment in agreement with charismatic principles as did the cloisters of our Middle Ages in Cistertian times: Hindu monkdom developed out of wandering magicians and sophists.[36] It remained at all times largely an itinerant mendicancy. Formally the monk was usually free to resign[37] from the monastery and in principle could do so any time. The discipline of superiors (*mathenats*) and the monastic rules and regulations therefore were often lax and relatively loosely defined.[38]

Given the nature of Hindu holy ways, whether orthodox or heterodox, any sort of work duties of monks could hardly exist.[39] No monk labored. The substantive rules for the monk's way of life were partially mere prescriptions of order such as prohibitions against wandering during the rainy season and instructions concerning tonsure and other externals. Otherwise, they represent an intensification of routine Brahmanical asceticism partly simply in degree, partly, however, also in nature and meaning. The last was determined by the interrelation with Brahmanical holy doctrine as developed in the Brahmanas and Upanishads.

The following represent merely intensifications of routine asceticism: the command of chastity; abstinence from sweet nourishment (confining nourishment to fallen fruit); the complete propertylessness; the prohibition of storing goods; and living from begging (later usually under restriction to accept only the remains of the donor's meal); the commandment to wander (later often intensified by the injunction to sleep only one night in a village or not to sleep there at all); the restriction of clothes to bare necessities.

The command of *ahimsa,* that is, to spare life absolutely of all creatures appears in some of the salvation religions in extreme form. Apparently, it was already honored prior to this among classical Brahmanical ascetics only with varying degrees of strictness. This command (*ahimsa*), however, was more than a mere quantitative sharpening of anti-orgiastic vegetarianism and did not merely flow from the restriction of eating sacrificial meat by the priests.[40] Rather, the religio-philosophical belief in the unity of all life evidently played a decisive part. To this came the universal diffusion of the worship and therewith immunity of the cow as an animal conceived to be absolutely pure. Animals also belonged to the sphere of *samsara* and *karma.* They also had, each according to its kind, their *dharma* and hence each was able, in its peculiar manner, to practice piety.[41] The way in which self-control, i.e., the control of eyes and mouth, was enjoined, was at first but disciplinary in nature, but commands such as to do nothing for one's bodily or spiritual welfare were determined beyond this by the general philosophic conception of asceticism as a holy path.

5. *Brahmanical Writings and Science*

THIS transformation of classical Brahmanical asceticism from magical to soteriological ends was consummated in the religious literature in the wake of the Veda collections, namely, the Brahmanas which deal interpretatively with sacrifice and ritual and especially the following Aranykas "works created in the forest." They are products of the contemplative, elderly Brahmans living in the retirement of forest retreats. The speculative sections, the Upanishads, "secret teachings" comprise the decisive soteriological parts of Brahmanical wisdom.[42] (They represent *juanakanda,* that is, gnosis in contrast to *karma-kanda,* the knowledge of ritual.) The Sutra literature contains the ritual prescriptions for practical use: the *Srautacastra,* the holy ritual, the *Smartacastra,* the ritual of everyday life (Grihyasutra), and the social order (Dharmacastra).[43]

This whole literature differs essentially from the Confucian. First, in some externals: the Brahmans, too, were in a specific sense "scholarly scribes." Also Hindu holy literature, orthodox Brahmanical at least, is written, as is the Chinese, in a sacred language strange to the laity,[44] that is, Sanskrit. However, Hindu intellectual culture was far less a purely written culture than Chinese. The Brahmans (and most of their competitors) have for an extraordinarily long time adhered to the principle that holy doctrine may only be transmitted orally. The specific literary character of Chinese intellectual life is to be explained in terms of the early impact of official courtly chronicalism and calendar-making, even when written symbols still were in the form of hieroglyphs. Further, it is to be explained in terms of administration based in principle upon written documents. This was lacking in India. Court procedure was oral and forensic. Speech always was an important means in the pursuit of special interests and power. Through sorcery one sought to secure victory in debate,[45] and all Hindu-influenced culture is familiar with religious disputations, with speech contests for prizes and debating exercises of students among its characteristic institutions. While Chinese writing addressed itself as a hieroglyphic, calligraphic art to the eye and ear at the same time, Indian speech was, above all, addressed to the (acoustic, not visual) memory. The ancient rhapsodists were succeeded by the vyasas (compilators) on the one side, but the speculative Brahmans on the other. Both were later replaced by poets and reciters who elaborated the kavaya forms, combining story-telling with instruction. These poets were partially *pauranikas* and *aithiasikas,* story-tellers of edificatory myths, myths for an essentially intellectualized urban public; partially, they were *dhampatakas,* the reciters of the law books, who probably took the place of the ancient law speaker (and with Manu and in the epics had a stake in commissions for expert opinions on doubtful cases). In about the second century A.D. out of these reciters there developed the guild of Brahmanical pundits, essentially a class of learned scribes. In any case, oral tradition and recitation played the main role into the Indian Middle Ages. In contrast to Chinese sacred literature, this had important ramifications.

All holy Indian literature (including Buddhistic) was fashioned for easy memorization and ready reproduction. It employed for this purpose, in part, the epigrammatic formulae, as in the ancient philosophical and Sutra literature which was learned by ear, the teacher providing the urgently required commentary. Versification was partially used, being prevalent in a large portion of the nonphilosophical literature. Extensive use was made of the refrain—unending literal repetition of a train of thought or of prescriptions with modification only of a single sentence or word in the respective strophe according to the progression of the discussion. Besides, number schematism and the play on numbers was utilized to an unusual extent; a Western teacher can hardly consider this application of numbers as anything else. Finally, however, rhythm was utilized as a quite pedantic system of presentation.

In its beginnings this kind of Brahmanical writing was probably determined primarily by memorization requirements. In connection with "organismic" peculiarities of Indian rationalism this style has been pushed to a mannerism, determining the whole nature of what are for us the most important aspects. In Chinese constructions brief, functional "rationalism" of linguistic means was conjointed to plastic, aesthetic elements of hieroglyphic script. It sought the charm of the epigram yet linguistically made a sober impression. Against this, in Indian religious and ethical literature, appears a luxuriant growth of incredible bombast serving only an interest in systematic completeness.[46] The Western reader is wearied by endless accumulations of ornamental adjectives, comparisons, symbols, great figures to cultivate the impression of grandeur and dignity, and by luxurious phantasies. A difficult journey is in store for the Western reader once he leaves the world of the Rigveda and popular fable, which are gathered in the *Panchatantra* and are the sources of almost all the fables of the world, or when he leaves the world of secondary art drama and lyric to enter the field of religious poetry and philosophical literature. Most of the Upanishads not excepted, the Western reader will find a mass of quite implastic, because rationally intended, symbols and images alongside inwardly dry schematism; and only at long intervals may he chance upon the fresh source of a truly and not apparently dead insight. The hymns and prayer formulae of the Vedas could not be changed because of their proven magical efficacy. Their original quality was preserved in the tradition. In contrast, the ancient epics of chivalry were taken over by the Brahmans and inflated into an unshapely code of ethical paradigms. The Mahabharatha is in form and content a manual of ethics in terms of examples—no longer a poem.

This peculiarity of specifically Brahmanical, but also similar heterodox Indian religious and philosophical literature which contains abundant thoughts, which the European thinker, too, will appraise as absolutely profound, contributed its part to those internal impediments which prevented further development. The Apollonian quest for absolute conceptual clarity did not develop the theory of knowledge beyond the very noteworthy beginnings of logic of the Nyaya school. This was partly due to the deflection of rational endeavor toward pseudo-systematization which, in turn, was codetermined by the technique of the ancient literary tradition. The sense for the empirical, plain, and sober fact was stifled through essentially rhetorical habituation to the search for significance in phantasy beyond the realm of facts. Yet, Indian scientific literature made excellent contributions in the fields of algebra, grammar (including declamation and drama and to a lesser extent metric and rhetoric). There are noteworthy contributions to anatomy, medicine, (excepting surgery, but including veterinary science) and music (*tosolfa!*). Historical science, however, for previously noted reasons, was altogether lacking.[47]

Indian natural science in many areas arrived at a level which Western science had attained about the fourteenth century. Unlike Hellenic science it did not even come near the beginnings of rational experimentation. In all disciplines, including astronomy, developed for ritual purposes, and in mathematics (outside of algebra), Indian science measured by the standards of occidental science has essential achievements to its credit. It had the advantage of not having to contend with certain prejudices of Western religious ideas, i.e., the belief in resurrection which blocked the dissecting of corpses,[48] and an interest in the sophisticated control of the psychosomatic apparatus implementing the technique of contemplation. Western science did not raise such questions nor have such interests. In India all science of social life remained in the form of a policing and cameralistic technology. This can well compare with the contributions of our seventeenth- and early eighteenth-century cameralism. Considering natural science and technical philosophy, however, one has the impression that noteworthy developmental beginnings were somehow hindered.[49]

All these natural science studies were also in large measure undertaken only to serve purely practical purposes (therapeutic, alchemistic, political) and the technology of contemplation. Moreover, natural science in India as in China and elsewhere lacked the mathematical thought of the Hellenes, their imperishable legacy to modern science. Even apart from all this, the custom of rhetorical and symbolical pseudo-systematization clearly contributed to this restriction.

The other most important restriction issued from the focus of attention of Indian thought. In the last analysis it was indifferent to the actualities of the world, and, through gnosis, sought the one thing needful beyond it—salvation from it. This perspective was formally determined by the techniques of contemplation of the intellectual strata.

CHAPTER V

ORTHODOX HINDUISM

1. *Holy technique (Yoga) and the Development of Religious Philosophy*

LIKE ALL methodologies of apathetic ecstasy, technologies of contemplation were based on the same theoretical principle the Quakers formulated, that "God only speaks in the soul when the creature is silent." In practice this doubtless rests on the ancient magical experience of auto-hypnosis and related psychological states, and is induced by physiological effects of controlled regulation and temporary stoppages of breathing and its reaction upon brain functions. The emotional states resulting from such practices were valued as holy and cherished as blissful removal of the soul. They formed the psychological basis of the philosophical holy teachings which in a framework of metaphysical speculations sought rationally to establish the significance of these emotional states.

Among the many varieties of techniques for inducing apathetic ecstasy, one stands out by the fact that it was championed by the orthodox philosophic school of Yoga. Yoga signifies exertion, asceticism, and represents the rationalization of ecstatic practice (of ancient sorcerers). It is not intended here to analyze the details of this much discussed phenomenon.[1] Originally it was a practice of specific lay asceticism. The Krishna Hero is alleged to have imparted this technique to Vivasvat, the tribal god of the Kshatriya caste and he in turn to the old sages of the warriors. It is necessary to mention this here because variations of Yoga appear in orthodox as well as heterodox teachings. It gained greater influence than any other equivalent technology representing the characteristic holy technique of the intellectuals. Whether it actually had its main origin inside or outside Brahman circles can hardly be decided. Historically it was diffused beyond these circles. In time it was superceded by the classical Brahmanical holy technique, and today Yogins form a stratum of magicians without Vedic education. While they are not large in numbers they are widely distributed. Since the Brahmans do not recognize them as their peers, the Yogins—corresponding to a developmental type described earlier—constitute a caste of their own.[2]

The Yoga technique places central emphasis upon controlled breathing and related means of inducing apathetic ecstasy. In this connection it concentrates the conscious psychic and mental functions upon the partly meaningful, partly meaningless flow of inner experiences. They may be endowed with an indefinite emotional and devotional character, but are always controlled through self-observation to the point of completely emptying consciousness of anything expressable in rational words, by gaining deliberate control over the inner motions of heart and lungs, and finally, auto-hypnosis. Intellectually, Yoga technique presupposes that the grasp of the godly is an irrational psychic experience available by irrational means which allegedly have nothing to do with rational, demonstrable knowledge.

Classical Brahmanical intellectualism has never completely accepted this view, for it places knowledge per se in the center of all holy means. In the first place, this includes knowledge of rituals peculiar to the Brahman guild. The salvation-seeking Brahman, however, beyond this, sought the metaphysical, practitional gnostic interpretation of its cosmological meaning. This conceptual goal developed gradually out of the rationalization and sublimation of holy practices. As in other religions the right (ethical) intention displaced mere externally correct conduct, so in Brahmanism, corresponding to the specific prestige of wisdom and thought, the right idea became paramount. As Oldenberg has pointed out, certain thoughts were presented to the officiating Brahman performing certain rites as prerequisite to the magical efficacy of the rites. Right thought and right knowledge were held to be the sources of magical power. Here as elsewhere, such knowledge did not retain the character of ordinary common sense. The supreme good could be achieved only through a higher knowledge: a gnosis.

Yoga technique, on the other hand, sought primarily to achieve magical states and miraculous power. Thus, for example, one sought the power to suspend gravitation and to gain the ability to float around. Moreover, one sought to gain omnipotence with power directly to realize imagined events without external action by virtue of the magical will power of the Yogin. Finally, omniscience was sought, that is, clairvoyance, especially of other men's thoughts.

Classical Brahmanical contemplation, however, sought the blissful rapture of a gnostic comprehension of the godly. All intellectualized holy techniques had one of two purposes: either (1) through the emptying of consciousness they attempted to make room for the holy, which then is more or less clearly felt because it is incommunicable; or (2) by combining internally isolating techniques, which concentrated meditation, they sought to achieve a state experienced not as feeling but as gnostic knowledge. The opposition is not sharp, but classical Brahmanical contemplation in agreement with the nimbus of wisdom, was unmistakably inclined to the second, so much so that the Nyaya school could even consider its pursuit of empirical knowledge as the holy path. This, of course, hardly corresponded to classical Brahmanical type which is firmly convinced of the metaphysical nature of gnosis. Hence it cherished mechanial meditation techniques of achieving "institution" as a psychic experience never to be gained via empirical proof. It therefore never completely rejected Yoga practices. In fact, Yoga was in its way also a supreme form of a specific, intellectualistic conquest of the godly. For the feelings intended through ever higher levels of concentration (*samadhi*) first had to be experienced with the greatest possible consciousness. To achieve this the sentiments of friendship (to God), sympathy (for creatures), beatitude, and, finally, indifference (toward the world) were planfully and rationally pursued in the self through meditative exercises. Thus only the highest step is catalepsy. Classical Yoga rejected the irrational mortification, the *atha Yoga* of pure magical asceticism. It was, for its part, a rationally systematized form of methodical emotional asceticism, and therein somewhat comparable to the exercises of Ignatius. Its systematization essentially represented a level of rationalization superior to that of contemplation. The latter, however, was more rational with regard to the intended "set," namely, knowledge, not feeling, was sought.

2. *Orthodox Salvation Doctrines*

IN THE end, classical Brahmanical teaching could never completely reject as heterodox the virtuoso-like self-mortifications of world-fleeing anchorites, because they too upheld the magical character of the gnosis. Furthermore, in early times the popular prestige of the *tapa* as a means of compelling the gods was unshakable. Brahmanical teaching preferred the temperate means of a contemplation technique only for the ordinary Brahman, so to speak, the "secular priest." The historical origin of devout concentration upon the sacred prayer—syllable *om*[3]—cannot be ascertained. The mechanical repetition of this magically efficacious word assists in emptying the consciousness of worldly thoughts. Use of this device prevails in orthodox as well as in heterodox soteriologies of India. In addition to this technique there are others with similar functions. The purpose is always to free one's self from the world of the senses, from anxieties, passions, drives and striving, and the purposeful considerations of everyday life, thereby preparing one's self for a final state signifying eternal rest (that is, the salvation [*moska, mukti*] from these pressures) and unison with the godly.

No eternal heavenly existence comparable to the Christian paradisical beatitude could appear as a goal in the classical soteriology of India. To the minds of its exponents the idea of eternal rewards and punishments for deeds and omissions of a creature in this ephemeral life would naturally have appeared to be stupid nonsense contradicting all ethically balanced and just compensation. The individuals could sojourn in Heaven only a finite time for finite merits.[4] Moreover, the Vedic as also, later the Hindu gods were as little virtuous as men. They differed primarily in being more powerful. Thus, heaven could hardly be the final aim of Brahmanical salvation-striving. In the realm of experience the soul was only truly detached from the world in deep and dreamless sleep. Where, at such times, was the soul sojourning—who could know? It was certainly not entangled at such periods in the vanities of the world. Hence it probably was sojourning in its extra-worldly home.

All salvation technologies of India stemming from the intellectual strata, whether orthodox or heterodox, involve a withdrawal, not only from everyday life but from the world in general, including also paradise and the world of the gods. Since residence in paradise is but for a finite time one must tremble in fear of the moment when the surplus of merits is used up, for one must inevitably enter upon a new rebirth on earth.[5] Moreover, the gods are subject to the magical influence of properly utilized ritual. In this sense they are inferior, not superior, to the wise man who knows how to coerce them. They are as little eternal as men, their desires are as passionate and they behave like men. Hence they cannot be identical with that godhead purused in their exercises by the technicians of salvation. In classical form Brahmanical salvation is always absolute salvation from the world. This differentiates it from all Chinese attitudes toward the world, including that of Lao-tzu and the other Chinese mystics.

The extreme radicalism in this denial of the world was determined by the world image of Indian religious philosophy which in its consistency left no choice other than yearning for salvation. The quest for salvation did not reject suffering or sin or the imperfection of the world, rather it rejected transitory nature.

Transitoriness adheres to everything, whether available to sense perception or to man's imagination as earthy, heavenly, or hellish forms and things. It is a quality of the world of forms as a whole. The world is an eternal, meaningless "wheel" of recurrent births and deaths steadily rolling on through all eternity. Only two nontemporal realities are discoverable in it: the eternal order itself, and those beings who, through escape of on-going rebirths, must be conceived as their subjects. They are the souls.

The central concern of all Hindu philosophy[6] was with the structure and relation of these beings to the world and the godhead. The one and only question of Hindu philosophy was: how could souls be untangled from the web of *karma*—causality tying them to the wheel of the world? An absolute presupposition of Hindu philosophy after the full development of the *karma* and *samsara* doctrines, was that escape from the wheel of rebirth could be the one and only conceivable function of a "salvation."

This conclusion, so fraught with consequences, was, of course, only gradually attained and, even then, it was by no means universal. Even though the *karma* and *sansara* doctrine have become the general property of Hindu thought, the concept of an impersonal godhead and the un-createdness of the world have not. Indeed, as a rule, the last was accepted even where people believed in personalized gods of the world.

The later cosmologies, such as are contained in the Puranas, ordinarily visualized the world as evolving through a series of ages. In the Vishnu Purana the various ages designated as Krita, Treta, Dvapara, and Kali unceasingly follow one another. In the Kali-age the upper castes disintegrate; the Shudra and the heresies come to the fore, for Brahma is asleep. Vishnu then assumes the form of Rudra (Shiva) and destroys all existent forms: the twilight of the gods sets in. However, then Brahma awakens in the form of Vishnu, the merciful god, and the world begins anew.

The early cosmologies either do not know such supreme deities or recognize them under different names and plural forms in a way of no interest here. Of more importance is the change of thought pattern. Very slowly the early, personal god-father and creator of the world (*prajapati*) has been displaced by the impersonal Brahman principle, originally the magical prayer-formula, then a magical world potency. There was, however, a growing tendency for this potency, in turn, to be endowed with the traits of a personalized, super-worldly god—Brahma—who, according to classical learning, no longer has created the world out of nothing. The world, rather, has emanated from him or appeared by individualizations. His supra-divine nature was perhaps established for theory by the fact that as the functional god of prayer, he could not himself be subject to the magical compulsion of prayer. Below the circles of philosophically schooled Brahmanical intellectuals, in fact, in their very midst, there always reappeared in some form the actually unclassical belief in a supreme, personal-creator God over and above the crowd of local and functional deities—the *ekantika dharma*—(we would say, "monotheism"). With this appeared belief in saviors and salvation in paradise.

Yoga, particularly, with its irrational asceticism and the personal emotional character of its holy states did not, at least in the form given it by Patanjali, eliminate the personal supreme God (*Isvara*, "ruler"). Of course, in strict logic his existence was hardly consistent with *karma* and *samsara*. Indeed, the question properly arose as to the consistency of the ideas of creation and reign of this world belabored with suffering, torment, and vanity and a supreme god. Alongside less consistent solutions to this question (in the Maitrayana Upanishad) the answer appears as follows: the supreme being called this thing to life for his own diversion and enjoyment. Nietzsche occasionally gives voice to the conception of the "artist-god" with the negative moralistic pathos which often betrays an embarrassing residue of bourgeois philistinism even in some of his greatest passages. Its intentions was to expressly renounce any "meaning" of the empirical world. A powerful, and at the same time, kind God could not have created such a world. Only a villain could have done so. This, in crystal-hard clarity, was the teaching of Samkhya philosophy.[7]

On the other hand, the orthodox assumption of a possible salvation of souls from the wheel of rebirth would certainly have led to the concept of a temporarily finite world. If not in this form, it would have led to the conception of an end to the process of unceasing rebirths under the assumption of a finite number of souls. Actually, to escape this conclusion the most consistent school[8] posited an infinitude of souls. Thus the redeemed ones who had attained beatitude were not only, as in Christianity, a remnant, but this number became infinitesimally small. The pathos of this representation necessarily worked toward utmost enhancement of the religious individualism characteristic of all mystical holy seeking, in the attainment of which the individual can and will, in the last analysis, help only himself. What could be the sense of any salvation task in the face of an infinitude of souls? Apart from the belief in predestination the religious solitude of the single soul has never been placed on such a sounding-board as in this conclusion from Brahmanical doctrine. In polar opposition to the belief in election by divine grace, this doctrine left it entirely to the individual soul to work out its own fate.

The basic teaching of the entire theory of salvation, namely, transmigration of souls and ethical compensation, were, as already mentioned, also only gradually developed. In the Brahmanas the first was still quite undeveloped.[9] The second only made its appearance in the Upanishads. Once conceived under the pressure of rational requirements of theodicy, these teachings decisively influence the interpretation of all ascetic and contemplative holy striving. It is these teachings which isolate the transitory nature of earthly things as the essential reason for the devaluation of the world. They also establish the idea that the manifold nature of the world, its forms and individuals, is the decisive sign of its apostasy or at least remoteness from Brahma (and no longer, as it once was, his creation). Consistent extension of these ideas imparts to Brahma the quality of impersonal oneness and—as this vanished behind the phenomenal pluralism of things—at the same time, the hidden negation of the world.

Also, ethically this was decisive for the quality and meaning of the devaluation of the world. In fundamental contrast to Christianity, sin and conscience could not be the sources of holy seeking. In popular thinking sin was a kind of magical-daemonic affair as was *tapas* (asceticism). In the Rigveda it was the trespass of commandments under the protection of Varuna.[10] In later literature the conception was completely eclipsed by that of "evil." It was not evil that devalued the creature but metaphysical worthlessness of the transitory, death-consecrated world and the fact that wisdom is weary of its senseless bustle.

The closer Brahmanical philosophy approached this standpoint the more its central theoretical question concerned the nature and ways of individuation and their sublimation.

Indian philosophy essentially represents a theory of the metaphysical structure of the soul as the vehicle of individuation. According to a widely-held version, the breath was originally considered to be the substance, so to speak, of the immaterial, of the "psychic" and "mental" in men. The originally related concept "*atman,*" therefore, represents the sublimation of such ideas into the concealed, immaterial, magical unity of the "self." In the Mudeka-Upanishad[11] the inner self still consists of "breath" which also in the Khandogya-Upanishad is conceived as something special in contrast to all other organs indispensable to life. In these sources it is already incorporeal. In this last source there is also found the "astral" body of a spiritual self.[12] In the Maitrayana-Upanishad[13] it becomes simply "what a man thinks that he is." Thoughts alone cause the cycle of rebirth when oriented to the world rather than to the Brahma.

Thought simply has magical power: "With knowledge, belief, and Upanishad one makes the sacrifice work," say the Upanishads. The single but important step toward identifying this magical agent of self-conscious individual life with the magical world potency, the Brahman, was already consummated in the esoteric doctrines of the early Upanishads. The famous passage in the Khandogya Upanishad (I, 1, 10) in which the teacher conducts the student through the realm of the living from the seed of grain to man, unceasingly calling attention to the inwardly turned "fine essence" of life, "by virtue of which all exists that has a self" (the Indian conception of "entelechy") with the constant refrain—"that is the essence that is the self—and that, O Svetakatu, is thou (*tat tyam asi*)," belongs to the most striking formulations of old Brahmanical wisdom.

The close relation of classical Brahmanical thought to magic hindered the transformation of the concept of the highest world potency into a "substance" as occurred in Hellenistic philosophy. This development readily suggests itself and is almost consummated in the advance passages. However, it could not occur, for the prestige of magical power was firmly established for Brahmanical thought. From this vantage point one can readily understand why all materialistic speculation was sharply rejected as heterodox. It would have led in a similar direction.

On the other hand, the rationalization of apathetic ecstasy into meditation and contemplation, as the (Yoga) technique of self-concentration, once carried out consistently awakened special and unsurpassed capacities among virtuoso-like, consciously intellectualistic Indians,[14] for various psychic processes of the self, particularly feeling states. The habituation of one's self to an interest in the events and processes of one's psychic life at the same time that the self is turned into a disinterested observer was achieved through Yoga technique.[15] This must have quite naturally led to conceptions of the "I" as an entity also standing outside all "spiritual" processes of consciousness, and, indeed, outside the organic depository of consciousness and its "narrowness."[16]

Similar to the Chinese dualism of *Yang* and *Yin*, the duality of world potencies appears therefore in the early Upanishads as sources of individuation. The masculine spiritual principle, the *purusha*, is entangled with the feminine principle, primordial matter, the *prakriti*. Therein the undeveloped, materially conceived psychic and mental powers of the empirical world are slumbering. They include, particularly, the three basic powers of the soul, the three *gunas: satva*, namely, divine brightness and benevolence; *rajas*, human striving and passions, and *tamas*, bestial darkness[17] and stupidity. We are not concerned here with the way in which they interpenetrate almost all Hindu literature, including the later literature. All conceivable modes of internal behavior in the usual schematism and pedantic-fantastic manner were reduced to the operation of mixtures of these three powers. More important is the fact that already in the Upanishads, *purusha* appears as the spectator who takes no active part in the business of the world and the soul as conjured up by the *prakriti*. But, of course, his part as spectator is to "endure" life, so long, at least, as he lacks insight into the interrelation, and finds himself with the erroneous belief that he acts himself and that his interests are the hub of his entire psychic life. Of course, as soon as he attains wisdom and views the *prakriti* and her doings for what they are, she will behave "like a woman from a good family, when seen naked": she will withdraw and leave him at liberty for that eternal immobile tranquility peculiar to his nature.

With these conclusions Brahmanical speculation found itself faced with several important difficulties which adhere to mysticism in general, but especially to gnostic mysticism. For one thing, from such mysticism no ethic for life within the world could be deduced. The Upanishads contain nothing or almost nothing of what we call ethics. For another, salvation through gnostic wisdom alone came into sharpest tension with the traditional content of holy writing. The gnostic doctrines led to the devaluation not only of the world of the gods but, above all, of ritual. From what has been said one can infer that essentially the orthodox remedied the situation through "organic" relativism. There is no universal "ethic," but only a status- and professionally-differentiated *dharma* according to caste. Surely one could and should not forego all and every formulation of a general teaching of virtue for the gentleman (*Arya*). The law books particularly (the books of house ritual, the *grihyasutras*) could hardly dispense with such. The eight virtues, once ten in number, are unusually colorless. Forbearance, patience, freedom from envy, purity, tranquility, correct life, freedom from desire, and freedom from covetousness are the eight good qualities of the soul in Gautama's law book (the oldest, perhaps pre-Buddhistic). The virtues listed by Manu are given a somewhat more positive turn: contentment, patience, self-control, nonstealing, purity, control of desire, piety, knowledge, truthfulness, and freedom from anger. These were also condensed into five commandments for all castes: to injure no living being, to tell the truth, not to steal, to live purely, to control the passions. Quite similar commandments appear as the first step of Yoga.

In all this the tension between this concept of salvation and Vedic ritual was by no means settled by such commandments.

The questions for the layman in search of salvation remained as to the value of Vedic ritual when he did not qualify for training in gnostic wisdom. It is to the merit particularly of E. W. Hopkins to have shown how these questions run throughout classical literature. For its agents, the Brahmans could hardly allow Vedic ritual to be deprecated, at least in the eyes of the laity. The books of house ritual (*grihyasutras*) remained all-important.

For the law books, too, the Vedic gods and sacrifices, the heavens and hells as means of compensation and punishment remained the decisive and mostly ultimate realities of man's life. Ancestor worship remained a central concern. While in the Upanishads ritual—the most important being the ancient, political soma-ritual of the knightly cult—was allegorically reinterpreted, there is no mention of this in the books on house ritual and law for which the fire ritual of hearth and home was of central concern.

In the course of the rationalization of early Brahmanism a "father god," *prajapati*, had been postulated as reigning over the many functional gods of the world. Only in esoteric thought was the impersonal "Brahman" moved into central location as world potency. The creation of the figure of Brahma as a supreme personal deity was, then, a concession to lay needs. However, this position was not uniformly sustained in the law books. Indeed, Brahma was accepted as a supreme deity and for the most part, as has been justly observed, often treated as identical with *prajapati*. But even then and later he was increasingly conceived as *roi fainéant*. Atman is, and indeed as a cult object, represented in the law books in the sense of philosophy, while the house rituals understandably make little of this idea. At least in the law books *samsara* and *karma* are taken as self-evident presuppositions, coming more into the foreground in the later books. The means of religious discipline, however, consist of a longer or shorter sojourn in hell and heaven, in addition to joy and good fortune of the ancestors in the beyond in the case of virtue, in contrast to their misery in the beyond in the case of evil deeds of the successor.[18] It goes without saying that when misery is caused by the successor the vengeance of the ancestral spirit is upon him.

In agreement with the significance of ancestor worship and, thus, of progeny for the death peace and ancestral bliss, an especially delicate question was posed: whether one could be permitted to be a *sramana* without having first produced progeny. Even if one believed it to be no longer needful to perform ancestral sacrifices in behalf of one's self, one must not leave his forebears unprovided for by successors.[19] Thus the law books generally take as self-evident the fact that the individual must pass through all the marital stages to attain merit in the beyond. With this emerged the conception that continued life or "immortality" consists in nothing else but continued existence in one's own progeny.[20] It may be noted that there were Brahmans who taught that an ascetic need not necessarily be a householder before taking up monastic life. There are occasional protests against this and against "wisdom" in general as the supreme holy path, and the sophistical hair-splitter is declared to have forfeited salvation[21] even as the man given to worldly pleasure. On the whole, however, the phenomenon is accepted as real and rules for the monks were given which were rather similar to those of heterodox (Jain) monks.[22] If a stand is taken at all it is roughly the following: there are simply several paths and also several goals of holy seeking. The monk strives for otherworldly personal holiness, while the ritually correct lay persons, remaining in the world, seeks this-worldly holiness now and rebirth for his forebears and descendants.

It is one of the most important and extraordinary of phenomena that the holy seeking of the *sramana* thus succeeded in breaking through the magical sib bonds of ancestor worship. This is to be explained only by one circumstance—that no one doubted the magical powers which the ascetic possessed. In India, and this is the most important contrast to China, the prestige of the *sramanistic* magical charisma outweighs the duties of piety to the family.

Today no one can say when this development occurred and against what obstacles. Probably things were in flux generally since the colonizing advance into Northern India went on during the entire Brahmana period, necessarily loosening family ties. This, perhaps, facilitated the development. Perhaps only then was the situation wide open for the unchecked formation of Brahmanical schools and ascetic communities, for monasteries and the philosophers' mystic quest for salvation.

Philosophical holy teaching, known as *cruti,* that is, "salvation," in contrast to *sriti,* i.e., "traditional ritual," has accepted the relativization of the holy paths according to intent and the personal charisma of the holy seeker. The gods are present and they are powerful. However, their heavenly world is transitory. By means of correct ritual the laity may join them. So, too, may he who properly studies the *Vedas,* because his mental power does not suffice for more. However, whoever has the charisma of gnosis can escape this world of ephemeral things. If gnosis is the highest soteriological means its substance may develop along two separate courses.

Either it is knowledge of the material-psychic-mental processes of reality as a world of the qualitatively particular, which is the forever becoming and passing away in contrast to the eternally unchangeable and quality-less self; the heterogeneous, but actually existing from which the self turns away. Then, the dualism of the knowing self and known matter (including the so-called "mental processes") is taken as the basic metaphysical fact.

Or knowledge is "gnosis" in a much more specific sense: the world of reality of eternal growth and decay simply cannot be "true." It is an appearance (*maya*), a phantasmagoria presented through the enchantment of knowledge by a daemonical creature, the demi-urge (Isvara). Thus *maya* "creates" the world. Reality is not an attribute to this apparent growth and decay, but of being which, in all this semblance of change, remains self-identical. Naturally, this is a transcendant reality; it is divine being; it is Brahman. By means of the organs of knowledge (belonging to the realm of semblances) this Brahman issues through individuation in the individual mind. When, by means of knowledge, this cosmic illusion is destroyed emancipation from suffering under this illusion is consummated. Once having attained gnosis the mind is no longer needful. The mind can be brought to this state only by suitable means for gnosis is no ordinary knowledge but a "possession."

The peculiar religious difference of both conceptions which is in practice more important than the formal theoretical contrasts, thus rests on this conception of the illusory nature of reality. Liberating knowledge can be attained only by a mystical reunion of the spirit, which has been individualized only through its cosmic illusion, with the divine All One, Brahman. For the dualistic points of view, recognizing reality as true, a Brahman is, in the last analysis, superfluous for the successful holy seeking attained through systematic schooling of knowledge in the sense of Yoga practice. Thus the dualistic doctrine does not concern itself with the Brahman and is, in this sense, "atheistic": the soul sinks into eternal dreamless sleep, but it doesn't vanish. Monastic Brahman doctrine might be called "pantheistic" if one intends this rather inappropriate term to cover adequately the quite specific metaphysical "superworldliness" of the Brahman as the truly real opposite for cosmic semblance.

The dualistic doctrine of reality was elaborated by the Samkhya school; which Kapila first systematically established. The monastic doctrine of cosmic illusion is known under the name of "Vedanta." Samkhya teaching is already anticipated in the Upanishads and is without doubt older and, before the Vedanta-doctrine, the classical philosophy of Indian intellectuals. This is proven by its relation to Yoga which technique furnished the preconditions for its constructions. Its age, moreover, is testified to by the influence it had on the formation of the early sects and heterodoxies, including Buddhism. Further proof is found in the fact that important parts of the Mahabharata were clearly first elaborated under the influence of Samkhya doctrines and only later revised in terms of Vedanta. Finally, also, extereral circumstances may be adduced, such as the time of the oldest systematic editorship[23] of the doctrine. Finally, the fact remains that still in the daily water libation of the Brahmans, Kapila and the ancient Samkhya-saint are called upon.

Vedanta which was written down[24] in the Brahmasutras of Badarayana, and later commented upon by Gankara, the preeminent philosopher of the school, later became the classical system of orthodox Brahmanical Hinduism. This is certainly not astonishing. The proud denial of any form of belief in God, and the acknowledgment of the reality of being in Samkhya doctrine were inevitably more congenial to a stratum of cultured Brahmans and lay intellectuals drawn from knightly circles in the time before the development of the great kingdoms, than it could be to pure priestly caste, especially when this caste stood under the protection of the great patrimonial kings. For this priestly caste the existence and mystical access to godly power was of central interest. It was able to bring its teachings easily into harmony with the presuppositions of Vedic literature, a goal which can be seen from its very name (Vedanta meaning end, conclusion of the Veda).

We must resist the temptation to analyze more closely the

conceptions of Vedanta though they are sublime in their way. In our context only the most general presuppositions are significant. We must avoid conceiving these tensions merely as rational elaborations of "pessimistic, word-rejecting" emotional dispositions such as is to be found among the Hellenes and which appears in ancient Brahmanical and even old Vedic literature. As a truly fundamental emotional disposition, however, it is first found in the late Upanishads.[25]

The great Indian doctrinal systems represented proud and rather rational conceptions of thinkers who were consistent in their ways. The mystic nature of the holy, so strongly determining their teachings, resulted from the internal situation of a stratum of intellectuals who as thinkers face life and ponder its meaning but do not share its practical tasks as doers. The kind of orientation, sensitivity, and "world feeling" that resulted was only in part derived from their rational image of the world. It was in part also determined by striving after holiness through contemplation. When, in one of the Upanishads[26] the three cardinal virtues of the Indian are named as self-control, generosity, and compassion, the second may be seen to be of knightly, the first of Brahmanical origin. "Compassion" however, was clearly the product of a worldly euphoria typically bound up with apathetic mystical ecstasy and later elevated to universal ethical significance in Buddhism.

Among the six official orthodox Veda-schools[27] Samkhya and Vedanta were so outstandingly important that the metaphysics of the rest can be ignored here. Also we are concerned with the doctrines of both great schools only insofar as they determined practical ethics in a manner important for our context.

The "orthodoxy" of all six schools was expressed in the fact that they recognized the authority of the Vedas, that is to say, as stated earlier, they did not dispute the binding character of ritual duties developed in Brahmanical literature and did not attack the position of the Brahmans.

The orthodox philosophic schools[28] have always recognized the pluralism of holy paths (*marga*). Ritual works, asceticism, and wisdom were the three they recognized as classical from the beginning. However, only the last two led beyond the bounds of the *karma*-chain. This holds above all for wisdom. This wisdom was gnosis, "illumination," for which the *expressions "Bodhi"* and *"Buddha"* occasionally appear. We have already seen its magical meaning, especially for the Yogins. Its soteriological significance lay in its capacity for dissolving the unfortunate linkage of spirit and matter, the "materialization" (*upadhi*) of the "I." The state of complete dematerialization or elimination of all "material basis" (*upadhi*) was designated later as *nirvana*,[29] a psychic state which sets in when all relation with the world has been severed. In extra-Buddhistic representation it is not, as in ancient Buddhism, equated with the complete "blowing away" of all individuality, but with the end of suffering through restlessness. It is not the extinguishing of the flame, but a steady smokeless and nonflickering burning, such as occurs when all the winds have ceased.[30]

Nirvana and similar states of bliss (designated by other words) are not necessarily other-worldly in the sense that they can be entered upon only after death.[31] Quite the contrary, they are sought in the present, as results of gnosis. The perfect attainment of gnosis imparted to the classical *sramana* the one important quality, the Hindu *certitudo salutis*. According to Hindu metaphysics this meant two things: first, already in the present it afforded the enjoyment of bliss.[32] Vedanta particularly placed decisive emphasis on this earthly joy attained through unison with Brahma. It also meant a this-worldly emancipation from the *karma*-chain. Through perfect knowledge the redeemed *jivanmukti*[34] escapes the ethical compensation mechanism. "No act clings to him." This means that he is "sinless" in the Hindu sense. "The question no longer torments him: what have I done for good and evil?" From this, the anomistic position, the conclusion, so characteristic of mysticism, has been drawn that ritual no longer binds him, for he stands above it and can do anything[33] without endangering his holiness. This conclusion suggested itself to the metaphysical thought of the Samkhya-school but was not confined to it for it was also drawn by the Vedantists (for example, in the Taittireya-Upanishad).[35] However, such conclusions seem not to have met with universal recognition. This is quite understandable for the devaluation which ritual suffered thereby was felt to be too fundamental a loss.

However, such representations may well have played quite a part in encouraging the emergence of the heterodox-nonritualistic salvation religions. Indeed, all mysticism as independent salvation of the self, because of just such consequences, usually becomes unavoidably dangerous to priesthoods. Actually, the *sramana* as "knowledgeable persons" felt themselves to be superior to the Brahmans as mere technicians of ritual, the more so since their personal visible holiness was far greater to the laity. This state of tension within the ranks of Brahmans and Brahmanically-influenced intelligence was as important in this case as the tension between secular priests and ordained monks of the recognized orders and lay-asceticism in the Occident.

The place of the religious virtuoso within Hinduism, despite some similarities, was somewhat different from that within Catholic Christendom after Christendom had definitely assumed the ecclesiastical form of a compulsory association of corporate grace. Indeed, the idea of the *opera supererogatoria* is also to be found in Hinduism, an inconsistent thought as evaluated over and against *karma*-determinism. But at least there is lacking the agency which could have imparted grace out of the Thesaurus of these accomplishments. Hence, as a rule, simple direct hagiolatry of old continued to exist in place of these conceptions: worship of and gifts to the *sramana* were ritually good works, bringing credit. The great ascetic became a *directeur de l'âme* (*guru, gosain*). There was, however, no fixed relation to the head of a church. At least as a principle it remained true that the individual could gain salvation only by acts of his own and not through institutional grace *ex opere operato*, hence the *sramana* became significant for salvation only as magicians or as examples.

Corresponding to the organically graded holy statuses there were: redeemed ones (*jivanmukta*); other-worldly aspirants to salvation by means of asceticism or contemplation; the ritually correct and Veda-educated Brahmans; and, further, the simple laity. In accord with this the attempt was naturally made to bring the steps of extra-worldly, soteriological, *karma*-free holy seeking and the inner-worldly *karma*-ethic together into organic relation. In the Samkhya soteriology, for example, the following stages, from lower to higher, were held to be means of perfection: (1) liberality—corresponding to the ancient Vedic virtue; (2) intercourse with wise friends; (3) personal studies; (4) instructing others; and finally, (5) meditation (*uha,* deliberation of reason). Whoever truly strove for the supreme goal should strive for unconditional physical detachment (*virage*). Desire and grief destroy receptivity. One should, therefore, give up possessions, and above all, withdraw from the company of all men save those possessing wisdom.

Of course, even ancient Hinduism did not lack the experience of all virtuoso religion, that of the unequal religious qualifications of men. According to the Samkhya doctrine it results from the dispositions of the organ of thought (belonging to *prakriti*): *aviveka* (nondiscrimination) is the obstacle to omniscience which varies in strength according to constitutional endowment. Meanwhile, through concentration (for which, later, the device of Yoga was borrowed), one can master this obstacle. According to pure Samkhya doctrine social acts were valueless for salvation. Even the recognition that the fulfillment of ritual duties also had positive value for holy striving seems to have been accepted only late by this teaching and in consequence of the influence of lay thought.

Vedanta-teaching has always esteemed rites and "work," i.e., traditional social duties as a valuable for salvation striving. In place of the ancient concept *rita,* this concept for the cosmic order derives from the inviolability of ritual, and at the same time represents the real basis of all being (hence it is close to the Chinese Tao-concept); in classical and later literature the concept of *dharma* came to the fore. For the single person this meant the binding "path" of social-ethical behavior, "duty." It was a concept which, in turn, tended to signify the "cosmic order." This turn was due to the increasing need for priestly regulation of the inner-worldly duties, especially ritual duties of the laity. Also Vedanta possessed the idea that the correct fulfillment of external duties of ritual and particularly sacrificial duties indirectly facilitated the attainment of right wisdom and not that they were themselves a path to salvation. According to classical Vedanta they are quite indispensable in this indirect sense. Also according to Vedanta, only he who has attained perfect wisdom and therewith bliss has no more use for the rites.

3. *Holy Teaching and Professional Ethic of the* Bhagavadgita

IF EVERYDAY duties and the holy path to Brahmanical understanding thus had been brought into a reasonably satisfactory mutual relation of organic stages, this solution was in no way satisfactory for the needs of the educated laity. This was particularly true for the knighthood. While the Brahman could pursue meditation alongside his ritualistic everyday profession as its meaningful enhancement inside the real or the extraordinary, or as an esoteric supplement, and, above all, could find these internally reconcilable, the warrior could hardly do so. His status *dharma* was irreconcilable with any sort of escape from the world. However, he was hardly disposed therefore to see himself treated as religiously inferior. The tension between everyday-*dharma* and holy striving partly contributed to the establishment of those heterodox salvation religions to be discussed later, and, partly, however, to a further development of soteriology within the orthodoxy.

This further elaboration of the soteriology is our concern for two reasons. On the one hand, its beginnings can be ascertained at a time preceding the establishment of the heterodoxies or, at least, contemporaneous with them.[36] On the other hand, this soteriology still bears characteristic traits of the ancient soteriology of the intellectuals, of course, in the only transmitted form, already bound up with beginnings of the later cult of a redeemer. Its classical literary source is, of course, the Mahabharatha (in definitive edition dating from about the sixth century B.C.), and especially one of the philosophical dialogue insertions with which this work abounds—introduced by priestly hands into a compendium of ethics. Obviously, they represent—at least in part—reminiscences revised and adapted by priests and residues of the discussions of the problem of theodicy[37] which took place in cultivated high society of the Kshatriya at the time of the petty princes. On the one hand we encounter residues of the belief in "fate" and an arbitrary play of chance with men,[38] a belief close to all warrior heroism. It is a belief which can hardly be harmonized with the *karma*-doctrine without difficulty. Further, especially in the conversations of King Yudhischthiras with his heroes and with the Draupadi, we encounter discussions of the "justice" of the fate of the individual hero and of the "right" of war. Many of them indicate that the purely autonomous (Machiavellian) conceptions of the *dharma* of princes resulted only in part from the political conditions of the later *Signorie*-epoch and partly from consistent Brahmanical ratiocination. In detail, and somewhat in the manner of the Book of Job, King Yudhischthira of the Epic in his blameless misfortune discusses with his spouse the reign of God.[39] The woman comes to the conclusion that the great God only plays with men according to his whims. A genuine solution is as little found here as in Job: one should not say such things, for by the grace of God the good receive immortality and, above all, without this belief the people would not practice virtue.

This has quite a different ring from the philosophy of the Upanishads which knows nothing of such a world regime by a personal God. It is taken over from the ancient father-God of the Brahmanas, who stands above the unethical deities of the Vedas. This borrowing was partially conditioned by sectarian religions with their personal gods and which experienced a revival during the time of the final revision of the epic. Brahma, personally conceived in this context, is identified with *prajapati*. The Vedic gods also are all to be found, but they are powerless. The hero does not fear them. They cannot even help him, they can only cool his forehead and admire him. He is himself—for example, Arjuna—a God's son. But the father-God too causes him little concern. He is convinced of the meaning of "fate," also he externally commits himself to the philosophy of the Brahmans.[40] The ancient Valhalla, India's warrior heaven, is, it seems, his true goal and therefore death on the field of honor, death which here as elsewhere is amenable. At least in one place it is stated that this is better than asceticism and the land attainable through asceticism. Virtue, gain, and pleasure are what man seeks, and action is better than doing nothing. Since the hero also practiced asceticism and since the power of the ascetic and the significance of holy knowledge is completely fixed for him as well, this pure heroic ethic can only be one aspect of the matter. So it is in fact.

The question of the ethical implications of hero *dharma* and war is discussed at length in the very famous episode belonging to the repertoire of every story-teller and known by the name of Bhagavadgita.[41] Externally it represents a discussion directly preceding the bloody battle between opponents related by blood, between the Hero Arjuna, who is concerned during battle about the justice of killing such close relatives, and his chariot master Krishna, who successfully disputes such worries. Krishna, however, is viewed already by the poet as a human incarnation (avatar) of the supreme divine being, the Bhagavat (the majestic) and we already find ourselves on the ground of those epiphanies which dominated the unclassical, folk savior religiosity of later Hinduism. The characteric emotional traits of this religiosity so important for the India of the Middle Ages —to be discussed later—were still in their beginnings.[42] In the most central points we meet with the product of the genteel intellectual stratum of ancient times.

The point is justly taken that there was an ancient community of Bhagavata worshipers who championed the kind of soteriology rendered by the Bhagavadgita.[43] As Garbe has proven, Samkhya doctrine formed the basis for the original version. Only later were correct Vedantic features added through a classicist Brahmanical revision. Then the poem was accepted as an expression of orthodox thought. This historical status of the figure of Krishna is disputed. While occasionally (even as Buddha before the documentary proofs of his historical personality) he has been held to be an ancient sun God, outstanding scholars have maintained that he was, rather, the deified author of the Bhagavata religion.[44] Nonspecialists cannot settle the matter. However, there are no compelling reasons against the simplest assumption: that the form has been taken from the ancient epic tradition and has been worshipped by the Kshatriya as a hero of their estate. The essential features of the Bhagavadgita holy doctrine in its present form may now be reviewed.

Upon close inspection it may be seen that to Arjuna's thoughts against fighting close relatives in battle, Krishna answered with several rather heterogeneous arguments. Firstly,[45] the death of these enemies was decided anyway and would occur even without Arjuna's doings. Moreover,[46] Arjuna's Kshatriya nature would drive him into battle even without his will; this being beyond his control. Here "causality" is read into the determinism of caste-*dharma*. This conclusion, so suggestive to the Samkhya in consequence of the purely material-mechanical nature of all components of action, has not usually been drawn even there. Furthermore, and theoretically this is the main argument, what is not really there one cannot really fight. This has the ring of the Vedanta illusion, in accordance, however, with the Samkhya interpretation maintaining that only the knowing mind "exists," all action and fighting adheres only to matter. For the sake of salvation, the spirit must emancipate itself from its entanglement in the affairs of matter.

The argument would seem to be weaker than when it was advanced from the standpoint of Samkhya thought, for it holds discerning "knowledge" to be precisely what works. Once the passive, life-suffering spirit comes to see clearly and definitely that it does not act but merely endures the action of matter it is no longer enmeshed by the *karma* mechanism of merit and default of matter. Like the classical Yogin, the devout person becomes the observer of his own action and of all psychic processes in his own consciousness and thereby emancipated from the world.[47]

However, the question remains: why then should Arjuna fight at all? This follows, in correct Hindu fashion, positively out of the warrior's caste *dharma* to which Krishna calls attention.[48] In the eyes of the warrior the fight is good; in one phrase still characteristic of epic times Krishna says "righteous" war.[48] To avoid battle is shameful. Whoever falls in battle goes to Heaven. Who conquers there rules the earth. Both things, Krishna opines, must be equally valid for the warrior. But this could hardly be the last word.

The very question is whether and in what sense action according to caste *dharma*, hence an act of matter and not of the salvation-seeking spirit, could have holy value. Only in answer to this is to be found the religious originality of the conception rendered by the Bhagavadgita. We are familiar with the minimization of entanglement in the world, the religious "incognito" of the mystic which issues from his peculiar way of receiving the holy. The early Christian had his goods and women, "as if he had them not." In the Bhagavadgita this takes on a special coloration, namely, that the man of knowledge proves himself in action better against his own action in the world by consummating what is commanded—that always means caste duty—while inwardly remaining completely detached. That is, he acts as if he acted not. In action this is achieved by performing everything without ever seeking success and giving up all and every wish for the fruits of endeavor. Such desires would lead to entanglement in the world, hence the emergence of *karma*.

As the early Christian "does right and leaves the rest to God" so the worshipper of the Bhagavata does the "necessary work"—we would say he yields to the "demand of the day"[49]—the "obligations established by nature." And indeed, corresponding to the exclusiveness of caste duties, he does these and no others[51] without any concern for the consequences, especially not for personal success.

One cannot dispense with works so long as one has a body

(such works include spiritual functions materially conceived by Samkhya doctrine), but one may well dispense with the fruits of such works.[52] Asceticism and sacrifice, too, are only valuable for salvation[53] when one inwardly renounces their fruits, hence when, as we would say, practicing them "for their own sake." Whoever in action gives up the desire for the values of the world, "does not through his action burden himself with guilt, for he acts only for the sake of the body and is content with what offers itself."[54] Such action remains *karma*-free.

It is evident that Vedanta authors, too, were capable of justifying these teachings in fact. From the standpoint of Vedanta, action in the world of illusory reality involves a weaving of the treacherous threads of the veil of *maya* behind which the godly All One is concealed. Whoever has once raised the veil and knows himself to be at one with Brahma can continue to take part in the illusory action without endangering his salvation. Knowledge, however, has protected him from the entanglements of *karma* and ritual duties supply the rules by which one can protect one's self from behavior offensive to the gods.

If this world-indifference precisely to inner-worldly conduct in a certain sense represents the crown of classical ethics of Indian intellectuals, the poem itself reveals the struggle by which this ethic gradually assumed its final form. In the first place there are discernible traces of the struggle against ancient ritualistic Brahmanhood. The Veda teachings are informed by the desire for happiness. It concerns the *gunas,* the material world and its coveted fruits.[55] There remained the further problem of the relative significance of action in agreement with the holy teaching, that is to say of action disregarding results, thus *karma*-free action in the world over and against the classical redemptory means of contemplation. Thus the question involves the position of inner-worldly to world-fleeing mysticism. In one place[56] it is said that action is better than the mere shunning of action.

The derivation of the Bhagavata religiosity from the Kshatriya ethic makes it probable that it is older than the official ethic which, in reverse gives a higher place to meditation as the business of charismatic saints. However, both holy paths are acknowledged to be correct: *jnanayga* (right knowledge) and *karmayoga* (right action), each corresponding to the respective caste *dharma* are ordered alongside one another. Also in the education of the cultured laity the place of methodical contemplation as the classical path to gnosis was no longer to be shaken. The derivation from the stratum of cultured intellectuals is clear throughout. This is obvious in the absolute rejection of orgiastic ecstasy and all active asceticism. In the Bhagavadgita, senseless asceticism full of desire, passion, and defiance is of daemonic character[57] and leads to ruin. Over and against that, the intimate relation of Bhagavata piety to classical Yoga is quite obvious and fully in agreement with the Samkhya dualism of known spirit and known content of consciousness evinced in numerous passages of the poem.

The Yogin is more than an ascetic and—characteristic of the original attitude of classical Brahmanical teaching—also more than a "knower."[58] Yoga technique, the regulation of breath and perception are extolled.[59] General Hindu principles find their correspondence in the commandments of world indifference: the avoidance of lust, rage, and greed as the three gates to hell,[60] the inner emancipation from attachment to home, wife, and children,[61] and absolute *ataxia*[62] are here again bidden to the redeemed. The statement that who knows spirit and matter will not be reborn "no matter how he has conducted his life"[63] is opposed at least to the classical principles of Yoga and is also non-Vedantic, representing, rather, an extreme Samkhya formula. The anomic consequence which we have come to know in classical Hinduism, in the last analysis, as resulting from the position of the redeemed believer (*jivanmukti*), in the Bhagavata religion, however, was brought into relation to a theme we have not previously encountered, and one which also actually represents an alien element in classical teaching. "Lay down all duties in me, your refuge," Krishna says occasionally.[64] Even a miscreant who truly loves Krishna became holy.[65] Dying with the syllable "Om" on one's lips and in thought of Krishna gives assurance against ruin in the future life.[66] The doctrine that inner-worldly action be not unholy but has, indeed, holy value when performed with absolute indifference to the world, thus proves the mystical state of grace of the spiritual Ego precisely against what appears to be one's own external and internal conduct and behavior as conditioned by entanglement in the material world. This doctrine easily harmonizes with the general presuppositions of early Hindu salvation conceptions and is found with the positive interpretation that action in the world is only of redemptory value if performed without attachment to the fruits of action and oriented toward Krishna alone, for his sake and in thought of him.

Here a type of religion of "faith" emerges. For "faith" in the typically religious sense does not necessarily intend facts and teachings to be true—such belief in dogmas can only be fruit and symptom of the actual religious sense. A religion of faith implies the religious devotion, the unconditional trust and obedience and the orientation of one's entire life to a god or redeemer. Krishna here appears as such a redeemer. He dispenses "grace" (*prasada*) to those seeking refuge in him alone. This concept, which except perhaps for weak traces in some of the Upanishads, is lacking in ancient classical Hinduism because it presupposes the super-worldly god and, at bottom, signifies also a disruption of *karma* causality or, at least, of the ancient principle that the soul should alone be responsible for its own peculiar fate. Originally, the concept of dispensing grace per se is not foreign to Hindu religion. The hagiology—worshipping magicians dispensing of grace by virtue of their charisma and the grace of the super-mundane, personalized God or deified hero—suggested itself as the transposition of the human into the divine. However, the thought that salvation from the world be available along this path is a new phenomenon. Yet it does not seem possible to attribute the emergence of this redeemer religiosity and faith to later times—after Buddha, during which time this religion, as will be shown, developed luxuriously. The first inscriptural mention of the Bhagavat religion[67] would seem to date only from the second century B.C.[68] However, upon close inspection the Bhagavadgita is uniformly pervaded by this belief, and is obviously understandable only in the paramountcy of just this element even in its origin. Furthermore, it appears so completely as an esoteric teaching of a community of religious virtuosos of high intellectual culture that it must be assumed that this very feature was characteristic of the Bhagavata religion from the beginning.

The impersonality of the godly has been the truly classical conception but presumably it has never consistently been the only one, even among the intellectual strata and the Brahmans. This held least for lay circles, particularly the strongly developed, cultured, but unmilitary citizenry in the time of emergent Buddhism. The *Mahabharata* as a whole, even in its old sections, represents a peculiar mixture of features of an ancient, humanistically intellectualized ethic of proud knights. "This holy secret I inform you; nothing is nobler than being human," says the epic,[69] with the bourgeois need for assurance in the grace of a God guiding man's fate according to his will and with priestly, mystical indifference to the world. In the Samkhya doctrine, which in its consistent form is atheistic and undoubtedly belongs to the rational religion of intellectuals, Vishnu, as a personal God, occasionally seems to play a somewhat obscure role. Yoga for reasons known to us always adhered firmly to the concept of a personal God. Among the great personalized deities of later Hinduism neither Vishnu nor Shiva were new creations. Shiva was only eliminated by silence in the literature of the ancient Vedic Brahmanhood because of the orgiastic character of the ancient Shiva cults. Later, and until today, precisely the most orthodox, distinguished Brahmanical sects were and are Shivaists; however, they expunged orgiastic elements from the cult. That the individual could find refuge with a redeemer as with a divine incarnation was a concept which was at least current in heterodox soteriology of the intellectuals particularly the Buddhistic from the beginning. It was hardly invented by the Buddhists. In proof we may adduce the position of the magical *guru* which of yore bore this absolutely authoritative and personalized character. What was first lacking in classical Bhagavata religion or, if it already existed, was not taken up by the strata of cultured literati was the ardent love of the redeemer of the later Krishna religion. This may have been similar to Lutheran orthodoxy which rejected the psychological identical pietistic love of Christ (Zinzendorf) as an unclassical innovation.

The Bhagavata religion also preserved its character as religion of intellectuals in its unconditional retention of gnosis, hence of the holy aristocracy of knowledge. Only the wise were holy. Indeed it carried these conceptions to their logical conclusion by relativizing the paths of salvation along organic status-group lines. All honestly and zealously pursued holy paths lead also to the goal, namely, the particular goal sought by the aspirant. One should not disturb the ignorant "who are attracted to action," that is to say, who never free themselves from striving for the fruits of action and do not attain world-indifference to things worldly. The knowing man, indeed, acts in an elevated state (Yoga) of indifference to the world, but he calls the work of the ignorant "good."[70] This is quite similar to the Chinese mystics who leave the masses with their material pleasures and personally strive for Tao. The reason is the same in both cases, namely that people vary in receptivity to religious experience, as every virtuoso knows.

The knower of the Vedas, the soma-drinking (the ritualistic Brahmans) go into the Heaven of Indra[70] with eternal gladness. To envision Krishna is, of course, not possible either through Vedic knowledge or through ascetic penance. And it is indeed difficult[71] to achieve Krishna as the Vedantists wished, directly through striving for unity with the Brahman. Krishna has power to grant attainment of that final holiness which the sincere worshippers cherish though enticed through desire—that is to say, by attachment to the beauty of the world—they are unable to approach him.[72]

Decisive for salvation is "constancy" in the state of grace. To be "immutable" (*aviyahicarin*) to have the *certitudo salutis* is all important. Then the individual will think of Krishna in the hour of death and reach him. This grace he grants to those who act rightly, that is to say, according to *dharma*, without regard to results and without personal interest in their acts. As regards one's own situation, speaking in occidental terms, he must have only the Fichtean "cold approval" of his rightful actions as measured by *dharma*. Then the individual is truly indifferent to the world, hence emancipated from it and *karma*-free.

What strikes the occidental about the redeemer Krishna, and what separates him from later redeemers who are presented as free of sin in the theology of the sects is Krishna's indubitable nonvirtuousness. In the Mahabharata he suggests to his protégés the grossest and most unchivalrous offenses against the mores. This is indicative of the relatively great age of the heroic epic, rather than astral, sun-god derivation of Krishna. His features bear the stamp by the old heroic ethos so basically that it could not be eliminated by retouching. Holy teaching accommodated itself to this fact by declaring, on the one hand, that words not acts are the one essential thing and, on the other, by interpreting indifference to the world to mean also that what happens is presumably decreed by fate (in orthodox conceptions, finally through *karma*) and it holds, at least for a god, no matter how it came about.

The inner-worldly ethic of the Bhagavadgita is "organismic" in a sense hardly to be surpassed. Indian "tolerance" rests upon this absolute relativizing of all ethical and soteriological commandments. They are organically relativized not only according to caste membership, but also according to the goal or end sought by the individual. It is no more a matter of negative tolerance but: (1) of positive—only relative and graded—appreciation for quite contrary maxims of action; (2) of the recognition of the lawful and ethical autonomy, the equal and independent value, of the various spheres of life which had to result from their equal devaluation as soon as ultimate questions of salvation were at stake. That this universal organic relativism was no mere theory but penetrated deeply into emotional life can be seen from the documents which Hinduism has preserved from the time of its rule. In the so-called "Kanausa-Verse-Inscription" of the Brahman Sivagana,[73] for example, Sivagana donates two villages in support of a hermitage built by him. He had through his power of prayer helped his king to conquer innumerable enemies and to butcher them. In these verses, as usual, the earth is soaked with blood. Then, however, "devoutly" he built this house and whoever in the world turns his eyes to it will be freed from the imperfections of the "Kali Age." He did this because he found that life is burdened with every sort of suffering, with aging, separation, and death and that this manner of using riches is the only good one known to all good people of the world. "He built it," the following verses continue, "in the season in which the wind bears the scent of the Acoka—blossoms and the mango shoots are sprouting. Swarms of bumble bees are everywhere and more than ever the gleam in the eyes of lovely women tells of their love. The sign which love impressed upon their round bosom is revealed and their bodies shatter the bodice when they are stirred sitting on swings face to face with their lovers. Laughingly they hastily avert their half-closed eyes and only the quiver of their brows betrays the joy in their hearts. The wives of the pilgrims, however, see the land lighted with the flowers of Mango trees and hear the humming sound of drunken bees. And tears come to their eyes."[74] There follows the listing of contributions for incense and other needs of the hermitage and their reimbursement.

One sees that here everything in life receives its due: the wild battle fury of the hero, then the yearning for salvation, for the ever-new pains of separation composing life, the place of solitude for meditation, and, again, the radiant beauty of spring and the happiness of love. In the end, all this is immersed in a melancholy dream-mood pervaded by resignation which the idea of the maya-veil must produce and into which finally everything is woven, the unreal and passing beauty like the horror of the struggle of man against man. In an official monumental inscription[75] is set forth the attitude toward the world which, in the last analysis, also pervades the most characteristic parts of Indian literature. Reality and magic, action, reasoning and mood, dreamy gnosis and sharp conscious feelings are found with and within one another, because ultimately all remains equally unreal and unsubstantial against the sole reality of divine being.

CHAPTER VI

THE HETERODOX SOTERIOLOGIES OF THE CULTURED PROFESSIONAL MONKS

1. The Two Great Heterodoxies

With a universalism based on the religious depreciation of the world and an organic relativism of "world affirmation," we find ourselves on the true grounds of the classical viewpoint of the Indian literati as created by the intelligence during the ancient epoch of nobles and petty princes. However, there appear two other forms of religion as well. First, there always existed that massive popular orgiasticism against which the intellectuals had closed the door and which they detested and scorned as a *pudendum* or which they ignored as they have done as far as possible into the present. Alcoholic, sexual, and meat orgies, magical compulsion of the spirit, personal deities, living and apotheosized saviors, ardent cultist love of personalized helpers-in-need, conceived as incarnations of great merciful gods—all these were familiar elements of popular religiosity.

We saw that Bhagavata religion, although in structure still native to the cultured stratum, nevertheless made extensive concessions to the redemption belief of the laity with its need for grace and help in distress. We shall see later how under quite changed power relations, the ruling intellectual stratum found itself compelled to arrange for much broader compromises with plebeian forms of piety which were the sources of the specifically unclassical Hindu sects. Located on this base were the Vishnu and Shiva religions of the Indian Middle Ages and modern times.

However, before turning to these it is first necessary to examine two other religious movements which in all essentials had grown on the soil of the ancient intellectual stratum, but which were regarded by the Brahmans not only as unclassical, but were fought, cursed, and hated as most base and objectionable heresies. It was said that it is better to meet a tiger than one of these heretics, because the tiger only destroys the body, but they destroy the soul. The two forms of belief are historically important because they succeeded for several centuries in winning recognition as the dominant competitors of Hinduism. Buddhism diffused to all areas of India; Jainism to considerable portions of India.

This was only transitory. Although Buddhism later completely disappeared from India, it developed into a world religion which partly exerted a culturally revolutionizing influence from Ceylon and India across Tibet to Siberia including China, Korea, and Japan. Jainism remained essentially restricted to classical Indian territory and shriveled to what today is a numerically small sect which often is claimed by the Hindus as belonging to their community. In our context Jainism is of some interest due to the fact that it is a specifically merchant sect as exclusive, or even more exclusive, than the Jews were in the Occident. Thus we here meet apparently with a positive relationship of a confession to economic motivation which is otherwise quite foreign in Hinduism. Of the two confessions which were in sharpest competition with one another and which emerged in classical Kshatriya times (in the seventh and sixth centuries B.C.), Jainism[1] is the older and more exclusively Indian and for reason of expedient presentation shall be discussed first.

2. *Jainism*

LIKE numerous other holy teachers of classical times, according to tradition the author of Jain asceticism Inatriputra (Nataputta), named Mahavira (died around 600 B.C.) was a Kshatriya noble. The origin of the sect within the sphere of the ancient distinguished intelligentsia is still expressed in the assurance of the transmitted biography,[2] that *arhats* (holy men) always stem from a royal family of pure lineage and never from lower families.[3] This is already expressive of a sharp opposition to Vedic-Brahmanical education on the part of the *sramana,* who originated in lay circles. The ritualistic commandments and teachings of the Vedas as well as the holy language are emphatically rejected. They have not the slightest significance for salvation which depends solely on the asceticism of the individual. The teaching rests solidly on the general presupposition that salvation consists of freedom from the wheel of rebirth attainable only by detachment from this world of imperfection, from inner-worldly action, and from *karma* attached to action.

In contrast to Buddhism, Jainism accepted the essentials of the classical *atman* doctrine.[4] Like ancient Samkhya, however, it bypassed the Brahman doctrine, the concept of the divine soul of the universe. It was heterodox particularly because of its rejection of Veda education, of rituals, and of the Brahmans. The absolute atheism of the doctrine, the rejection of any supreme deity and of the total Hindu pantheon[5] would have been no absolutely compelling reason for the charge of heterodoxy, since other ancient philosophies of the intellectuals, particularly the Samkhya doctrine, were of the same bent.

Certainly Jainism rejected all orthodox philosophies, not only the Vedantic but also the Samkhya doctrine. Yet it was close to the last in certain metaphysical presuppositions. This holds especially for its view of the nature of the soul. All souls, i.e., the actual, ultimate I-substances of the Ego, are alleged to be equal and eternal essences. These and only these, not an absolute divine soul are *jiva,* the carriers of life. And indeed they are (in sharpest contrast to Buddhistic teaching) a kind of soul-monad which is capable of infinite wisdom (gnosis). The soul is no mere passive, receptive spirit as in the case of orthodox Bhagavata religion, but, corresponding to a far more strongly accentuated interrelation with the ancient active asceticism and self-deification, the soul represents an active principle of life to which the inertia of matter is opposed as a contrast (*ajiva*).

The body of such is evil. Within Jainism the interrelation with mortificatory magic remains close within the qualitative limits established through its intellectualistic anti-orgiastic origin. The tie was closer than in any other salvation religion of India. An expression of this is the fact that Jainism in place of the world of completely dethroned deities gives divine honors to great virtuosi of asceticism: The *arhat,* the *jina,* and, as supreme, the *tirthankara.* They are worshipped during their lifetimes as magicians and after death as exemplary helpers in virtue.[6] From a total of twenty-five tirthankars, Parsvanatha (allegedly in the ninth century B.C.) was, according to the legend, the next to the last. Mahavira, however, was the last. With them the "prophetic age" came to a close. After them no one has attained the stage of omniscience or the penultimate stage (*manahparyaya*).

As the quality of Brahmanical gnosis increases by steps, so Jain charisma is graded, according to the Kalpa Sutra[7] into seven statuses according to the stages of knowledge: from knowledge of the writings and holy traditions to the stage of enlightenment concerning the things of this world (*avadhi*), the first stage of supernatural knowledge; then the ability to have visions (*Hellsehens*); then to the possession of magical powers and the ability of self-transformation; then (fifth step) to knowledge of the thoughts of all living beings (*manahparyaya*, the second stage of supernatural wisdom); and freedom from all suffering (sixth step); and, therewith, finally, (seventh step) to certainty of the "last birth." Therefore, says the Acharanga Sutra[8], the soul of the perfectly redeemed is qualityless, bodyless, soundless, colorless, tasteless, without feeling, without resurrection, without contact with matter, knowing and perceiving "without analogy," hence directly and without imagery thus leading an "unconditional" existence.

Whoever in life has attained the proper intuitive knowledge sins no more. He sees, like Mahavira, all deities at his feet, and is all-knowing. Mahaviras is the (earthly) final state which the perfect ascetic enters and is also[9] called *nirvana* (in this case identical with the later *jivan mukti*). This state of Jainistic *nirvana* means, however—as Hopkins has correctly seen—in contrast to Buddhist *nirvana* not salvation from "existence" in general, but, "salvation from the body," the source of all sin and lust and of all limitation of spiritual power. One may clearly discern in this the historical relation to miraculous magic. For the Jains, too, knowledge is the supreme, in fact magical means of salvation, as with all classical soteriologies. However, the path to this, in addition to study and meditation, is asceticism to a higher degree than was the case with other sects of literati.

Indeed, with the Jains asceticism has been pushed to an extreme point. He achieves supreme holiness who starves himself to death.[10] On the whole, however, this asceticism, as compared to the primitive asceticism of magicians, is spiritualized in the direction of "world renunciation." "Homelessness" is the basic holy concept. It signifies the break of all worldly relations, thus, above all, indifference to all sense perceptions and avoidance of all action based on worldly motives.[11] It aims at seeking to cease to "act,"[12] to hope, and to wish.[13] A man who only feels and thinks "I am I"[14] is "homeless" in this sense. He yearns neither for life nor for death.[15] Both desires would be lust capable of awakening *karma*. He has no friends and declines the aid of others toward himself (for example, the usual foot-washing which the pious perform for the holy man).[16] He acts according to the principle that one should not resist evil[17] and that the individual's state of grace in life requires proof through the endurance of hardship and pain. Therefore, the Jains were from the outset not a community of individual wise men who, as old men or temporary students, devoted themselves to ascetic life. Nor were they individual virtuosi of life-long asceticism; nor did they represent a plurality of schools and monasteries. Rather they were a special order of "professional monks." Perhaps they were the first, certainly they were among the older confessions of cultured intellectuals who were the most successful in carrying out the typical dualistic organization of the Hindu sects: the community of monks as the nucleus, the laity (*upasaka*, adorers) as a community under religious rule of the monks.

The reception of the novitiate into the community of monks in classical times took place under a tree,[18] after the laying aside of all jewels and clothes as a sign of the renunciation of all possessions, and it consisted of tearing of the hair and smearing the head, and ended with the communication of the *mantra* (the magical and soteriological formula) by the teacher[19] into the ear of the novitiate. The severity of the flight from the world appears to have varied. According to the tradition, it must have increased; originally it entailed neither absolute lack of possessions nor unconditional chastity. It is controversial which of the two forms was introduced at a late time as an absolute commandment. As this supplementary introduction is ascribed to the Mahavira, in contrast to the milder commandments of the penultimate tirthankara, it is identical with the formation of the order of monks itself.

A lasting schism of the order occurred through innovation in the first century A.D. when one part of the monks followed the commandment of absolute nakedness, at least for holy teachers, and another part, indeed the majority, declined.[20] As the gymnosophists in many points of their ritual followed more archaic practice and were also mentioned by Hellenic writers—they disputed with the Hellenic philosophers—and as their later name was originally known only to Indian sources, whereas the name "Jaina" would seem to be of later origin, the case probably represents an accommodation of the majority of the monastic community to the world in the interest of easier propaganda, which in the following centuries had great external successes. The gymnosophists seceded with the claim that only they were the true *nigrantha* (unfettered ones). As *Digambara* (those clothed with the width of the world) they separated themselves from the rest—the *Swetambara* (white-clothed)—and ended by excluding women completely from the possibility of salvation.

A further split occurred when Islam, here as once before in Byzantium, carried on the struggle against idols into the community and led to the emergence of an anti-idolatrous sect. Naturally, the Swetambara sect composed the bulk of the Jains. During the nineteenth century the Digambara were driven from public life by the British police.

Lest he be entangled in personal or local relationships, the classical rules of Jainism laid upon the monk the duty of restless wandering from place to place. A painstaking casuistry regulated the manner of his mendicancy such that the voluntary nature of giving and the avoidance of all *karma*-engendering action of the giver (for which the monk could become answerable) seems to have been secured. To avoid all "action" the monk should live as far as practicable from what nature freely and abundantly offers or from what the householder (laity) without any intention has as a surplus on hand, hence, to that extent, resembles nature's gift.[21] The commandment of wandering homelessness quite naturally gave the order a strong missionary power. In fact, propaganda was expressly recommended.[22]

In complete reversal of the duty to wander for the monks was the rule for the laity against travel, for travel puts them in danger uncontrolled and ignorant as they are, of falling into sin. The familiar Hindu suspicion of change of place, at least any change of place without the accompaniment of the controlling religious man, was pushed to extremes among the Jains. For any trip the *guru* had to give permission and instructions, to determine in advance the route of travel, maximum duration of travel as well as the permissible maximum of travel expenses. These prescriptions are characteristic for the position of the Jain laity in general. They were treated as incompetent minors and held under disciplinary control by means of inspection trips of the clergy and the guardians of morality.

In addition to "correct knowledge," the second "gem" of the Jain was "correct insight," which meant blind submission of the laity to the insight of the teacher. In contrast to the rather far-reaching "organic" relativism of orthodox Hinduism, in classical Jain soteriology there was only the one absolutely holy goal of perfection over and against which all other things represent but way stations, provisional arrangements, immaturity, and inferiority. The holy was achieved through a series of steps—according to the most widely diffused Jain doctrine, after eight rebirths reckoned from the time one set out upon the proper path.

The laity also was required to meditate for a definite time (forty-eight minutes) daily. On definite days (usual four times a month) it was required to lead a full monkish existence. The lay individual was also compelled to take upon himself special austerity on definite days, not to leave the village, and to eat only one meal a day. Lay *dharma* could only mean a possible approach to the *dharma* of monks. Hence, above all, the laity by special vows should take up obligatory duties. Thus, the Jain confession acquired the typical character of a "sect" into which one was especially received.

The discipline of the monks was severe. The *acharya* (superior) of the monastery[23] was ordinarily designated by age. Originally, however, he was chosen because of his charisma, by the predecessor, or by the community.[24] He accepted confessions of the monks and imposed penance. The competent monastic superior[25] controlled the life of the laity, which for this purpose was divided into *samghas* (dioceses), these further into *ganas* (subdioceses) and these, finally, into *gachchas* (parishes). Any laxity on the part of an *acharya* was revenged through magical evil, loss of charisma and particularly, impotence against demons.[26]

In substance, the commandments of Jain asceticism, the third "gem," "right practice" placed supreme importance on *ahimsa,* the absolute prohibition of the killing (*himsa*) of living beings. Without question the Jain principle of *ahimsa* originated in the rejection of the meat sacrifice which the Brahmans had illogically preserved out of ancient Vedic sacrificial ritual. As well as the sharp polemic against this Vedic practice is the proof that the Jains carried through this commandment of nonkilling with unheard-of vehemence. The Jain was allowed to take his own life and, in the opinion of some, should do so when either he could not control his worldly lust or, in reverse, had reached the holy.[27] But he must not touch another's life, not even indirectly nor unwittingly.

Perhaps this prohibition was first transposed in meaning from the anti-orgiastic origin of vegetarianism to the meaningful unity of all life. When Jainism became the official state religion in some kingdoms an accommodation had to occur. Even today correct Jains refuse to sit in criminal courts while they are quite useful in the administration of civil law. However, some safety valve had to be provided with respect to military service, in this case similar to ancient Christianity. Thus, according to the revised doctrine conduct of the king and the warriors was just in "wars of defense." The ancient prescription was now reinterpreted to mean that for the laity it precluded only the killing of "weaker" beings, that is, unarmed enemies. In this form the *ahimsa* of the Jains has been pushed to the extreme. During the dark season the correct Jain will burn no lights as it might burn moths. He kindles no fire, because it would kill insects. Water is strained before boiling. The Jain goes about with his mouth and nose covered with a cloth to prevent the inhalation of insects.[28] Only after carefully sweeping every bit of earth with a soft broom does he step on it. Lest he kill lice with the scissors he does not cut the hair on his head or body (instead, he plucks the hair out by the roots).[29] He never goes through water lest he step on insects.[30]

The practice of *ahimsa* led to the exclusion of the Jain from all industrial trades endangering life, hence from all trades which made use of fire, involved work with sharp instruments (wood or stone work); from masonry; and, in general, from the majority of industrial callings. Agriculture was, of course, completely excluded: ploughing, especially, always endangers the lives of worms and insects.[31]

The second most important commandment for the laity was the limitation of possessions. One should have no more than "necessary." Personal effects in some Jain catechisms are restricted to twenty-six definite articles.[32] Moreover, the possession of riches in general beyond those necessary for existence is dangerous to the holy. One should give his surplus to the temple or the veterinary in order to gain service merit. This occurred in Jain communities famous for their charitable institutions. It may be noted that the acquisition of considerable wealth was in no way forbidden, only the striving after wealth and attachment to riches; this was rather similar to the ascetic Protestantism of the Occident. As with Protestantism, "joy in possessions" (*parigraha*) was the objectional thing, but not possession or gain in itself. The similarity extends further: a Jain commandment forbids saying anything false or exaggerated; the Jains believed in absolute honesty in business life, all deception (maya)[33] was prohibited, including especially all dishonest gain through smuggling, bribery, and any sort of disreputable financial practice (*adattu dama*).

All this excluded the sect, on the one side, from typical oriental participation in "political capitalism" (accumulation of wealth by officials, tax farmers, state purveyors) and, on the other, it worked among them and among the Parsees, just as for the Quakers in the Occident, in terms of the dictum (of early capitalism) "honesty is the best policy." The honesty of the Jain trader was famous.[34] Their wealth was also famous: formerly it has been maintained that more than half the trade of India passed through their hands.[35]

That the Jains, at least the Swetambara Jains, nearly all became traders was due to purely ritualistic reasons, as we shall see later—a case similar to the Jews'. Only the trader could truly practice *ahimsa*. Their special manner of trading, too, determined by ritual, with its particularly strong aversion against traveling, and their way of making travel difficult restricted them to resident trade, again as with the Jews to banking and moneylending. The compulsory "saving" of asceticism familiar from the economic history of Puritanism worked also among them toward the use of accumulated possessions, as investment capital rather than as funds for consumption or rent.[36] That they remained confined to commercial capitalism and failed to create an industrial organization was again due to their ritualistically determined exclusion from industry and as with the Jews their ritualistic isolation in general. This must have been added to by the now familiar barriers which their Hindu surroundings with its traditionalism put in their way besides the patrimonial character of kingship.

The commandment to retain no more than is "necessary"

(*parigraha viramana vrata*) provided but a very elastic restriction[37] to their extensive accumulation of wealth. As with the Puritans the strict methodical nature of their prescribed way of life was favorable to such accumulation. Abstinence from intoxicants and from the enjoyment of meat and honey, absolute avoidance of any sort of unchastity and strict loyalty in marriage, avoidance of status pride, of anger, and all passions are, among them as among all cultured Hindus, self-evident commandments. Possibly the principle that any emotion leads to hell is even more strongly applied. And even more strongly enjoined than for the Hindu laity is the warning against naïve surrender to "the world." One can avoid entanglement in *karma*[38] only through rigid, methodical self-control and composure, through holding one's tongue, and studious caution in all life situations.

Among merits their social ethic counts the feeding of the hungry and thirsty, the clothing of the poor, the forbearance of and care for animals, care for the monks (of their own confession),[39] saving another's life, and kindness toward others. One should think only good of others, not hurt their feelings, and seek to win them through high morality and politeness. However, one should not bind oneself to others.

The five great vows of the monks contain, in addition to *ahimsa, asatya tyaga* (prohibition of dishonesty), *ashaya vrata* (prohibition against taking anything which is not freely offered), *brahmacharya* (chastity), and *aparigraha vrata* (the renunciation of love for anyone or anything). Love must be eliminated for it awakens a desire and the processes of *karma*. Despite these ritualistic commandments there is completely lacking the Christian conception of "neighborly love," as well as any equivalent to the "love of God." For there is no grace and forgiveness, no repentance which wipes out sins, and no effective prayer.[40] The well-reasoned redemptory advantage which the act yields to the doers is the lodestar of action: "The heart of Jainism is empty."

Externally viewed, this proposition for the Jains as for the Puritans may seem erroneous. For the mutual solidarity of the very members of the Jain parishes was always strongly developed. As with many American sects their economic power position depended also on the support of the individual by the parish; and when he changed place, he soon had personal contacts with his sect again. To be sure, in essence this solidarity was rather remote from the early Christian "brotherliness," and similar to the functional rationalism of Puritan welfare work, more in the nature of a discharge of good works than an expression of a religious "acosmic" love of which Jainism, indeed, knows nothing.

In spite of the strict disciplinary subordination of the laity (*cravaka*) under the monk-clergy, the former have always exerted strong influence in Jainism. Just like Buddhistic classical writing, their literature is addressed in their own language to circles ignorant of Sanscrit. It was the laity—here as in Buddhism—which for want of cult objects introduced hagiolatry and idolatry and through comprehensive constructions and foundations contributed to an extraordinary flowering of hieratic architecture and handicraft.[41] The laity could do so because it represented the possessing, pre-eminently bourgeois classes. Guild chiefs were mentioned even in the older literature as lay representatives. To the present day the Jains are most strongly represented in the West Indian guilds. Nowadays, lay influence is mounting again and finds expression especially in the attempt to organize hitherto isolated parishes scattered throughout India into a single community. The strong organization and ties between the lay parish and the monks, however, has always existed and formed for Jainism—in contrast to Buddhism—the means of enduring the competition of the Brahmanical restoration of the Middle Ages and the Islamic persecution.

The origin of the sect was closely contemporaneous with the rise of the Indian city. Anti-urban Bengal, on the other hand, was least receptive to the Jains. One must, however, guard against the notion that it was "product" of the "bourgeoisie." It stemmed from Kshatriya speculation and lay asceticism. Its doctrine, especially the demands addressed to the laity, and its ritualistic prescription formed a workable routine of the everyday life only for a stratum of merchants. But it imposed also on such a stratum, as we saw, quite burdensome restrictions, which it could neither have developed nor tolerated because of economic interests.[42]

Doubtless, the rise of Jainism like all orthodox and heterodox Hindu communities was due to the favor of princes. Also it is extremely suggestive and rightly assumed[43] that the wish by these princes to be free of Brahman power was one of the most important (political) motives for supporting the Jains. The great flowering of Jain religion does not occur in the time of the rising bourgeoisie but coincides precisely with the decline of city politics and guild power, somewhere between the third and thirteenth centuries B.C.—a time also of the flowering of Jainist literature, which gained especially at the expense of Buddhism.

The sect appears to have been founded in the region East of Barnares, hence it expanded West and to the South while remaining weak in Bengal and in Hindustan. In some southern Indian areas and in the realm of the Western Chalukaya kings it was, at times, accepted as the state religion. In the West the main sects of practicing Jains have continued to exist right down to the present.

After the Hindu restoration Jainism to a large extent submitted to the fate of Hinduization. At the beginning it had ignored the castes. The castes had no relation, even indirectly, to Jainist soteriology. This changed even as, under the influence of the laity, the temple and idol assumed even greater dimensions.

The genuine Jain monk could not possibly take care of temples and idols since the practice produced *karma.* Preoccupied with his own salvation, he could assume appropriately only the position of *guru* and teacher. The task of taking care of temple idols thus fell into the hands of the laity. We find the peculiar phenomenon that the temple cult was preferentially placed into the hands of Brahmans,[44] for they were trained for such tasks.

The caste order now overpowered the Jains. In South India the Jain sects are completely organized into castes, while in the North, Hinduistic theory is inclined—according to the familiar type—to treat them as sect castes, which they have always expressly denied. In the cities of Northwest India, however, they have maintained intermarriage with peer groups from the times of guild power. Hence they are above all trader strata. The modern representatives of Hinduism are inclined to claim them for their own. The Jains themselves have given up propaganda proper. Their "service comprises a sermon in which no "God" appears and the exegesis of sacred scriptures. The belief of their laity[45] seems inclined to the view that there is indeed a god but that he does not trouble himself with the world and has contented himself with revealing how to redeem oneself from this world. The number of believers, as has been said, is relatively declining.

This peculiarly shifting situation of the sect rests in part in the Hindu conditions we have recognized, in part, however, in the original and intrinsic peculiarities of Jainism itself. Its ritualistic attitude was not completely clear and could not be in the absence of a supra-mundane God and an ethic anchored to his will. While the sect is constituted on the principle of strict separation and while the laity is bound to the monks, it has not been provided with a fixed ritual of its own.

There were uncertain elements in its whole teaching; it was contradictory so far as its teaching consisted in an initial state available only through contemplation, whereas its specific holy path was asceticism. At least, radical ascetic means had equal standing with meditation and contemplation. Magic was never entirely given up and the anxious control of ritualistic and ascetic rectitude took the place of a perfect and consistently unified method be it contemplative mysticism or active asceticism.

The Jains themselves have always viewed themselves as a specifically ascetic sect and especially in opposition to those who were from this standpoint scorned as "worldly" adherents to Buddhism.

3. *Ancient Buddhism*

LIKE Jainism, but even more clearly, Buddhism presents itself as a product of the time of urban development, of urban kingship and the city nobles. The founder of Buddhism was Siddharta, the Sakya Simha or Sakya Muni, called Gautama,[46] the Buddha,[47] who was born in Lumbini in the present-day Nepal territory at the foot of the Himalayas.

His flight from the house of his parents into solitude, "the great renunciation" (of the world) is considered by Buddhists as the time of the founding of Buddhism. He belonged to the noble (Kshatriya) sib, the Sakya of Kapilavastu.

In the ancient literary documents of the Buddhists, just as with the Jains, and still more in the inscriptural names of donors to Buddhistic cloisters, guild leaders play an outstanding role. Oldenberg drew attention to the fact that rural surroundings, cattle and pasture, were characteristic of the ancient Brahmanical teachers and schools, at least in the early times of the

Upanishads, whereas the city and the urban palace with its elephant-riding kings were characteristic of Buddha's time. Moreover, the dialogue form reflects the advent of city culture. Even in the later Upanishads all this is underway. Obviously a difference in age cannot be readily deduced from literary character. It would be easier to do so by comparing the sequence and development of ideas here and there. Early Buddhism, like Samkhya teaching and the Jain sect know nothing of Brahman. In opposition to both, however, it also denies the *atman* and, in general, the problems of "individuality" which had been the preoccupation of philosophical school soteriology.

The opposition to *atman* doctrines occurs, partially, in so pointed a form against the whole complex of problems that it must have been thoroughly worked over before it could be dismissed as vain and without substance. The character of Buddhism as a quite specific soteriology of cultivated intellectuals appears on the face of it, not to mention the fact that all Buddhist documents place it there.

Tradition has it that the founder was a generation younger than Mahavira, the founder of the Jain order. This is probable because not a few Buddhistic traditions presuppose the competition of the new order against the old and the latter's hatred of the Buddhists. Occasionally Jain traditions, too, mirror this hate. Feelings of competitiveness were combined with feelings that arose from the inner opposition of Buddhistic holy striving not only against the classical Brahmanical path, but, also and especially, against the Jainistic.

The Jain order represents essentially an ascetic community in the specific sense we attribute here to "active asceticism." As with all soteriologies of Indian intellectuals, tranquility is the holy goal. The way, however, is through detachment from the world, and self-denial through mortification. Mortification, however, is not only bound up with extreme exertion of will power, but easily entails emotional, and under certain circumstances, quite hysterical consequences.

In any case active asceticism does not readily lead to that feeling of security and tranquility which must have had for the holy, seeking after detachment from the toil and trouble of world, decisive emotional value. This *certitudo salutis,* however —the present enjoyment of the tranquility of the saved—is indeed, psychologically, the psychic state sought, in the last analysis, by the religions of India. As *jivanmukti,* the Indian holy seeker, as noted, will enjoy the bliss of the world-detached life even here and now.

It is important for the assessment of early Buddhism to keep in mind the fact that its specific accomplishment consisted in having pursued this and only this goal, abolishing without consideration all holy means which had nothing to do with it. Buddhism has expurgated all the ascetic features peculiar to Jainism, all speculation about such problems—be they worldly or other-worldly, social or magical—so long as they are unrelated and of no value to the achievement of this particular goal. The true holy seeker is not attached even to the desire for knowledge.

The peculiarities of "primitive" Buddhism—whether this term is understood to mean the teaching of the master or the practice of the oldest community makes no difference to us—are an object of study in the most recent literature containing a whole series of distinguished works of Indologists. Unanimity has not been reached in everything. For our purposes it is advisable first to present early Buddhism according to the oldest sources,[48] systematically, with regard to points important to us, stating the ideas in as close connection as possible, and disregarding whether in its original phases it contained this rational closure actually and fully—a question which only the expert can decide.[49]

Ancient Buddhism[50] represents in almost all, practically decisive points the characteristic polar opposite of Confucianism as well as of Islam. It is a specifically unpolitical and anti-political status religion, more precisely, a religious "technology" of wandering and of intellectually-schooled mendicant monks. Like all Indian philosophy and theology it is a "salvation religion," if one is to use the name "religion" for an ethical movement without a deity and without a cult. More correctly, it is an ethic with absolute indifference to the question of whether there are "gods" and how they exist. Indeed, in terms of the "how," "from what," "to what end" of salvation, Buddhism represents the most radical form of salvation-striving conceivable. Its salvation is a solely personal act of the single individual. There is no recourse to a deity or savior.[51] From Buddha himself we know no prayer. There is no religious grace. There is, moreover, no predestination either.

According to the *karma* doctrine of the universal causality of ethical compensation, which replaces the theodicy, and which Buddhism does not doubt, man's ultimate fate depends entirely on one's own free behavior. And *karma* doctrine does not take the "personality" for its point of departure, but the meaning and value of the single act. No single world-bound act can get lost in the course of the ethically meaningful but completely cosmic causality.

One might think that an ethic based on these premises must be one of active conduct, be it within the world (like those, each in its particular way, of Confucianism and Islam), or in the form of ascetic exercises, e.g., Jainism, its main competitor in India. Early Buddhism, however, rejected both alike because its salvation "from what?" and "for what?" precluded both alternatives. Out of the general premises and viewpoint of the soteriologically-minded Indian intelligentsia, Buddha's doctrine as expressed even in the first address after the "illumination," and penetratingly interpreted by Rhys David, drew the ultimate conclusion that the basic cause of all illusions inimical to salvation is belief in a "soul" as a lasting unit. From this the doctrine concludes that it is senseless to be attached to all or any inclinations, hopes, and wishes connected with belief in this-worldly, and above all, other-worldly life. All this means attachment to imperfect nothing. To Buddhistic thought an "eternal life" would be a *contradictio in adjecto*. "Life" consists precisely of the fusion of the individual constitutive elements (*khandas*) in the form of the self-conscious, willful individuality which by its very nature is completely transitory.

To attribute "timeless validity" to individuality in Buddhistic, as in all Indian thought, is as an absurd and ridiculous presumption, the very peak of creature worship. What is sought is not salvation to an eternal life, but to the everlasting tranquility of death. The basis of this salvation-striving for Buddhism, as for the Indians in general, was not any sort of "satiety" with the "meanness of life" but "satiety" with "death." This is indicated most clearly in the legend of the experiences preceding Buddha's flight from the parental home, from the side of the young wife and the child into the solitude of the woods.

Of what use was the splendor of the world and of life when it was incessantly beset by the three evils—sickness, age, and death; when all surrender to earthly beauty only enhances pain and, above all, the senselessness of the departure ever and again in an infinity of new lives? The absolute senselessness of ephemeral beauty, happiness, and joy in an everlasting world is precisely that which in the end devalues the goods of the world. For him who is strong and wise and only for him, Buddha repeatedly explains, is his teaching.

Buddhism negates the ordinary conceptions of salvation. A concept of sin based on an ethic of intentions is as little congenial for Buddhism as it was for Hinduism in general. Certainly there were sins for Buddhistic monks, even deadly sins which excluded the offender forever from the fellowship. And there were sins which only required penance. However, everything that hinders salvation is by no means a "sin." In fact, sin is not the final power inimical to salvation. Not "evil" but ephemeral life is the obstacle to salvation; salvation is sought from the simply senseless unrest of all structures of existence in general.

All "morality" could only be a means, hence, could have meaning only insofar as it is a means to salvation. In the last analysis, however, this is not the case. Passion per se, passion for God, even in the form of the loftiest enthusiasm is absolutely inimical to salvation because all desire means attachment to life. Basically, hatred is no more inimical to salvation than all forms of passion. It is on the same footing as the passionately active devotion to ideals. The concept of neighborly love, at least in the sense of the great Christian virtuosi of brotherliness, is unknown. "Like a mighty wind the blessed one blows over the world with the wind of his love, so cool and sweet, quiet and delicate."[52] Only this cool temperance guarantees the internal detachment from all "thirst" for the world and men. The mystic, acosmic love of Buddhism (*maitri, meta*) is psychologically conditioned through the euphoria of apathetic ecstasy. This love and "unbounded feeling" for men and animals like that of a mother for her child gives the holy man a magical, soul-compelling power over his enemies as well.[53] His temper, however, remains cool and aloof in this.[54] For in the end the individual, as a famous poem of the master states,[55] must "wander lonely as the rhinoceros"; that means, as well, that he must be tough-skinned against feeling. The "love of enemies" is necessarily quite foreign to Buddhism. Its quietism could not stand such virtuoso powers of self-domination, but only the equanimity of not hating one's enemies and the "tranquil feeling of friendly concord" (Oldenberg) with community members. This sentiment is not born purely out of mystical experience, but feeds also on the egocentric realization that the expurgation of all aggressive tendencies benefits one's personal salvation. Buddhistic *caritas* is characterized by the same impersonality and matter-of-factness as Jainism, and, in another manner, also that of Puritanism. The personal *certitudo salutis,* not the welfare of the neighbor, is at issue.

In Buddhism, too, salvation is achieved through "knowledge." Naturally this is not in the sense of broad knowledge of earthly or heavenly things. On the contrary, early Buddhism demanded an extreme restriction of the quest for knowledge, namely, the conscious renunciation of the search for what will occur after the death of the saved. A concern for knowledge is also a "desire," a "thirst," and does not benefit the holiness of the soul. The monk Malukya, who wished to know whether the world was eternal and infinite, and if Buddha would live on after death, was mocked by the master. Such questions from one who was unredeemed were compared to those of someone lying deathly sick from a wound who demanded to know from the doctor, before allowing him to treat the wound, his name, whether or not he was of noble birth, and who had inflicted the wound upon him. Inquiry into the nature of *nirvana* was, indeed, held by correct Buddhists to be heresy.

In Confucianism speculation was rejected because it was of no use to the present perfection of the gentleman and was, viewed in utilitarian terms, sterile. In Buddhism it was rejected because it bespeaks of an attachment to mundane intellectual knowledge and this is of no use for future perfection. But salutary "knowledge" is exclusively the practical illumination by the four great truths of the nature, origin, conditions, and means of destroying suffering.

While the early Christian sought passion as an ascetic means or perhaps as martyrdom, the Buddhist flees passion by all means. "Passion," however, is equated to the transitoriness of all forms of existence. What is the nature of passion? It is the fight without prospects of success against the transitoriness of all forms of existence resulting from the nature of life, the "struggle for existence" in the sense of striving to maintain one's own existence which yet is consecrated to death from the outset.

Still later Sutras of the "world-friendly" Mahayana school operated with the proof of the complete senselessness of life that it was unavoidably to end in old age and death. The illumination definitively liberating one from passion is solely secured through meditation, through the contemplative absorption in the simple practical truths of life. "Knowledge," which is denied to active men and available only to the aspirant of enlightenment, hence is also practical in nature. However, it is not "conscience" —which Goethe, too, denies active man, conceding it only to "contemplative" man. Buddhism knows of no consistent concept of "conscience" and cannot know it because of the *karma* doctrine substructuring the Buddhistic denial of the idea of personality.

Buddhism elaborates this with special consistency, somewhat in the manner of the Machian soul-metaphysics. What is the "ego" that salvation teachings hitherto took no trouble to destroy? The various orthodox and heterodox soteriologies had given different answers to this question, from the primitive, more materialistic, or spiritualistic linkage to the ancient, magical soul power of the *atman* (in the Buddhistic Pali: *attan*), to the construction of an immutable constant, but merely receptive mind of the Samkhya doctrine, which referred all that happens to matter, that is to say, to transitory events.

Buddha turned back from these intellectualistic constructions, which did not satisfy him soteriologically and psychologically, to what in effect amounts to a voluntaristic construction, with however, a new twist. In addition to all sorts of residues of more primitive views is to be found the nuclear sense of the new teaching, particularly rich in spiritual implications in "The Questions of King Milinda."[56] Introspective experience shows us no "ego" at all and no "world" but only a stream of all sorts of sensations, strivings, and representations which together constitute "reality." The single elements as experienced are bound together into wholes (by meanings). If one has "swallowed" something with a "taste," for example, the substance is afterward still there—but no more as "taste." And "salt," that is to say, salty quality of taste is not discernible (III, 3.6). A bundle of all sorts of heterogeneous single qualities are perceived as true external "things," and, especially by way of self-consciousness, also as that which appears to us as an "individuality." This is the sense of the discussion.[57]

What is it that establishes the unit? Again, external things are taken as a point of departure. What is a "chariot"? Clearly, it is not any one of its single component parts (wheels, etc.). And, obviously, the chariot cannot be thought of as all its parts together as a simple sum. Rather, we experience the whole as a chariot by virtue of the unity or "meaning" of all the single parts in interrelation. Exactly the same holds for "individuality." Of what does it consist? Certainly not of the single sensations; also not of all of them together: but of the unity of purpose and meaning governing these sensations, as the meaningful purpose of the chariot constitutes the object. But wherein is the purpose and meaning of individuality? In the unified will of the existing individual. And the content of this will? Experience teaches us that all individual wills are in hopeless, manifold striving against and from each other and only in one single point is there unity: the will to exist.

In the last analysis the will is nothing other than this. All men's toil and trouble, whatever illusory cover they may use to clothe themselves before themselves and others has, in the end, this last single meaning: the will to life. This will in its metaphysical meaninglessness is what ultimately holds life together. It is this which produces *karma*. The task is to destroy the will if one wishes to escape *karma*. The will to life, or, as the Buddhists say, the "thirst" for life and actions, for pleasure and joy, above all, for power, but also for knowledge or for whatever it be—this will alone is the *principium individuationis*.

Will alone produces out of the bundle of psychosomatic events, which, empirically, is the "soul," an "ego." This occurs in the manner of (we would say) a "law of the conservation of individuational energy."[58] The will exerts influence beyond death and the grave. Thus the individual who dies can rise again—but not through the "transmigration of souls," for there is no soul substance. However, when an ego is decomposing in death, "thirst" at once joins together a new Ego burdened with the curse of ineluctable *karma* causality, which demands an ethical compensation for each ethically relevant event.[59] Thirst alone handicaps the appearance of redemptory illumination leading to divine tranquility. In this specific sense, with that intellectualistic turn which somehow distinguishes all salvation religions of Asia, all desire is made equivalent with "ignorance" (*avidya*). Stupidity is the first, lust and evil will only the second and third of the three cardinal sins. The illumination, however, is not a free, divine gift of grace, but the wages of incessant meditative absorption by the truth for the sake of giving up the great illusions from which spring the thirst for life. Whoever achieves that illumination enjoys—note this—bliss here and now.

The tone to which the hymns of ancient Buddhism are attuned is triumphant joy. The *arhat* who has reached the goal of the methodical, contemplative ecstasy is *karma-free*[60] and feels himself[61] replete with a strong and delicate (objectless and desireless) experience of love, free from earthly pride and Philistine self-righteousness, but possessed by an unshakable self-confidence which guarantees a lasting state of grace, free from fear, sin, and deception, free from yearning for the world and—above all—for a life in the hereafter. He has inwardly escaped the endless wheel of rebirths which in Buddhistic works of art takes the place of the Christian hell.

From the role that "love experience" plays in this description of the condition of *arhat* one might conjecture a "feminine" trait. That however would be false. The attainment of illumination is an act of the spirit and demands the power of pure, "interest-free" contemplation on the basis of rational thought. The woman, however, at least in later Buddhistic doctrine is not only an irrational being incapable of supreme spiritual power and the specific temptation for the aspirant to illumination—she is, above all, quite incapable of that "objectless" mystic love mode which psychologically characterizes the state of *arhat*. A woman, rather, will fall into sin wherever the opportunity is offered. Where she does not sin in spite of the given opportunity it is surely to be credited to some conventional or other egotistical reason. This is the express view of later monastic moralists. Apparently the master did not express himself in this manner. On the contrary we find in early times—at least according to legend—women in the circle of the master himself, just as in all other sects of intellectuals of the time. All sects were still less conventionally bound. There were also women who became wandering teachers, spreading the teachings of their masters. The quite inferior place of the Buddhistic nun-order, which is throughout subordinate to the monks, therefore, was a product of later monastic development.[62] The frankness of the intersexual exchange in the intellectual circles in no way signifies a "femine" character of the master's message. The message rejects mundane pride and self-righteousness. It did so in favor, not of edifying self-humiliation or emotional love of man in the Christian sense, but in favor of manly clarity about the meaning of life and the ability to draw the conclusion with "intellectual honesty."

A sense of "social" responsibility resting on a social ethic which operates with the idea of the "infinite" value of the individual human soul," must be as remote as possible from a salvation doctrine which, in any value emphasis upon the "soul," could discern only the grand and pernicious basic illusion. Also the specific form of Buddhistic "altruism," universal compassion, is merely one of the stages which sensitivity passes when seeing through the nonsense of the struggle for existence of all individuals in the wheel of life, a sign of progressive intellectual enlightenment, not, however, an expression of active brotherliness. In the rules for contemplation, compassion is expressly defined as being replaced, in the final state of mind, by the cool stoic equanimity of the knowing man.

Of course, it strikes one as highly sentimental when that victorious Buddhist king (ninth century), to honor Buddha, let his elephants go free, and who now, as the quoted inscription states (Ind. Ant. XXL 1892, s. 253) "with tears in their eyes" sought to join again their companions in the woods. Meanwhile, this consequence from *ahimsa* is in itself a purely formal act—like the modern veterinaries and animal pensions of the monasteries. And at least in the early times of ancient Buddhism "tears" were relatively strange and flowed more freely in India, generally first with the pietistic (*bhakti*) devotion.

For characterization of the influence upon external behavior of the Buddhistic type of salvation the following is decisive. Assurance of one's state of grace, that is, certain knowledge of one's own salvation is not sought through proving one's self by any inner-worldly or extra-worldly action, by "work" of any kind, but, in contrast to this, it is sought in a psychic state remote from activity. This is decisive for the location of the *arhat* ideal with respect to the "world" of rational action. No bridge connects them. Nor is there any bridge to any actively conceptualized "social" conduct.

Salvation is an absolutely personal performance of the self-reliant individual.[63] No one, and particularly no social community can help him. The specific asocial character of all genuine mysticism is here carried to its maximum. Actually, it appears even as a contradiction that the Buddha, who was quite aloof from forming a "church" or even a "parish" and who expressly rejected the possibility and pretension of being able to "lead" an order, has founded an order after all. The contradiction remains unless the institution here, in contrast to Christendom, was rather the mere creation of his students.

According to legend the Buddha did not commit himself to preach his redemptory doctrine because he wished to, but he took it upon himself at the special request of a deity. In fact, the ancient fellowship of the order offered the brethren only modest support in the form of correct teaching and supervision for the novice, edification, confession, and penance for the full monk. For the rest the fellowship appears above all to have served the concerns of status decorum, of the monks' deportment lest their charisma be compromised in the eyes of the worldly. As will soon be discussed in general the organization of this social community and the ties of the individual to it, were "minimized" with great consistency and studiousness.

The restriction of the prospect of salvation to him who has fled from the world was in agreement with Indian custom. In Buddhism, however, it resulted from the specific nature of its salvation doctrine. For salvation from the endless struggle of eternally renewed individuality in order to achieve everlasting tranquility could be achieved only by giving up every "thirst" linking man to the world of imperfection and the struggle for existence. Naturally, such salvation was accessible only to the "homeless" (*pabbajita* that is to say, economy-less) status group, according to parish doctrine only the wandering disciples (who in later times were called monks, *Bhikkshu*).

In the parish doctrine the status group of "house-dwelling people" in a manner somewhat similar to the tolerated infidels in Islam, existed only for the purpose of sustaining by alms the Buddhist disciple who aspires to the state of grace until he has reached it. Wandering homelessly, without possessions and work, absolutely abstemious as regards sex, alcohol, song, and dance, practicing vegetarianism, shunning spices, salt, and honey, living from door to door by silent mendicancy, for the rest given to contemplation, the Buddhist sought salvation from the thirst for existence. Material support of the holy seekers fell on the laity and ultimately this alone constituted the highest merit and honor available to the *upasaka* (adorer).[64] The refusal of his alms, through the turning of the beggar pots upside down, was the only sanction with which the monks threatened him. *Upasaka*, however, was he who acted as one. Originally, there was no official recognition of this. Later the explanation was accepted as sufficient that one took refuge with Buddha and the parish (of monks). While for the monks there are quite unambiguous moral rules, the founder limits himself as regards the pious adorers to a few advisory recommendations which were only later and gradually developed into a sort of lay ethic. Thus, there were no *consilia evangelica* here for the *opera supererogatoria* of the charismatics, as in Christianity, but the reverse obtained as an insufficiency ethic of the weak who will not seek complete salvation.

In their original substance the advisory councils were roughly in agreement with the Decalogue, but with a broader understanding of the prohibition against killing (*ahimsa*), extending it to all injury of live beings, the commandment of unconditional truthfulness (in the Decalogue it applied only to court witnesses), and the express prohibition of drunkenness. For the loyal observance of these commandments of lay morality (especially of the five cardinal prohibitions: not to kill, steal, commit adultery, lie, or get drunk), prospective worldly goods are held out to the pious laity such as riches, a good name, good company, death without fear, and betterment of rebirth opportunities. Thus, in the best case, one may be reborn into one of the (to be sure transitory) godly paradises scorned by those entering *nirvana*, which, however, might be more agreeable to the worldly-minded than that condition whose close definition Buddha perhaps had left open to controversy, but which in the ancient teaching was doubtlessly identified with absolute annihilation. Early Buddhism of the canonical Pali text, hence, was merely a status ethic, or more correctly speaking, the technology of a contemplative monkhood.[65] The laity ("house-dweller") can only practice the "lower righteousness" (*adi-brahma-chariya*); unlike the "*reverend*" (*arhat*) it does not qualify for the decisive works of salvation.

It is, of course, questionable whether Buddha's teaching from the onset was conceived as a "monk's" religion. Perhaps, better, it is as good as certain that this definitely was not the case. It is clearly an ancient tradition that the Buddha in his lifetime permitted numerous lay persons who were not in his order to reach *nirvana*. In the *Questions of King Milinda*[66] the teaching still maintains that a layman could at least envision *nirvana*, like a promised land, through direct visual contact. Also, the question is discussed how salvation of the laity through Buddha could ever have been possible and why Buddha, in spite of this, had founded an order of monks.[67]

Initially the community of Buddha represented the following of a mystagogue, being, in any case, more a soteriological school than an order. The discussions of experts[68] make probable what suggests itself, per se, that after Buddha's death the disciples, at first over and against their followers occupied positions similar to that of Buddha to themselves. They were the spiritual fathers of their followers, in the usual Indian terminology, *guru,* and authoritative interpreters of his teaching. In the council of Vaicali, which led to the schism, the "father of the fellowship," the hundred-year-old disciple, Ananda, the loved student of the master, was brought thither. Formal regulations specifying who was entitled to a seat in what were later occasionally called councils, the general meetings of the fellowship to decide doctrinal and disciplinary disputes, were doubtlessly lacking and a "vote" in our sense was out of the question. Authority was decisive. The charisma of the *arhat*-hood, the sinless revered man who was endowed with magical power, was the decisive criterion. In fact, one of the disciples[69] even admitted by Buddha himself had been responsible for a schism. Any sort of rules initially needed were possibly given by the Buddha from case to case. It is said that after his death the rules should be the impersonal "master" of the community. But it is uncertain whether a systematic rule of the order, such as the late *Pratimoscha,* was developed by Buddha himself. The unavoidable discipline, then, forced a fixing of forms. Hence the community became an order, precisely because important parts of the teaching were transmitted as secret doctrine,[70] as in the case of most ancient Indian soteriologies. A sign of membership was desired. Very soon after Buddha the order must have been constituted with head-shaving and yellow costume. Only in the relatively loose organization were retained the traces of a once free fellowship of ancient lay disciples. It soon became a fixed principle that one could never attain full insight[71] and achieve the dignity of *arhat* without having been a formal monk.

A rational economic ethic could hardly develop in this sort of religious order. In fact, a rational economic ethic had not even developed when ancient Buddhism was already on the way toward developing into a lay religion, as in *Mahayana* (great ship to another shore: namely, salvation), in opposition to pure, monkish, "sectarian" Buddhism, Hinayana (small ship). In the *Lalitavistara* advice is given to the pious cultured laity (*arya*) concerning progress in their calling (*magra*) but only—and on account of the denial of the holiness of work—in a studiously indefinite form. Ascetic rules are absent. Also low regard for riches and gifts appears in the decalogue of the Hindu Yoga-Sutra which concerns general, binding, social-ethical rules of life (the five *yamas*), and the soteriological, personal-ethical rules of the higher ethic of religious professionals which include among the five *niyamas* sobriety and ethical rigor. The usual later Buddhistic decalogue (*decacila*) says nothing of the ascetically negative attitude to riches, but restricts the five, generally valid commandments to: murder, stealing, lying, fornication, and enjoyment of alcohol; the aspirants to holy orders, however, are absolutely forbidden to eat more often than the permitted time of once daily or to participate in worldly pleasures, use finery, jewelry, and soft beds, or accept gifts of money.

The later Buddhistic *suttas* which deal more thoroughly with moral problems (often the respective doctrines are placed into the mouth not of Buddha himself but of his disciple Ananda) seek to treat lay morality as a preliminary step to the higher spiritual ethic. Within the degrees of moral doctrine ascending from lower to higher morality the disdain for finery of dress and the nonparticipation in theatrical plays and tournaments was commanded for the "superior" moral degree. But this "higher" morality does not lead—this is the decisive point—to increasingly rational asceticism (extra- or inner-worldly) or to a positive life method. Every satisfaction of work (*kriyavada, karmavada*) is and remains heretical. Rather the opposite holds; active virtue in conduct recedes more and more into the background as against *cila,* the ethic of nonaction, for the purpose of eliminating *rajas* (drives) in the interest of pure contemplation.

In the writings of the orthodox "southern" (Hinayana) Buddhists, the recognition is expressly attributed to the sayings of the master himself that his ethic is "dualistic" and as much formulates a quietism as an ethic of active workaday life. The explicit manner of solving the contradiction is spiritual sophistry: quietism with respect to the bad, work with respect to good will. In truth, an insolvable gap yawns between the ethic of action and the technical rules of contemplation and only the latter yields salvation. Unlike the later Christian ethic, Buddhistic monastic ethic simply does not represent a rational, ethical endeavor supported by special gifts of grace to surpass "inner-worldly" ethical conducts as channelized in the social order, but it takes precisely the opposite direction, principally an asocial course. Therefore no true reconciliation between the worldly and monastic ethic by way of "status" relativism as in the Bhagavata belief and Catholicism could ever be consummated with comparable success.

The later soteriology, fashioned for the laity, therefore could not follow the course of an inner-worldly puritanical asceticism, but only that of a sacramental, hagiolatrous, idolatrous, or logolatrous, ritualistic religion. In any case, the principle always remained, "whoever would do good deeds, should not become a monk."

Moreover, ancient Buddhism lacked almost all beginnings of a methodical lay morality. Upon acceptance by the order, the lay person was required to avoid murder, impurity, lies, and drink. How old these commandments are is, however, not quite certain. For religious reasons certain trades were early considered nonpermissible for the *upasaka:* trade in weapons, poison, and alcohol (similar to certain trades related to pagan cults in early Christendom), caravan trade (considered suspect in all Hinduism), the (sexually and morally dangerous) slave trade, and the butcher's trade (as an offence against *ahimsa*). From these occupations correct lay persons, at least, were excluded. However, the specifically objectionable nature of tillage for the monk (again because of *ahimsa,* the prohibition against the wounding of living beings, unavoidable in ploughing and hoeing, beings who are bound together forming a community with man in the cycle of rebirths) hindered the monks in no way from accepting farm products as alms. It has had no influence whatsoever upon the lay economy.

The extremely sharp prohibition of all possession of money by the monks had just as little influence for lay morality. Any kind of individual moral or social-ethical protest against gaining wealth or against the use of luxuries, so far as the mundane ethics came into consideration, is not to be found in ancient Buddhism. There was no requirement of disdain for the vanity of the world, hence of riches and finery, such as the cited Suttas, written later, contain. Such things are not an injustice but a temptation to acquire a "thirst." On the contrary, riches per se, as noted, were promised as a fruit of lay morality and the "advice of Sigala" specifically enjoined parents to leave their children an inheritance. Any sort of religious premium for a specific economic behavior was lacking completely. There were also no means to control lay conduct. The one, previously noted punishment of "refusal of the alms pot" was not a punishment for vice, but exclusively for lack of respect for the monastic community. The oldest rules, perhaps dating back to the founder himself, originally have exclusively this significance. There was, for the laity, neither confession nor church discipline, neither lay brethren nor tertiaries.

The Buddhistic monastic mores not only exclude work but also the otherwise usual ascetic means, except for auxiliary practices for deepening contemplation, edification for securing self-control through confession, and admonition of the student by the teacher, the junior disciples by senior monks. Buddhism denies any form of rational asceticism. Just as every rational asceticism does not constitute flight from the world so not every flight from the world represents rational asceticism—as convincingly shown by this example.

For Buddhism the "thirst" for a hereafter constitutes as much an attachment to the world as a thirst for things worldly. Accordingly, the ascetic's mortification of self, or work for the sake of happiness in a hereafter is on the same footing with surrender to happiness in the present. Against both, Buddha takes the "middle way." According to the most reliable tradition, the great turning point in his life was the giving up of the attempt, hopefully developed in Indian soteriological method, to mortify the body through undernourishment and other physiological means for the sake of attaining an ecstatic charisma. In this, Buddhism historically stands near to the Jesuitical denial of the means of ancient monastic mortification.[72]

This very innovation in his life conduct, was, according to ancient tradition, experienced by his ascetic comrades as representing the same degree of a break with the most elementary presuppositions of salvation as Jesus' anomistic behavior was by the Pharisees. At first it brought open scorn, and doubt of his gifts of grace among these very circles. The unquenchable hatred of the Jainist monks, who were set on a course of ascetic mortification and sanctifying works, fastened precisely on this. In principle Buddhistic salvation is anti-ascetic if one conceptualizes, as we wish to do here, asceticism as a rational method of living. Certainly Buddhism prescribes a definite way; through it alone one can achieve illumination. However, this way is neither through rationalistic insight into the principles on which it metaphysically rests, in themselves, indeed, timelessly simple, nor a gradual training for ever higher moral perfection. The liberation is, as we noticed, a sudden "leap" into the psychic state of illumination, a leap which can only be prepared for through methodical contemplation. The nature of this leap is such that inner experience is set in harmony by theoretical insight, giving the holy seeker, thereby, the Buddhistic *perseverantia gratiae* and *certitudo salutis;* the certainty that he is freed from "life thirst" definitively and without backsliding, hence, in this sense, also giving him "holiness."

As all traditions indicate, this was Buddha's own self-conscious state of grace. All Buddha's prescriptions were designed for the practical attainment of this state, being as it were, prescriptions for novitiates. All those statements of Buddha which must be considered authentic, especially those concerning the "noble eight-fold path," contain only general prescriptions for the proper salvation disposition. And it is quite possible that Buddha, just like Jesus, drew direct anomistic conclusions for the state of attaining lasting grace (to use a Christian expression).

The opponents (including the modern confessional Christian critics) have always rebuked him for his "merry life" and according to tradition he died from eating spoiled pork. Be that as it may, Buddhistic method restricted itself to instructions for securing successful contemplation and methodical conduct, be it oriented toward a this-or other-worldly goal, for Buddhism does not point toward salvation but to "world thirst," the very thing from which Buddhism wishes to bring salvation. Perhaps it is expedient to summarize Buddhistic soteriology in rational form, as it is done by modern, European-schooled Buddhists.[73]

The basis for this is the famous sermon of Buddha in Benares concerning the four holy truths. The four holy truths are concerned with (1) suffering; (2) the basis for suffering; (3) the end of suffering; and, finally, the means thereto (4) the noble eight-fold path.

(1) Suffering and grief are attached to transitoriness per se,

bound up with imperfection as such, which is, in turn, bound to individuation. All the splendor of life is not only transient but rests upon the struggle with other lives and originates only at the cost of these. (2) The basis of all life and therewith all suffering is the senseless "thirst" (*trishna*) for life, for the preservation of individuality even beyond death in an "eternal" life. The belief in the "soul," and its duration is only the consequence of this unquenchable thirst with all the meaninglessness this brings with it. It is also the source of the belief in a "god," who hears our prayers. (3) The end of thirst for life is the end of the suffering in imperfection and in life. The way thereto, however, is (4) the noble eight-fold path. Its steps are: *sammadikhi*, (correct insight)—namely, first rational understanding, then, however, insight permeating one's entire being to the effect that all constitutive elements of life by nature bear the predicates of suffering, transitoriness, and the absence of any "eternal" kernel in the way of the Brahmanical *atman*, the "soul." The second step is *sammarsankappa*, (right will), the compassionate wise renunciation of all pleasures of life, which generally are only possible at the expense of others. The third step is *sammavaca*, (right speech), the avoidance of untruths and loveless speech through mastery of one's own passionate nature. The fourth step is *sammakammanta*, (proper life conduct), the elimination from conduct of all impurities and particularly all interest in the results or fruits of one's own correct action. Whoever fully attains this, wins the fifth step, which, in Christian terms, provides *certitudo salutis* the no longer alienable holiness of life: *sammo ajivo*. The tremendous exertion of all his powers in the service of the holy goal gives him a spiritual power of the holy will, which surpasses by far what is attainable for others: *sammavayano*, (the right "power of will"), the sixth step. He had this power over himself not only while waking but also when sleeping; he knows who he is and was. And this inner attitude of holy knowledge leads him to the seventh step of perfection, *sammasati*, in which he is no longer available to anything but holy thoughts and feelings. And though this ability far exceeding normal consciousness he inwardly reaches the "shores wrested from death," *nirvana*, in the right concentration, *sammasamadhi*, the last and highest step.

Also in this already quite modernized[74] and hence watered-down form, the holy teaching still permits insight into what is practically the essential peculiarity of Buddhism, the complete elimination of any form of inner-worldly motivation to conduct or rational purpose in nature. For all rational action ("goal directed action") in compliance with the principle is expressly rejected. Thus, there is lacking an element which in occidental monkhood increasingly developed and signified so much, namely, the strain toward rational method in life conduct in all spheres except that of the pure intellectual systematization of concentrated meditation and pure contemplation. This, on its side, has been increasingly developed to that level of sophistication, also otherwise characteristic of things Indian. The later development took many aids from Yoga technique with which the master was certainly acquainted. These techniques varied from breath regulation to the submergence of thought step by step through the forty *karmasthanas;* all means were methodologically rationalized to the successive attainment of the four degrees of salvation.

According to the teaching, at least of the parish community, as we saw, the highest degree was attained only by the monks. The pious lay person, however, was excluded even from the one cult-like event of this originally and necessarily completely cultless piety—the bi-monthly gatherings and the *Uposatha*-festival, which were essentially disciplinary confessional meetings of the monks. There remained to him nothing but the honoring of the monk's personality and the relics by making foundations of *viharas* (rest shelters in ancient times still without the character of monasteries). In the course of the construction of *stupas,* with their increasing accent on objects of art, there was soon joined to the single possible form of lay piety the cult of relics proper. Precisely the absolute extra-worldly character, the cultlessness of the monkish piety, and the lack of any kind of planned influence on life conduct of the laity—a very important difference between ancient Buddhism and Jainism—must have pushed the lay piety increasingly in the direction of hagiolatry and idolatry as it was practiced by the later Mahayana sects.

Ancient Buddhism was indeed thoroughly disinclined to sorcery. But it never doubted the existence of "spirits" (*devata*) and from this there soon developed the art of compelling spirits—geomancy.[75] On the other hand, the ease with which the changeover was accomplished— from the fellowship of disciples, provided for by donations from case to case, to monastic life, endowed with permanent real estate, buildings, permanent rents, possession of grounds, slaves, bondsman, in effect, monastic landlordism—is shown by the history of ancient Buddhism in India and the neighboring lands and in the thoroughly established form of monastic landlordism acquired by Buddhism in Ceylon and Tibet. (All this will be discussed at a later time.) Counter to this almost unavoidable development, ancient Buddhism upheld, in addition to the prohibition of possessions (on this, there were infractions, at least the stores of clothing for which special managers appeared from the beginning), the commandment that the monk wander, and the refusal of an hierarchical, parochial, and, in general, any binding organization. The dioceses (*sima*) for which, in former times, the bi-monthly and *Uposatha* festivals were arranged by the respective senior monk on behalf of the monks who happened to sojourn there, were not exclusive parishes. Any residence duty or membership in a definite monastery was originally lacking. In the gatherings only seniority of a full monk, not rank by age, gave precedence. All "officers" were only technical aids without imperium. And the so-called "patriarchs" or "fathers," who later disappeared, of the ancient Buddhistic church were apparently *Arhats* qualified exclusively by seniority and charisma in a cloister, which, in turn, was charismatically esteemed according to its traditions. For the rest it appears that nothing is known for certain about their position.

The reception into the order after a preliminary novitiate (consisting of apprenticeship to a monk as *directeur de l'âme* and formal admission upon request of and recommendation by the teacher), contained no sort of lasting bond. Also the member was free to resign at any time and rejection was recommended to anyone who lacked sufficient power.[76] All in all, in consequence of this intentional and consistent minimization of ties and regulation, Buddhism persisted in an unstructured state which from the beginning was dangerous to the uniformity of the community and which actually soon led to heresies and sect formation. The single countervailing means—the calling of councils—soon failed, and the unity of the community was apparently possible only through the support of secular authorities. It looks as if even the few, finally created elements of organization and discipline, hence the establishment of an order, and likewise the fixing of the teaching, occurred only after the death of the founder and against his own intentions.

Ananda was his beloved disciple, hence, the "John" of primitive Buddhism was his designated successor. Likewise, one can deduce with certainty from the otherwise so little serviceable tradition of the "first council" (after his death) that Ananda was not only pushed aside by the other disciples but deemed sinful, required to do penance, and that others took the leadership of the community from his hands—quite like the original Christian community. The primitive community of monks clearly did not wish to permit either spiritual succession or, in general, the aristocracy of charisma to gain ascendancy in their midst. Therefore it emphasized the seniority principle (of the fully saved and hence sinless) *arhats* and beyond this a certain minimum of fixed order, while Ananda presumably was considered the representative of charismatic descendants free of all organization. Down to the present the rank order of the monks, who for the rest are strictly considered to be peers in orthodox Burmese monasteries, is determined solely by the number of *was* credited to them, i.e., the annual seasons of joining (hence years) gone by since they entered the cloister: after ten *was* the individual became a full monk. That is certainly very old tradition.

The orthodox teaching of the community, as it continues to live a thousand years later in the Hinayana-Buddhism, recognized besides seniority only one absolute and highly efficient element of structural cohesion, the teacher-disciple relationship. The novice has to abide by the strict rule of piety of the Indian *bramacharin* toward his *guru.* Also, the received monk, as late as the times of J-Tsing (seventh century A.D.), was permitted to leave his teacher only after five years, after, in the teacher's view, he had thoroughly mastered the content of the Vianya-canon. Even then he required permission for each and every act from the teacher from whom he must not withhold any emotion of redemptory significance. This tutelage ceased only after ten years and with full memorization of the Vianya. But whoever was not completely capable of this, remained under this absolute tutelage for the rest of his life. Precisely the Hinayana-orthodoxy appears to have preserved this piety relation with special severity.

In India the following of ancient Buddhism, which rejected the later development of cloisters into landlordships and of the salvation doctrine into a lay soteriology, was recruited from the outset, not exclusively but predominantly, like the founder himself, from among great noble families and from rich burghers. Also Brahmans appear to have been taken up; but they were the distinguished representatives of a cultured laity—a secular strata of nobles who formed the majority of Buddha's disciples.[77]

Accordingly, beginnings of the development of status conventions go far back. Even the prescribed form of mendicancy was adapted to the sense of honor and standard of good taste of a well-educated intellectual. Buddha's disciples were never a horde of uncivilized beggars. In contrast to other sects, not only was dress regulated from the beginning, but also subject to planned provision. But the attractiveness of Buddhism, especially for the upper strata, is to be explained, in part at least, exactly in terms of its concern for decorum. The Pratimokkha of Southern Buddhism is replete with purely conventional rules of etiquette for monks in intercourse with one another and with the "world," down to the prohibition against smacking one's lips when eating.

This suggests the inner peculiarity of the teaching. Immense and basic—as has been observed repeatedly (especially by Oldenberg)—is the difference between the preaching of Buddha, of which, after all, one can gain a rough idea from the tradition, and that of Jesus on the one hand, and Muhammed on the other. The typical form of Buddha's teaching is the Socratic dialogue, by which the opponent is led through a considerable argument to a *reductio ad absurdum* and then forced into submission. Neither the short parable, the ironic dismissal, or the pathetic penitential sermon of the Galilean prophet, nor the address resting on visions of the Arabic holy leader find any sort of parallels to the lectures and conversations which seem to have constituted the true form of Buddha's activity. They address themselves purely to the intellect and affected the quiet, sober judgment detached from all internal excitement; their factual manner exhausts the topic always in systematic dialectical fashion. It was simply impossible to follow these lectures—and one can easily convince himself of this—without extensive schooling in specific Hindu thought, although Buddha insisted, and, indeed, for a Hindu thinker with justice, that his teaching be so simple that any child could understand it. In any case this held only for a child, as understood in the ancient Hindu sense, who had an excellent upbringing.

Buddhism had no sort of tie with any sort of "social" movement, nor did it run parallel with such and it has established no "social-political" goal. The ignoring of the status order was not new. In the regions where Buddhism originated—Magadha and the neighboring North Indian territories—the might of Brahmanhood was relatively weak. The four old "estates" had doubtlessly long since fallen into decay—particularly had the free peasants (Vaishya) become a fiction. The sources in Buddhistic times held the merchants to be typical Vaishya, and the religious closure of castes against one another, especially the organization of the Shudras into professional castes was apparently, at least in this part of India, only in its beginnings and was carried through with full consistency only by later Hinduism. Individual holy seeking of the *sramana,* whose ascetic accomplishments had long won religious esteem and had made them the peers of the Vedic-educated priests, was here a widely diffused phenomenon. So far as it actually took place, the disregard of Buddhism for status differences meant no social revolution. That members of the lowest strata were to be found among the adherents of early Buddhism is not traditional and very improbable. For it was precisely *sramana* who came predominantly from distinguished circles of lay culture recruited from the city-dwelling Kshatriya patricians, somewhat as in the case of our Humanists, who constitute its membership. In fact, it appears rather certain that originally Buddhism, exactly like Jainism, first firmly adhered to the conviction that only one born in the Brahman or Kshatriya castes was qualified for full gnosis. Also Buddha himself was soon elevated by legend from a scion of rural nobility which, historically, he was, to a son of a prince. The rich city patricians and also quite a few rich Brahmans, according to tradition, were proselytes of his first preaching. The stratum of cultivated intellectuals to whom Buddha's teaching was addressed—and which, indeed, as Oldenberg puts it, could in no way be meant for the "poor in spirit"—strongly experienced themselves, as we have already noted, as a pervasive unit amidst the petty states of India, comparable to the intellectual stratum of our Middle Ages. The fortuitous and changing political structures could hardly have permanently favored only such a class. Buddhistic teaching itself originated in a region in which there was relatively considerable development of noble and bourgeois fortunes. Moreover, there was no ruling priesthood comparable in extent to that of later Hinduism or, which like the ancient Brahmans, might have prevented these patricians from conducting their lives as they pleased, and believing or disbelieving as they wished—and secular authorities could in no way find cause against an absolutely unpolitical movement such as existed in the main. For the rest the rule of Buddha, whom the tradition considered as a protégé of king Bimbisara, who adored him, is to avoid all suspicion of worldly power: soldiers and slaves, indebted bondsmen and criminals found no sort of reception in the order. A "struggle" against the Brahmans somewhat in the manner of Christ against the Pharisees and scribes cannot be traced in Buddha's preaching. He left aside the question of the Gods as well as the meaning of the castes. According to tradition he would insist, after the energetic quizzing of a Brahman, only that not birth but right acts make a true Brahman. Likewise there is to be found no true struggle against sacrifice, such as was peculiar to the Jains. It simply had no value for the goal pursued by the strong and wise.

As a whole early Buddhism was the product not of the underprivileged but of very positively privileged strata. There can be no doubt, however, that its anti-hierocratic feature, namely, the devaluation of Brahmanical knowledge of ritual and of Brahmanical philosophy made the princes and patricians sympathetic to its teaching. That against the Brahman hierocracy in time only the still stronger hierocratic power of the mendicant monks would be exchanged, was an experience which dawned only upon later generations. The conviction of the specific holiness of the wandering monks and ascetics was long a common view of all social strata in India, and existed also in quite a few other epochs and among other peoples. The rules of the order prescribed expressly, indeed, not without intention, that monks while begging should without differentiation knock upon the doors of poor and rich. But to change the social order in this world neither early nor later Buddhism has attempted to do. The monk was indifferent to the world. Not, as in the case of ancient Christendom, because escatological expectations stamped it so, but the reverse, because there were no sort of escatological expectations. At least according to later doctrine, there was neither salvation for him who wished not to become a monk nor, on the other hand, was there for the monk a human fate which in any way could influence his chances of salvation.

The kind of salvation which was promised to the mendicant monk certainly was not one to the taste of the socially oppressed strata, which would have rather demanded compensation in the hereafter or this-worldly hopes for the future. The lay morality, however, bore the character of an extremely colorless "bourgeois" ethic as did its present rewards of riches and an honorable name. A religious "natural law" of peasant bondsmen or guild artisans would have looked quite different. A salvation religion rooted in these strata natively or in general, a specific lay religion of the lower strata would have had a basically different character as is indicated by later developments.

Propaganda through teaching belonged quite personally as a specific way of life to the restless wandering Buddha. Whether it was originally regarded as a peculiar "duty" for the monks may remain an open question, though it is rather improbable. The express duty of the missionary work as such was probably more connected with the transformation of the salvation ideal in later centuries.

However, Buddhism became one of the greatest missionary religions on earth. That must seem baffling. Viewed rationally, there is no motive to be discovered which should have destined Buddhism for this. What could cause a monk who was seeking only his own salvation and therefore was utterly self-dependent to trouble himself with saving the souls of others and engaging in missionary work? Besides such work could only have appeared sterile to the mystic under the influence of the *karma* doctrine with its determination of the salvation chances through *karma* and its dependence on differences in religious qualification. For a long time Buddha was uncertain whether or not, at the request of Brahma, he should preach salvation to man. Finally, he was determined to do so by the fact that he saw next to those qualified for holiness and those destined for evil, quite a few men of ambiguous qualification whose future destiny, hence, could be influenced by preaching the holy.

Nevertheless, this was but a dogmatic interpretation. Where, however, were to be found the actual practical motives? First, presumably in that psychological circumstance which is not rationally further explainable (perhaps physiologically conditioned circumstance) which we know to be peculiar to the great virtuosi of mystic piety. For the most part there is a compassionate acosmic love which almost always goes with the psychological form of mystical holy state, the peculiar euphoria of god-possessed tranquility. This drove the majority of them, as over and against the rational consequences of mystical holy seeking, on the road toward saving souls. This motive which is quite apparent also in the Buddhistic ethic of compassion is to be found also in other Indian mystics. Besides this operated the custom of migratory disputation which Buddha shared in characteristic fashion with all Indian soteriological representatives of the old stratum of intellectuals.

But this, too, was a general phenomenon of all soteriologies of his time. Decisive for the success of the propaganda as with the Jains was the appearance of the "professional monks" in the form of communities. The decisive motive for the propaganda activities was naturally given by the material interests of the monks in the increase of the givers of subsistence, the *upasaka*. Also this interest was shared by the competing monkish associations, the Buddhists and especially the Jains. In the time of its expansion Buddhism was favored by several circumstances which on the other side, practically viewed constituted weaknesses, circumstances which later, in India itself at least, were to bring misfortune to Buddhism in competition with orthodox professional monks.

On the one hand, the monastic community lacked all firm organization and therewith also fixed prebendal interests. Each confession met crises in its missionary expansion in the moment when the typical process of "prebendalism" is completed. That is, it occurs when its organization is so far developed that its income, on the one hand, its help offering, on the other, are firmly allocated to stable parishes in terms of a clientele of patrons or a "rent" for its professional holy mediators (priests, preachers, monks). It was unavoidable, then, that the monopolistic interests of such holders of clienteles, of patrons, and prebends prevail over the joint interest in the winning of new land. The community, itself, then, makes more difficult the reception of novices in order not to endanger the customary income of the present parish holders. It is interested, indeed, in the avoiding of competition for its income area, but its prebendaries are not fit propagandists for missionary endeavor in foreign territories.

In one or another form this transition can be found for most formerly missionary confessions. In Buddhism the ancient acosmic organization (or lack of organization) in connection with the rejection of all ordering of lay relations at first directly precludes the development of prebendalism. Initially, the following circumstance, at least externally, offered quite considerable advantage: the purely parasitic character of Buddhistic income seeking, so offensive to the ascetic of older observance, the attachment to the flowering cities and larger places generally in connection with a very tenuous commitment to ritualistic rules on the part of the monks as well as the supporting laity. As shown, ancient Buddhas, using the firmly given differential qualification for salvation as a basic fact and point of departure, imposed almost no other duties upon the laity than the support of the monks. Originally it knew no contributors to the community, which necessarily would have quickly been transformed into prebends of the monks and would have led to quota regulations of their number. Original Buddhism knew only gifts to individual monks.

Gradually this changed in the direction of the usual monastic organization. Doubtless, the *avasika,* i.e., the no longer migratory monks who are in residence in the monastery not only during the rainy season but permanently, represent, like the more stable definition of church parishes (*sima*), steps in the course of the development toward monastic landlordism. These resident monks were engaged in the study of the Sutras and other scientific work, as well as in meditation. Early Buddhism, however, had no esteem for scientific or other work. Moreover, the emergence of a literature as an object of study was, in terms of the purely oral tradition, undoubtedly secondary. So long as the older situation lasted it must result in an overflow onto the land of missionary disciples and monks, and it did indeed.

Yet Buddhism would hardly have been able to embark at least upon its career of international conquest without the historical accident that one of the first great kings, ruling almost over the entire Indian cultural area became its ardent adherent, as we shall soon see.

PART III

THE ASIATIC SECTS AND THE REDEMPTION RELIGIONS

CHAPTER VII

THE TRANSFORMATION OF ANCIENT BUDDHISM

1. General Reasons for the Transformation of Ancient Buddhism

Ancient Buddhism was, if not the last, at least the most uncompromisingly consistent and to this extent represents the perfection of the soteriology of the distinguished Hindu intellectuals.[1] Externally, Buddhism has been the only salvation religion which, at least for some time, namely, under the Maurya Dynasty, became the official religion of all India. To be sure, this was not permanent. Its inner consequence, and thereby also its external weakness, lay in the fact that in practice it confined salvation to those who actually followed the path to the end and became monks, and that at bottom it hardly bothered about the others, the laity. One can see from the prescriptions created for the laity that they represented external accommodations without an internally consistent point of view. Above all, there was lacking what Jainism had produced—a parish organization of the laity. Indeed, even the monastic organization was, as we saw, restricted to the barest essentials.

Historically, this lack of a lay organization has had the consequence that Buddhism has completely disappeared in its native land. Despite all accommodations, which we shall examine, it could not withstand the competition of other orthodox and heterodox Hindu sects which were able to structure the relationship between the laity and its leaders. Similarly, Buddhism proved to be incapable of resisting external force, particularly that of Islam.

In addition to the frightful destruction of the idols of all Hindu religions, the Mohammedan conquerors sought, quite naturally and particularly, to undermine all leading strata of the conquered people. This included the noble, so far as he could not be converted, and the monk, whom Islam justly considered to be the actual representative of organized communal religious life. As we shall see later, in the nature of Mohammedanism there was an initial antipathy to monkish asceticism. The "shorn Brahmans," the monks, and indeed, particularly Buddhistic monks were, therefore, the first whom the Mohammedans inconsiderately butchered.

In Buddhism, however, the very substance of the confession was concentrated in the cloisters and the community of monks. If these were destroyed so was the community. Actually, the Islam invaders permitted only traces of its existence to survive. So thorough was the destruction that even the location of the holy places, above all, of Lumbine, the "Indian Bethlehem," were completely forgotten until European archeological excavations again uncovered them. However, long before this external catastrophy the formal rule of Buddhism in India had been broken through the competition of other soteriologies. Moreover, in its vain, competitive struggle with them, Buddhism had itself deeply transformed its inner structure. This, however, did not allow it to maintain its domination in India, but essentially in this changed form it became, outside of India, a "world religion."

The driving factor of the transformation, alongside the unavoidable accommodation to actual conditions of the world, was the interest of the laity. Indeed, it was a laity essentially different from the Kshatriya and Shreshthi families in the time of its establishment.

Buddhism, as well as Jainism, first ascended with the support of the city nobles and, above all, the bourgeois patricians. The refusal of priestly knowledge and the intolerable ceremonious rules and regulations for living, the substitutions of the folk language for the incomprehensible dead Sanskrit language, the religious devaluation of caste relations for connubium and social intercourse, bound up with replacement of the unholy secular priesthood and its power of the keys by strata of holy seekers pursuing an earnest holy life—these were all features which must have gone far to meet lay culture halfway. This included both lay culture generally and particularly that of the patrician bourgeois strata of the time of the first flowering of the cities.

At the time, caste barriers were loosened, at least for admission to religious holiness. Only the Brahmanical Vedanta school stood fast on the principle that only a member of the "twice-born" castes could attain salvation. The Samkhya school had no scruples against viewing even the Shudra as capable of salvation, and Buddhism formally ignored caste membership, at least for admission into the monk order, though great importance was placed upon good manners and also—according to education—on good family, though it emphatically stressed the descent of most of its members from distinguished status circles.

2. *King Ashoka*

SOON after the expedition of Alexander had brought about the first, albeit transient contacts between North India and Hellenism, there arose for the first time, so far as is known, a great king in India in the Dynasty of the Maurya. The standing army and the officers, the kingly bureaucracy and its many bureaus of scribes, the kingly tax farmers, and the kingly police then formed the ruling powers. The city patricians were used as givers of loans and commissioners of supplies and services but they were gradually thrust into the background and the traders brought forward as bearers of liturgies and taxes in relation to the new administrative powers.

The patrimonialism of the great king took the place of the ancient petty kingdoms. Therewith the situation of nobles and bourgeois patricians was unavoidably changed. The Brahmanical tradition ascribes a low origin to the members of the Maurya Dynasty and, at least in the bureaucracy and officers' corps, a patrimonial prince must have been inclined to give the lower strata opportunities to rise. At first, this was in perfect agreement with the circumvention of status barriers by the Buddhistic salvation religion, and actually the great king Ashoka of the Maurya Dynasty who first succeeded in uniting the entire culture area of India into a unified empire, changed over to Buddhism first as a lay person, then even formally as a member of the order.

The relative leveling of the political power of the distinguished status groups, and especially the apparent elimination of the ancient Kshatriya stratum with its numberless small castles as independent centers of an eminent knightly culture, must have had profound ramifications for the social conditions of the competing religions. The souls of the laity for whom these religions struggled were no longer made up exclusively of educated nobles, but of courtiers, the literate officials, and the petty bourgeois and peasants. Princes, priests, and monks alike had an interest in how religious needs were met. The holders of political power saw in it an instrument to domesticate the masses. The champions of religion saw an opportunity to win pillars of spiritual power and a source of prebends and causal fees. Thus opened a plebeian epoch of orthodox Indian soteriology or, more correctly speaking, an epoch aimed at satisfying plebeian religious needs. The period can be compared to the time of Counter-Reformation in the Occident, and the following epochs, too, which coincided with the formation of great patrimonial states. To be sure, there was an important difference. In Europe the fixed hierarchical organization of the Catholic Church drew the conclusion, first in the emotional character of its propaganda-agitation, then in the bureaucratized structure of its administration resulting in a "chaplainocracy." In India, by contrast, a far more complicated adaptation had to be consummated by a hierarchy which represented only a cohesive status group or a loose association of monasteries but which was otherwise unorganized.

In early Buddhism court society missed the distinguished literary culture and opportunity for artistic stylization. It also missed the means for the domestication of the masses.

The petty bourgeois and peasant could make nothing of the products of the soteriology of educated gentility. Least of all could they find satisfaction from early Buddhistic soteriology. The petty bourgeois or peasant could as little think of yearning for *nirvana* as he could of uniting with the Brahman. Above all, he did not have the means at hand to attain these holy objects; it required leisure for the meditation necessary to achieve the gnosis. He had no such leisure and, as a rule, saw no reason for gaining such leisure by living as a penitent in the woods.

To some degree both orthodox and heterodox soteriology had prepared for this contingency: the orthodoxy through holy promises of caste ritualism; heterodoxy through a secondary lay morality, for which premiums in this and the future life were promised. However, all this was essentially negative and ritualistic in nature. It in no way satisfied the specifically religious need for emotional experience of the superworldly and for emergency aid in external and internal distress. Such unsatisfied emotional needs were and are always decisive for the psychological character of religion for the masses, in contrast to the rational character of all soteriologies of intellectuals.

For emotional mass religiosity there have been and are but two possible types of soteriology: magic or a savior. Or both may occur together, the living savior as magician and helper in physical and psychic need, the dead, deified savior as helper in need, as intercessor and super-earthly object of ardent devotion and emotional ecstatic reawakening in the experience of having the holy or being possessed by it. Almost all Indian soteriology took the course which showed adjustment to these specific plebeian religious needs. This is fundamental for the understanding of the developments which are now to be sketched.

In its relation to the laity ancient Buddhism was relatively, perhaps even absolutely, inimical to magic. The strict commandment (violation being punishable as a deadly sin) to the monk (fourth vow) not to boast of super-human abilities as his own, must, no matter how one restricts its bearing by interpretation, have precluded or at very least devalued the monk as a magical helper and therapist. Likewise, ancient Buddhism was at least relatively inimical to images. The Buddhist prohibition against pictorial representation is reliably transmitted and many genuine ancient Buddhistic reformers introduced into church art a certain reliable puritanism somewhat of the character of the Cistercians. This very often occurred, again as with the Cistercians, not to the injury of their art. Finally, ancient Buddhism had been simply apolitical. An inner relation to political power was hardly discoverable for it. In this last point appears the first change.

Ancient Buddhism reached its acme in India under the reign of the great Maurya king Ashoka, the first monarch who in the Egyptian and Assyrian manner saw to it that his deeds and arrangements were carved forever in countless mountain caves.[2] They report that the king received the opportunity to be a novice, then an official member of the order.[3] That he remained a king indicates the order's extensive accommodation and the king himself[4] emphasized how difficult it is to win this world and the future. The monarch, after all, was not considered to be an ordinary monk, but he accepted a special position. With this, for the first time in Buddhism, the beginnings of political theory emerge. The power of the world monarch (*tshakravati*) must necessarily supplement the spiritual power of Buddha, which necessarily leads away from all worldly action. The monarch is patron of the church somewhat in the sense claimed by the Byzantine monarchs.

Ashoka's edicts also indicate some of the peculiar ramifications of a semi-theocracy. The conversion of the king took place after the bloody conquest of the Kalinga-realm. The king declared[5] that he regretted the unavoidable butchery and the fact that many pious people were destroyed, that forthwith it would not belong to the *dharma* of his descendants to conquer by the sword and by and for the power of true belief, and that more important to him than even these peaceful conquests was the salvation of the soul in the next world. With this pacifistic-religious turn from the traditional kingly *dharma* came, as could not be otherwise, the development toward a patriarchal ethical and charitable ideal of a welfare state. The king who has[6] to care for country and people must work for the public welfare in order that the subjects be "happy" and "attain heaven." Allowance is made for reports to him at any time of those of his affairs which require speed.[7] He personally conducts an exemplary life, forswears war and the hunt, which was until then, as everywhere, propaedeutically linked to war service, taking the place of it in peacetime. Instead of this,[8] in his journeys he will engage in the propaganda of piety.[9] Corresponding to *ahimsa,* he prohibits slaughtering in the capital city of Pataliputra and festivals (*samaja*) bound up with meat orgies, and he announced, that in the royal kitchen forthwith no cattle would be slaughtered.[10] Hospitals for men and animals, as well as the required apothecaries, should be established. Fruit and shade trees should be planted[11] on the streets. Rest houses should be set up for men and animals and alms given them.[12] Unjust torture and imprisonment should cease.[13]

The most important peculiarity in this was the "tolerance" which results from the ancient Buddhistic prohibition against violence. The king declared that all his subjects, regardless of what belief, were his "children" and—with a turn of phrase which reminds us of the *Bhagavadgita*—that only the honesty and the earnestness of piety matter; the practical conclusions drawn from their teaching was that ceremonies and external rites are of little avail.[14] Of such things much mischief is made especially by women whom the king maligns;[15] probably sexual orgies are thought of and, indeed, morally corrupting practices that go with them.

The king does not think much of gifts and external reverence of religion but appreciates only that "the nature of the case" be carried out.[16] He honors all sects and all status groups, rich and poor, Brahman, ascetic, Jain, Ajivika (Vishnuistic ascetic-sect) and others like the Buddhists, if only each really adhere to his particular sect in true sincerity.[17]

And actually Ashoka supported all of the sects by foundations. Especially in the early edicts he expressed reverence of the Brahmans. The sects should desist from debasing one another which under all circumstances is wrong,[18] and turn to the cultivation of the ethical substance of their teaching. Obviously this seemed to the king to be essentially the same in all confessions, although it is most perfectly contained in the *dharma* of Buddha. He summarizes these generally binding rules as "laws of piety" and reportedly enumerated them as: (1) obedience to parents—(and the aged as such[19]); (2) liberality towards friends, relatives, Brahmans, ascetics; (3) respect for life; (4) avoidance of bad temper and excesses of all sorts.[20] Not everyone can fulfill the whole law. Each sect, however, can endeavor to control the senses, cultivate and spread purity of heart, thankfulness and loyalty.[21] Each good deed bears its fruit in the next world, often already in this one.[22] To control and carry out these ideas the king created special officials, usually called "censors" (*dharmaraharatra*). Apparently their first duty was to watch over the kingly and princely harems.[23] Furthermore, the provincial officials were to hold gatherings of the people who "are mild and patient and esteem life"[24] in all districts every five years. Through these gatherings, and certainly through other inspections of the censors, the laws of piety were to be propagated.

The conduct of women, further offenses against piety, and against the faithfulness requested by the king were to be censored.[25] The clergy[26] through instruction in the law should help the faithful. Thus we see a form which resembles the Carolingian system of emissaries and judicial censorship, without however, any formalistic basis which makes the whole set-up reminiscent of Cromwell's "Tryers" and, in general, his state of saints.

The king must have met with tangible resistance to this ethical syncretism. Against political rebellion the former criminal law in all its horror remained in operation. The three-day delay prescribed by the king before every execution, so that the sinner through meditation could at least save his soul,[27] will hardly have been experienced as a mitigation. One edict complains that the king had found to be disloyal[28] those whom he had trusted. Moreover, the side from which opposition developed seems also to have been discernible. In another edict[29] the king says that no fame is worth anything unless it be earned through the piety attainable only through complete renunciation of the goods of the world. But this is very difficult for the highly placed. And in the Rupnath edict[30] the king finds it necessary to emphasize especially that not only the great, but also the little man, through renunciation of the world, can achieve the heavenly goal. That the king considered these stipulations which were cumbersome to the ruling strata to be conclusions from Buddhism is indicated by the very dating of the Rupnath edict itself; the document is dated[31] from the time fixed for Buddha's historical flight from the world.

Thus, Buddhism is quite intentionally treated here as a specific leveling and, in this sense, a "democratic" religion, especially in connection with the very derogatory treatment of ritual, including caste ritual. Such purposeful opposition to the ruling strata was thoroughly lacking in ancient Buddhism. It was merely a latent possibility of its devaluation of the worldly order in general. The possibility cannot be completely rejected that precisely the linkage to patrimonial kingship first developed this latent possibility in Buddhism. If not this, patrimonialism certainly intensified it. Obviously, for the patrimonial kingship, Buddhism appears specifically valuable as a means of mass domestication.

The zeal of the king for Buddhism appears gradually to have increased. In similar form he also felt himself to be lord and patron of Buddhism, as the Byzantine monarchs did with respect to the Christian church. In the so-called Sanchi edict, he turns against the schismatics in the community (*samgha*), and prescribes that they wear not yellow but white cloths "for the *samgha* should be united."

However, formally, the greatest innovation, which most likely goes back to this king, who presumably first changed over to systematic administration by scribes and to the church council (allegedly the third) under him, was the fixing in writing of the two-and-a-half century long, orally-transmitted tradition. The Chinese pilgrim Fa-Hien, sent out by the Emperor to procure authentic (copies) of the holy books found in all India written scriptures only in the monasteries of Pataliputra (the seat of the kings and, allegedly, of the council) and in Ceylon and elsewhere only oral tradition. It is clear how much the writing-down meant for the preservation of the unity of the church, likewise, however, what it meant for the mission. In a land of literati like China, Buddhism could gain a footing only as a book religion. And actually the staging, or at least the programmatic pronouncement of the Buddhist world mission, goes back to Ashoka. He threw himself into the project with fiery zeal. Through him Buddhism received its first great push toward becoming an international world religion.[32]

Next the wild tribes were to be converted. Ambassadors were sent to foreign powers, particularly to the great Hellenistic powers of the West, to Alexandria, to make known the pure teaching in all the world; and a mission with the support of the king went to Ceylon and outlying Indian territories. No matter the actual results, at first success was considerable only in Ceylon and to the North. The great international expansion of Buddhism in Asia in any case had its ideal beginnings at that time. It has become and has remained the official confession of Ceylon, Burma, Annam, Siam, and other outlying Indian states, and of Korea, in a changed form later of Tibet, and for quite some time, Buddhism held sway over China as well as Japan. In order to qualify for this role the ancient soteriology of the intellectuals had to undergo deep transformations.

In the first place, it constituted a completely new situation for the order that a worldly ruler as such took its legal affairs into his hands. These legal affairs and their influence were not insignificant. Especially do the later classical areas show distinct features of the ancient, orthodox (Hinayana) Buddhism peculiar to the theocracy of Buddhistic monarchs. Throughout, the king appoints or (at least) confirms a "patriarch" of the Buddhistic territorial church (in Siam he is called *Sanharat,* in Burma *Thatanabiang,* and he is always an abbot of a charismatically distinguished cloister). It is, of course, quite contrary to the tradition—quite possible that this dignitary first emerged under Ashoka; previously, it appears, simply, that seniority (of the monastery and within it of the monk) was decisive. Besides, the king granted titles (as in Siam) to distinguished monks. Obviously this has developed out of the position of the king's chaplain.[33] He had the monasteries and their discipline supervised by secular officials and called monks to account for offences.

Thus Ashoka had an official position, at least in matters of church discipline. In fact, the king himself donned the monkish garb. However, he was himself dispensed by his *guru* from the full content of the vows: perhaps this is (though no proof is at hand) also a creation of Ashoka or of his successors. It served the purpose for the king of securing for him the ecclesiastical rank of monk. It has led to the general practice in orthodox (Hinayanistic) territories of temporarily joining the monkish community, considered to be a custom of social distinction and part of the education of young people; temporarily or partially the fulfillment of monkish duties by the laity became a specifically meritorious work furthering rebirth chances. Thereby a certain external approximation of lay piety to monkish holy seeking was brought about.[34] Elementary popular education, which in connection with the cloister education of gentility and in imitation of it had been set up by the monks for the mass of the laity, might have had more extensive ramifications had it been rational in nature. For at least in Burma popular education was almost universal. There, and in Ceylon, it included, corresponding to its purpose, reading and writing (in the local and sacred speech) and religious instruction (however, no mathematics for this was religiously useless). Again, it is not improbable that Ashoka's missionary zeal had given the first push toward this work with the laity, which was by no means close to ancient Buddhism.

For the first time in the Hindu culture area there appeared the idea of the "welfare state," of the "general good," (the promotion of which Ashoka regarded as the duty of the king). "Welfare" was, however, partially understood to mean spiritual welfare (as the furtherance of salvation chances), and partially to mean charities, but also rational and economic action. The tremendous irrigation works of the Ceylonese kings, however, like those of Northern India (Tschandragupta) even, were throughout fiscal in orientation, i.e., intended to augment the number of taxpayers and the capacity to pay taxes, not to implement welfare politics.

The transformations of the ancient Buddhistic monkhood was not exhausted with these theocratic ramifications. Given the momentum of the masses who took to the ancient monk community, it had first to soften the austere, world-fleeing character and to make extensive concessions to the abilities of the average monks, and also to the requirements of cloisters, which were not places established for the holy seeking of eminent thinkers but centers of religious mission and culture. For the rest, Buddhism had to meet halfway the needs of the laity, which in ancient Buddhism, given its nature, had essentially played an incidental role. Hence, soteriology had to be bent in the direction of faith in magic and saviors. The first of the two tendencies appears first clearly in the sources.

An edict of Ashoka speaks of the "schismatics" within the *samgha*. The Mahayanistic tradition[35] has it that the great schism first broke out (perhaps,[36] however, only under Ashoka and at his instigation) in the council (Sanghiti) of Vaicali, (allegedly, the second) which is supposed to have occurred 110 years after the death of Buddha. Independently of the historical accuracy of the details, the basis of the oldest schism is essentially clear according to the tradition as well as to the nature of the cases. The famous "ten theses" of the Vajji monks, over which agreement was not reached, were throughout disciplinary rather than dogmatic in nature. Along with some details of monastic conduct, all aimed at relaxing the discipline, an organizational question formed the prelude of the schism.[37]

There was one fundamentally important point at issue. It was the very same point over which, at the time, the Conventualists and Observants were divided in the Franciscan order, namely, the economic. The statutes of the founder forbid any sort of money possession, hence, as well, the acceptance of money donations. Now—the tradition relates—a strict observant rejected money donations. The majority of the monks declared this to be an insult to the laity. The man used the opportunity offered to him to recant publicly for protesting his rights. Whereupon, having preached to the community without an order to do so, he had to do penance. For the rest, according to the Hinayanistic tradition, the council presumably confirmed the orthodox tradition. Agreement, however, was not secured.

Along with the problems of discipline there soon appeared dogmatic controversies, and, indeed, first in connection with the doctrine of this-worldly salvation. It is transmitted that the chairman submitted three questions to the first council held under

Ashoka, namely, (1) whether an *Arhat* could fall from grace; (2) whether existence (of the world) was real; (3) whether *samadhi* (gnosis) could be attained by way of continuous thought. The first question had an important ethical aspect: Anomism (also fought by Paul Párta) would result from affirmation. The two other questions were connected with the doctrine of salvation. Above all, they indicate distinctly the appearance of speculation—corresponding to the Hellenistic penetration of ancient Christianity. Even the Mahimsashaska school was opposed by the Sarvastivada school which the chairman of the council joined and which sought to dam the advance of speculation. In vain. The later councils concerned themselves with dogmatism. The respective minorities refused to recognize them, charging biased composition of the councils. Thus, in one form, the schism was at hand.

In the course of time, the parties were essentially distributed geographically, in such a way that the ancient Buddhist strict observance (Hinayana) finally prevailed in Southern India; the lax direction (Mahayana, the "great ship," i.e., the universal church) since the first century A.D. dominated in the North.[38]

3. *Mahayana Buddhism*

THE tradition suggests, as is probable, that the laity, either from the beginning or later, stood on the side of the more lax form of Buddhism, which was originally called Mahasamghika (great community),[39] currently Mahayana in opposition to Sthaviras, the "elders," i.e., proven charismatic *arhats*. As a specialty of the Mahasamghika is transmitted the co-operation of the laity in the councils. Of course, this did not concern the "lower" classes—who never were or could be spoken of as an active driving element—but, precisely, the ruling strata. Also, distinguished ladies are said to have excelled as partisans of the Mahayana school. This is just as conceivable as the partisan stand of the Holy See in the fourteenth century in favor of the conventualists and against the Observants of the Franciscans.

The dependency of the monks on the ruling strata was the greater the less world-denying they were. The almost unrestricted clerical sway of the Hinayana-orthodoxy in Ceylon and Burma over the laity, against which the secular rulers often proved to be completely powerless, had—as indicated in the soon to be mentioned reports of the Chinese pilgrims—repeatedly occurred in Northern India under the dominance of ancient Buddhism. The same struggle between lay power and the monkhood, which went on for centuries in the Byzantine Empire, was also fought in India, though in different forms. Secular authorities were interested in using the monks as a means of domesticating the masses. Although the masses have never been an active force of Buddhistic religiosity, they have, of course, played a decisive role here as the object of rule by means of religious belief, as is the case in all religious postures of the ruling strata. By way of hagiolatry, however, the Buddhistic monks, too, often attached the masses strongly to themselves.

Alongside this political factor there appeared the growing influence of Brahmanical school speculation and its concepts on Buddhistic thought. J-Tsing's description from the seventh century[40] still permits us to recognize that the linkage was primarily sought for pedagogical-technical reasons. He thought the technique of learning the Vedas was unsurpassed as a means for formal training of the mind, particularly for retention of one's own, but also of one's opponent's arguments.

Literary interests demanded simply the pursuit of science and of the five *vidya:* grammar (always most important), medicine, logic, philosophy, and, also, the theoretical pursuit of "fine arts" (*silpasthanavidya*) which had been demanded by the literary circles of artists. These emerged—even in the Hinayana school itself—and willy-nilly had to make use of ancient Brahmanical speech. Monastic schools for the laity and primers for children were created. The express recognition of the caste organization,[41] which had previously been ignored, provides sufficient proof of the influence of cultured strata not only on the whole development but particularly on Mahayana. The influence of cultured strata is also shown by the external circumstance that this school, in opposition to the ancient Hinayana Buddhists, participated in the renaissance of Sanskrit which had Kashmir as its point of departure. Its holy scriptures were written in the ancient scholarly language. The Pali-canon remained in possession of the Southern Buddhists.

Gradually, the sacred literature was divided completely as between the two Jain sects. For in every respect the antagonism of the schools very soon spread beyond the initial disciplinary point of departure. The picture which one derives from the travel descriptions of Fa Hien's (around 400 A.D.)[42]—who, though personally a Mahayanist, stayed for two years in Ceylon, the stronghold of orthodoxy—is still one of relative peace. The teaching had spread as far as Turkestan. Completely corresponding to the edict of Ashoka, the kings there[43] arranged for the five-year assemblies. In Nagrak (near Jelladabad) the king attended divine service each morning; similarly, in Takshasila.

A century later, accounts[44] indicate that the kings in the Punjab, partly as late as the sixth century, continued to live as strict vegetarians and did not mete out capital punishment. For the region of Mathura, Fa Hien[45] relates that the officers of the king had fixed incomes, that people were not tied to the soil, that taxes were low, and that the system of head and tax registration, usual in great patrimonial Indian states, did not exist, that all creatures were spared, no meat was eaten, no swine were kept, no cattle trade tolerated, no intoxicating drinks were permitted, and onions and garlic were enjoyed only by the (impure) Tschandala caste, also, capital punishment was lacking.

Ashoka's empire had long since disintegrated. However, relatively pacifistic principalities prevailed in Northern India. In Oude (between Kashmir and Kabul), as well as in Kanouj, the Hinayanistic school held sway. In the ruins of Ashoka's capital city, Pataliputra (Patna) were monasteries of both schools and in the region of Farakhabad they shared the same residence.[46] In the area of Mathura where political conditions have just been reported, the Mahayana school ruled, though not exclusively. Buddhistic Brahmans are described[47] as *gurus* of the kings in the neighborhood of Pataliputra. Sung Yun even stated that, whereas a conquering king in Gandhara scorns Buddha, the people "belonged to the Brahman caste" and have the greatest respect for the laws of Buddha.[48]

Buddhism was and continued to be the doctrine of genteel intellectuals. All these pilgrims were interested (just as two centuries later was the pilgrim Hiuen-Tsang), solely in the behavior of the kings and their court officials. Obviously, by the time of Hiuen-Tsang (628 and the years following) quite a few things had changed. First, there is the opposition of the Mahayana school against the Hinayanistic orthodoxy. A Hinayanist became sorely sick because he reviled Mahayana.[49] Actually, Mahayana is discussed and Hiuen-Tsang thought it was not necessary to go to Ceylon. In addition, there was a growing interpenetration of specifically Brahmanical elements into the increasingly dominant Mahayana doctrine. India was called by Hiuen-Tsang the "Kingdom of the Brahmans" (*To-lo-man*).

Statues of Brahma and Indra stood in the holy temples of the Ganges Valley beside the statue of Buddha.[50] The Vedas (*Wei ho*) are termed "subaltern," that is to say, lay literature,[51] but they are read. The king of Kosala honored beside Buddha, however, in the Brahmanical temple, the Hindu Devas.[52] Although there were still kings (Ciladitya) who yearly called the great councils of Buddhistic clergymen,[53] this is clearly not the rule. One gets the impression of an increasingly sharpened antagonism of the schools. The Hinayana in North India is pushed back, but Buddhism generally is declining.

For the sharpening of the antagonism between Mahayana and Hinayana the ancient disciplinary differences were no longer decisive.

In Hinayana, too, the ancient prohibition of money possession by strict observance was circumvented by the same means as with the Franciscans. Lay representatives received the money and managed it for the monks; even in the old orthodox church of Ceylon the alms bag finally held sway.

Monastic landlordism and permanent monastic residence (not, as originally, restriction of monks to the cloister in the rainy season), appeared here and there, and for a time quite extensively—as is yet to be explained. This occurred even in Ceylon, the seat of strict observance. In the Mahayana church, antagonism and adaptation needs of a different religious type have been much more decisive for the further development away from the ancient soteriology. In first line were the religious interests of the laity, who required consideration for reasons of propaganda. The laity had no wish for *nirvana* and could not be satisfied with an exclusively exemplary prophet of self-salvation such as Buddha. The laity demanded helpers-in-need for life here and now and paradise in the hereafter. Therefore, in Mahayana the process began which is usually described as the replacement of *Pratyeka-Buddha* and *arhat* (self-salvation) with the *bodhisattva* (redeemer) ideal.

While the Hinayana school divides its adherents into *cravakas* (laity) and *pratyeka-Buddhas* (self-savers and *arhats,* the saved) as religious status groups, the *bodhisattva*-ideal became the peculiar and common characteristic of the Mahayana sect. It presupposed an inner transformation of the salvation theory. In the early times of Buddhism, as we saw, there occurred a struggle between the "elders" (*sthaviras*) that is to say, the charismatic representatives of the parish tradition and the *mahsamghika,* the speculatively schooled thinkers, the intellectuals. From the questions of discipline and practical ethics, speculation moved to questions of the "*sattva*" problems, questions concerning the nature and state of salvation and hence first, concerning the person to be saved. The old school maintained Buddha's human quality. The Mahayanistis developed the "*Trikaya*" theory, the doctrine of the supernatural character of the Buddha. He has three appearances: first, the *nirmana kaya,* the "Transformed body" in which he wanders on earth; then he might take the form of the *sambhoga kaya,* somewhat like the "Holy Ghost" the all-pervasive "ethereal" body constituting the community; and, finally, Buddha appears as the *dharma kaya,* of which more below.

Thus the typical Hindu deification process took its course first with regard to the person of Buddha. To this was joined the Hindu incarnation apotheosis. Buddha was represented as an embodiment of (impersonal) divine grace, which appeared ever anew on earth in a series of rebirths and for which, often, also an *Adi-buddha* was thought to exist. From there it was no great step to fashion the Buddha into a type, the representative of the saint who has fully achieved salvation and is thereby deified and who could have appeared and still may appear in as many copies as one wishes. "Self-deification" was the ancient Indian meaning of asceticism and contemplation, but with these conceptions, the living redeemer had entered the belief. However, the living redeemer is the *bodhisattva.* Formally, the *bodhisattva* was bound up with the Buddha, first through the theory of rebirth and the concept taken over from the Hindu philosophy of world epochs.

The world is eternal. However, its course—as earlier indicated —runs forever in new and finite epochs. There was now thought to be one Buddha in each world epoch and all together there were an infinite number of Buddhas. The historical Gautama Buddha of the present epoch had passed through 550 rebirths before his entrance into *nirvana.* With the penultimate rebirth as the saintly *arhat,* who in the next rebirth would be Buddha, the state of *bodhisattva* (whose nature, *sattva* is illumination, *bodhi*) is attained. He dwells in *tuschita*-heaven where even now the future Buddha, Maitraya is sojourning as *bodhisattva.*

By a miraculous incarnation in the body of his mother, *maya,* the historical Gautama Buddha himself had come from the *tuschita* to his last journey on earth in order to bring his teaching to man before his entrance to *nirvana.* Clearly, with his "blowing away," interest had to turn to the coming savior, the *bodhisattva.* Also, it is clear, that in this simple and rational scheme per se of the *tuschita*-heaven and the plurality of Buddhas and *bodhisattvas,* there were subtle points of departure for the formation of a pantheon, for rebirth mythologies, and miracles of all sorts.

We shall not concern ourselves with the mythologies swollen to fabulous dimensions, but rather with its ethical-soteriological aspect. As noted, a *bodhisattva* was, ideally, a saint who has attained "perfection," and who with the next rebirth can be a Buddha and arrive at *nirvana.* When this does not happen and he remains, rather, a *bodhisattva* it was held to be an act of grace which he dispenses so that he may work as a helper-in-need to the believer. Hence he became the peculiar object of Mahayanistic hagiolatry. It is clear this change went far toward meeting lay interest in the holy.

Active goodness (*paramita*) and grace (*prasada*) are the attributes of the *bodhisattva.* He is not only there for his own salvation but at the same time and primarily for the sake of man. As it is expressed in Mahayanistic terminology, the Buddha is not only a *pratyekabuddha* but also a *sammasambuddha.* He could not possibly resolve to achieve his own salvation alone from this world of suffering so long as there were still others left there to suffer. *Upaya* (the duty, actually, in characteristic ceremonial terminology "propriety") hindered him.

The speculative doctrine of a trinity which had emerged in the Mahayana school made this easier for the *bodhisattva.* He had experienced *nirvana* only in the first of his forms of existence, the *nirvana kaya.* The difference between the Buddhistic and Christian trinity is characteristic. The Buddha becomes a man, such as the second figure of the Christian Trinity, in order to save men. He saves them, however, not by suffering, but through the mere fact that now he, too, is transient and as a goal has only *nirvana* before him. And he saves them by example, not as the representative sacrifice for their sins. For it is not sin, but transitoriness which is evil.

All these examples point out the third direction of the adaptation process to which Mahayana was subject. In addition to adaptation to economic conditions, and adaptation to the needs of the laity for a helper in time of stress, was adaptation to the needs of Brahmanically-schooled intellectuals. The simple banning of all speculation on things useless for salvation, as Buddha had consistently done, could not be upheld. A whole religious-philosophical literature came into existence, increasingly and exclusively employing the classical language (sanskrit), establishing universities, holding debates and religious disputations, and developing, above all other things, a somewhat complicated metaphysics in which all ancient controversies of classical Indian philosophy were revived.

With this, however, the rift between the knowledgeable theologians and philosophers and the illiterates, valued only as exoteric fellow-travelers, was in quite Brahmanical manner, imported into Buddhism. Again, schoolbook knowledge rather than personal gnosis was strong in the community. As in the literati circles of China, India was considered to be only the "land of the Brahmans." From the standpoint of Mahayana literati under Hiuen-Tsang it was held that China was a barbarian (*mlechcha*) country. That is why Buddha was incarnated on Indian cultural territory and not anywhere else.

And Hiuen-Tsang's characteristic counter-argument took for its point of departure the fact that in China, too, the old and wise were first. Science, including astronomy, blossomed there and the power of music was known.[54] This concept was completely fashioned for the theology of Brahmanical, or, let us say, Asiatic or perhaps even antique intellectuals. Ancient Brahmanical concepts and, indeed, by this time also Vedantic ones—above all, the central concept for Vedanta, "*maya*" (cosmic illusion)—served to substructure the theology of Mahayana Buddhism only in reinterpretations.

It is hardly an accident that Mahayana Buddhism in Northern India developed increasingly next door to the ancient centers of Brahmanical philosophy and soteriology, while the orthodox Hinayan doctrine, after a number of ups and downs held its own in the missionary work of the South, namely, in Ceylon, Burma and Siam—similar to the way in which Rome and the West always represented the stronghold in all the councils against the innovations of Hellenism in the ancient Christian Church, while in the Orient the neighbors of Hellenistic philosophy let loose dogmatic speculation.

Perhaps reminiscences of Samkhya doctrine are to be found in the Mahayana theory of the *alaya-vijnana,* the soul which is not strictly opposed to all nonspiritual things. Here we touch a fundamental opposition to ancient Buddhism. Precisely the denial of the "soul" concept had been one of its essential peculiarities. But this idea was certainly soon given up. As the "metempsychosis" of Buddhism turned into the Brahmanical concept and did not retain the ancient pure doctrine, so, too, was the case of the concept of divine potency. As in Vedanta, it is the conception of the "pan psychic" and the extreme spiritualization of the world, conceived as an emanation closely approaching the *Maya* doctrine which occasionally appears explicitly. Everything is but subjective appearance; supreme knowledge dissolves it. Finally, the beginnings of a revival of an organic relativism of ethics is reminiscent of the Bhagvadgita.

The *bodhisattva* appears, like Krishna, ever anew on earth and can, corresponding to the *trikaya* doctrine, according to the ethical needs of the world, appear in any form and profession according to demand. He can appear not only as a man but also as an animal—to save souls lost among animals—and if as a man, then in each ritually respectable profession. Hence he appears also, above all, as a warrior. According to his nature he would fight only just and good wars. But when he does fight he will be unhesitatingly free of scruples. This theory, in practice, represents the most extensive adaptation to the needs of the world.

Theoretically, these accommodations were predicted on the introduction of some sort of super-worldly divine being, and we saw, indeed, that even in the deification of Buddha himself this was consummated. However, Buddha was in *nirvana,* forever vanished from the world, and could not himself or at least alone represent the supreme godhead. Corresponding to the canonical starting point of the teaching, once it had been established, the World God could not be a personalized world deity in the manner of Vishnu or Shiva. The absolute infinity and supernatural quality of the divine was supplemented by his strictly impersonal attributes: *bhutatathata,*[55] the quality of being and through the opposition of *ashunya* (the "void," the "non-real") as the specifically holy, over and against *cunya* (the "complete," "real"), quite in the manner of occidental mystic attempts and also of the Upanishads to describe the possession of godhead. The ultimately inexpressible divinity thereby displayed, naturally, an inclination, corresponding to the *triratna* of ancient Buddhism, in which *dharma* appears as a divine potency[56] to assume features of the Chinese "Tao," namely, coming to be the order and real ontological basis of the world, to equate eternal norms and eternal being. The absolute had to be found beyond the sharp dualism of eternal being, and the absolute transitoriousness of the phenomenal world was ordered by eternal norms (or *karma*). In this, the inviolability of *karma* was the point where it could be seized by Hindu metaphysics. The mystical experience embodies here as everywhere not "norms" but, on the contrary, a felt "being." The supreme godhead of Mahayana Buddhism, the *Kharmakaya,* was, because of this unbridgeable, rational, but quite unavoidable opposition, self-evidently not only beyond any "Word" but able to embody rationally heterogeneous predicates. The fact that *karuna,* supreme love, and *bodhi,* supreme knowledge, unite in the relation of the saint to the godhead is explainable only in terms of the psychological qualities of mystical ecstasy.

If *nirvana*—a condition which moves into a derivative secondary position—was at the same time negatively conceived as the destruction of all desire and positively as "all-love," there remained, as before, *avidya,* stupidity as the source of all evil. This is explainable in terms of the strict intellectual origin of this soteriology. Mahayana is again simply an esoteric salvation doctrine for the gnostics, not for the laity. The principle of Buddha's teaching, so important in practice, that generally speculation over unsolvable problems is evil and dangerous to salvation, is given up in a characteristic manner. After-effect consisted only in the following: according to orthodox Mahayana teaching the last great cosmic mystery—the question of how the peculiar great root of all evil, the *avidya* (stupidity, obtuseness, or cosmic illusion) could have come into the world—remained unsolvable for human wisdom, just as the why of the specific qualities of *bhutatathata* revealed itself only to the last and highest, verbally incommunicable gnosis of a *bodhisattva.*

The redeeming gnosis, however, is characterized by the peculiarly dualistic features which combine a practical sentiment of love with controlled concentration of thought. According to the orthodox Mahayana doctrine, such gnosis passes through continual *exercitia spiritualia,* rising in ten stages of warm love (*pramudita*), the purification of heart (*vimala*), the clarity of cosmic insight (*prabakhari*), the striving for perfection (*arcismati*), the meditation over the nature of *tathagata* (*sudurjaya*), over the nature of world emanations (*abhimuki*), the production of world estrangement in spite of inner-worldly acts (*durangam*, the "going far away"—which is closely related to the inner attitude of the Bhagavata familiar to us), the attainment of full composure as a personal quality become unconscoious and part of one's nature and effortlessly practised (*achala*), the full *gnosis* of transcendant truths (*sadhumati*), and, finally the vanishing of the "clouds of *dharma*" (*dharmamegha*): omniscience.

One can readily observe the crossing of gnostic and practical elements of acosmic love. The *nirvana* conception of the Mahayana school also has traces of this crossing. Besides the absolute escape in *dharmakaya* with death, which now, in Vedantic manner replaced complete extension, there were distinguished two kinds of this-worldly *nirvana:* (1) *Upadhicesa nirvana,* the freedom from passion which, however, has not yet been freed from *samsara* because intellectual gnosis was lacking—always the characteristically relational element in Buddhism;[57] and (2) *Anupadhicesa nirvana: upadhi* (materialization), free *nirvana,* which through full gnosis is a this-worldly state of bliss of the *jivanmukti,* freed from *samsara.* However, what is characteristic for the Mahayana school is that the concept of inner-worldly *nirvana* is not thereby exhausted. Besides world-fleeing mysticism there is found (3) the inner-worldly mysticism of a world-indifferent life, which proves itself precisely within and against the world and its manipulations. Inwardly it escapes from the world and death and accepts birth and death, rebirth and renewed death, life and action with all their apparent joys and apparent griefs as the eternal forms of being; it is in this that the mysticism maintains its assurance of salvation (*ceritudo salutis*).

The Buddhistic turn of the scholarly form of inner-worldly world indifference which appears in the Bhagavadgita represents the wisdom and feeling of the absolute nothingness of those events over and against the timeless value of the conscious unity with *dharmakaya,* and thereby with all creatures who are encompassed with acosmic compassionate love. Traces of this point of view extend far back[58] and it is understandable that this approach should be represented at present as the truly authentic Mahayanistic one[59] for it allows for the interpretation of the *bodhisattva* idea in the sense of a very modern mysticism.

In any case, even in about the fifth century of our calendar, Vasubandus' "*Awakening of the Bodhicitta*" seems already to have been translated into Chinese and to embody the doctrines for this turn of the *Bodhisattva* idea. *Bodhicitta*[60] is the capacity slumbering in each human heart for "knowing love" which awakened wakes *pranidhana,* that is, the unshakable will to work as *tathagata* (redeemer) through the whole sequence of one's own births for the salvation of the brethren. The *bodhisattva* who has attained this quality wins thereby the capability not only to produce his own salvation but—and this is what matters to him—to accumulate a treasure of merits from which he can dispense grace. Thus he is in this sense sovereign against the brazen power of *karma* compensation.

Thus the theoretical basis was won for satisfying the religious needs of the aliterary lay strata which ancient Buddhism had been unable to offer, namely, living redeemers (*tathagatas* and *bodhisattvas*) and the possibility of dispensing grace—self-evidently and primarily magical grace for the here and now, and only secondarily grace for the future, for rebirth and the hereafter. While the spiritualistic form of the Mahayana doctrine, as produced in North Indian philosophic schools exists here, yet it is obvious that in the practice of religious life the ubiquitous, customary, lay representations gained the upper hand. Nagarjuna, who in the first post-Christian century founded the Mahayana teaching had in his *prajna paramita* (transcendal wisdom which has attained the shore of the future) indeed taught the "void" as the specific form of existence (*sattva*) of the saved. Besides a combination "of all means of self alienation described as the "middle way" (*madhyamika,*[61] including particularly alms-giving and readiness to die for the suffering creature), he held continuous meditation and knowledge (*prajna*) as the last and highest means of achieving the holy. However, even he considered the sage to be endowed with magical power. With verbal spell (*dharani*) and mystical finger-placing he compels men and natural spirits. Finally, with Vasubandhu's teaching, four hundred years later *tantra* folk magic, namely, the attainment of the ecstatic *samadhi* state imparting magical power (*siddhi*) was introduced alongside the Hindu pantheon. With this the development was completed; Vasubandhu was held to be the last *bodhisattva.*

A rational inner-worldly conduct was not to be established on the basis of this philosophically distinguished, spiritualistic soteriology of Mahayana. The elaboration of the ancient lay ethic does not go beyond recommending the customary virtues and the special Hinduistic-Buddhistic rituals—elements which in our context it is not worth-while to analyze in detail. For obedience to the superhuman miraculously qualified *bodhisattvas* and magic was, of course, the dominant trait. Magical therapy, apotropaic and magical homeopathic ecstasy, idolatry and hagiolatry, the whole host of deities, angels, and demons made their entrance into Mahayana Buddhism. Above all, it accepted Heaven, Hell, and a Messiah.[62] In the seventh heaven enthroned on high, beyond "craving" for life[63] and for "name and form" (individuality),[64] dwells the Bodhisattva Maitreya, the future savior, the bearer of specific Buddhistic messianic belief.[65] Moreover, the terrors of Hell are at hand. And, finally, part of the Mahayanistic steps of salvation were transformed into a formal career of salvation in which the *arhat* was sub-ordered into three steps of which the highest answered rebirth in heaven as an *arhat;* the next, rebirth as an arhat after still other death, and the lowest rebirth as *arhat* after seven more deaths.[66]

Mahayanism, first through formalistic prayers, finally, through the techniques of prayer mills and prayer ships hung in the wind or spat-upon idols, attained the high point of cult mechanism and joined it to the transformation of the entire world into an immense magical garden. In this development we must not overlook those traits of inwardness and charitable compassion for all creatures which Buddhism and in Asia, Buddhism alone, wherever it went has incorporated into the sensitiveness of peoples. In this, its impact resembled that of the mendicant monks of the Occident. Typically such traits are also explicit in the very virtues of Mahayana religion. They are, however, by no means specific to Mahayana religion as over against the Hinayana school.

In Mahayana, however, there was development toward a rational life-method of the laity. Far from such a rational lay religiosity, Mahayana Buddhism has combined only an esoteric and essentially Brahmanical intellectual mysticism with coarse magic, idolatry, and hagiolatry or edifying prayer formulas for the laity.[67]

The Hinayana school had its origin in the soteriology of a cultured laity in so far as it developed a form of systematic monastic education of the laity, which soon generated into convention. The sons of good families were accustomed—presumably since Ashoka's entrance into the order—as in correct Hinayanistic communities they are, to spend some time (nowadays, to be sure at times only four days, hence, essentially symbolically) in the monastery as a *bhikshu.* With Hinayana Buddhism, however, monastic schools for lay needs in the form of elementary schools existed, presumably since Ashoka. Such are reported for Mahayana Buddhism, at least as systematically maintained institutions, only of single sects in Japan. One may well assume that the clerical zeal of King Ashoka has left this strain toward "inner mission" as a lasting imprint upon the Hinayana school.

While the actual doctrine of salvation of Buddhism represented the soteriology of genteel intellectuals, one cannot deny that its indifference to the castes also had practical ramifications. Some of its ancient schools are expressly recorded as having been founded by Shudras.[68] And during the time of its origin, coinciding with an epoch of guild power, doubtless there existed also a demand among the bourgeois strata for literary education. Instruction represented, so far as is known, no school of rational thought and life, but always aimed merely at the diffusion of the most necessary religious knowledge. Still, with the Hinayana school, since its writings were in the vernacular, reading was possible under certain conditions.

CHAPTER VIII

THE MISSIONS

1. *Ceylon and Outlying Indian Territories*

A DIRECT foundation of Hinayanaism, perhaps more rightly, of the preschismatic ancient Buddhistic orthodoxy is to be found in the Singhalese (Ceylonese church).[1] This occurred a few centuries after the Aryan conquest (345) when (presumably) Malinda, a son of Ashoka, made his appearance as a missionary. In spite of frequent reverses, repeated conquest by Malabars and especially the South Indian Tamils and once by the Chinese, the rule of the Buddhistic monastic hierarchy has yet been permanently maintained. This was supported by kingship based upon a magnificent irrigation system and the requisite bureaucracy which made Ceylon the grainery of southern Asia. The hierarchy, in turn, served the kings in the domestication of the people. Very extensive land grants and the inculcation of the reader with the authority of the monastic hierarchy fill up almost the entire epigraphic[2] and chronistic[3] legacy of the time of the Ceylonese rulers.

The decisive feature of Ceylonese Buddhism was a monastic landlordism pre-empting about one-third of the land. Primarily this institution facilitated at least formal obedience to the canonical prohibition of pecuniary possessions. Daily mendicancy characteristically practiced in ancient genteel forms has clearly turned into a ritual act. All the requirements of the cloister and the cult established for the laity and the maintenance requirements of the temple were apportioned among the peasants who, as hereditary tenants, lived on land grants allotted to them. The institution is reminiscent of the ancient Carolingian Fisci and monastic landlordism somewhat in the manner of the *Kapitulare de villis*. However, its consistent consummation of the principles of natural economy was superior in that the specified taxes in food and handicraft products of all sorts did not (or should not have) required purchases of any consumer goods. The tax burden of the hereditary tenants was so light in this that even the British rulers, after an intensive investigation and in agreement with the copy holders themselves, at first abstained from changing the taxes. Naturally, adjustments in details have repeatedly been made. On the whole the descriptions of earlier and modern travelers have confirmed the picture. The life of the monks in the monasteries, particularly their lodgings (*pansala*), was modest, more modest than that in an Italian *certosa*, and was based on the essential rules of the *pratimokka*. The notorious covetousness of the order as such concerned essentially the augmenting of its holdings.

So far as it to be viewed as Buddhist at all, lay piety found its point of gravity in the worship of relics (above all, the cult of Buddha's tooth) and in hagiolatry, in agreement with the nature of the relation of Buddhism to the laity. The influence of the clergy in the form of *gurus*, exorcists, and therapists must have been rather significant politically[4] so far as non-Hinduistic (heterodox) castes like the Kammalars (royal artisans) did not resist it.

Nowhere, outside Burma, did the practice of Buddhistic lay rules so nearly approximate theoretic demands. These rules, however, placed quite modest and essentially formalistic demands on the laity. Instruction in reading and writing, listening to the sermons, temporary asceticism, the mantic art, and the consultation of the monks as magicians exhausted the Buddhistic life content. In practice, belief in demons dominated the life of the laity and there were heterodox magicians (especially exorcists for sickness). Certainly the monastic community itself has always been held in high honor as guardian of the pure tradition and the canonical writings.

It is usual to consider the outlying Indian territories as pure mission territory of Hinayana Buddhism. This does not hold without qualification. The diverse political structures which arose there through repeated conquests were exposed to Hinduistic (Brahmanical) and Hinayanistic as well as, apparently, Mahayanistic religious influences. Brahmans, Vedic education, and at least the beginnings of caste formation (castes of artisans) were to be found. Indeed, only the nearness of Ceylon as a missionary center determined the fact that in the end the Hinayana school won the field, particularly after the conquering Mongolian princes had joined it, and their advance in the Middle Ages determined the prevailing distribution of political power of the single states down to the time of European occupation. Meanwhile, as the inscriptions indicate, everything was repeatedly in flux.

As a rule the need for domestication of the subjects and for rational administration based on written records supplied the occasion for the kings to call scribes into the land: these were, indeed, either Brahmanical, Mahayanistic, or, at last, Hinayanistic. Very soon even in folk belief *samsara* and *karma* were generally self-understood presuppositions. However, for quite some time Brahmanical and Buddhistic education were to be found side by side. In the eighth century in a Buddhistic inscription in Siam, Brahmans were mentioned and still in the sixteenth century a King supported the "Buddhistic and the Brahmanical religion."[5] Meanwhile, in due form, Ceylonese Buddhism had become the state religion.[6] *Gurus* and *acharyas* (teachers) are mentioned in a kingly edict from the tenth century.[7] Great donations of slaves and real estate to cloisters took place at various times. However, only since the fifteenth and sixteenth centuries has it been unambiguously clear that this concerns Buddhistic, and indeed, Hinayanistic cloisters.[8] What occurred meanwhile is shown rather distinctly in the inscription of a great Siamese king of the fourteenth century.[9] The king describes himself as one informed in the Vedas. He yearns, as he says, for Indra's Heaven but he is striving also for *nirvana* at the end of the transmigration of souls. Therefore he founds and builds extensively by means of his own artisans. Not withstanding the Buddhistic character of the inscription the main objects of construction were two statues and temples to the great Hindu gods Shiva (Paramesvara) and Vishnu. As the crowning act of merit the king then sent to Ceylon and has a Ceylonese sage import the first Tripitaka-canon. In so doing the king declared himself to be willing to renounce the Heaven of Indra and Brahma and to become a Buddha, who brings to all his subjects the good of salvation from the world.[10]

He personally joined the order—doubtless in order now as pontifex to guide the church and by this means to lead his subjects. However, according to the inscriptural account, in consequence of his excessive piety such dangerous wonders occurred that the mighty of the kingdom urged him again to leave the order and rule the empire as a lay person. He followed the advice with the consent of the holy man. As one can see, quite essential considerations of political power were involved, and, at the occasion of his entrance into the order, matters of the usual Hinayanistic reception and dispensation.

The monastic organization was and always remained correctly Hinayanistic. After the novitiate (*shin*) the monk is received as *u pyin-sin* and after having proven himself in about ten years, during which time he dedicates himself merely as a prebendary in the cloister to the spiritual exercises, he becomes a full monk, *bonze*, or in Burmese, *pon-gyi* ("great renown") and acquires qualification to cure souls as a *guru*. Even the inscriptions from thirteenth-century Siam indicate that this principle of grading the dignity and titles of monks according to seniority even then was just as correctly practiced in agreement with the ancient Buddhistic principle.

Accordingly the monks in Siam were honored by the titles of *Guru, Thera,* and finally as *Mahathera* and were in part cenobites, in part eremites. Their functions, however, were always the same: to serve as *gurus,* spiritual advisors to the laity, and as teachers of the holy wisdom. An upper-*guru,* called *sankharat* (teacher), was appointed by the king and headed them up as patriarch of the church.[11] Here the king, as once Ashoka did, claimed the position of secular patron, *membrum eminens* (*tschakravati*) of the church. However, the king expressly preserved the ancient cult of the mountain spirits because its omission might endanger the well-being of his subjects.[12]

Primarily the king had also called the Buddhistic sages for the sake of inventing a national system of writing.[13] Doubtless, this was desirable in the interests of administration. As the monuments plainly show, the Siamese kings, especially at the time of the reception, were engaging in military expansion in all directions and were fighting against Chinese attempts at expansion.[14] The administration developed a royal army and a bureaucratic administration. A star-chamber judicial procedure was employed.[15] And the administration strove to break the power of the presumably feudal—notables.[16]

Standing under the patronage of the monarchs, monastic Hinayana Buddhism had to help in this and doubtlessly did so with success. The significance of the ancient sib-relationships was greatly reduced by the power of the hierarchy. In large parts of the outlying Indian territories, obviously, the prerogatives of kingship were no longer restrained by the sibs as was the case elsewhere in Asia. The power of the monks compensated for this.

The monastic priest held almost absolute sway over the people also in things political under the Buddhistic rulers. The rather especially strict (external) discipline in the hands of the abbots (*sayah*) facilitated this. A monk excommunicated for an offence against one of the four great commandments or because of disobedience was boycotted and not able to exist. Also, the obedience of the laity to the monks was boundless. This spiritual stratum was—particularly in Burma—the real champion of the native civilization and was, therefore, one of the strongest opponents of European rule, which threatened their position.

For a time each young lay person from a good family in Burma—as with us daughters are sent to a boarding school—is sent to a monastery. He lives there for a short time (one day to a month) as a monk and receives a new name. In this manner the "rebirth" of ancient magical asceticism was transposed into this purely ritualistic cloister internment.

In lay life, however, the *nal* (spirits) hold unbroken sway. Each household had its *nal* (protective demon). For the rest, they correspond to the *deva* of the Hindus. After death the king was still thought of as entering the "village of the spirits," (*Nal-Ya-tsane-thee*).

Economically the domination of Hinayanism in the outlying Indian territories may well have been co-responsible for the overwhelming importance of tranditionalistic husbandry and, in comparison to India, visible inferiority of technical and industrial development. The Buddhistic monasteries were as little places of rational work as were any other Asiatic monasteries. At that, Hinayanism depreciated caste *dharma* even more strongly than did Mahayanism, or where Hinayana was introduced into new land did not permit its development. Therewith all incentives embodied in caste toward being "loyal to one's vocation" (in a traditionalistic sense) were eliminated. The mere theoretical praise of the vocationally stable worker as it is found under Hinayanistic influence in the literature of the Southern and outlying Indian territories lacked the strong psychological incentive which, as noted, was embodied in the sacred order of castes.

In the ramifications of Buddhism this would seem to be quite tangible. For example, in Burma Hinayanistic monastic education has indeed produced a degree of elementary education which, on the basis of percentage, is quite high for Indian and Asiatic conditions; qualitatively, of course, by European standards it is very modest. (On this point see the Census Report of 1911, Vol. IX, Ch. VIII); this agrees with the exclusively religious purposes of the schooling. The extent of local predominance of Buddhism, is, after all, decisive for the amount of literacy. For intensive modern types of labor (cotton seed oil making, oil refineries) it was necessary to import lower-caste Hindus (Census of 1911, *op-cit,* Ch. XI, XII), proof of the strong training for work by the caste but lacking in Burma. This is also proof of the fact that the caste regime on its own does not engender modern forms of work. Siam has remained an almost purely agrarian land although preconditions for its industrial development are not unfavorable.

With the elimination of Brahmanhood and the castes through the introduction of Buddhism as a state religion (fourteenth century), the ancient artistic tradition of caste-schooled royal artisans disappeared throughout the outlying Indian territories. The practice of the arts, stimulated by Buddhistic influence, has clearly not been able to produce works of the same value, however considerable their accomplishments.[17] Given its nature, correct Hinayanistic Buddhism simply could not well be other than inimical to or at best tolerant of industry. Only the needs of the laity, which almost exclusively had to depend on this way of acquiring merit, has made for the creation and conservation of religious art—typical of Buddhism—also in Hinayanism. In Burma as elsewhere the religious interests of the correct Buddhistic laity were oriented primarily to rebirth opportunities as indicated by source inscriptions of recent times.[18] The queen mother prays always to be born again as a high personage, endowed with devoutness and good qualities. Again the prayer is expressed that when the future Buddha Maitreya comes, to be permitted to go to *nirvana* with him.[19] Some wish to escape rebirth in a base family.[20] There is the wish to be born again always as a rich man and adherent to Buddha. Finally there is the hope of achieving omniscience and attaining *nirvana*.[21] Still another would like to be born again and again together with his present family (parents, brothers, children).[22] And another wishes in a future life to possess a particular woman as a wife.[23] In case they should be reborn as lay persons, monks often wished, in any case, to have pretty wives.[24] And besides such hopes is the prayer that good works be conferred on dead persons, especially those who are in hell,[25] the familiar late-Buddhistic representation of the *karma* doctrine also appearing in Hinduism.

The truly great missionary religion of Asia was not the Hinayana, but the Mahayana church.

Mahayana Buddhism, too, like the Hinayana school first won its missionary tendency through a king,[26] Kanishka of Kashmir and Northwest Hindustan, shortly after the beginning of our era. Under him the presumably third and last of the canonical councils which Mahayana Buddhism recognizes took place in a city of Kashmir. It was clearly first through the power of this king that Mahayanism was diffused throughout North India, where Ashoka once had held the orthodox council. Finally it prevailed and Hinayanism became a Southern branch.

The process leading up to this was, of course, already in motion, and the development of esoteric Mahayana soteriology had long since begun. Acvagosha wrote his still standard Mahayanistic works at least a century before the council. Nagarjuna is considered to have been the driving power of the council itself. Almost all other philosophers cited as authoritative by the Mahayanists lived in the centuries following the council, none after the first millenium of our era.

The main expansion of Mahayanism took place in the time up to the seventh century. Ever since the fifth century the star of Buddhism in India began slowly to pale. In addition to the reasons already adduced, perhaps one of the factors is also the prebendalizing process which, in one sense, sets in with all religions, and which the Mahayana school could promote. Settled hierocrats dispensing grace, i.e., prebendaries appeared in the place of wandering mendicant monks. It appears, too, that later Buddhism, like Jainism, often and preferentially employed ritually schooled and devoted Brahmans for the temple services proper. Given the original enmity to the Brahmans, these play a surprising role in many of the legends. Hence, in India too, there rather soon appears a Buddhistic secular priesthood composed of individuals who are married and are hereditarily appropriating the monastic prebends. At least, Nepal and the North Indian border territories display this development still today.

As soon as a strictly disciplined organization with missionary purposes came onto the scene in competition, not only the external but the internal weakness of Buddhism became apparent. This was the lack of a firmly outlined lay-ethic such as that represented by Brahmanical caste ritualism and also Jainistic parish organization. The travel accounts of the Chinese pilgrims, in comparative time perspective, permit insight into the inner decay of Buddhistic organization, with its want of any hierarchical or status unity.

Obviously, the renaissance of Hinduism found an easily tillable field and has, as noted, eliminated almost every trace of the ancient Buddhist church. However, before we turn to this new rise of orthodox Brahmanism, we shall have to consider briefly the expansion of Mahayanism beyond India; it was promoted with tremendous success only since the time of king Kanishka and it allowed Buddhism to become a world religion.

The great expansion territories of Mahayana Buddhism were China, Korea, and Japan.

Generally, in the course of its expansion, Mahayana Buddhism had to take account of more politically different conditions than did the Hinayana school. In those culture areas which Mahayana conquered at least partially during its mission, it encountered dynasties which either were more firmly bound up with a non-Buddhistic stratum of literati (China and Korea) or with a non-Buddhistic state cult (Japan) and so preserved its ties.[27] Thus, secular power in general here assumed more the role of a "religious police" than that of a "patron saint" for the church, hence, theocratic clericalization was very slight.

2. *China*

SOME statements concerning the fate of Buddhism in China, which were made in another connection, must be supplemented here. After some missionary failure, Buddhism was imported by missionary monks during the reign and at the instigation of Emperor Ming Ti shortly after the beginning of our era. It took root, however, only during the fourth century and found expression in the more frequent appearance of native Chinese monks. Then in the fifth, sixth, and seventh centuries Buddhism was officially supported by the state through numerous pilgrimages and missions, official translations of Buddhistic writings, entrance of some emperors into the monastic order, and finally—

in 526 under Emperor Wu Ti—the resettlement of the "patriarch" *bodhidharma* from India to Nanking and further to Honanfu. With the eighth and finally ninth centuries, through great persecutions of churches instituted by the Confucians, which also have already been mentioned, the back of the order in China was broken, without, however, its permanent or complete destruction. From the outset the attitude of the Chinese government has always been shifting, also after the great persecutions up to the time of the Holy Edict of Kang Hi.

The decisive opponent of Buddhism in China was, of course, the Confucian literati. Their views were that duty, and not fear and hope of transcendental reward and punishment should be the source of virtue and that devotion for the sake of obtaining remission of sins was no expression of true piety. Finally they thought that *nirvana* idealizes inactivity. To these views the apologists of Buddhism rejoined that Confucianism showed consideration only for the present world, or, at best, for the happiness of descendants, but not for the future hereafter. They argued, furthermore, that Heaven and hell are the only effective disciplinary means to human virtue.[28] Especially this last argument may have made an impression on the Emperor.

In addition to this was the belief as well in the magical power of the Buddhist literati. For it was as the teaching of genteel literati that Buddhism first came to China. Permission to become a monk was first given in one of the Warring States in the time of the great interregnums, 335 A.D. Idols were destroyed in 423 in the San Kingdom and again in 426 in the Wei Kingdom. In 451 idols were allowed once again. Around 400 Emperor Yas sent out an army expedition to procure fully qualified literary priests, and at the same time, Fa Hien went on the official mission to India to procure translations. After an emperor of the Ling Dynasty became a monk and the immigration of the patriarch to China occurred the peculiar mysticism of Indian Buddhism made its appearance.

As late as 515 the employment of magical art was subject to capital punishment. This did not, however, prevent the luxuriant growth of magic everywhere. Since this period government policy wavered between support or toleration, and the closing of all monasteries, a quota regulation of monks with the surplus compelled to resume secular professions (714), and confiscation of temple treasures for purpose of coinage (955). Under the

Ming Dynasty the government adopted the formerly prevailing role of systematic toleration with restrictions of land possession, limitation of monasteries, and the numbers of monks and control of reception by means of state examinations. Kang Hi's "secret Edict" finally prohibited (at the end of the seventeenth century) the further acquisition of land and completely rejected the Buddhistic teaching as unclassical. There matters have remained.

Buddhism in China has undergone the inner transformation into a pure book religion in agreement with the impact of the scribe upon the character of the whole of Chinese culture. The disputations and religious controversies peculiar to India disappeared. The Chinese government would never have permitted this and they thoroughly contradicted the nature of Chinese literary culture. Furthermore, Chinese Buddhism—corresponding to the strictly anti-orgiastic policing of religion by Chinese officialdom—remained immune to any penetration of Sakti religion which had, after all, not left Indian Mahayanism completely untouched.

From the outset Chinese Buddhism[29] has been a purely monastic church of wandering monks. The Buddhistic monastery—in contrast to the Confucian Temple (*miao*) and the Taoistic sanctuary (*kuan*) designated by "*si*"—contained also the temples with the images of the original and five secondary Buddhas (*fo*), five *bodhisattyas* (*pusa*), the *arhats* and patriarchs, and a whole band of tutelary deities borrowed from the folk hagiolatry of the Chinese (including also as apotheosized war gods the aforementioned *kuanti*). The primarily Chinese element in all this is the appearance of a feminine *bodhisattva, kwan, yin,* the protectoress of charity. And, indeed, this figure would seem to have received its feminine character only in the course of time,[30] probably under the influence of sect competition which like most apolitical confessions, count on feminine followings. The form is the counter-image of the occidental mother of god as helper-in-need and represents the single concession which was made to Sakti piety in China. Evidently the monasteries were originally organized according to the typical filiation system. Chinese regime had established special officials for the supervision of the monasteries and the management of discipline. Later, no organization separate from this hierarchy existed. Also, after the great persecutions, the patriarchhood which was in its beginnings did not develop further, doubtless for political reasons. The community of the cloister, however, was preserved by the fact that each monk had the right to be a guest in any monastery. In general, there remained only the charismatic prestige of single monasteries as ancient, known places of ritual correctitude.

Quite in the Indian manner the monasteries split into schools. Obviously, this was essentially in agreement with the waves of Mahayana revivals which, under the influence of the great leaders of India, spread out over the missionary territory. At the time of the first import and as late still as the time of the resettlement of the patriarch bodhidharma, the later conclusions of Mahayana doctrine (through Nagarjuna and Vasubandhu) had as yet not been elaborated. Hence, the oldest school, the Tschan sung, still had a strong Hinayanistic character in the form of its holy seeking.

The ancient meditation (*dhyana*), the seeking to "empty" consciousness, the denial of all external cult means, remained in a large measure peculiar to it. For a long time it was held—indeed because of its relationship with the Wu-Wei teaching—to be the most distinguished, and the greatest of Chinese Buddha sects. The Mahayanistic teachings of Nagarjuna and Vasubandhu, earlier described, found their representatives in the sects of the Hsien-schon-tsung and Tsi-jen-tsung. The fantastic revelling in supra-mundane splendors, by the first sect, the acosmic love of the *bodhisattva* by the second, perfected through the eight-fold steps of concentration, characterized them. Accordingly, the second-named sect had become in large measure the champion of the specific Buddhistic charity in China.

Among the other sects the Tien-tai-tsung may well have achieved the greatest literary popularity through the translation and the commentary of the Mahayanistic Saddharma pundarika.[31] In essence it represented an electic mixture of Hinayanistic meditation with rites and idolatry. Over and against this the Lutsung-sect was the most strictly ritualistic (in the sense of the Vinayana pitaka). The Tsching-tu-tsang sect was most closely adapted to lay needs. The glorification of paradise in the West under the guidance of Buddha Amithaba and of the Kwan-yin, presumably, also the very reception of this figure, was its doing.

Chinese Buddhism has in part attempted to achieve a unified religion (*San chiao i ti*) through reception of the great saints of both other systems. In the sixteenth-century Buddha, Laotse and Confucius may be found in the same monuments. Similar things can allegedly be ascertained many centuries earlier. Meanwhile, official Confucianism at least has rejected these attempts and has always viewed Buddhism in the same way that ancient Roman office nobles looked at oriental "superstitions."

The character of later Chinese Buddhistic monkdom was essentially established through its increasingly plebeian nature. Nowadays, no man of rank from a good family would join a monastic cloister. This may well have been the case since the century of the great persecution. It is certainly so since the Holy Edict of Kang-Hi. The monks were recruited from the aliterary strata, mainly from among peasants and petty bourgeois. This in itself first necessitated a thorough, ritualistic elaboration of monastic life; offenses of the monks against ceremony and discipline appear—in agreement with the nature of Chinese formalism—often to be rather severely punished. On the other hand "moral" offences, in our sense of the word, were relatively lightly received. Gambling, drinking, opium, and women presumably played a considerable role in some monasteries. Any beginnings of a systematic ethical rationalization of conduct of the laity was out of the question. There were in existence few monastic schools for the laity and the literary education which the novice received before ascending to the rank of a monk and aspirant to the dignity of a *bodhisattva*, had very little rational character. The point of gravity of monastic life lay in three things:: (1) a daily cultus—a reading aloud of holy scriptures—grown out of the ancient *Upostha* festivals; (2) in solitary or more characteristically joint meditation by sitting and, as a specialty in China, by running persons[32]; and (3) in ascetic virtuoso accomplishments which Mahayanism had borrowed from the ancient Hindu folk-asceticism of magicians.

The higher ordination of old monks to *bodhisattva* candidates was bound up with the practice of being branded. And as accomplishments of virtuosity, a monk[33] either had single parts of his body burned or, assuming the prescribed posture of praying man, sat down in a wooden stall and personally lighted the materials heaped around him for burning, or, finally let himself be immured for life. After death such virtuosi became great saints of the monastery.

All in all, the Buddhist monasteries in China which were administered by a crowd of officials and were occasionally quite important, were seats in part of irrational asceticism, in part of irrational meditation, but they were not places of rational education. Throughout China, the older the monastery the more completely it lacked the tremendous and magically understood nimbus of the literati although (and in part because) in the interest of propaganda they were the main centers of book printing concerned with edificatory writings and magically important tablets. The Chinese called upon Buddhistic deities and dead or living Buddhistic saints as helpers in case of sickness or other misfortune. The death mass was also esteemed in high circles and the primitive fate-oracle in the sanctuary played no inconsiderable role with the masses. But that was all.

The monks had to make the most diverse concessions to different lay beliefs; among others, introducing correct ancestral tablets and offering ancestral sacrifices for dead monks. Also the Chinese pagoda, which from India was diffused throughout all Hindu-influenced territories, represented, with the necessary modification, the form of the temple; and in China, through connection with the Fung-Shui teaching, it changed from a Buddhistic place of worship into an apotropaic means against the air and water demons for which purpose it was constructed at suitable sites determined by magicians.

The great importance of ceremonies of Buddhistic derivation in folk customs has been mentioned before. The belief in ethical compensation was carried by older Taoism and Buddhism to the masses and has doubtless reinforced obedience by commandments of the old neighborhood ethic and the special piety commandments of Chinese folk-ethic. As already mentioned, whatever inwardness, charitable feeling for man and animals, and sensitivity are at all to be found in China had to some degree been promoted by the mass of translated and familiarized Buddhistic legendary literature. However, Buddhism never won a controlling influence over conduct.

3. *Korea*

CLEARLY, Buddhism had even less influence in Korea than in China.[34] The Korean social order was a copy of the Chinese. Merchant guilds (*pusang*) and artisan guilds were to be found as in China. Moreover, feudalism was replaced by the rule of mandarins. The support and promotion of officials on the basis of successive literary examinations, like the propagation of Buddhism as a domestication means, was the work in Korea of the Mongolian dynasty in Peking.

Even before the Mongolian Conquest, since the sixth century, missionary Buddhists from China were to be found in Korea. They achieved the high point of their power after the tenth, particularly, however, in the thirteenth century. Occasionally the monasteries served as organizational centers of warrior orders, for the Buddhistic monkdom in Korea had exactly the same opponent as in China—the literati.

The literati, indeed, had not attained equivalent prestige to that in China. The literati had to contend, on the one hand, as in China with the eunuchs, on the other with the (finally six) "generals" of the army, that is to say, the condottieri who had the entrepreneurial commission to recruit the army. The rent, which the long, quite unwarlike purveying of soldiers yielded, was much desired and position in the army an object of purchase. The army chiefs stood on a footing of almost equal privilege with the monarchs with whom they divided the income.

In religious respects the original magic of the professional sorcerers, above all, the ecstatic magic of the therapeutic and apotropaic dance, practiced by women (*mudang*) appears quite independently alongside the Buddhistic monasteries which ascended only through the support of former rulers.

An insurrection that undoubtedly had been fanned by the competitors of the monks finally broke the power of the church and therewith all beginnings of a particular culture in Korea. The recently reported initiative of the Japanese government in the founding of big monasteries appears at first glance to be in contradiction to its anti-Buddhistic policies on the Japanese home island. However, in this the idea of pacifying domestication of the conquered land by means of this religion of peace may play its part as with the building of a warlike spirit at home by supporting the ancient official rites.

4. *Japan*

AS IN Korea, all intellectualism in Japan[35] was Chinese in origin. At the time Confucianism seems to have exerted a quite considerable influence on the Japanese ideal of a gentleman.

However, this influence was modified by the heterogeneous conditions of the Japanese status structure which will be discussed below.

The conception of the Chinese soldier-God was borrowed by Japan. Besides this, direct and tangible Hindu elements have been imported. But primarily, China was mediator of all cultural borrowing of ancient Japan. Thus, when Buddhism made its appearance in Japan during the first decades of the sixth century, it was first imported through the Korean mission and later, about the eighth century, from the Chinese mission. Thus it was essentially Chinese Buddhism that influenced Japan.[36] In fact, the whole of Japanese court literature was originally tied to the Chinese language, as, for a long time, was her sacred literature.

Here as elsewhere, cultural borrowing occurred, for typical reasons, on the initiative of the government. The much celebrated Prince Shotoku, who consummated the process, certainly and particularly aimed at taming and disciplining the subjects. Furthermore, the literate Buddhist priests served as officials, a function they often monopolized as late as the end of the eighteenth century. In addition, Shotoku enriched Japan with Chinese culture to which, as one of Japan's foremost literati, he was devoted. The numerous women, who occupied the throne in the following period, were all enthusiastic adherents of the new religiosity with its emotional appeal.

Here we deal in passing with Japanese Buddhism and religion, and in general terms, in spite of the considerable interest the subject has in its own right. This is because the particular properties of the "spirit" of the Japanese way of life relevant here have been produced through entirely different circumstances than religious factors.[37] Rather, they originated in the feudal character of the political and social structure.

For a time Japan has had a social order based on a strictly executed "clan charisma." Moreover, the Japanese government represented a very pure type of "familistic state." Later the rulers shifted toward the feudalization of political offices, essentially in order to overcome the inflexible form of this social order. Thus a social order developed which has dominated medieval Japan up to the threshold of the present.

Japanese feudalism strangled export trade (by restricting trade to imports in a treaty harbor) and putting brakes upon the development of any "bourgeois" strata in the European sense of the word. The concept of the "city" as a seat of jurisdictional prerogatives was entirely absent in Japan. To be sure, there were large and small settlements with heads of villages and urban districts. But with the exception of two, the cities were neither royal fortresses nor typical seats of princely administration as in China. In contrast to China, it was legally immaterial whether a princely vassal took up residence in a "city" or in a rural castle. There was no bureaucratic apparatus comparable to the Chinese administration, no stratum of mandarins shifting from office to office under a system of examinations. Nor did Japan have a patriarchal theocracy with its theory of the welfare state. From the time of the Tokugava rulers the theocratic head of the state was confined in hierocratic seclusion in Kyoto.

The Shogun was *primus inter pares* of the crown vassals, hence *major domo*. He directly controlled the jurisdictional area of his household and the administration of the princely vassals. In the feudal hierarchy[38] there was to be found a particularly sharp cleavage between the *daimyo* and the *samurai* of varying rank orders. As territorial princes, the *daimyo* were accoutered with sovereign prerogatives as was the shogun. They were considered direct vassals of the Emperor. The *samurai* were vassals and subvassals of the *daimyo* and the shogun. Among the various rank orders the *daimyo*, knights serving on horseback, preceded in rank. The footmen (*kasi*) were simple office nobles who often took care of administrative routine. The *samurai* alone were entitled to bear arms and to hold fiefs. They were sharply set off from the peasants, merchants, and artisans, the latter two groups being of still lower rank, in feudal fashion. The *samurai* were free men.

The *samurai* could give notice to terminate the hereditary fief (*han*) and they forfeited it through felony or serious mismanagement as determined by verdict of the feudal court. The verdict could also adjudge demotions to a lower fief. In order to determine the number of combatants which the lord was obligated to raise, the fiefs were registered according to the amount of their traditionally owed rice rent (the *kokudaka*). This rent determined the rank of the chief holders.

All this makes the Japanese fief comparable to the typical Asiatic military prebends, which were either dependent upon the income of a district (*tsyga-fiefs*) or upon the storehouse (*hyomono*) of the overlord. The decisive obligations of the vassal, however, remained personal loyalty and service in war, besides traditional honorific gifts. The act of making the amount of rice rent the criterion of rank, even of *daimyo* status, is, of course, the reverse of the original clan charisma, a reversal which occasionally occurred elsewhere. According to the clan principle, the traditional rank of the sib provided the claim to the rank of office to be enfeoffed and therewith entitled to the authority and prerequisites traditionally going with the office. This appears clearly, even under the Tokugava rule, in the claim of certain families to the high office positions (*karo* positions) which were subject to recall.

Similarly, the army command which could be given an officer was determined by his *kokudava.* Furthermore, only a man from a *Samurai* family could be enfeoffed with criminal judiciary functions.

The Shogun's chancellory (*bakuhu*) controlled the administration of the *daimyos,* their politics, and their politically important private actions, for instance, their marriages, which required consent. The *Daimyos* controlled those of their subvassals.

The Shogun especially exercised his control by holding the minister (*karo*) in the employ of the crown vassals directly responsible to himself. The personal character of the feudal hierarchy, on the other hand, is evidence that no direct relation of the subvassal to the lord paramount existed. The aging vassal, or the vassal declared unfit to serve by the judge's verdict, had to go into retirement (*inkyo*). The successor had to apply for investiture. The same held for the case of escheatage. The fief was not transferable and could only temporarily be mortgaged.

Trading monopolies and certain workshops (*ergasterion*) for the manufacture of luxury goods appear as elements of the princely *oikos.* Important guilds appeared in the treaty harbor of Nagasaki and occupational associations were to be found well nigh everywhere. But there existed no considerable stratum which could function as a political force and promote a "civic" development in the occidental sense. The regulations of foreign trade maintained a highly static economy and did not provide for the emergence of capitalistic dynamics. Political capitalism was almost wholly lacking as the preconditions of political finance were nonexistent. There was no stratum of state contractors, state creditors, or tax farmers. Army requirements were essentially met by the summons of vassals and knights and feudal self-equipment, hence without separation of the warrior from the means of warfare. Besides, the long era of peace under the Shoguns of the Tokugava dynasty did not allow opportunities for the rational conduct of war to emerge. Only private feuds prevailed, as in our Middle Ages. The lower classes of vassals and office nobles, the *samurai* and *kasi,* represented the strata typical for Japan. The exaggerated, purely feudal notion of honor and the vassal's fealty were the central emotions around which everything ultimately turned—at least in literary theory. In practice, the rice rent was the typical form of material provision of this class.

The merchant, artisan, and the broad stratum of peasants had no political rights. The latter existed for raising taxes for the lords. Among them the principle of redivision of holdings in connection with the tax obligation operated at least in partial measure. There was a strict closure of villages against those bound outside its area, for here, also, the right of the soil was correlative with the obligation to the soil. The *midzunomi* (the "water drinker"), i.e., the stranger who had no claim to land, had no rights in the village. A system of joint responsibility (*gonungumi,* five sibs each) was carried through. The dignified role of the village head man was an hereditary form of clan charisma. Above him stood the *daikwan,* a *samurai* enfeoffed with feudal jurisdiction.

At important occasions every prince called his vassals together for a plenary meeting. Such assemblies of the *samurai* in some of the princely realms during the great crisis of the sixties of the last century have determined the transition to the modern army system and the direction of policy in general, leading up to the downfall of the Shogun's office. The further course of restoration then led to the introduction of the bureaucratic, in place of the feudal, administration in the army and in the state administration and to the dissolution of and compensation for feudal rights. The latter process transformed the broad stratum of the *samurai* class into a middle class of petty rentiers, partly even into paupers. The high notions of honor of ancient feudal times had already been tempered in the direction of rentier mentality under the impact of the system of rice prebends. From this no relation to an ethic of entrepreneurial acquisitiveness could have been autonomously established. European traders in the post-restoration period have often complained about the "low business morals" of the Japanese, in contrast to the great Chinese traders. Insofar as such "low business morals" existed, this fact could easily be explained in terms of the universal estimation of trade as a form of mutual fraud as evidenced in Bismarck's phrase "*Qui trompe-t-on?*"

Japan's condition most closely resembled China's feudal period of the Warring States. The differences consisted particularly in the following: in Japan the greatest weight in social affairs was carried by a stratum of professional warriors rather than a non-military stratum of literati. Practical life situations were governed by a code of chivalry and education for knighthood as in the occidental Middle Ages, not by examination degrees and literary education as in China, nor by worldly cultivation as in occidental antiquity, nor yet by a philosophy of salvation as in India.

A people among whom a stratum of the character of the *samurai* played the decisive role could not attain a rational economic ethic on their own, quite apart from all other circumstances, especially the closure against the outside. Nevertheless, the feudal relationships making for recallable, contractually-fixed, legal relationships offered a basis much more favorable to "individualism" in the occidental sense of the word, than did Chinese theocracy. With relative ease Japan was able to take over capitalism as an artifact from the outside, though it could not create capitalism out of its own spirit. But Japan could not produce a mystic intellectual soteriology on its own, nor the rule of *gurus* in Indian fashion. Rather, the status pride of the feudal *Iamuri* inevitably had to revolt against absolute obedience to clerical leadership. And so it came to pass.

At the time of the introduction of Buddhism the dominant religion of Japan consisted in the belief in functional spirits. Also among its forms were phallus cults (however carefully prudish modern rationalism obliterates their traces), and the belief in amulets and similar magical apotropaic and homeopathic procedures. The main element of the religion was the cult of the spirits of one's own ancestors and of apotheosized heroes. These were the powers to which the noble felt responsible for his life.

The official cult bore the typical stamp of the refined ritualism of a stratum of knights. The essential elements consisted in the recitation of hymns and food propitiations. Orgiasticism and ecstasy had undoubtedly been eliminated by the sense of dignity characteristic of a knightly status group. Only moral "sin" was the basis for exclusion from participation in the cult (similar to the exclusion from the Elysian mysteries). Ritual impurity meant blood guilt and incest as well as bodily defects. Very strict prescriptions for ritual purity compensated for the lack of a religious "ethic." Any sort of compensation in the beyond was lacking. The dead live, as among the Greeks, in Hades. The sovereign, descending from the spirit of the sun was, as in China, supreme priest. In a manner similar to that found elsewhere, the ordeal and oracle functioned in political decision-making.

Among the mass of deities, the majority, even today, are apotheosized heroes and benefactors. The priestly positions of the numerous plain temples were and are mostly hereditarily transmitted in the sibs of the "divinity officials" who fall into eight rank classes. Just as in China ranks were assigned to proven gods. Similarly the rank-order of the temples was fixed. In addition to the official temple cult, there was the private cult of the household. The old form of the cult of one's own ancestors' spirits later was almost completely displaced by the Buddhist death mass. Here, as everywhere, Buddhism in the doctrine of compensation and salvation in the beyond had its desmesne. On the other hand, the ancient religiosity designated as the "Shinto" cult (cult of the Gods of the land, of the *kami*), in opposition to this foreign doctrine, put all cult, even the cult of ancestral spirits, exclusively into the service of one's own interests in this world.

Buddhism first made its entrance into Japan under the protection of the cult as a genteel soteriology of the literati. Mahayanism then soon unfolded its various potentialities by forming schools and sects.[39]

According to its nature, Buddhism brought about a relatively rational and religious regulation of life, other-worldly goals and paths of salvation. It also brought about an enrichment of the emotional content of the experience of these phenomena. This was in contrast to all those essentially animistic and magical cults which were devoid of any direct ethical demands.

Whatever sublimation of impulsive and emotional life occurred in Japan beyond the feudal conception of honor has undoubtedly been the work of Buddhism. Here, too, Buddhism has retained the soteriology of Indian intellectuals. This soteriology obviously was fused with the Confucian code of "countenance" and "propriety." In Japan the latter, again, had been completely transposed into feudal attitudes. This fusion issued in the gentleman ideal attuned to a dignity of bearing and courteous distance. In the face of the unbroken coarseness, emotional sentimentalism, and lack of distance of the European, educated Japanese usually experience themselves as representatives of this gentleman ideal. Only expert analysis could in the special instance tell how strongly Buddhism has contributed to this complex. Japanese Buddhism, nevertheless, evinces some evolutionary trends peculiar to Japan in spite of the borrowing of most of the sects of China.

We shall be concerned here with only some of the Buddhistic sects (*shu*). They are usually enumerated in round numbers, ten being the customary figure. This, however, includes small sects that are changing. Among the larger sects existing down to the present time, the Shingon is the oldest. It was founded during the ninth century. For the Shingon sect the prayer formula (the Hindu *mantra*) is at the same time the formula of magical sorcery and an esoterically interpreted means of union with the divine. The Vagrskhedika is usually counted among the sect's scriptures.[40] The watchwords of argumentation are "*dharma*" and "*samgnas*." The first is here understood as *eidos*, from individuality; the second is understood to mean "name," the designation for "concept." There is no "dog," but only "this" dog. Hence, as concepts are only abstractions, the objects only "names," everything is but illusion. Only the soul is real and only the *bodhisattvas* know the illusory world of empirical existence.

The Jodo-shu was founded toward the end of the twelfth century. The great and small Sukhavati-Vyuha belong to its sacred books.[41] It promises the western paradise in the manner of Chinese Mahayanism (in Indian the Sakhavati). As a means for the attainment of paradise the sect recommends the formalistic and enthusiastically faithful invocation of Amida. Amida was the most popular disciple of Buddha throughout Eastern Asia. Here he belongs to the five highest deities (Buddhas). The western paradise is described in the most glowing colors. "Faith," however, is the absolute prerequisite. According to the great Skhavati-Vyuha,[42] no sceptical man enters paradise. Even doubting bhodisattvas (!) damages their salvation chances. The small Sukhavati Vyuha expressly rejects righteousness based on good works as a path to salvation. Faithful prayer to Amitaya, sustained for days before death and unto death is the sole guarantee of salvation.

However, more important than the Jodo-shu and Shingon are the Zen and Shin sects. They were founded somewhat later than the Jodo-shu.

The Zen sect consists of three independent branches. It cultivated a religiosity of inner-worldly edification and faith especially by engaging in exercises of mystic significance. The Shin sect's religiosity, on the other hand, was free of all such feats of religious virtuosity. The religious practices of the Zen sect relatively approximated those of the ancient Hindu type of the Buddhistic Kshatriya religiosity. Correspondingly, the branches of this sect were long preferred by the status group of the *samurai* as being genteel forms of Japanese Buddhism which were especially rich in temples. The Zen sect, like ancient Buddhism, rejected all book knowledge and placed decisive emphasis upon mental discipline and the attainment of indifference toward the external world, especially one's own body. For the Zen monks this training meant liberation from the world through contemplative union with the divine. The layman, particularly the professional warriors, cherished the exercises as a means of hardening and discipline for their vocation. Japanese authorities claim that the sect discipline has made a considerable contribution to the military value of the Japanese by breeding an atmosphere of disregard for life as such.

The Tokugava-Shogun, Yiesyasu, protector of Buddhism, who had been restored after persecution by Ota Nobunga, seems to have essentially cherished his soldiers' hope for the Buddhist paradise as a heaven of heroes.

The Shin sect, founded at the beginning of the thirteenth century, in sharp contrast to the Zen sects, may be compared to occidental Protestantism, at least insofar as it rejected sanctification by good works and upheld, rather, the sole significance of the faithful devotion to the Buddha Amida. In this it is similar to the *Bhakti* religiosity of India, to be discussed below, which grew out of the cult of Krishna. It differs, however, in that it rejects all orgiastic-ecstatic elements, a rejection characteristic of all religions which have developed from the ancient soteriology of Hindu intellectuals. Amida is helper-in-distress; trust in him is the only attitude bringing salvation. The Shin sect was the only Buddhist sect, therefore, abolishing not only priestly celibacy but also monkdom. The *busso* corrupted by the Portuguese into "*bonze*" were married priests, wearing a special costume only when officiating. For the rest, their way of life is identical with that of laymen.

The way of life of the priests of the other Buddhist sects of Japan resulted from the disintegration of discipline. Among the Shin, however, the identity of the way of life of priests and laymen, appears as a deliberate policy, perhaps for the first time. Sermon, school, instruction, and popular literature were developed in many ways similar to the occidental Lutheran manner, and the sect, which has a great number of followers among the "burghers" belongs to those strata which were most favorably disposed to the reception of elements of occidental culture.

The sects, however, developed just as little of a rational innerworldly asceticism as did Lutheranism, and for the same reasons. Zen religion was a religion of a redeemer. It was adaptable to the soteriological and emotional needs of the middle classes under feudal control, but it did not accept the orgiastic-ecstatic and magical turn of the old Hindu and popular piety, nor did it accept the strong emotional ardor of later Hindu piety or of European pietism. Their tempering of feeling was apparently more conducive to "moods" than to "sentiment" or "emotionality" as we understand it. This tempering, after all, was the product of genteel priests.

Finally, the sect of the Nitchires was founded in the middle of the thirteenth century and was a counter-reformation movement of monks. They advocated a return to Gautama, the true Buddha, who was conceived as a world-permeating magical force of illumination. The redeemer Amida was sharply rejected as a false idol. The movement sought to restore the typically Mahayanistic linkage of contemplative mysticism of monks with the magic of prayer formulae and ritualistic sanctification of good works (*hoben*) among laymen.

The restriction of the laymen to somewhat irrational and occasional acts of piety is far removed from all education for a method of rational living. This restriction is peculiar to the majority of the sects with the exception of the Shin. Actually, these forms of Buddhism have produced among laymen only a certain general mood of indifference to things worldly, the conviction of the vanity of the ephemeral, that is, of the world including life itself. For the rest, they have diffused the doctrine of compensation (*ingwa,* approximately corresponding to *karma*) and ritualistic magic as the means of escape.

The external organization of the monks at first did not differ from that of other mission areas. The sharp competition among the sects was encouraged by individual princely vassals and parties of nobles who exploited their competition and played off one against the other. However, given the thoroughly feudal character of the country, this competition often gave the monastic communities of Japan the character of military communities of crusaders, of monastic orders of knights, especially as long as the monks, or at least the abbots, were recruited from noble strata. They fought at the same time for their own position of power in the population.

During the eleventh century, for the first time, an abbot, whose example was followed by others, formed an army of disciplined soldier-monks (*tonsei*). This development reached its climax during the fourteenth century. With the exception of some branches of the Zen sect, the whole of monkdom was militarized. Accordingly, the monasteries mostly were turned into hereditary prebends and the code of celibacy disintegrated. The war lord of the crown, Ota Nobunaga, restored political sovereignty and restricted this power of the *ecclesia militans.* An enormous massacre broke the politico-military power of the Buddhistic monk orders forever, and the victors had no scruples about making use of the assistance of Christianity, above all, of Jesuit missionaries, for this purpose. The Christian mission has attained no mean results.

The ascension of the Tokugava Shoguns put an end to this. They did not wish to exchange Buddhistic clericalism for the rule of a clergy directed from abroad. The members of this dynasty of *major domi* were and remained to the end, personal adherents of Buddhism, especially of the ritualistic Jodo-shu. The religious edict of 1614 and the subsequent persecution of Christians finished the Christian mission in Japan and its establishment. Therewith, all clericalism in Japan was broken. The Buddhist church was restored and for the first time systematically organized. But this occurred entirely under the auspices of the state. As in late antiquity one could offer proof of not being a Christian by merely sacrificing to the Emperor, so under the Tokugava it was possible by merely registering in a Japanese temple. Since the Tokugava Yiemitsu, no priest was allowed to officiate without having passed an examination in the Chinese manner. The function of preacher and the directorship of the temples was linked to certain long periods of monastic life following in this the Buddhist principle of seniority. The filiation principle determined the rank order and the hierarchical rights of the monasteries and of their superiors. Monastic discipline, namely celibacy and vegetarianism, was inculcated in the priests by the state but without lasting success. To be sure, the number of Buddhist monasteries and temples increased tremendously, but the social power of the monks declined. The purchase of priestly offices seems to have been widely practiced.

As regards the religiosity of the common people, it approximated general Asiatic and ancient conditions insofar as Shintoist, Confucian, Taoist, and Buddhist deities and redeemers were called upon according to function and occasion. A formal connection between Shintoist and Buddhist religion was undertaken under protection of the court. (Though this is not without interest in itself, it does not contribute anything essential to our context.) To a large extent, the genteel strata turned toward Confucian ethics. This had social reasons. Buddhist monkdom, during the course of the centuries, underwent a strong internal transformation inasmuch as the recruitment of the monks became more and more democratic, probably under the pressure of the propagandistic competition of the sects. In the end, after persecution and regulation by the state, they belonged, as in China, predominantly to the illiterate lower strata.

In the monastic schools in general, they acquired only what was necessary for the practical management of the cult. Therewith the prestige of monasticism and Buddhism decreased; socially to a considerable extent. Aside from political reasons, this has probably been one of the reasons for the "disestablishment" of Buddhism at the time of the restoration of the legitimate dynasty (1868) and the systematic restoration of Shintoism as the state religion. It was decisive that once Shintoism was considered the "national" form of cult as over against Buddhism, it then guaranteed the legitimacy of the Emperor. Also, in the constitutional state of Japan, the descent of the legitimate dynasty from the sun and the superhuman quality of the Emperor belong to those basic presuppositions which the Japanese, at least the correct Japanese, must not overtly doubt.

Confucianism had numerous adherents among the genteel strata, as we have observed above. But in Japan it could not fulfill the same task of legitimating the dynasty as did Confucians for the Chinese emperor in establishing him as world monarch and *supreme pontifex*. Confucianism in Japan did not have, as in China, the support on an academically organized stratum which through the system of examinations and, above all, the use of state offices as prebends, was politically and economically firmly organized and motivated by homogeneous interests. Confucianism in Japan was rather a literary hobby of individual circles.

Buddhism, on the other hand, lacked the very strong support of the charismatic *guru* as a magical redeemer, a support which Buddhism, like Hindu sects, had in other Asiatic areas. The Japanese, like the Chinese government, undoubtedly for political reasons, blocked the development of this institution. The establishment of the *guru* in general has not grown beyond relatively modest beginnings. Thus in Japan there was no stratum carrying the prestige of magical-soteriological redeemers such as was enjoyed by the literati in China and the *gurus* of the sects in India.

The revolution of the army and technical administration, under the pressure of external threat, overthrew the feudal military and office organization. They were, from a purely political point of view, in the agreeable situation of a political vacuum, or, at least, not faced by the magical or soteriological entrenched power of religious traditionalism, which might have been crossed in its intentions in the field of economic conduct.

5. *Inner Asia: Lamaism*

A VERY different form from that displayed in the penetration of Buddhism into outlying Indian and other East Asiatic missionary territories is found with the establishment of Buddhist missions from North India to the North. Indeed, in the neighborhood of its origin, in Nepal,[43] it underwent the typical prebendalizing process in the course of which it was penetrated by *tantristic* magic and its blood sacrifices. Beside this, it had to compete with the Hindu propaganda of the Shivaists and was in the Mahayanistic North Indian fashion amalgamated with the Hindu caste system.

Of the three main social classes the Banhar (priests) and the Udas (industrial workers) were viewed as orthodox; because they were *tantristic*, the rest were heterodox. The Banhars dwelt in cloisters, however, without celibacy; the prebends were hereditary. Their highest class was the priestly (*gubhaju*), to which one belonged only through ordination after examination. Whoever was not ordained belonged to the simple *Bhikkshu*, serving as lay assistants in certain ceremonies also, however, pursuing a craft, namely goldsmithing.

There were seven divisions within the first class including silversmiths, carpenters, founders, copper and iron workers (apparently ancient kings' handworkers). Also, ordained monks were, after a four-day consecration as *gurus*, released from their vows. The *udas*-class was divided into seven subclasses of which the most important were the merchants, the rest craftsmen. Between the *banhars* and the *udas* intermarriage and commensality did not occur. The *banhar* could not receive water from *udas* craftsmen.

The lower folk strata made use of Buddhistic or Brahmanical priests as benefactors. Buddha was united into a trinity with Shiva and Vishnu. Beside them appeared all the Hindu gods, as well as the ancient snake-cult. The developments were in motion the beginnings of which are discernible in the accounts of the Chinese pilgrims. Through prebendalization and incorporation in the caste organization the transformation of the nature of Buddhism was completed. Other trends appear in Central Asia, where beyond Nepal very ancient trade relations maintained, especially in Tibet.

Here was to be found, in sharp opposition to the lack of organization of the former territory, a hierarchy of such unity that the religion of its representatives, the Lama-monks, is often described as a different system of religion, Lamaism.[44] Hindu, and indeed also wandering Buddhistic monks must have appeared very early as benefactors in Inner and North Asia; the expression "shaman" for the magico-ecstatic exorcist is an East Turkestan transformation of the Indian *sramana* (Pali: *samana*). The genuine Buddhistic missions in these territories began in about the seventh century of our time calculations and in the eighth century were officially established. As was usual, the king in the interest of administration (the importation of writing skill) and of domestication of his subjects imported a holy man as a *guru*[45] from the neighboring Indian territory (in this case from Udayana, which is next to Kashmir). The missionary was a representative of pure *tantristic* (magical) Mahayana religion: alchemy, magical drinks, and the usually Mahayanistic formula-magic appears to have been brought together with him. After him the mission no longer had to compete with the reactions and struggles of other sects. At the time East Persia and a large section of Turkestan was won over to Mahayana Buddhism, which remained until the Islamic conversion of the Western Mongolian Khans; then these missions were again destroyed. The Mongolian world empire was, however, on the other side, the source which the holy church of Tibet, the representatives of "Lamaism," had to thank for support.

"Lama," the "Elevated," "Holy One," was first the name for the superior (*Khan po*) of a monastery. Later, as a form of courtesy, each fully ordained monk was so named. The Buddhistic monastic establishment at the beginning progressed in quite the usual way. However, the power position of some of the monastic superiors, mounted to such an extent that, corresponding to the pastoral nature of the land, the political structure fell apart into small principalities. Like the bishops of the European Occident in the time of the migrations of the nations, the monastic superiors here held the single, rationally organized power in their own hands. The education of superiors was accordingly spiritual as well as secular.[46]

The monasteries had become pure prebends. The "monks" married and formed an hereditary caste. In Tibet, as in India, at least in some monasteries, particularly in the Saskya monastery close to the highest point of the Himalayas, the position of superior had become hereditarily charismatic. The Lamas of Saskya for the first time in the twelfth century formed a liaison with the dynasty of Genghis Khan, and in the thirteenth century they secured the conversion of the Mongol emperor Kublai Khan, the conqueror of China, who now became the secular patron (*tschakravati*) of the church. Again, the need for writing in the Mongolian political administration was clearly decisive.

The Mongols were interested as well in the domestication of inner-Asiatic peoples, who were difficult to dominate. The Lamas of the Saskya monastery brought theocratic political power to this purpose (while as representatives of a writing culture they were also indispensable for the administration). This domestication of Mongoloid tribes, which formerly lived chiefly by war and thievery, actually succeeded and had important world historical consequences. For only with the beginning of the conversion of the Mongols to Lamaistic Buddhism had the perpetual military expeditions to East and West of the peoples of the steppes been instrumented with a goal; they were pacified and thus, finally, was quieted the ancient source of all "folk migrations"—of which the last was the Timurs in the fourteenth century. With the downfall of Mongol dominion in China in the fourteenth century, the theocracy of Tibetan Lamas also declined. The national Chinese Ming Dynasty, with no idea of permitting a single monastery alone to dominate, played the many charismatic Lamas off against one another. An age of bloody cloister feuds broke out, the orgiastic ecstatic (*Sakti*) aspect of magical Mahayanism again appeared in the foreground until the new prophet Tson-ka-pa, the greatest holy man of Lamaistic Buddhism, a church reformer in the grand style, made his appearance. An understanding with the Chinese emperor concerning monastic discipline was again arrived at. In religious colloquy the Lama of the Saskya monastery (who was symbolized by a yellow cap) was supported. Thus the "yellow" church, as it is usually called, of the "Virtuous Sect" (D Ge-lugs-pa) was secure in its supremacy.

For the disciplined this new teaching signified the restoration of celibacy and the devaluation of *tantristic* ecstatic magic practice of which was forbidden the monks of the Virtuous Sect. They had a relation to those who wore red caps—similar to that of the Taoists to the Confucians—as monks of lower rank tolerated as adherents to the ancient teaching. It shifted the point of gravity of monastic piety from meditation and prayer formulae to capability for sermonizing and missions through disputation, for which they were prepared in monastic schools, a source of the reawakening of scientific studies in the monasteries.

However, decisive for the characteristic *Lamaistic* hierarchy of monastic organization was the connection of a special form of universal Hinduistic and especially also Mahayanistic Incarnation teaching. In the Lamaist comprehension, it was bound up with the charisma of certain famous monasteries of the Yellow Church. This development was completed in the generation after Tsong-ka-pa, while in place of the hereditary superior, now another form of successorship had to appear.

This, however was only a special case of a generally valid manner of representation. The nature and significance of Lamaistic incarnation teaching are in themselves simple.[47] To be sure it stood in strictest opposition to all ancient Buddhistic philosophy with the view that the charismatic quality of a holy man is strengthened in transmission with the rebirth of the individual, which seems to be simply as a consequence of the Mahayanistic theory of the nature of Buddha as one who from his early births to the penultimate, the *bodhisattva*-birth, achieved holiness by increasing steps to this last birth (as Buddha). The doctrine of holy steps of Mahayanism, earlier described, which generally computes the degree of holiness according to the number of deaths the holy man had undergone before reaching the dignity of *arhat*, was simply a consequence of this. Now this same reasoning was extended: each *Lama* who had enjoyed the status as ascetic, magician, teacher, would after his death be reborn. The *Khubilgan* reincarnated in some child rose again. Each succeeding *Khubligan*—birth of the holy man—was normally accompanied by mounting holy prestige. And, on the other hand, traced backward it represented by rebirth the original possessor of charisma who was always some sort of missionary, magician or wise man of ancient Buddhistic times. Each *Khubilgan* is a benefactor by virtue of his power of magical charisma. A monastery which has a famous *Khubilgan* in its walls or has a number of them is certain of a large income, and the *Lamas* were therefore always on the hunt to discover new *Khubilgans*. This theory of holiness lies at the basis of the *Lamaistic* hierarchy as well.

The superiors of highly qualified charismatic monasteries are incarnations of great *bodhisattvas*, who, after the death of the former possessor, was incarnated anew in a child after seven times seven days and also—somewhat in the manner of the search for the *Apis-Stier**—now must be located according to definite oracles and signs. The two highest of this sort of incarnations are the superiors of the now great *Lama*-monasteries—the Potala near Lhasa, the Gryal ba, later in accordance with the title given him by the Mongol Khan after the re-establishment of the Lamaistic church in Mongolia in the sixteenth century

* Apis the Bull, deity of Egyptian mythology, capable of incarnation as a bull or a man with the head of a bull. *Eds.*

called the *Dalai-Lama*, and the superiors of the monastery usually called the Teeshoo loombo, the Pan-c'en rin-po-ce, at times called by his monastery the *Taschi Lama*, the first as an incarnation of the *bodhisattva* Padmapani, also Buddha himself, the last the incarnation of Amithaba.

According to the theory, the discipline lay more in the hands of the Dalai-Lama than in those of the Taschi-Lama. Corresponding to the specific significance of Amithaba as an object of ardent mystical meditation, the Taschi Lama had more significance for the exemplary conduct of the religious life. However, political significance of the Dalai-Lama is considerably greater than that of the Taschi-Lama of whom it is said that after the downfall of the first he will re-establish the religion.

The incarnation of the Dalai Lama is taken into the monastery where for seven years he is trained as a monk and educated in rigid asceticism till he comes of age. Against the divine office of the Dalai Lama, and other incarnated possessors of high Lamaistic charisma, the Chinese regime imposed the necessary political guarantees establishing: (1) an upper limit on (the strictly incomparable) competing incarnations, particularly of Dalai Lama and Taschi-Lama; (2) residence duty of a number of the highest *Lama* (now only one remains) in Peking; (3) with the incarnation and usual hieratic monastery of the Dalai Lama, the conduct of the worldly administration through a *major-domo* whom they set up; (4) the duty of certain higher incarnations to appear in the court in Peking and to receive the exequatur from there.[48]

The new conversion and Lamaistic organization of the mongols took place in the sixteenth century and more incarnations of great holy men appeared as representatives of the Dalai-Lama. The most important of them was Maidari Hutuktu, in Urga. Despite the great difficulty of the Mongols in supervision, after the downfall of Dsungaren the practice was retained by the Chinese. But the Chinese regime prescribed that the incarnations of this hierarchy could take place and be sought only in Tibet, not in Mongolia itself. The final distribution of rank classes of *Lamas*, corresponding to the rank classes of Mongolian nobles likewise occurred with the new conversion of the Mongol Khans.

The recruitment of Lamaistic monasteries,[49] which normally had between 200 and 1,500 Lamas—the larger even more—followed in large measure (as is also usual in many Buddhistic monasteries in China) through gifts of children, in part, as well through their purchases by the cloister. In Tibet the fixed limits of subsistence possibilities created a permanent demand for monastic service.[50] Due to the high power position of Lamaistic monasteries, the influx of propertied strata is not inconsiderable and monks of this type often bring hereditary private means with them. It is self-evident, but apparently in *Lamaistic* monasteries developed to an exceptional degree, that a strong plutocratic organization of *Lamas* exists.[51] Monks without means work for propertied monks and serve them, practice crafts such as basket-making and others similar, gather horse manure for dunging, and enter business.[52] Chastity as a duty was demanded only by the orthodox "Yellow Church," which permitted the enjoyment of meat and alcohol. Instruction was also customarily given in small monasteries and indeed to four faculties: (1) the theological faculty, the most important, because at the same time that it provided leadership of the monastery[53] it imparted consecration; (2) the medical faculty (empirical herbalism for the monastic house physician); (3) *Tsing Ko* (ritual), the ancient classical teaching, here in essentials reduced to inculcation of knowledge of the rules for the death mass;[54] (4) *Tsu pa* (mysticism), schooling in *tantra*-asceticism for shamanistic purposes.[55] Corresponding to the character of all Indian relations in the instruction, a considerable role was played and is still today played by the pure debate (as a monthly test).[56]

Consecration brought the student (*dapa*) from novitiate (*getsul*) to *Gelong* (full monk) and through further steps (five in all) to *Khan po,* which in the ancient literary hierarchy was the highest step of the lower clergy and as monastic superior of the discipline (with power over life and death). The ranks of the higher clergy beginning with *Khubilgan* (from there to *Hutuktus,* finally *Dalai lama* and *Pon c'en*) were not to be achieved through consecration but only through rebirth. The monks fought with bravery against the beliefs of Islam and were, and perhaps also today, are armed, in contrast to the laity. Generally far more extensively than in any of the other Buddhistic monasteries, the time of the *Lama* was taken up by communal cult practices.

A survey of the Lamaistic pantheon is of no special value in this context.[57] It is a modification of the Mahayana pantheon with extensive enrichment by non-Buddhistic, Vedic, Hinduistic (particularly Shivaist), and local Tibetan gods and demons. The Lamaistic pantheon also contains ancient Indian folk female (Sakti) goddesses as (latter briefly to be discussed) magical *tantrism* had formed them. Also here the Buddha was supplied with a divine spouse, in the manner in which, in later Hinduism, a spouse is to be found beside Vishnu. The intellectualized monastic character of all Buddhistic religiosity had also here tempered the orgiastic-ecstasy, namely, sexual-origastic elements of *tantrism,* as we have already seen in Hinduism and will have occasion to see further. However, practical religion, above all, lay religion, was pure hagiolatry, above all, deification of the *Lamas* themselves;[58] magical therapeutics and divination occurred without the ethical rationalization of the conduct of the laity. Beside their holy occupations and tribute to the monastery, the laity came into consideration only as pilgrims and dispensers of alms.

The holy seeking of the *Lama* himself took a Buddhist and also Hinduist direction insofar as also here the highest holy way was achieved by methodologically regulated meditation. In practice it became almost pure ritualism, especially *tantrism* and *mantrism,* and the mechanization of the cult of prayer-formula through prayer mills and prayer sticks, for the cause of which rose wreaths and similar means were first in Lamaism developed to their full consequences.

The former degree of ethical monastic disciple was essentially dependent on the order of political relations and is most narrow.[59] As shown by the mountain monastery Potala near Lhasa, today fallen into decay, the cultivation of science itself in monasteries of second rank was extensive. The development of an ever more inclusive religious literature, like the ever increasing storing up of first rank works of art in the pasture and desert territory, some 5000 meters above sea level with a frozen earth eight months of the year and with a pure nomadic people is under the circumstances so significant an achievement that it only could have been achieved under the hierarchic, rigidly organized Lamaistic monastic Buddhism with its boundless power over the laity. The ancient Chinese sacred military organization on the one hand, the Lamaistic monastic ascetic-organization with its tribute-paying and dispensing subjects on the other, here achieved culture on territory, which from the standpoint of capitalistic rentability was partially extensive eternal pasture, partly simply desert, therefore not the sort of place to support great construction and artistic production; with the downfall of that organization presumably it will once again silt over with the shifting sands of fate.

CHAPTER IX

THE ORTHODOX RESTORATION IN INDIA

1. General Character

We turn back once more to India proper.[1] There Buddhism in all its forms in the course of the first millenium of our era was pressed back step by step and finally was almost completely exterminated. In South India it gave way to Jainism. This may, as earlier indicated, be correlated with the superior community organization of this confession. However, Jainism, too, shriveled within the area of its diffusion, finally being reduced to the cities of West India where it still lives on today.

The field was won by Hinduism with the Brahmans on the top. It almost appears that the restoration of Hinduism proceeded from Kaschmir, the classical land of the magical science of the Atharva-Veda, as of Mahayan teaching. In the land of its origin the course of the renaissance is indicated already by Sanskrit speech—which, of course, did in no way simply develop parallel to the renaissance of Brahmanhood. In reality, Brahmanhood, as we saw, never disappeared.[2]

The Brahmans were only rarely displaced by the heterodox salvation confessions. This had purely external bases. The Jain *tirthankara* and the Buddhistic *ahrat* performed no sort of rites. The laity, however, demanded a cult, as well as definite representatives of such. In general that could be accomplished, where the need was present, only by monks, who gave up their meditation and teaching or by trained Brahmans, who submitted to the heterodox soteriology, and who, however, supervised the rites for the laity and appropriated the temple prebends for themselves. Brahmans therefore usually served as temple priests for the Jains, as we saw, and also in many Buddhistic communities Brahmans were found performing this function. The caste order furthermore had indeed loosened its hold, and large sections of its present territory were only won since the restoration.

However, the caste order never really disappeared in its ancient North Indian dominion territory. Buddhism, particularly, ignored it, but did not attack it. There was no epoch discernible in Indian literary or monumental sources in which it was not presupposed in practical concerns. However when the power of the guilds in the cities began to preponderate, particularly under Buddhistic influence, a genuine "welfare state" ideal begin to develop. The conditions which belong to the earlier mentioned description in the Vellala-Charita, of the conflict between King Vellala Sena and a Bengal trader of the king from whom a war loan was requested, belong also to the general heterodox conception that the *dharma* of the king lies not in conducting war but in concern for the welfare of the subjects.[3] This shy beginning of the concept of a city-bourgeoisie, looking away from the caste organization, corresponds to similar shy beginnings of teaching about the primitive status condition, which leads to the quite un-Hinduistic thought of an original equality and pacifistic golden age of men.

The growing princely power sought at the same time to fetter the Buddhistic plebeian hierocracy—that had developed, as we saw, in Ceylon and Burma and also in North Indian States—and to free themselves from the plutocracy of the bourgeoisie of the cities. They (the princes) revived the ties with the Brahmanical intellectual strata and the caste organization over and against the ancient Buddhistic monkdom and the guilds, and completed the partial receipt first of Mahayanaism, then later of pure, ritual, orthodox Brahmanhood. As the inscriptural sources indicate throughout, the power of the kings was decisive for the restoration of the new orthodoxy.[4] Through external and internal reorganization the Brahmanical hierocracy completed this process, which appears in classical form especially in Bengal, under the Sena Dynasty.

The Brahmans, indeed, as we have seen, never disappeared. However, so far as they had not assumed Buddhistic monastic rules they had been depressed into the subaltern situation of ritualistic temple priests. In general, from the time of Ashoka (around the fourth century) until about 300 years after Christ, it was only rarely that an institution in the inscriptions was favorable to Brahmans. The intention of the Brahmans, as a noble secular priesthood, became more than anything else to free themselves from their situation as subordinates to the congregation of monks, which also occurred in Mahayanism the more it developed contrary to the Brahmanical tradition. From the standpoint of the Brahmans, it was a strange body in the social system of Hinduism.

The restoration took place with the decay of the heterodox intellectual soteriologies, on the one side, in the stereotyping of caste ritualism, namely, in the form in which it appears in the law books of the first century of our time calculations. On the other side, the restoration occurred in the propagation of the ancient classical Hindu sects dating to the epoch of prior great kingdoms. And indeed it took place through the same means to which the heterodox communities owed their success: an organized professional monkdom.[5]

It is to these sects that we now turn. Even their rise signifies a turning away from the soteriological interests of the ancient intellectual strata which receded in Kschatriya times, and the fostering of that religion, which was adequate to the plebeian, aliterary strata which Brahmanhood had to reckon with only as clients. The "Rajputs" were indeed different from the ancient Kschatriya, their namesake.

Literarily the Brahmanical restoration manifested itself in the final editions of the epics. In practice, however, it appeared as a mission, in the rise of Purana literature. The final editions of the epics are the products of eminent Brahman editors. Quite the contrary is the case for Puranas. It was no longer the ancient, scholarly, pre-eminent Brahmañ families who composed this species; ancient bardic poets, it appears,[6] left the material. It was procured by temple priests and wandering monks (concerning whom more follows) eclectically organized, and contained the holy teaching of the particular sects; the epics, however, above all, the Mahabharatha, were still a kind of interconfessional, ethical paradigm. And as such it was recognized by all great sects.

Leaving aside, for the moment, the particular sect gods and the specific holy objects of sect religion, one already finds in the epics the types of officially accepted conjuring and animist practice greatly developed. Sympathetic and symbolic conjuring which approaches fetishism, spirits of holy rivers (particularly the Ganges), ponds, and mountains, the quite exceptionally developed word formulae and finger-pointing magic and after the introduction of writing into the tradition, writing magic as well—these all appear. All these elements stand beside the worship of ancient Vedic gods and the increase of diverse divinities and spiritually conceived abstractions.[7] The worship of the ancestors priests and of the cow stood beside one another, as Hopkins made evident. It continues into present-day folklore.

Since the development of the great kingdoms there has appeared the characteristic patriarchal development that patrimonial bureaucracy demands of its subjects. In the latest sections of the epics the king is already a kind of earthly god to his people despite the unsurpassed rise in power of the Brahmans. This Brahman power was somewhat different throughout and essentially greater than in the ancient Brahmanical writings. The patriarchal place of the elders, after the death of the oldest son, was strongly asserted. Doubtless through this teaching above all did the new Brahmanism recommend itself as a buttress to kingly power. For Buddhism in spite of all its developments was less patriarchally oriented throughout. Thus patriarchal power, in spite of its failure to follow a course similar to the Chinese, was finally responsible for the division of highest power—both aspects of which remained orthodox—and, above all, for the powerful position of ascetics and *gurus,* concerning whom there is more to be said.

The holy values were also enriched. In addition to the hero's heaven of Indra and the high universal heaven of Brahma, final absorption in the unity of Brahma is found in the epic as well as the ancient folk belief that the souls of good men will be transformed into stars. Also a varied combination of Hinduistic elements now was offered by the sects. They are partially contained in the later editions to the Mahabharatha, in which the Brahmans apparently tried to achieve a kind of equipoise and adjustment to the sects; they are contained particularly in the Puranas, which were pure sect catechisms.

Like the learned rewritten sections of the epics, which in their latest editions are already developing into this genre of literature, so are the Puranas, above all, the Bhagavata Purana even now an object of recitation for the broad Hindu public. What then were the new elements of content? There are two new personal gods—in themselves ancient but at last within the official intellectual culture for the first time grown to influence—Vishnu and Shiva.[8] There are some new holy values. Finally, the construction of the hierarchical organization of the sect development of medieval and contemporary Hinduism has made its appearance. We turn now to the holy values.

The ancient, cultivated, intellectual soteriology, as we saw, ignored and banned all orgiastic-ecstatic and emotional elements together with the correlated magical practices belonging to original folk belief. Below the level of those seeking Brahmanical gnosis there was a scorned substratum of disreputable magicians preoccupied with the problem of folk religiosity. However, in the interests of their power position, the Brahmans could not completely ignore the influence of this magic and the need for rationalizing it, as, indeed, had been accomplished already in the Atharava Veda with its concessions to unclassical magicians. In *tantra* magic folk ecstasy made its entrance into Brahmanical literature, and the *tantra*-writings[9] were viewed by many as the "fifth Veda." While in India, as in the Occident, the systematic rationalization of magical art, namely, alchemy and nerve physiology for ecstatic purpose, formed the anticipations of rational empirical science, we cannot here pursue the consequences further.

Tantra-magic was originally a form of orgiastic-ecstasy called forth through common indulgence of the five *nukara* [in later terminology was known as the "holy circle" (*puruabhishaka*)] the five things beginning with the letter "M": *madia,* alcohol; *mamsa,* meat; *matsya,* fish; *maithura,* sexual intercourse; *mudra,* holy finger gestures (presumably originally pantomines). The most important was alcohol bound up with sexual orgies,[10] and next, the bloody sacrifice beside the concluding meal. The goal of orgy was doubtless ecstatic self-deification for magical purposes. He who has attained possession of god, *Bhairava* or *Vira,* has magical power. He was united with the feminine creative power of *sakti,* which later appears under the names *Lakschmi, Durga, Devi, Kali Sana,* etc., represented by a naked woman eating meats and wine (*Bhairavi* or *Nayika*).

In some of its forms this cult was certainly ancient. As everywhere, here also the orgy as a form of holy seeking of the lower strata, especially also the Dravids, remained for a long time, particularly in South India where the Brahmanical caste order only developed late. The Jagannath-festival in Pari was an occasion, until the very threshold of the present, when all castes still ate together. Lower castes, e.g., the Parayans and the somewhat higher Vellalar in South India, had special rights in famous temples of the ancient, orgiastically-honored deities. Numerous residues are retained from the time when the upper castes also honored these deities. Even the very energetic moral policy of the British was only able with difficulty to control the sexual orgies and at least suppress their public manifestation.

The symbol of the ancient fertility-spirit with which the sexual orgies were homeopathically tied was here as everywhere else in the world the phallus (*lingam*, actually the combination of male and female genital parts). In all India it is lacking in almost no village. The Vedas deride the cult as an evil custom of the underprivileged. We are here not interested in this orgiasticism in itself.[11] More important for us is only its indubitably ancient and unbroken existence; without exception all important Hindu sects in their psychological peculiarity represent an often extensive sublimation of the universally diffused, orgiastic holy seeking by Brahmanical or non-Brahmanical mystagogues. In South India the process of this blending can still be seen in its residues because it is only incompletely achieved. Some of the lower castes of immigrant kings' craftsmen resist the regimentation by the Brahmans and, thus, there is a schism of Valan-gai (*Dakshinacharas*) and *Idan-gai* (*Vamacharas*)—castes of the "right" and "left" hand. The latter retain their own priests and their ancient orgiasticism; the first adjust themselves to the Brahmanical order.[12] The cult of those held to be validly orthodox castes of the "right hand" have concealed orgiasticism and especially, also, the bloody sacrifice. In place of this rice is employed.

In the course of amalgamation the ancient feminine fertility spirits were first elevated to the status of wives of the Brahmanical gods. A particular godly-form illustrating this process is the ancient Vedic fertility god,[13] Shiva (the Vedic Rudra). Ranged beside him was Vishnu as sun and fertility god. The feminine fertility demons came to be ordered beside one of the three orthodox gods or, better, subordinate to them. So, for example, Lakschmi was located beside Vishnu, Parvati to Shiva, Sarasvati (as patroness of lovely music and writing) to Brahma. Other goddesses followed. The ancient legends, which in many ways suggest Hellenic myths, prove that apotropaic or, in reverse, homeopathic orgiastic rituals were received. Many gods and, above all, goddesses not even represented in ancient literature now appear as "orthodox." This process appears throughout India and the Puranas are its literary expression. Thoroughly eclectic philosophically, they attempt to gird up and extend the sect doctrines cosmologically.

The driving motive of the Brahmans in this reception and accommodation process was in part quite grossly material. They wished to protect the many prebends and incidental fees which were available if one accepted the service of these ineradicable folk deities. As well, there was the force of competition against the powerful salvation confessions of Jainism and Buddhism which had managed to get into the saddle only through adaptation to the folk tradition. The formal method of the reception was as follows: the folk demon or god was identified directly with a Hinduist or—if an animal cult was involved—as an incarnation of such. In this respect essentially the fertility gods, Shiva and Vishnu, came into consideration. These were deities, who, indeed, themselves had orgiastic elements in their cult past. The cults, however, were if possible tempered in interpretation by orthodox vegetarianism, and alcohol and sexual abstinence. We will not develop the details of the accommodation process which Brahmanhood underwent with folk religion, nor the widely diffused cult of snake and sun spirits.[14] Here we will consider only the more important phenomena.

The decisive form of the unclassical but orthodox Brahmanical reception of worship of feminine fertility goddesses is illustrated by the customarily designated "Sakta" sect. Important parts of *tantristic,* magical-esoteric literature, whose significance for Buddhism we have already examined, formed its literary expression. The religious-philosophical connecting point for those Brahmans who sought to rationalize *tantrism* and thereby serve the popular Sakti-goddesses was sought in the teaching of Samkhya-philosophy of the *prakriti* and in the Vedanta concerning *maya,* which they conceived monistically as the original material, or dualistically as the feminine principle in opposition to masculinity, represented through Brahma as world creator.

This religious philosophy is throughout of such secondary character that we can completely ignore it although it could have functioned in the creation of exact science. The intellectual spiritualization of the orgy was developed into meditative worship of the holy circle (instead of the feminine sexual organs). The urban Sakta-cult also developed into the adoration of the naked woman as representative of the goddess cult act. Bound up with the alcoholic and sexual orgy of the folk cult was often the specifically Sakta-cut form of blood sacrifice, the *puja*—originally, and until the threshold of the present, a human sacrifice and a meat orgy. Such cults negative to the rationalization of conduct are also found, namely, in east North India (Bihar and Bengal), to be bound up with the middle classes. Such was the Kayasth (scribe) caste which for a long time was predominantly *tantristic.* The distinguished strata of Brahmanhood always remained remote from this accommodation, although they too had to seek a relation to folk cults. There were found different stages of crypto-erotic sublimation along the way to ascetic reversal of sexual orgiasticism.

2. *Shivaism and the* Lingam *Cult*

THE Brahmans succeeded in concealing the alcholic and sexual-orgiastic character of the adoration of the phallus (*lingam* or *linga*) and transformed it into a pure ritualistic temple cult which—as already observed—was diffused throughout the whole of India.[15] This cult recognized as orthodox commands the interest of the masses through its very cheapness which is not to be underestimated. Water and flowers serve for the normal ceremonies.

Brahmanical theory thoroughly identified the spirit which the Linga possessed as a fetish or—according to sublimated conceptions—the symbol of this, with Shiva. Perhaps already in the Mahabharata the reception had been completed. In characteristic opposition to the ancient sexual orgiasticism, the god was happy when the *lingam* remained chaste.[16] The *tantra* literature consists almost completely, corresponding to its orgiastic origin, of dialogues between Shiva and his bride. Through compromises with both tendencies Shiva became the particular "orthodox" god of medieval Brahmanhood. In this very general sense Shivaism also encompassed great oppositions for it was in no way unified.

The Brahman and Mimamsa teacher Kumarila Bhatta, named Bhattacharya, in the seventh century of our time calculations is the first great polemicist against the Buddhistic heterodoxy. The first established extensive and lasting workable solution, however, the renaissance of Brahmanhood in the sense of a joining of the ancient philosophical tradition of intellectual soteriology with the propaganda needs, took place under an (apparently) Malabar Brahman half-breed and learned commentator on classical Vedanta-writings of Sankara, named Sankarachrya[17] in the eighth or ninth centuries. He presumably died at the young age of thirty-two years (in truth, thirty-two years after the beginning of his reformation). He appears to be the first to have systematically developed the particularly incongruous Vedanta doctrine that Brahma-Para-Brahma was—the personally highest, and at bottom single, God.

All other divine beings were appearance-forms of Brahma. Of course, though he was himself regent of the world he was not its final basis. In the Hindu system this must unavoidably remain super-personable and inscrutable. In the Hinduistic hagiolatry Sankara stands at the peak. All orthodox Shivaistic sects consider him leader and many conceive him as an incarnation of Shiva.

In the most eminent Brahman school of India, the *Smarta* (from *smriti*, tradition), especially in the South with the famous monastic school in Shringerie, in the North primarily with the monastic school in Sankeshwar, Sankara is made central to doctrine and the schools adhere rigidly to his teaching. Since his work each new Brahmanical reform movement has had to acknowledge a personal god as world regent and the syncretistic orthodoxy has then formed Brahma with both folk gods Shiva and Vishnu into the classically Hindu trinity.

Corresponding to his origin as a construction of the philosophic schools Brahma himself remained, of course, an essentially theoretical figure and in the nature of the case subordinated to both other deities. Cult was organized around him only in a few temples for distinguished Brahmans. In general, he receded in importance before Shiva and Vishnu, who in orthodox syncretism were viewed as his phenomenal appearance forms. Actual sect relations inevitably considered either Shiva or Vishnu to be the highest and particularly in fact, the single God. The peculiar classical neo-Brahmanical soteriology develops almost completely in the name of Shiva. More important, however, than Sankaracharya's eclectic teaching was his practical efficacy. In essentials, he proposed a monastic reform in the grand style, with the conscious intention of fighting the heterodox Buddhistic and Jainistic monastic orders. The monastic order, according to official tradition divided into ten schools, which he called into being which he headed as "Dandi" the name taken from the pilgrim's staff. According to strict observance only a family-less Brahman (without parents, wife, or children) could be taken into the order. The mendicant monk of the Puranas was different from the ancient classical forest hermit (*vanaprastha* and *asrama*). It was his *dharma* in the time of wandering not to stay more than one night in a village.[18] "*Atit*," the "unexpected guest" is an old name for the wandering monk. The rules for ethical conduct were throughout bound up with the traditional prescriptions of Brahmanical soteriology: "self-control," also controlling the word, body and soul in action and thought were basic. As in the case of Jesuits of the Occident, the new element was the specific intention of a mission and care for souls. For the purpose of these the prohibition of the receiving of money—indeed, quite according to the Buddhistic model—was sharpened, while at the same time, however, for each of the four great monasteries, which Sankara personally founded a "novitiate" was established, *Brahacharin* order whose members did not beg on their own but only as "serving brothers"; they accompanied the *Dandi* and eventually were allowed to receive money—a form of circumventing the formal prohibition of begging for money which also appeared in European begging orders. After twelve years as monks the *Dandi* and *Sanyasi* achieved the dignity of "Para Hamsa" who were settled in the monastery with preponderantly literary obligations and at whose head stood a superior called a "*Swami*."

Through the ritual reception in the order the monk experienced a rebirth and indeed as an earthly god. Only the deified full monk was originally permitted to serve the laity as *guru*. From former times the power of the monk over these was very significant, namely, that of the monastic superiors. The superior of the monastery in Shringeri, the mightiest until the present, could through excommunication outlaw any Shivast from the community of believers in the whole of South India. Each monk and also each correct lay person who belonged to a sect had his *guru*. The home of the *guru* was for the adherent, so to speak, a spiritual dwelling place. Only in terms of the seat of this *guru* and only after the spiritual affinities of other *gurus* can the sect adherence be indubitably identified; among correct Sankarites also through their "*tirtha*" (place of pilgrimage—somewhat like Mecca for the Islamites—in this case the seat of the cloister or the *guru*). This was also true for others, for example, the late sect adherents of *Chaitamitic,* through the *sripat* (the seat of the "*sri,*" of the *guru* whom the individual worships).

According to Sankara's intention, the literarily cultivated, wandering monk should destroy opponents through religious speech; and, settled in the monastery, the *guru* should take over the spiritual needs of the believer. Nevertheless, both should remain in the hands of the spiritual leader of the school founded by Sankaracharya. The external organization of the monastic and temple service was assisted by the native rulers of the time partly through kingly institutions.[19] Often, however, these were so organized that the prince possessed formally free will and private institutions were accoutered with definite compulsive rites which secured their external existence and their monopoly.[20]

Before our time calculations indication is found in the monumental sources for temples at least of the present practice in India as in China of foundation through subscription,[21] and the creation of an entrusted committee (*goshti*) which conducted the administration and mostly supported itself. Spiritual leadership, mostly in the monasteries and at times in the temples, as well as economic activities lay in the hands of the superiors designated by the spiritual founder. In order to achieve the closure of the monkhood the Sankaracharyas school appears to have placed greatest importance on the celibacy of the *gurus.* Three of the first ten schools held to be classical firmly held to the principle that the soul benefactor must remain single. However, in general this is no longer the rule. The Sankaritistic, ritually consecrated *Grihasthas* today are *gurus* of the laity as earlier were the monks of the cloister. Now there is the practical difference—that they are no longer able to choose outside the order the *purohita* (house chaplains) or bring Brahmans in to serve as practicing priests. Vegetarianism and abstinence from alcohol dominates in correct *sankaritic* circles. Likewise Vedic (Sanskrit) education is pursued and the basic principle observed that only "twice-born" castes can be received into the sect, only Brahmans into the order. This, of course, is not strictly observed. The monks at present designated "Sanyasi" are often illiterate, serving members castes not "twice-born," taking money, and conducting an empirical (in general not unworkable) therapeutic which they propagate as a secret teaching.

Each Brahman of higher caste today has a *lingam*-fetish in the house. However, the Shivaistic revival was not by its own power able to interpenetrate the people with its orthodox holy teaching and achieve the elimination of heterodoxies. Nagendra Nath Vasu[23] analyzed the strata of religions as they appeared in Bengal in the twelfth century and discovered that as well as the 800 immigrant orthodox Brahman families, the Hinayana school dominated west of the Ganges, in general Mahayanism in the upper circles of the monks and laity, Yogaism and some Buddhistic and hagiolatrous sects in the middle classes, pure Buddhistic ritualism and hagiolatry in the lowest strata; *tantrism,* however, was diffused through all the classes. It was primarily the activities of a king, namely, Vellala Sena, which brought the Brahmanical orthodoxy to dominance.

Shivaism shared with late-Buddhism the peculiarity of drawing together the upper intellectual strata on the one hand, and the lower on the other. For as Buddhism, in addition to the salvation doctrine of the intellectuals, had received *tantrism* and *mantrism* as the most usable ritualisms of the masses, so the Shiva cult alongside the ancient-classical Brahmanical tradition, which it received via the epics, accepted the phallic and apotropaic ecstasy and magic. From these sources Shivaism developed a peculiar scholastic asceticism (*charya*), which is mentioned, namely, in the *Mahabarata,* corresponding to the origin of the Pasupata school, to a high degree taking on an irrational character, mind wandering and other paranoid states being held as the highest holy achievements which were thought to contain magical power[24] for the destruction of suffering.

The chastity asceticism generally known from the epics was transformed by Shivaism into a mass phenomenon within the sect as well as for the laity. In the middle of April each year all correct Shivaistic lay persons of lower class are gathered together by their *guru* and engage in week-long holy practices of a number of kinds. They are of no interest here except that they are of a thoroughly—in opposition to Yoga contemplation—irrational type, often pure, nervous virtuosity performances. The most frightful spirits and the fertility god were represented powerful magical virtuosos thirsting for sacrificial blood. With these things, gradually freed from its symbolic origin, the phallic *linga*-fetish came to play a major cultic role for the masses.

The eminent Smarta school considered itself to be the representative of the ancient tradition because it retained in purest form the Vedantic holy value of self-negation through unification with the deity and the Vedantic holy path: contemplation and gnosis. The ancient Hindu teaching of the three *gunas—satra, rajas, tamas*—lived on in the sect. So did the impersonality of the divine spirit in the three forms—being, wisdom, holiness—live. Within the maya world of cosmic illusions, they could be manifested as a personal god and as an individual spirit which can be conscious (*viraj*). The wakeful spiritual state of the individual soul is the profundity of divinity—dreamless removal of the highest type because the holy object is approached.

With this teaching, naturally, the popular *lingam* cult had only slight relation. For the simple worshiper of the *lingam,* in general it was not Shiva but the *lingam*-fetish, and in all cases the ancient masculine or more often feminine and strongly animistic local deity which was familiar to him as the object of the cult. In this the ancient Shiva cult and, namely, the ancient Sakti cult, in a manner originally peculiar to his wife the goddess Durga, received the orgy and blood sacrifice as an unclassical form of folk cult.

Sex and blood orgies were at times amalgamated in a sadistic manner. Individual Shivaistic holiness was detached from this, for it was often of a strong ascetic character, requiring most virtuous chastity. Shiva himself appears in the literature as a rigid ascetic. With the reception of customary holy seeking through the Brahmans, precisely the most extreme forms of monastic asceticism were represented as Shivaistic. Doubtless this was because the ancient prestige of charisma achieved through chastity was advanced as a means of competition against the heterodoxies.

A range of practices from extreme and pathological chastity to pathological orgies was apparent in popular Shivaism, in part of the native fertility form; also human sacrifice was not lacking until the most recent times.[25] Finally, common to all Shivaist religiosity in general was a certain coldness of temper in the feeling-relation to God. Shiva was no god of love and mercy. His adoration took neither a ritualistic nor ascetic nor contemplative form, except so far as it retained an ingredient of heterodox orgiasticism. Precisely that quality of cool contemplation had made this god acceptable to the Brahmanical intellectual soteriology. For Brahmanical soteriology found theoretical difficulties only in the fact that Shiva was precisely a personal God and equipped with the attributes of such. For this purpose Sankarachrya had provided the connecting link.

The introduction of the entire unclassical *lingam* cult into classical ritual which knew nothing of it, was of course, difficult in practice. The greatest Shivaist festival on the 27th of February is even now purely the worship of a decorated *lingam* bathed in milk. The entire "spirit" of this cult was in tension with the tradition of intellectual soteriology as well as to that of classical Vedic ritual. In fact the danger of a breach always remained, as the split between orgiastic and ascetic orientation as Shivaism today indicates. It resulted in a large number of controversies, above all, in the heresy of Basava, the founder of the Lingayat sect, which in the general view is the most bigoted of all Hindu religious communities. The founder, a Southwest Indian Shivaistic Brahman (twelfth century) came into conflict with the hierarchy because he held that the ceremony of girding of the holy cord, which ended with sun worship, was heretical and he refused to believe it. He was at the time a court Brahman and prime minister of a Kanaristic King. His adherents were and remained strongest in Kanaristic territory but the views diffused widely over Southern India. The denial of Vedic ritual by Basava resulted in breaking loose from the Brahmans and splitting the caste order.[26]

The religious equality of all men, also of women was preached. The rational anti-orgiastic course of Shivaism was intensified. Part of the sect was "puritanical" in sexual respects. Yet it appears that this was not firmly held. They were and are more strict in other ritual respects. They not only banned the enjoyment of meat but declined to take part in any type of meat- or cattle-trading or in the breeding of cattle for war service. They not only rejected *tantra*, but belonged, at least in their beginnings, to the few sects which doubted the *samsara* teaching. The holy objective of the intellectuals consisted of meditation on the theory and symbols of the supernatural potency of Shiva's spiritualized *lingam*, leading to complete indifference to the world and the highest achieved of grace (*prusada*).[26] The customary soteriology, however, was of a purely magical and sacramental type. The *guru* carried the newcomer through the steps toward full membership, the eight (*ashtavarna*) sacraments which alone gave the right of full membership. In doctrine it was strictly "monotheistic," recognizing only Shiva and denying the Brahmanical-Hinduistic pantheon and the trinity of the highest gods.

However, Shiva was worshipped essentially in magical-ritualistic form. They carried the *lingam* as an amulet (*Jangama-lingam*). The loss of this object was held to be highly dangerous to one's luck. Beside the adoration of this amulet and the temple-phallus (the *sthavara lingam* that is to say, the firmly fixed, non-portable *lingam*), they recognized the devotion to the holy word and syllable (*Om*). Its priesthood, the Jangama, were in part wandering and monastic ascetics, in part *lingam*-temple priests. The latter belonged at times to an "establishment" of Lingayat villages.[27] In general they served as *gurus* for the laity. Obedience to the gurus was strong in the Lingayat, stronger than in any other Indian sect, namely, in ritual and ethics, including sexual ethics. In abstinence from alcohol the most rigid observants were the Visesha Bhakta. Besides the usual drinking of water used to wash the holy man's feet and similar hagiolatrous practices the idea appeared here that the divine picture of a *guru* symbolized his superiority. The same groups have also strictly adhered to the ancient castelessness.

In contrast to this, as mentioned earlier, in general the Lingayat, in accordance with the general fate of the sects, was once again pressed back into the caste order by the power of the environment. It did not escape again. First, there developed an aristocracy of the sibs of the ancient believer over and against the newer converts. Only to them were the eight sacraments fully available. Then status differentiation according to profession occurred. Indeed, according to Lingayat ritual its occurrence in different degrees was inconceivable. Finally, as we saw, the sect was organized simply according to the traditional castes.[28] The Samayanya, the "usual" Lingayat sects (in opposition to the pietistic observants) easily accommodated itself in these respects. All in all, the rationalistic course which expressed itself in the purism of the sect was not able to shatter the massive hagiolatry and traditionalism of its predominantly peasant adherence.

3. *Vishnuism and Bhakti-Piety*

IN SPITE of all contrary influences and nuances a significantly different type of religion (or group of religions) of the Hindu renaissance, different from that of genuine Shivaism, is indicated by Vishnuism. Orthodox Brahmanical Shivaism reduced the orgiastic ritualism of the *lingam*-cult to chastity. It took over the ancient classical Vedanta soteriology and introduced a personal world-regent into the system. In its inwardly highly heterogeneous form it won adherents, on the one hand, from distinguished Brahmans as a new orthodoxy; on the other hand, among the masses of peasants it appeared as a village temple cult. In truth, of course, though not recognized by the orthodoxy, blood, alcohol, and sexual orgies remained the domain of the actual folk cult of Shiva.

Vishnuism, on the other hand, tempered orgiasticism through passionate devotion and, indeed, primarily in the form of the love of the redeemer. The bloody sacrifice of ancient Shivaism and the radical virtuosity of chastity were strange to it. Vishnu as an ancient sun god, a vegetation deity, was celebrated by a nonbloody cult, rather than with sexual (fertility) orgiasticism.

Throughout the connection, which always is close, of the sun cult with an incarnated redeemer assumed the form of the specific savior religiosity which India produced and found thereby, so it seems, its basis primarily in the middle class burgher strata of Indian society. Each intensification of fervor and of genre form finds its best comparisons in those trends which in Italian plastic art one can observe between the Pisanos, father and son, and which goes hand in hand with the expansion of mendicant monkhood. Further comparisons are naturally to be found in the attitudinal aspects of similar phenomena in the Counter-Reformation and in Pietism.

In India it was primarily the Krishna cult which provided the basis from which this development could proceed. Vishnuism was the religion of "Avatars." It was the religion of the incarnation of highest gods come down to earth. Krishna was not alone: ten, then twenty, then twenty-two, then even more deities were found. Ranking beside Krishna appeared a second important and highly popular incarnation of Vishnu: Rama. Rama was perhaps a victorious historical king, the hero of the second great Indian epic, Ramayana.

He was occasionally represented as the brother of Krishna. He was even occasionally (in the Mahabarata) described as one of Krishna's appearance forms and in three different figures, all held to be the *incarnations* of the same hero, as benefactor and savior. In contrast to Krishna, who in all his acts is throughout unethical, Rama is far more moralistically accoutered. The relation to the ancient cult of the sun, Surya, was far more strongly retained in his cult than in that of Krishna.

It appears that the vegetation festival and the nonbloody sacrifice, which was characteristic of Vishnuism, in opposition at least to the ancient Shivaist meat orgy, stem from this cult. And, on the other hand, that sexual orgiastic ingredient which lived on in sublimated form in the Krishna-Vishnuistic cults appears in more raw form in the Rama-cult. Also the Ramayana provided occasion for philosophical speculation. Rama is thus an important universal benefactor, appealed to ritualistically through prayer-formulas, partly by the philosophically educated, partly, in reverse, by the quite uncultured masses. The peculiar pietistic redemption piety of an aliterary but wealthy middle class, it appears, was from the beginning closely tied to the erotic or crypto-erotic adoration of Krishna.

It was indicated how the "belief" in a personal inner relation of trust came to the foreground, e.g., in the Bhagavat-religion. Further development led to the concept of an all powerful personal god, Vishnu, the ancient Vedic sun and fertility god, with whom the ancient deity of the Bhagavat was identified. Krishna was held to be the most important incarnation of the mythical redeemer.[29] The main point, however, was that a new quality of piety already appears in late interpolations in the Mahabarata. Holy knowledge and gnosis, ritual and social fulfillment of duty, asceticism and Yoga-meditation are in no case the decisive means of holiness. This was obtained through *bhakti,* the passionate inward devotion to the redeemer and his grace.

It is possible that this meditative piety was peculiar to a sect, the Bhaktas, who were different from the Bhagavats already in earlier times. In the last edition of the epics it is bound up with the doctrine of grace. The orgiastic, and indeed sexual-orgiastic origin of *bhakti* ecstasy, is clear beyond all doubt, for the sexual orgies of the Krishna worshipers persisted even after the Brahmanical sublimation to god-contemplating devotion, remaining until the present. The Mahaprasada eucharist in which all castes ate together at a sacrificial meal was—quite similar to the earlier mentioned Jaganath orgy of the South Indian castes of the left hand—an apparent residue of ancient pre-Brahmanical rites, and was found in almost all *bhakti*-sects.[30]

The very tangible residues of sexual orgiasticism among the Vishnuites are still to be accounted for. Especially for the Chaitanyas, a popular revival later to be described, the basis of *bhakti* was recognized to be the coarse sexual orgiasticism of the masses, accompanying cultivation of the earth, and thereby was itself of a sexual-orgiastic character. Above all, the psychological quality of *bhakti* itself supplied the clue; the prescribed steps should lead through three or four other states of feeling to an inner emotional relation to the redeemer.[31] This emotional relation was interpreted as similar to that of the erotic experience of lovers. In place of the real sexual orgiasticism appears also the crypto-erotic enjoyment of fantasy. To this end the crudeness of ancient erotic Krishna mythology was increasingly turned in a crypto-erotic direction.

The youthful adventures of the hero who was, according to the legend, a shepherd (*Govinda*) with the shepherdess (*Gopis*) stood from early times at the center of the Krishna myths and also, indeed, of Krishna mimes. The famous Gitagovinda, first made available to the West in Ruckert's translation, was a glowing, erotic, poetic representation of these adventures. However, it is beyond all doubt that this was important also for the inner quality of the later developed, Christian legends—the history of the Bethlehem youth, above all—which represented a sublimation and enrichment of the redeemer eroticism.[32] In the intellectual soteriology of the ancient Bhagavata religion *bhakti* meant somewhat the same as piety, namely, Zinzendorf Pietism, of the Wittenberger orthodoxy in the seventeenth and eighteenth century. In place of masculine believing—trust—a feminine emotional relation to the redeemer made its appearance.

In contrast to *certitudo salutis* which this salvation circumstance provided, all the other holy paths receded. The *advaita* salvation of the Vedantists, as well as Mimamsa justification by work, are minimized while the "cool" wisdom of the Samkhya salvation did not even come into the consideration of the *bhakti* practitioners. All ritualistic or other holy practices of Hindu piety only had value so far as they were addressed to the redeeming god or savior. This had already been taught by the

Bhabavata religion. Such religious manifestations were important, finally, only as technical devices subordinate to the single decisive holy circumstance.

In this interpretation anything, at least so long as the right attitude is present may serve as a religious means. The theology of this religion of grace was subject to the same discussion as occurred in the Occident. The theory of the *gratia irresistibilis* the one who is saved like the cat which carries its young in its mouth stood over and against the other that of *gratia cooperativa* in which grace operates like the ape mother of whom the young hang about her neck.[33] Once again the "sacrifice of the intellect" was demanded. The individual is required "not to doubt the commandments of the Vedas with human reason." "Works" are valuable only if it—corresponding to the teaching of the Bhagavatgita—they are "disinterested" (*niskama*). "Interested" (*sakama*) works cause *karma*, the "disinterested" works lead to *bhakti*.[34]

According to the sublimated form of *bhakti*-theory,[35] the true *bhakti* adherent preserved himself in the love of god finally in the absence of unpure thoughts and drives, particularly anger, envy, desire. This inner purity gave *certitudo salutis*. This consequence must have resulted where instead of the acute ecstatic unification with the God or the Redeemer one sought a permanent holy condition. This occurred particularly in the intellectual strata.[36] Beside *karma marga*, the holy path of the ritualistic Brahmans, and *inana-marga*, the holy way of the contemplative Brahmans, and beside *Yoga marga*, the holy path of the (increasingly) aliterary ecstatics appeared also *bhakti-marga* as an independent holy means. Meanwhile the most sublimated and ethically rationalized forms were opposed to one another which the *bhakti*-state essentially crudely included. For *bhakti* became a form of holiness which was diffused in all strata of Vishnuistic Hinduism—and partially also beyond these.[37] And of the nonritualistic pure forms of holy seeking, it is even today, in general, the most broadly diffused in India. This is true even though by the classical Brahmanical tradition each of its forms is held only to be an unclassical holy path.

As a form of emotional redemption religion it quite naturally became the primary form of holy seeking of the aliterary middle classes. Almost all Hindu reformers of Vishnuistic preference have in some way or other seized upon the crypto-erotic sublimation,[38] or, in reverse, the popularization of *bhakti* holy seeking and its combination with ancient Vedic ritualism.[39] In South India the professional teachers of *bhakti*, the *alvar*, distinguished themselves from the teachers of disputation, the *acharya*. Naturally, from the latter derive the least "pietistic," emotionally-oriented reformers.

Particularly to them belong both of the most significant Vishnuite sect founders on the basis of the Rama cult: Ramanuja (twelfth century) and Ramananda (fourteenth century). Both were Brahmans who led wandering lives as teachers and who conducted the organization and instruction of mendicant monks, quite in the manner of Sankaracharyas, as a means of the mass propagation of their holy teaching and the retention of adherents.

Ramanuja is supposed to have left behind him seventy-four (or indeed eighty-nine) *gurus* as personal disciples and *directures de l'âme*. And it appears that the stability of his organization essentially rested on the fact that it was a hereditary hierarchy. In addition to the *dandis* and *sanayasins*—names which forthwith were used for the Shivaistic mendicant monks—there appeared the *vairaghis* as (most) of its Vishnuite competitors were described.[40]

The doctrine which Ramanuja constructed out of the Vedanta system of Sankaras held that behind the personal God belonging finally to the *maya* world is the inscrutable, attribute-less Brahman. Insofar as the world is no cosmic illusion but the limbs and appearance of the divine, the personal God (*Parabrama*) is a reality and world regent, not a part of the *maya* world but substantially different. In fact he is as much different from the spiritual (*chit*) as from the nonspiritual (*achit*). *Maya* and impersonal divinity were held to be products of "love-less" doctrine. Accordingly, as a holy value, immortality and not reception in the divine was promised. The influence sphere of the sect was therefore called "dualistic" (*dwaitawadi*) because it taught the substantial difference of God from the soul substance and thereby the impossibility of reception in God (the Vedantic *nirvana*).

Around the final section of the Bhagavadgita, philosophical speculation was much more developed by the intellectual strata of the Ramaistic Vishnu sect than by Krishnaists, that is, the struggle raged mightily between the Vadagala (the adherents of the *gratia cooperativa* which characterized the Sanskrit-educated monks), and the Tengala (the adherents of the *gratia irrestibilis* practiced by monks with Tamil as a holy speech). The last-named school inclined to strong indifference toward caste distinctions. According to the genuine teaching of Ramanujas the achievement of the true *bhakti* was connected with *upasana,* the ancient classical meditation, also with Vedic education. Consequently, it was not immediately available to the Shudra. *Bhakti* could be achieved only through *piapatti,* unconditional devotion to God out of a feeling of complete helplessness; therefore, holiness was available only through guidance of the Vedic-cultured *guru.* Thereby the lower strata who were drawn to it, in consequence of the lack of sentimental motives, were turned toward pure, prayer-formula ritualism combined with all sorts of animal cults (as the holy ape of the epics).

The competition against the Shivaists was at times, namely, under Ramanuja, very sharp and bitter with counter-persecutions and expulsions, religious disputes, competing monastic establishments or monastic reforms. The discipline of the Vishnuite *gurus* was partially anomalous and on the whole less ascetic than that of the Shivaists. Vishnuism to a large extent applied the principle of hereditary charisma to each Hindu. Also from the beginning Vishnuism established the *gurus* as a hereditary hierarchy. Personal *guru* power was particularly strong in general in the Vishnu sect. On the whole, it was more strongly developed than for the Shivaists. It corresponds to the character of Vishnuite religion, which, on the one hand, demands adoration of authority,[41] on the other, the continual incitement to pietistic "revivals."

Hereditary *guru* power first appears in large measure in the sect of Ramanujas. *Guru* families were established who are even now to be found (in Conjeveram). Ramanuja's reform consisted particularly in actions counter to the phallus (*lingam*) cult. In place of these practices, which in his eyes were unclassical fetishism, he advanced forms of sublimated orgiasticism, namely, the cult meal often practiced as the Arkan-discipline. Corresponding to the redemptory character of Ramaistic piety appeared, the calling on the benefactor by means of prayer formulae. Such is found among the Ramats, the sect of Ramanandas, alongside other details which distinguish its observance from that of Ramanujas. The *"mantra,"* the invocation formula consisting of a few words or a meaningless syllable, occasionally acquired an overwhelming significance as a result. Krishna and the ancient residues of sexual orgiasticism were conceived in terms of propitiousness to Rama and eliminated by this sect in its devotion in words. In general, the Rama cult is sexually pure. The feminine deity is the true goddess, in opposition to the Krishna cult with its orgiastic eroticism and preoccupation with Krishna's lovemaking.

On the other hand, an important social innovation was to be found for the first time as a principle in the mission of Ramananda. This was the disruption of the castes. Such disruption did not concern everyday social organization and everyday ritual. In this, with some exceptions, all sects accepted the caste restrictions without question. However, the question was opened as to the possibility of lower castes achieving *guru* status. The ancient wandering and teaching philosophers, sophists, and holy wise man of the Kschatriya epoch, as we saw, were largely eminent lay persons. Very often they were old men who had for the first time taken up the life of the ascetic and wandering teacher, as others who had assumed it temporarily. The heterodoxy, namely, Buddhism, had principally ignored the caste memberships of those whom it took into the order and had created the "professional monk." The Brahmanical restoration took these over, indeed, but once again required for reception into the philosophic schools and monasteries Brahman caste membership as prerequisite to becoming a *guru*. The Shiva sect, at least officially, on the whole adhered to this.

Ramananda, for the first time, expressly rejected this. Here, indeed, a role was played by the Islamic foreign domination which had in the meantime broken over India. It had, as earlier indicated, through destruction, conversion, or political displacement of the secular nobility left in the field, only the ancient native religious tradition indeed intensified it. The spiritual power of the Brahmans was multiplied. However, the external means of power of the Brahmans decayed and the founders of the sects sought more than ever to join forces with the masses.

All eminent founders of Hindu sects until Ramananda were Brahmans and, so far as is known, accepted only Brahmans as students and teachers. Ramananda broke with this principle. Among his immediate students were found—according to tradition—alongside a Rajput, Pipa, and a Jat; Dhuana, a weaver,

Kabir; even a Chamar (leather worker); Rai Das. Finally, and more important than this, however, was a phenomenon not without consequences for the infiltration of mendicancy with non-Brahmanical elements. Henceforth sects developed in all on the basis of status and professionally diverse aliterary strata. That the Smarttas was in essentials a pure Brahman sect was bound up with its character as a "school." The sect which stems from Ramananda and bears his name (the Ramanandi), in characteristic reaction to the "democratic" tendencies of his reform, later appears to have restricted admission to members of the aristocratic castes—the Brahmans and those classed as Kschatriyas. The esteemed Ramaistic mendicant strata—the Achari—were even recruited exclusively from Brahmans. They are ritualistically pure. On the other hand, the Rai Das Panthi sect founded by his student the Charma, Rai Das, had, corresponding to its social situation, developed social, charitable acosmic love out of *bhakti* piety; out of opposition to the Brahmans it had developed a denial of priestly power and idolatry.

Congruent to the social situation of these despised professional castes is traditionalism and a conviction of the unchangeable nature of the order of the world. It is the basic attitude of many sects.[42] The Maluk Dasis developed the consequences of quietism, while the Dadu Panthi, a Ramanandic sect of cotton-washers established in the seventeenth century, drew extremely deterministic consequences from the doctrines of the Bhagavadgita. One should not intentionally seek either heaven or hell, for everything is pre-established and only the capacity for spiritual love of Rama is a guarantee of grace, freedom from illusion and pride, and the suppression of desire. In addition to the mendicant monks (*virakata*), believers in strict possessionlessness, was a stratum which the Indians class as Rajas, soldiers (Naga), and a third, (Bhistu Dhari), which pursues bourgeois callings. This cult restricted itself almost completely to formal invocation of Rama. Finally, the sect widely diffused among the weaver castes—the Kabir Panthi, established by Ramananda's student Kabir—came to deny Brahmanical authority and all Hindu deities and ritual. It was strongly pacifistic, suggesting the Quakers. It advocated ascetic techniques of holy seeking—displaying forbearance to all forms of life, avoiding lying, shunning all worldly lust. Here, as in the Occident, textile handwork, with its relation to the household and opportunity for meditation, appears to have demanded such almost completely nonritualistic religiosity. Corresponding to Hindu tendencies, however, was the fact that it did not assume an active ascetic character, but led to the devout worship of the founder as a helper-in-need, and unconditional obedience toward the *gurus* as a cardinal virtue. An "inner-worldly," autonomous, life methodology of occidental stamp was not possible here.

A division of this sect was scornful of communal economic work, naturally, above all, of the specifically military.

The mendicants and ascetics of the neo-Hindu religions have also displayed that phenomenon found in Asia, particularly among the Japanese Buddhists, most extensively, however, among the Islamic Dervishes—the monastic conflict of belief, a product of the sect competition and of the foreign dominions of Islam and then of the English. A great number of Hindu sects develop the Naga type of outright weaponed propaganda of their ideas under the strict control of an ascetic *guru* or *gosain*. In caste affiliation they were rather "democratic," however, some like the Nagas of the Dasu Panthi sect, were exclusively restricted to the "twice-born" castes. They have made the role of the English difficult, but also have fought each other in bloody feuds. So, for instance, in 1790 under Hindu dominion a battle occurred between the Shiva Nagas whom the Vairaghis had excluded from the great market of Hardwar; the Shiva Nagas gave battle, leaving numerous dead on the field. As well, they have repeatedly attacked English troups. In part they developed into robber bands, living by the contributions of the people, or into soldiers of fortune.[43] The most significant example of this development of orders of propaganda fighters were the Sikhs ("students," of the founder of the sect and his *guru* successors), which for a time until the defeat of 1845, retained sovereignty over the Punjab, having established there a kind of pure warrior state. We shall not here pursue further this very interesting development.

Far more important for us is another kind of sect formation on the basis of Vishnuistic salvation religiosity, particularly that of Vallahba and some extending back to the student Chaitanyas. All were renaissances of orgiasticism against the single dominion of Brahmanical contemplation as a holy technique. Both display in the turning away from Brahmanical ritualism and world-fleeing contemplation not an active, inner-worldly asceticism but an inflaming of irrational holy seeking—and this despite the introduction of a super-worldly god.

The sect founded at the beginning of the sixteenth century by the Brahman Vallabha, the Vallabhachari or Maharadscha or Rudra Samperadaya, is still today, at least in point of gravity, a merchant and banker sect, primarily found in Northwest India, but diffused over the entire land. It adheres to the Krishna cult and seeks the holy, in opposition to the intellectual tradition, not in asceticism or contemplation but in refined sublimated Krishna orgies, together with a rigid ceremonialism. The founder taught that not abstinence, loneliness, dirt, scorn of beauty, but the reverse was the proper direction to glory. The means for becoming worthy of the honor of God was enjoyment of the beauties of the earth and achieving community with him (the *pushui marga,* doctrine of the holy dinner).

Meanwhile, he intensified mightily the significance of the *guru* through the prescription that only in the *guru's* house were certain, most important ceremonies possible in valid form. An eight-fold daily visit was under certain circumstances necessary. He left his son Vittala Nath as leader, from whose sons the dynasty of *gurus* developed in many branches. The most distinguished was the successor Gokula Naths, the Gokulastha Gosains. The temple Steri Nath Dwar in Ajmer is the central holy place of the sect to which each believer must make a pilgrimage once in his life (patently in imitation of the Mecca pilgrimage).

The power of the *gurus* over the laity is great. A scandalous trial in 1862 in Bombay brought to light the fact that occasionally the *jus primae noctis* was practiced on the wives of the members and that holy conception, according to ancient orgiastic custom, is still realized among the community members in the present.[44]

The meat and alcohol orgies were sublimated into chaste culinary dinners; and similar changes took place in sexual orgies. It is self-evident that the plutocracy—the richest Hinduistic trader castes, above all, the Baniya—was able, in such terms, to find a taste for the service of God. An extraordinarily large number of them belonged to this somewhat socially exclusive sect.[45] It is strikingly evident here that ascetic religiosity absolutely does not, as is generally maintained, develop out of the imminent "nature" of bourgeois capitalism and its professional representatives—quite the contrary. The Baniyas, "the Jews of India," represent indeed[46] the main contingent of these outspoken, antiascetic, partly hedonistic, partially ceremonial cults. The holy object and holy path were graduated. Corresponding to the *bhakti* principle, grace, "*pusti*," becomes the single principle. The attainment of *pustibhakti* is only possible through inner-worldly, ritualistic righteousness of work (*pravaha-pustibhakti*) or lasting devotion in the service of God (*maryada-p*), which leads to "*sayujya*," or the attainment of holy-bringing "wisdom" out of particular power (*pusti-p.*), or, finally, it can permit salvation through pure grace, giving passionate belief (*suddha-p.*). Then one achieves paradise and the eternal bliss of Krishna. This holy path is in no way ethically rational.

Though the "spirit" of this cult corresponds little to the Brahmanical tradition yet it has recruited relatively distinguished Brahmans like the Derschaschth, out of interest in the generally fat prebends which the stations in the temples of the sect represent. The spiritual patriarchs proper of the community, the *Gosains,* were indeed permitted to marry, corresponding to the general type, but were obligated to continuous inspection journeys in their dioceses. Since they were themselves mostly important business people, this ambulatory life was favorable to the development and extension of business relations. The established interlocal organization of this sect in general was of some importance for it served the immediate business operations of its members. Alongside the Parsis and the Jains, but on quite other grounds from these, it (the sect) included the largest number of the important Hinduistic business people.

The exclusion of the lower castes from the Vallabhachara sect, however, outside of the great expenditures which its *pushuimarga* required, gave this essentially moralistic sect, founded by Swami Narayand, the possibility of doing considerable damage in the lower and also in the middle strata.

Exactly the opposite phases of Krishna-orgiasticism to those of the Vallabhacharis were developed in Northeast India in a number of sects which had their origin at about the beginning of the sixteenth century with the Brahman Chaitanya. He was himself, apparently, an epileptic and ecstatic. He taught the identity of Krishna with Parmaturu, the uncreated spirit of the world, which endlessly manifests itself in countless temporary appearances. His important new innovation was Sankirtan, the great singing procession which particularly in the great states was elevated to first rank as a folk festival. Pantominic or dramatic dances appeared therewith. Vegetarianism and abstinence from alcohol was retained at least among the upper strata, to which the Kayasth (scribes) and the Satsudra (ritually pure industries) belonged in Orissa, for example; however, also the ancient brewer caste were numbered (now mostly merchants), representing a significant contingent.

The principle of hereditary *guruhood* was also retained by this reform sect. It is the most popular, at least in North India, primarily in Bengal. In contrast to *tantrism* a peculiar esoteric was lacking and unlike the aristocratic intellectual strata it lacked all need for holy wisdom (no Sanskrit!). Each individual is able to practice the *bhakti* attitude without help. In mass religion crass sexual orgiasticism dominated. The adherents recruited from the lower-caste Chaitanitic sect formed the numerically most significant strata of Vishnuites (in Bengal ten to eleven million) and practiced jointly the orgiastic invocation of Krishna (Hari, Hari, Krishna) and Ramas. At least for most of them, the sexual orgy was the primary means of self-deification, the device by which they sought absolution.

The Sahaya held that during the sexual orgy each man was Krishna, each woman Radha (his favorite). The Spashta Dayaka had intersexual monasteries as places for sexual orgies. In a less sharpened form were found residues of the Krishna orgies in other things. In a number of cults, and indeed not only for Vishnuistic sects, rituals were celebrated which place Radha beside Krishna himself. They appear today as general folk festivals. There is an account of the love life of Radha in the tenth book of the Bhagavata Purana—corresponding to the "Song of Songs" in the old Testament—as a symbol of reciprocal mystic love of the divine and central point of the human soul. These rituals are celebrated with song, dance, mimicry, confetti, and some orgiastic sexual freedom.

The estimation of pure, inner-worldly behavior as a holy technique appears only by some small disappearing Vishnuite communities. This was at first perhaps the case in the sect described by H. H. Wilson,[47] of Madhava, whose adherents were drawn from the Brahman (and ministers of king Vijayanagar). Madhava, abbot of Shringeri, founded the doctrine in the thirteenth or fourteenth century. He was[48] a Vishnuite, opponent of the Vedanta and adherent of the unclassical Ramaistic *dwaita* (dualistic) doctrine. Naturally, for him dualism was not the opposition between "good" and "evil" or between "God" and "creature," rather it lay between temporary life and eternal being. It was not eternal being alone that, for the human striving at least, is real, but exactly the opposite, life. It is eternal and irreversible. An absorption in formal eternal "being" in the sense of the Brahmanical doctrine, namely, the Vedanta, holds nothing for man.

Thus all presuppositions of Brahmanical soteriology are cast aside. Within this life man has to create his own holiness. A self-deification is unattainable, an attainment of unity with the godly impossible, for the eternal god is absolutely super-worldly and super-human. Yoga and all the exercises of intellectual soteriologies are meaningless; god dispenses his grace for correct behavior. With this the way was clear for an ethic of active, inner-worldly behavior in the sense of the Occident. Meanwhile, meditation as the highest holy path and "disinterested" behavior were held alone to be free from sin. There remained only the general presuppositions of Hindu theodicy—*samsara* and *karma.* Beyond this there was also retained the absolute authority over the believers of the knowledge of those soul helpers equipped with the holy (Vedic) wisdom. Indeed, the charisma of the qualified *guru,* as a personal quality of the qualified possessor, is in this doctrine, elevated to its highest point and treated as an alienable or purchasable property.

The unconditional dependence on the *guru* was held to be indispensable for lay salvation; only from him, not from books, could one win knowledge.

4. The Sects and the Gurus

THE place of the *guru* with respect to the believers was, in general, most widely extended in the Hindu community since the Brahmanical restoration. The position of the *guru* was modeled after the original absolute authority of the distinguished teacher of the Vedas (*guru*) over the scholar (*bramacharin*). At the time, however, this held only for conduct within the school. These ancient cultivated Vedic *gurus,* of whom the law books still speak, were employed as house chaplains by kings and nobles and as tutors of their sons. They imparted the genteel culture of the Kschatriya time.

However, since the church reforms of neo-Brahmanism, they were interpenetrated by essentially plebeian, less literary mystagogues and soul helpers, although it was precisely against this that Sankarachrya had directed his reforms. The creation of schooled and monastically-organized wandering mendicants, and the universal extension of the *guru*-conception were quite obviously—in addition to the connection with the court—the means by which the Brahmans had been victorious. As the Counter-Reformation churches through the mounting intensity of their confessions and the establishment of orders asserted anew their spiritual dominion over the masses, so these means brought in Hinduism by competition with the Jains and Buddhists. At least at first, the majority of mendicants and *gurus* were Brahmans. In essentials it is also so today.

The income, at times princely, which the *gurus* obtained from the mass sects must have led to the sharp resistence of the Brahmans to the usurpation of these positions. Not new doctrines but the universality of the *guru* authority symbolized the restoration of Hinduism. Quite apart from the Krishna and Rama cult which it embodied, it was a "redeemer" religiosity in a special sense. It offered the masses the corporal living savior, the helper-in-need, confession, magical therapeutic, and, above all, an object of worship in the form of a dignity-bearing *guru* or *gosain*—be it through the designation of successors, be it hereditary.

All sect founders were deified and their successors became and are objects of worship. The *guruhood* now constituted the typical role of the Brahman. As a *guru* the Brahman is a living god (*thakur*). No correct Shudra would fail to drink water in which a Brahman had touched his toe or to eat the left-overs procured from his table. The eating of the excrement of the *gurus* in the Gayatri-Kriya-Sacrament (presumably by the Satnami sect established by a Kschatriya in North India) and still practiced for short periods, was only an extreme case. The leading *guru* in a territory is similar to a bishop of a Western church, visiting his diocese accompanied by his following. He had power to excommunicate individuals in the case of the grosser sins. He bestowed absolution for penitence, placed a tax on the believers. In all and every consideration the *guru* was the most decisive advisor and father-confessor authority.

Each sect-believer had his *guru* who imparted religious instruction to him, and who taught him the *mantra* (prayer formulae). The *guru* took the believer into the sect with the drawing of the sect signs through branding or painting. The believer turned to his *guru* for advice in all life situations. In the Krishna sect children were brought to the *guru* in the sixth or seventh year and a crown of roses placed on them. Confirmation took place in the twelfth to the thirteenth year with corresponding (*samupana*) ceremony, for which the ancient form of girdling with the holy belts (the *samavartana* ceremony) supplied the rite. However, in terms of its significance it represented consecration of the particular body to Krishna.

Economically, as we saw, the diocese of the *guru* also viewed as the personal property of the *guru,* was not only—as most—hereditary, but also alienable, like the *"jajmani"* of a craftsman. Religiously, among the masses the worship of the *gurus* replaced all other forms of redemption religion. The living savior or god among the believers displaced all transcendant objects of worship. The practical measure of *guru* authority in the affairs of everyday life varied in the various sects, but quite understandably it was most extensive among the specifically plebeian sects. The institution also offered heterodox mystagogues the chance to represent themselves as soul leaders and gather adherents to themselves—namely, since exclusive political support of the Brahmans was lacking. The Hinduistic reformation had to take this in the bargain. On the whole, the popularization of Brahmanical teachers signified an extensive strengthening of their power. In the days of the Islamic foreign dominion and persecution, the *gurus* at times were the fixed support of the masses of Hindus in all inner and consequently also external needs. They were thus like the bishops of the Catholic Church in the time of the folk migrations.

Tied up with this increasing popularization was a marked change, accomplished during the restoration,[50] in the place and organization of Brahmanhood. The aristocratic Brahman of early times was the house chaplain of a king (*purohita*), or a noble, as they remain, namely, in Rajputana. Of equivalent honor to the *purohita* was the position of independent teachers of descendants of Brahmans, and after these of nobles compensated by *dakshina.* A Brahman of high caste was and is permitted to receive *dakshinā* only from the aristocratic castes.[51]

On the other hand, the distinguished caste which, according to rank was aristocratic and Vedic-cultured (Vaidika), claimed a monopoly in the taking of *dakshina* (therefore named *dakshina-charas*). Medieval developments brought for Brahmans, as we saw, the great prebend foundation of the princes and nobles in return for ritual service, writing administrative knowledge, and teaching power. The princes and nobles thus secured these services.

Naturally the capacity to receive pay for ritualistic instruction was monopolized by the Vaidika-Brahmans of full caste rank. As living *bhikkschu,* despite the retention of these signs later as in the case of the *bonzen* of the Buddhists, they often developed into a clergy without celibacy. These were different only by descent and Vedic schooling from the lay Brahmans called the *Laukika* or *Grihastha,* who had no share in the opportunities for prebends. Among these lay Brahmans the most distinguished were those who received secular wages for the performance of administrative service, for example, the Bhuinhar-Brahmans (from *bhum,* fiefs) in Bihar and Benares, and similar strata elsewhere.

As mentioned earlier all temple priests were degraded, (in Bengal they were called *madhya*). This was partly because their subaltern manipulations did not presuppose Vedic schooling, which most of them were lacking; partially, however, also because they lived on the gifts of undistinguished, often impure castes or on fees of alien pilgrims of uncertain purity.[52] Among the full Brahmans the highest-ranking individual, according to his own claims, took the ranked position of *pandit*. They were responding jurists and judges; the highest among them in the time before the foreign dominions was often held to be the first man of the land. In the restoration period, the position was further developed, indeed apparently like so many other Hinduistic institutions from Kashmir. Competing with them for power were the superiors of the great charismatic monasteries of whom the "Srimukh" of the Fetwa Decree (corresponding to the Islamic Mufti) was decisive and binding in all questions of ritual for the adherents of respective doctrines.[53] But this was only within respective spheres and, of course, under the circumstance of a doctrinal community including the majority of the sect.[54]

In all these ancient historical Brahmanical power positions, it was the possession of holy wisdom which constituted the quality which decisively lent a monopoly to the spiritual prebends. Profane juridical wisdom and the literary schooling constituted properties affording claim to worldly place.

So, among the students of Bikkshu-Dershashths in Maharanshthna, there stood beside the Vaidika the Castri (jurists), who had equal rank with one another and with the Jotishi (astrologers); Baidya (doctors); Puranika (recitors of the Purana). Next to heraldic rank[55] often but not always decisive for social estimate, was the interrelated[56] traditional degree of Vedic and Sanskrit schooling. In addition to this, the degree of esoteric, namely, *tantristic* "wisdom," was an important source of power, particularly of the Shivaistic Brahmans. In contrast, Yoga-schooling, for example, in present-day South India (Telinga), where it is usually found among Brahmans (Niyogin), constitutes no more than formerly a qualification for prebends.[57] The difference between spiritual and lay Brahmans is not completely uniform.[58] Cult procedures are variably interpenetrated by traditional rituals. In Bengal, Orissa, Mithila, and in Punjab there are genteel Brahman Saktis, who actually participate in bloody sacrifice but do not use alcohol or tobacco. The "extremists," that is to say, the alcohol-drinking Sakti-Brahmans, for example, in Sindh and Maharashtra are held to be of lower rank. The fact that in South India the pre-eminent Dravidic (Dravira) Brahmans are almost all Shivaists has a purely historical basis. In Rajputana the Vishnuite Srimali are especially distinguished (because they are purely Aryan). Only those forms of Vishnuism are degrading which give up Sanskrit or which accept *dakshina* from lower castes, both of which often occur together. Such was the case of the Chaitanitistic *guru* in spite of abstinence from alcohol.[59] Indeed, in Orissa the Chaitanitistic (Adhikari) Brahmans hold a rank between the Vaidika and lay Brahmans, under whom is to be found a ritually contaminated undercaste (the Mathan). However, as a general rule the Brahman is degraded as a Chaitanitistic *guru* because, like the *tantristic,* Vedic and Sanskrit wisdom is rejected and because the Brahman (generally) accepts *dakshina* from all (or almost all) castes.

These popular Vishnuite (mainly going back to Ramananda and Chaitanya) sects have now displaced the Brahmans in a most permanent fashion. To begin, while each had in itself only a small measure of unified organization, which for Shivaism was the work particularly of Sarkaracharyas, for Vishnuism it was completely ruptured. North India's weak form of Shivaism even lacked such a figure as the Abbot of Shringeri in the South; and in addition other monasteries were also present in South India. The power position of Sankeshwar was restricted to some distinguished Brahman castes. Vishnuism, that is, Chaitanitistic, mass Vishnuism was completely without this. Each *guru* dynasty in any way recognized formed a mainly hereditary hierocratic community in itself. In addition to increasing sect schisms, there appeared transformations in the form of power mechanisms. Vedic ritual wisdom, *tantristic* and Sakti esoteric as a basis of charismatic power position fell before the democratically oriented sects.

Emotional confessional agitation and competition in public, with its specifically plebeian means of recruiting and assemblage, appear. As well as processions and folk festivals, collective pilgrimages and similar forms made their appearance. The increasing number of small burghers and proletarian masses, and the increase of wealth among the burgher strata in the cities raised the chances for fees for the *guru* demagogue who was oriented toward them. Eminent Brahmans' deep suspicion of this competition could not spare them the bitter experience of developing out of their own circles the inclination to incorporate elements from *tantristic* and other such esoteric elements of Vishnuism. The authority of the *pandits,* even as the use of eminent cultivated Sankaristic and other Brahmans held to be completely classical declined before that of the aliterary (i.e., non-Sanskrit cultivated) hierarchies of the masses.[60]

The slow capitalistic development furthered by the English dominion—by opening quite new sources of accumulation of wealth and economic ascent—demanded this transformation. The old address *"Thakur,"* God, for the Brahmans was not only given up, but in general, also depreciated by the fact that it is the *guru* of the plebeian sect who is earnestly and really honored as a god.

This development is generally present where the neo-Hinduistic holy means is bound up with the Buddhistic—which occurs with special intensity among the Yogaistic- and mantristic-influenced Mantrayana school (those diffused in Java). Also this occurred: the authority of the Hinayanistic *guru,* already vast in the missionary territory, was elevated to the point where unconditional obedience to him became an absolute means of salvation.[61]

Such a divine or godlike place of the *guru* appears most strongly in precisely the kind of Hindu sect which radically set aside all idolatry and all other irrational, ecstatic, orgiastic, or ritualistic cult means. Adoration of the living savior was the last word of Hindu religious development.

The difference from the Catholic form of church was in organization; externally viewed, the monks and charismatic or hereditary mystagogues were finally its representatives. They differed also in their formally free will. Just as in China, there were nonprincely origins for official sacrifice. Moreover, temples for Brahman schools were established as a rule by subscription and with the formation of a committee, which took the external order and the conduct of the economy into its own hands. Under the Hindu princes this manner of instituting new cults could hardly prevail. However, under the alien beliefs of foreign dominions they were almost exclusively the external form of the propaganda of sect-cults. These developed in greatest number under the dominion of the bourgeois occupational strata. For the first time they achieved the possibility of emancipating themselves economically from official orthodox Brahmanism or of forcing this Brahmanism to accommodate itself to them.

The inscriptions show that these organizational forms remained the same for long centuries until the present. Just as typical is the spiritual domination of the *gurus.* Also the political power of the clergy was self-evidently great. The mendicants served the kings as spies (such an aspect played a typical role in the early history of Bombay). The Brahmans generally served as their officials and advisors.

It is established that apparently the most extreme forms of *guru* veneration were first realized in the last part of the fifth and sixth centuries. And this is understandable. So long as the kings had an interest in the Brahmanical secular priesthood the power of mystagogues and magicians and of monkdom in general could not become excessive. The kings were not inclined to permit the power of sect heads, even where their domestication of the masses exceeded their own.

It was first the foreign domination of Islam which shattered the political power of the distinguished Hindu castes, which gave the development of *guru* power free reign, permitting it to grow to grotesque heights.

This development of *guru* power to the point of human deification is instructive about the powerful significance in the Occident of the development of papal power. First, it brought under subjection the monastic churches of the mission areas, above all the Irish. At the same time, it legitimated them. It took under rigid official discipline the founding of monastic orders. It was not the personal super-worldly God, known also, indeed, to Hindu sect belief, but the inheritance of ancient Rome, the bishop office-church, which hindered the development as in India of monkdom through human adoration. It was not, it must be noted, the strong hierocratic power of the papacy as such—for the Dalai Lama was also powerful and great monastic superiors of the Indian sects were highly powerful hierarchs, but the rational office-character of the administration that was decisive over and against the personal or hereditary charismatic property of the *gurus*. We shall have more to say about this later.

In addition to the ritualistic and traditional inner relation anchored through the caste order to the *samsara* and *karma* teaching (undermined by none of the sects which comes into consideration[62]), there also appeared the religious anthropolatry of the Hindu laity against the naturally strong, traditionalistic, charismatic clergy of the *gurus*. These hindered the rationalization of life conduct throughout. It is quite evident that no community dominated by inner powers of this sort could out of its substance arrive at the "spirit of capitalism." It was also unable to take over the economic and technically finished form as an artifact, as occurred in Japan. There appeared here clearly and undoubtedly greater difficulties than in Japan, despite the English domination. When, today, the penetration of Indian society by capitalistic interests is already so extensive that they can no longer be eliminated, it is still possible for some eminent English students of the land to argue on good grounds that the removal of the thin conquering strata of Europeans and the *Pax Britannica* enforced by them would open wide the life and death struggle of inimical castes, confessions, and tribes; the old feudal robber romanticism of the Indian Middle Ages would again break forth.

Let us once more make clear which "spiritual" elements outside the caste ties and the *guru* domination of the masses served to fix the economic and social traditionalism of Hinduism. In addition to authoritative fixity, within the intellectual strata there was above all the dogma of the unalterability of the world order, common to all othodox and heterodox Hindu thought forms. The devaluation of the world which each salvation religion brought with it could here only become absolute flight from the world. Its highest means could be nothing other than mystic contemplation, not active ascetic conduct. The prestige of this holy path as the highest of all was not modified by the mass of various different ethical teachings. Always the extraordinary quality and irrationality of the holy means remained. Either they were of an orgiastic character and linked quite immediately in anti-rational manner to the course of each alien life methodology, or they were indeed rational in method but irrational in goal. The professional fulfillment, however, which, was demanded for example, in highest measure by the Baghavadgita was "organic."[63] That is to say, it was rigidly traditionalistic in character and thereby mystically oriented as an activity in the world but yet not of the world. At any rate, it would occur to no Hindu to see in the course of his economic professional integrity the signs of his state of grace or—what is more important—to evaluate and undertake the rational constitution of the world according to empirical principles as a realization of God's will.

Allowance must always be made for the thinness, past and present, of the India intellectual strata proper and, in general, the strata interested in "salvation" in some sort of rational sense. The masses, at least, of the contemporary Hindus know nothing about "salvation" (*moksha, mukti*). They hardly know the expression, let alone its meaning. Except for short periods, it must have always been so. Quite crude and purely this-worldly holy interest, gross magic, along with the betterment of rebirth chances were the values for which they did and do strive. Moreover, the sects, at least today, do not address themselves to the real "masses." If one takes as a standard the public membership of a sect (through imparting of the *mantra,* and painting or branding), according to previously mentioned instructions, they comprise scarcely more than 5 per cent of the people. There are probably even fewer Vishnuites, Shivaists, Jains, and Buddhists.[64]

Indeed, the thesis has been proposed and zealously defended that every nonheterodox Hindu, without realizing it himself, is either Shivaist or Vishnuist. That is to say, he strives either, in the first case, for absorption into the whole, or, in the last, for eternal life. This in indicated in his conduct in the death hour—in the formula for appealing to the benefactor (*mantra*) that he uses at that time. However, such a special *mantra* for the hour of death was actually not generally employed; also the Shivaistic striving for immortality in the form of a usual and customary formula (above all, the appeal to Rama)[65] is so meaningless that out of it some sort of relation to a God and of his special community cannot be concluded. The mass of the Hindus sometimes do not even know the names of Shiva and Vishnu.[66]

By "salvation" (*mukti*) the mass of Hindus understood all events effecting rebirth and precisely, corresponding to old Hindu soteriology, according to the individuals own work, not that of the God. From his local village god the Hindu expected the dispensation of rain and sunshine. From his family god, the Mailar Linga or Kedar Linga (fetish), he expected help in other everyday needs. Of the "confessional" relation to the *guru,* whom he consulted as an advisor, hardly anything can be said, for the *guru,* indeed, beside ritualistic formulae had learned a Brahmanical theology quite meaningless for the mass of the laity. Precisely here is the cleft between intellectual religion and the everyday needs of the masses. Adherence to a sect derived from a Brahmanical *guru* who alone understood something about it. The mass in no way bound itself to a confession. But, like the ancient Hellen adherent of Apollo and Dionysus, he worshipped according to the occasion. The Chinese Buddhistic mass, Taoistic magic, and Confucian temple cult devoutly dwelt together. In similar manner, the simple Hindu who was not especially received into a sect behaved toward the cult and divinities. And, indeed, this did not only hold for those held to be orthodox. Not only Jainistic and Buddhistic but also Islamite and Christian holy men (such as holy Francis Xavier, the first Jesuit missionary) rejoiced at the patronage in their festivals.

The sects and their redemption religiosity were and are an opportunity for the mainly middle strata advised by intellectuals, to achieve salvation through the power of contemplation in the same manner as the intellectual strata. Wherefrom, to be sure, the point has well been made, that perhaps it does not follow that the peculiarity of intellectual religion and its promise does not have most enduring indirect influence on the life conduct of the masses. However, in its effects, this influence never operates in the sense of an inner-worldly, methodological rationalization of the life conduct of the masses but generally exactly the reverse. Riches and especially money enjoy an almost overwhelming valuation[67] in Indian proverbial wisdom. However, beside the alternatives self-enjoyment or giving of gifts there stands a third loss.[68] Instead of a drive toward the rational accumulation of property and the evaluation of capital, Hinduism created irrational accumulation chances for magicians and soul shepherds, prebends for mystagogues and ritualistically or soteriologically oriented intellectual strata.[69]

Essentially, an opportunity is provided in the modern reform movement within Hinduism for the intellectual strata and indeed, in this case, the modern, European-educated or-influenced intellectuals. This appears in the community of "Brahmo Somaj," much discussed by us, and perhaps still more importantly in the "Arya Somaj." Their history belongs in our study as little as that of the Anglo-Indian university–educated, political, and journalistic bearers of the gradually developing modern Indian nationalism. Such is emerging in this land of schisms into countless bitter enemy castes, sects, speech and blood groups. This is an appearance which is necessarily foreign to the basic Indian character here portrayed. It grows only on the basis of a unified bourgeois class in connection with a national literature base and above all a press. In general, it establishes a sort of unified (external) life conduct. Historical Hinduism is in precise opposition to all this.

CHAPTER X

THE GENERAL CHARACTER OF ASIATIC RELIGION

IF WE LOOK behind the surface with its unprecedented richness of forms to the Asiatic cultural world something remains to be said.

For Asia as a whole China played somewhat the role of France in the modern Occident. All cosmopolitan "polish" stems from China, to Tibet to Japan and outlying Indian territories. Against this India has a significance comparable to that of antique Hellenism. There are few conceptions transcending practical interests in Asia whose source would not finally have to be sought there. Particularly, all orthodox and heterodox salvation religions that could claim a role in Asia similar to that of Christianity are Indian. There is only one great difference, apart from local and pre-eminent exceptions—none of them succeeded in becoming the single dominating confession, as was the case for us in the Middle Ages after the peace of Westphalia.

Asia was, and remains, in principle, the land of the free competition of religions, "tolerant" somewhat in the sense of late antiquity. That is to say, tolerant except for restrictions for reason of state, which, finally, also for us today remain the boundary of all religious toleration only with other consequences.

Where these political interests in any way came into question, in Asia as well they had religious consequences in the grand style. They were greatest in China, but they also appeared in Japan and, to some extent, in India. As in Athens in the time of Socrates, so in Asia a sacrifice could be demanded in behalf of Deisdaimonie. And, finally, religious wars of the sects and militaristic monastic orders also played a role in Asia until the nineteenth century.

However, we observe that on the whole cults, schools, sects, and orders of all sorts adapted to each other as in occidental antiquity. Of course, the competing directions could hardly have been valued equally by the majority of ruling strata of the time or, often, by the political powers either. There were both orthodox and heterodox religious forms and the orthodox included some more or less classical schools, orders, and sects. Above all—and this is especially important for us—they were also differentiated socially—on the one side (and in small part) indeed in terms of the stratum to which they were native; on the other side, however, (and primarily) in terms of the form of hope they offered different strata of their adherents. The first phenomenon was partly expressed in such a manner that the upper social strata stood against the folk soteriology of the masses, abruptly denying all salvation religiousity. China presented this type. It was partly the case that different social strata cherished different forms of soteriology. This phenomenon is in most cases, namely, in all those in which it did not lead to the formation of racial-historical sects, identical with the second. The same religions dispensed different forms of holy values and in terms of these they made demands of variable strength on the different social strata.

With very few exceptions Asiatic soteriology knew only an exemplary promise. Most of these were only accessible to those living monastically but some were valid for the laity. Almost without exception all Indian soteriologies were originally of this type. The bases of both phenomena were equivalent. Above all, both were closely interrelated. Once and for all, the cleft between the literary "cultivated" and the aliterary masses of philistines rested on this. Hanging together with this was the fact that all philosophies and soteriologies of Asia finally had a common presupposition: that knowledge, be it literary knowledge or mystical gnosis is finally the single absolute path to the highest holiness here and in the world beyond.

This is a knowledge, it may be noted, not of the things of this world or of the everyday events of nature and social life and the laws that they hold for both. Rather, it is a philosophical knowledge of the "significance" of the world and life. Such a knowledge can evidently never be established by means of empirical occidental science, and in terms of its particular purpose should by no means be confused with it. It lies beyond science.

Asia, and that is to say, again, India is the typical land of intellectual struggle singly and alone for a *Weltanschauung,* in the particular sense of the word, for the "significance" of life and the world. It can here be certified—and in face of the incompleteness of the representation this is to ask acquiescence in an incomplete certification—that in the area of thought concerning the "significance" of the world and life there is throughout nothing which has not in some form already been conceived in Asia.

Each, according to the nature of its own apprehension, unavoidably (and, as a general rule, actually all genuine Asiatic and that is Indian soteriology) found gnosis to be the single way to the highest holiness, and at the same time, however, the single way to correct practice. Therefore, in no way is the proposition so close to all intellectualism more self-evident: that virtue is "teachable" and right knowledge has quite infallible consequences for right practices. In the folklore itself, for example, of Mahayanism, which plays a role for the pictorial arts somewhat similar to our biblical history, it is everywhere the self-evident presupposition.[1] According to the circumstances, only wisdom provides ethical or magical power over the self and others. Throughout the "teaching" this "knowledge" is not a rational implement of empirical science such as made possible the rational domination of nature and man as in the Occident. Rather it is the means of mystical and magical domination over the self and the world: gnosis. It is attained by an intensive training of body and spirit, either through asceticism or, and as a rule, through strict, methodologically-ruled meditation.

That such wisdom, in the nature of the case, remained mystical in character had two important consequences. First was the formation by the soteriology of a redemption aristocracy, for the capacity for mystical gnosis is a charisma not accessible to all. Then, however, and correlated therewith it acquired an asocial and apolitical character. Mystical knowledge is not, at least not adequately and rationally, communicable. Thus Asiatic soteriology always leads those seeking the highest holy objectives to an other-worldly realm of the rationally unformed; and even because of this lack of form alone available, to a godlike beholding, possession, property, or obsession of a holiness which is not of this world and yet can, through gnosis, be achieved in this life. It was conceived by all the highest forms of Asiatic mystical belief as an "emptying." This is an emptying of experience of materials of the world. This corresponds throughout to the normal significance of mysticism and in Asia it is only carried to its logical conclusions. The devaluation of the world and its drives is an unavoidable psychological consequence of this. It is the meaning-content of mystical holy possession which rationally cannot be further explained.

This mystically experienced holy circumstance, rationally interpreted, takes the form of the opposition of peace to restlessness. The first is "God," the second, specifically creature-like, therefore, finally, either illusory or still soteriologically valueless, bound by time and space and transitory. Its most rational interpretation, dominant throughout Asia, of the experientially-conditioned inner-attitude to the world was conditioned by the Indian *samsara* and *karma* teachings.

Through these Indian doctrines the soteriologically devalued world of real life won a relatively rational meaning. According to the most highly developed rational representations, the world was dominated by the laws of determinism. Especially in the Japanese form of Mahayanistic teaching, causality in our sense appears in external nature. In the fate of the soul the ethical value-determinism of *karma* obtained. From it there was no escape other than flight, by means of gnosis, into that otherworldly realm. Thereby the fate of the soul could simply take the form of an "extinction," or as a circumstance of eternal, individual rest the form of a dreamless sleep. Or it could take the form of a circumstance of an eternal peaceful state of holy feeling in the countenance of god or as a reception into divine individuality.

Similarly, the idea that for transitory deeds of transient beings on this earth "eternal" punishment or rewards in the future could be assigned, and, indeed, by power of the arrangement of a simultaneously all-powerful and good God, is for all genuine Asiatic thought absurd, appearing spiritually subaltern and so it will always appear. Therewith, however, disappeared the powerful emphasis which, as already noted, the soteriology of the occidental doctrine of the beyond placed upon the short span of this life. Given its world indifference, it could now assume the form of a flight from the world or, indeed, in an innerworldly manner, with however, world-indifferent behavior: a protection against the world and one's own acts, not in and through both.

Whether the highest holiness is personally or, naturally, as a rule, impersonally represented—and this is for us not without importance—is a matter of degree rather than kind. The implications of the rare, however still occasionally occurring, superworldliness of a personal God was not carried through. Decisive for this was the nature of the striving for holy values. This was finally determined by the fact that thought about the meaning of the world formed a soteriology corresponding to the needs of literary strata.

These intellectual soteriologies now found themselves confronted by the practice in the life experiences of Asiatic strata. An inner connection of performance in the world with the extraworldly soteriology was not possible. The single, inwardly consistent form was the caste soteriology of Vedanta Brahmanism in India. Its conception of calling had to operate politically, socially, and economically in an extreme, traditionalistic manner. However, it is the single, logically closed form of "organismic" holy and societal teaching which could occur.

Cultivated lay strata, in a manner corresponding to their inner situation, took up characteristic relations with respect to the soteriology. So far as they represented distinguished status levels, there were further possibilities. They could form a literarily cultivated, secular knighthood, standing over and against an independent, literarily schooled priesthood, such as the old Kshatriya in India and the court knighthood of Japan. In this case they partly developed a soteriology free of priests, partly yielded to a religious skepticism as did the cultivated laity of old India and a considerable part of the distinguished intelligentsia of Japan.

In the last case, despite skepticism, and so far as it had occasion to make a settlement with religious usage, this occurred as a rule purely ritualistically and formally. Such was in part the case with cultivated strata of old Japan and old India. Or they were officials and officers as in India. Then merely this last-named relation appeared.

It became the peculiar objective of the priesthood, when these had the power—ritualistically—as was the case in India—to organize the social order to their personal situation. After the downfall of the Shogun in Japan the priesthood was no longer powerful enough to regulate the life conduct of the knighthood more than in a purely external sense. Or, in contrast to the previously mentioned cases, the distinguished laity not only constituted secular officials, or prebendaries and candidates in a patrimonial bureaucracy, but at the same time were bearers of the state cult without competition from a powerful priesthood. Then they had developed a particular, narrow ceremoniousness, a pure inner-worldly life conduct; they conducted ritual as a status ceremonial, as occurred with Confucianism in China for a whole (relatively), democratically recruited literary strata.

In Japan distinguished, secular, cultivated strata relatively free from the power of the priests despite the fact that they also were the political lords lacked the obligated ritual duties of the Chinese patrimonial bureaucratic and office-expectant character: they were knightly nobles and courtiers. In consequence of this they were lacking the bookish and scholarly element of Confucianism. They form a stratum of "cultivated men" strongly disposed to the reception and syncretism of all sorts of cultural elements and anchored, at least in the inner core, to a feudal concept of honor.

The situation of the aliterate "middle classes" in Asia, the merchants, and those belonging to the middle-class segments of craftwork, was, in consequence of the peculiarity of Asiatic soteriology, to be distinguished from occidental equivalents. Their upper strata partly took over the rational reworking of the intellectual soteriologies, that is, negatively, so far as it represented a denial of ritualism and book wisdom, but positively with respect to the general significance placed upon personal salvation-striving. By itself the finally gnostic and mystical character of these soteriologies offered no foundation for the development of an adequate, rational methodology for inner-worldly life conduct. So far as its religiosity was sublimated under the influence of the savior doctrines the religion was transposed into a different form.

Here also there worked the penetration of the gnostic and mystical character of all Asiatic intellectual soteriology and the inner relationship of God intoxication, the possession of God and Godly possession so decisive for mysticism and magicians. Everywhere in Asia where it was not, as in China and Japan, politically suppressed, savior religiosity assumed the form of hagiolatry and indeed a hagiolatry of living saviors: the *gurus* and their equivalents, be it as mystagogues or as magical dispensers of grace. This gave the religiosity of the aliterary middle classes its decisive stamp.

The often completely unrestricted power of these (mostly) hereditary bearers of charisma was somewhat reduced only in China and Japan on political grounds and by force. In China this occurred in favor of the obedience of the political literary strata. In Japan it occurred by way of a weakening of the prestige of all clerical and magical power in general.

In Asia generally the power of a charismatic stratum grew. It was a stratum which established the practical life conduct of the masses and dispensed magical salvation for them. The gift of the "living savior" was the characteristic type of Asiatic piety. Beside the unbroken character of magic in general and the power of the sib appears the impregnability of charisma in its oldest form: as a pure magical power. These determined the typical course of the Asiatic social order.

In general, in circles of distinguished political or hierocratic literary strata, the massive orgiasticism and savior belief was denied along with adoration or hagiolatristic formalism and ritualism. The attempt was made to sublimate them or denature them, in general with very differential success. It was most successful in China, Japan, and Tibet and in the Buddhistic outlying Indian territories, and least successful in India proper. However, these strata succeeded in breaking the dominion of magic only occasionally and only with very temporary success.

Not the "miracle" but the "magical spell" remained, therefore, the core substance of mass religiosity. This was true above all for peasants and laborers, but also for the middle classes. This concerns both miracle and spell in a two-fold sense. One can easily determine this by comparison of occidental and Asiatic legends. Both can be seen as very similar to each other and, the old, reworked, Buddhistic and Chinese legends stand at times inwardly near to the occidental. However, the two-sided division shows the contrast. The "miracle" in terms of its meaning always appears as the act of some sort of rational, world-linked, godly gift of grace, seen and practiced, thus inwardly motivated as a "spell"; in terms of its sense it stands as a manifestation of magical potencies manipulated by irrational, operational arts and by charismatically qualified beings. However, such manipulation occurs in terms of the particular free will behind nature, human or super-human, stored up through asceticism or contemplative performances.

The rose miracle of holy Elizabeth appears meaningful to us. The universality of the spell breaks through every meaningful interrelation of events. One can in the typical, average Asiatic legend, such as the Mahayanistic, determine the presence of this inner-worldly *Deus ex machina* in clearly most enigmatic form. It often appears in connection with the complete opposite, with deep, unartistic though rationalistic needs; to some extent equivalent details of legendary events are tempered by historical motives. So it is for the old treasure of Indian fairy tales, fables, and legends, the historical source of the literary fables of the entire world, produced through this religiosity of the spell-casting savior. Later it took the form of a literature constructed in an absolutely unartistic character whose significance for its reading public corresponded somewhat to the emotional and popular romance of chivalry against which Cervantes took the field.

This most highly anti-rational world of universal magic also affected everyday economics. There is no way from it to rational, inner-worldly life conduct. There were spells not only as therapeutic means, but especially as a means aimed at producing births and particularly male births. The undergoing of examinations or endurance tests was contemplated for achieving all conceivable sorts of inner-earthly values—spells against enemies, erotic or economic competition, spells designed to win legal cases, spiritual spells of the believer for forced fulfillment against the debtor, spells for the securing of wealth, for the success of undertakings. All this was either in the gross form of compulsive magic or in the refined form of persuading a functional god or demon through gifts. With such means the great mass of the aliterary and even the literary Asiatics sought to master everyday life.

A rational practical ethic and life methodology did not emerge from this magical garden which transformed all life within the world. Certainly the opposition of the sacred and the secular appeared—that opposition which in the West historically conditioned the systematic unification of life conduct, describable in the usual manner as "ethical personality." But the opposition in Asia was by no means[2] between an ethical God and the power of "sin," the radical evil which may be overcome through active life conduct. Rather, the aim was to achieve a state of ecstatic Godly possession through orgiastic means, in contrast to everyday life, in which God was not felt as a living power. Also, it involved an accentuation of the power of irrationality, which the rationalization of inner-worldly life conduct precisely restricted. Or the aim was the achievement of apathetic-ecstatic Godly possession of gnosis in opposition to everyday life as the abode of transient and meaningless drives. This, too, represents an orientation that is both extra-worldly and passive and thereby from the standpoint of inner-worldly ethics it is irrational and mystical, leading away from rational conduct in the world.

Where the inner-worldly ethic was systematically "specialized," with great consequences and with sufficient, workable, soteriological premises, in practice, for the corresponding relations in the Hindu inner-worldly caste ethic, it was simultaneously traditionally and ritually absolutely stereotyped. Where this was not the case, indeed, traces of "organismic societal theories" appeared, however, without psychologically workable premises for the corresponding practical behavior. Consequently, a psychologically workable systematization was lacking.

The laity to which the gnosis and also the highest holiness is denied or which it refuses itself, is handled ritually and traditionally in terms of its everyday interests. The unrestricted lust for gain of the Asiatics in large and in small is notoriously unequalled in the rest of the world. However, it is precisely a "drive for gain" pursued with every possible means including universal magic. It was lacking in precisely that which was decisive for the economics of the Occident: the refraction and rational immersion of the drive character of economic striving and its accompaniments in a system of rational, inner-worldly ethic of behavior, e.g., the "inner-worldly asceticism" of Protestantism in the West. Asiatic religion could not supply the presuppositions of inner-worldly asceticism. How could it be established on the basis of a religiosity which also demanded of the laity life as a Bhagat, as a holy ascetic, not simply as an ancient ideal goal but a contemporary existence as a wandering beggar during workless times of his life in general—and not without consequences[3]—as a religiously recommended service?

In the Occident the establishment of a rational, inner-worldly ethic was bound up with the appearance of thinkers and prophets who developed a social structure on the basis of political problems which were foreign to Asiatic culture; these were the political problems of civic status groups of the city without which neither Judaism nor Christianity nor the development of Hellenic thought is conceivable. The establishment of the "city," in the occidental sense, was restricted in Asia, partly through sib power which continued unbroken, partly through caste alienation.

The interests of Asiatic intellectuality, so far as it was concerned with everyday life, lay primarily in directions other than the political. When political intellectuals such as the Confucians appeared they were aesthetically cultivated literary scholars and conversationalists (also in this sense salon-men) rather than politicians. Politics and administration represented only their prebendary subsistences; in practice these were usually conducted through subaltern helpers.

The orthodox or heterodox Hinduistic and Buddhistic educated classes, by contrast, found the true sphere of their interests quite outside the things of this world. This was in the search for mystic, timeless salvation of the soul and the escape from the senseless mechanism of the "wheel" of existence. In order to be undisturbed in this, the Hindu avoided the fineness of the aesthetic gesture.

In order not to become vulgar the Confucian gentleman avoided close community with the Western barbarian. He separated himself from the Westerner who, represented to his understanding, a distended, untamed, and unsublimated unrestrictedness of passion; the need to shun him was necessary for his life conduct. Failure to do so could only mean lack of self-control. Asiatic self-control found its point of gravity precisely at a point negatively evaluated in the Occident. For on what central point was all alert Asiatic self-control erected, basic and without exceptions to the life methodology of the educated intellectual strata and holy seekers? What was the last content of that intensely concentrated "meditation," or that life-long literary study which were striven for, as the highest good against distractions from the outside?

The Taoistic Wu wei, the Hinduistic "emptying" of consciousness of worldly relations and worldly cares, and the Confucian "distance" of the spirit from preoccupation with fruitless problems, all represent manifestations of the same type. The occidental ideal of active behavior—be it in a religious sense concerning the beyond, be it inner-worldly—centrally fixes upon "personality." To all, highly developed Asiatic intellectual soteriology this could only appear either as hopelessly onesided philistinism or as barbaric greed for life. Where it is not in the beauty of the traditional, refined, salon-sublimated gesture as in Confucianism it is in a trans-worldly realm of the salvation from transience that all highest interests of Asia are located and therewith "personality" also finds its worth.

In the highest, and not only orthodox Buddhistic conception salvation is called "*nirvana.*" Neither grammatically nor actually would it be thinkable that this—as popularly often is done—be equated with "nothing." From the aspect of the "world" and seen from it, it could only be "nothing." But from the standpoint of the holy doctrine, the holy circumstance is quite different and very positively evaluated. However, it must not be forgotten that the striving of the typical Asiatic holy man is centered in "emptying," and that each positive holy circumstance of unspeakable, death-defying, this-worldly holiness is in the first place only evaluated as a positive complement of success. However, success is not always achieved. In fact, to actually attain possession of the godly was the high charisma of the blessed. However, how do things stand with the great mass that never attains it? For them, in a very practical sense, "the end was nothing, the movement everything"—a movement in the direction of "emptying."

The Asiatic, the wholly or semi-intellectual Asiatic, easily makes the impression on the occidental of being "mysterious" and "secretive." One seeks to penetrate the presumed secret through "psychology." Naturally, without in any way denying that psychical and physical differences of disposition do occur,[4] in general, certainly there are no greater dispositional differences than those between Hindus and Mongols. Yet both, nevertheless, find the same soteriology agreeable. It must be observed then that psycho-physical difference is not the primary way to understanding. Factors imprinted through education, and the objective elements of the respective interest situations, not "capacity for feeling," are first palpable. What was for the occidental pre-eminently irrational was for the Asiatic a ceremonial, ritual, and habitual condition whose meaning he did not understand. As generally for us, so in Asia the original sense of the customs that grew up were in themselves often not clear.

The reserved dignified countenance and silence which seems so highly significant of the Asiatic intellectual tends to taunt the curiosity of the occidental. To glean what finally stands as content behind this silence it is perhaps useful to consider a related proposition. Before the cosmos of nature we think: it must still—be it to the analyzing thinker, be it to the observer contemplating its total picture and its beauty—have some sort of "last word" as to its "significance." As W. Dilthey has observed this is to prejudge the issue. Whether there is such a "last word" as to the meaning of nature is a metaphysical indeterminable. Similarly, it is often equated with the belief that whoever, because of taste, remains silent has, indeed, much to be silent about. That, however, is no more the case true for the Asiatic than for anyone else. The soteriological product of Asiatic literature, which rested on the particular territories of these emergent problems, were not more ruthlessly worked through, than was done in the Occident.[5]

The lack of economic rationalism and rational life methodology in Asia is, so far as other than psychological historical causes play a part, pre-eminently conditioned by the continental character of the social order as developed in terms of the geographic structure. Occidental culture was throughout established on the basis of the foreign or transient trade: Babylon, the Nile delta, the ancient polis, the Israelite Confederation was dependent on the caravan traffic of Syria. It was different in Asia.

Asiatic peoples have predominantly excluded or extremely restricted foreign trade. Such was the case until the forceful opening of trade with China, Japan, Korea. It is still true for Tibet. While it is less, it is discernible in most Indian territories. The restriction of foreign trade in China and Korea was conditioned by prebendalization which automatically led to the traditionalistic stability of the economy. Any change could endanger the income interests of a mandarin. In Japan feudalism operated in a similar manner toward stabilization of the economy. Further—and this was also valid for Tibet—ritual reasons worked toward this end. Entrance of holy places by strangers disturbed the spirits and could have consequences for magical evil. Travel descriptions (that is, for Korea) permit us to recognize how the appearance of Europeans in the holy place could lead to frantic anxiety.

India, the territory of least closure, still had strong ritual restrictions on travel, while with ritually impure barbarian territory, there were restrictions against active trade. Political considerations also operated toward the restriction of strangers. These existed everywhere, but especially in East Asiatic territory, were they the last decisive reason why the ritual fear of foreigners was given free rein.

Can this strong closure of local culture be viewed as a form of "nationalistic feeling"? The question must be answered negatively. The character of the Asiatic intellectual strata had in essentials hindered the emergence of a "national" political form of the type developed since the late times of the medieval Occident—when for us the full implications of the idea of the nation were fully developed by the modern occidental intellectual strata.

The Asiatic culture area lacked in essentials a speech community. The cultural language was a sacred one or a speech of the literary: Sanskrit in the territory of distinguished Indians; the Chinese mandarin speech in China, Korea and Japan. Partly corresponding to these languages is the place of Latin in the Middle Ages; partly it corresponds to the Hellenistic language of late oriental antiquity or Arabic in the Islamic world; and partly to Church Latin or Hebrew in their respective cultural areas.

In Mahayanaistic cultural territory it remained in this state. In the territory of Hinayanaism (Burma, Ceylon, Siam), which basically recognized the folk idiom as a missionary language, the *guru*-theocracy was so absolute that there cannot be talk of any sort of secular political community formation of intellectual strata outside the monks. Only in Japan did the feudal development bring about the presuppositions of a genuinely "national" community consciousness, if also primarily on a knightly-status foundation.

However, in China the cleft separating Confucian aesthetic literary culture from all popular culture was so great that only an educated status community of literary man appeared, and the consciousness of commonality in general extended only as far as the unmediated influence of the status group itself. The Imperium was, as we saw, conceived in terms of its foundations—a confederation state of provinces, melted to unity through the periodic transfer of the high mandarins to other than their home districts for their official service. There was also in China as in Japan a literary stratum wedded to purely political interest. Even this was lacking, however, everywhere in Asia where specifically Indian soteriology set its feet, except as in Tibet, where it dominated the masses as a monastic landlord strata; even then, however, having no "national" relation to it. The cultivated Asiatic strata remained quite "confined" to its own interests.

Wherever an intellectual stratum attempted to establish the meaning of the world and the character of life and—after the failure of this unmediated rationalistic effort—to comprehend experience in its own terms, indirect rationalistic elements were taken into consideration. It was led in some manner in the style of the trans-worldly field of formless Indian mysticism. And where, on the other side, a status group of intellectuals rejected such world-fleeing efforts and, instead, consciously and intentionally pursued the charm and worth of the elegant gesture as the highest possible goal of inner-worldly consummation, it moved, in some manner, toward the Confucian ideal of cultivation.

Out of both these components, crossing and jostling one another, however, an essential part of all Asiatic intellectual culture was determined. The conception that through simple behavior addressed to the "demands of the day," one may achieve salvation which lies at the basis of all the specifically occidental significance of "personality" is alien to Asia. This is as excluded from Asiatic thought as the pure factual rationalism of the West, which practically tries to discover the impersonal laws of the world.

They were, indeed, protected by the rigid ceremonial and hieratic stylization of their life conduct from the modern Occidental search, for the individual self in contrast to all others, the attempt to take the self by the forelock and pull it out of the mud, forming it into a "personality." To Asia this was an effort as fruitless as the planned discovery of a particular artistic form of "style." Asia's partly purely mystical, partly purely inner-worldly aesthetic goal of self-discipline could take no other form than an emptying of experience of the real forces of experience. As a consequence of the fact that this lay remote from the interests and practical behavior of the "masses," they were left in undisturbed magical bondage.

The social world was divided into the strata of the wise and educated and the uncultivated plebeian masses. The factual, inner order of the real world of nature as of art, ethics, and of economics remained concealed to the distinguished strata because this was so barren for its particular interests. Their life conduct was oriented to striving for the extraordinary, for example, in finding throughout its point of gravity in exemplary prophecy or wisdom. However, for the plebeian strata no ethic of everyday life derived from its rationally formed missionary prophecy. The appearance of such in the Occident, however—above all, in the Near East—with the extensive consequences borne with it, was conditioned by highly particular historical constellations without which, despite differences of natural conditions, development there could easily have taken the course typical of Asia, particularly of India.

NOTES

India and Hinduism

1. Basic for the knowledge of contemporary India and the caste system are the excellent statistical and sociological studies of the ten-year censuses of India (Census of India, Reports). These consist always of a general report containing text and summary tables for each presidency. There are, in addition, numerous purely statistical volumes. These are published at Calcutta. The Census of 1901 is of particular value for it provided for the first time comprehensive data for all India, supplemented at important points by the Census of 1911. The general and provincial reports of Risley, the author of *Castes and Tribes of Bengal,* (Calcutta, 1891-2), Blunt, Gait, and others belong to the best general sociological literature available.

The *Imperial Gazeteer* of India represents an alphabetically organized encyclopedia of India which is exemplary in its way. Its four systematic introductory volumes entitled *The Indian Empire* (New edition, Oxford Clarendon Press, 1908-9) deal with the natural, historical, economic, social, and cultural conditions of India. The census experts also discuss the numerous theories of caste origin of Senart (*Les Castes dans L'Inde,* Paris, 1896); Bouglé (*Essai sur le Regime des Castes, Travaille de L'Annee Sociologique,* Paris, 1908); and the older work of Nesfield (*Brief View of the Caste System of the Western Provinces and Oudh,* Allahabad, 1885). The best modern work is Baines, "Ethnography," in Bühler *Grundriss der Indo-arischen Philologie* (Strassburg, 1912). These works are used throughout the following in addition to the well-known great works on Indian cultural history by the outstanding German Indologists A. Weber, Zimmer, H. Oldenberg. They are, however, only cited separately when a special occasion warrants.

R. Fick's *Soziale Gliederung im nordestlichen Indien zu Buddhas Zeit* (Kiel, 1897), belongs to the best treatises on Indian social history. It is supplemented by the essays of Washburn, Hopkins, to be cited on the proper occasion (particularly *India Old and New,* (New York, 1911), of Caroline Davids, and others. Especially noteworthy in the historical literature is Vincent A. Smith's *Early History of India from 600 B.C. to the Mohammedan Conquest* (Oxford, 1904), Grant Duff, *History of the Mahrattas,* (London, 1911), and works such as the *Rulers of India Series,* Oxford.

Good introductory surveys are to be found in *The Indian Empire.* Other literature is cited at the proper occasion.

For modern military history most convenient is P. Horn's *Heer-und Kriegswesen der Gross Moghuls,* (Leiden, 1894).

The literature used for economic history is cited at the respective sections of the following presentation.

The abundant inscription on monuments contain masses of information for historical monographs and thus far have been but little used for comprehensive treatises. Most of the translated inscriptions are published in the original and translated version with linguistic and topical commentaries, partly in the archeological journal *Indian Antiquary* (thus far 45 quarto volumes), partly in the purely epigraphical journal *Epigraphia Indica.* Both magazines contain excellent monographs by Hultzsch, Fleet, and especially Bühler. Unfortunately at this time the author did not have available Hultzsch's *South Indian Inscriptions* and the *Corpus Inscript. Indic.*

Of the abundant literary sources the most important parts of the Vedas are available in English and German translations. For sociological purposes important are the excellent *Vedische Studien* by Pischel and Geldner; for the development of the Brahmans: Bloomfield, *The Atharva Vedar,* (Bühler's *Grundriss der Indo-arischen Philologie,* Strassburg, 1899); for religious development, H. Oldenberg, *Die Religion des Veda.* The epic literature parts of the *Mahabharata* and the *Ramayana* are translated. For the former see S. J. Dahlmann, *Das Mahabharata als Epos und Rechtsbuch,* (Berlin, 1895). Translations of the Sudra literature are to be found in the *Sacred Books of the East.* The aforementioned works of Frick, Mrs. Rhys Davids, W. Hopkins concerning Hindu society of early Buddhist times are based upon the very important early Buddhist legends, especially the *Jakatas* which have been translated into English. Further sources are the law books of Apastamba, Manu, Vasishtha, Brihaspati, Baudhayana in the *Sacred Books of the East.* For Indian Law we used especially Jolly's book in Bühler's *Grundriss der Indo-arischen Philologie,* and West and Bühler *Digest of Hindu Law,* (Bombay, 1867-69). McGrindle has collected and edited the Greek sources in English. Legge has translated Fa Hien's Chinese travel report.

What has been translated and used from the great mass of religious literature proper of the Brahamana and Purana Period will be cited under Part II.

The aforementioned census publications contain comprehensive and, for introductory purposes, useful presentations of contemporary Hinduism as a religious system. Historical presentations are to be found in the various collections concerning comparative science of religions and in *The Indian Empire.* See also Barth, *Les Religions de*

L'Inde, (Paris, 1897), and Monier Williams, *Religious Thought and Life in India,* Part I, (1891). Other works and monographs used will be cited under Part II. Most monographical articles are to be found in the *Journal of the Royal Asiatic Society,* abbreviated J.R.A.S., and the *Journal Asiatique* (J.A.) and in the *Zeitschrift der Deutschen Morgenländischen Gesellschaft* (Z.D.M.G.) Unfortunately, the author had no access to the *Gazeteers* of the various presidencies. Also had available only parts of the *Journal of thè Asiatic Society of Bengal.* For Indian literature in general see Winternitz, *Geschichte der Indischen Literature,* (Leipzig, 1908).

2. There is no need for us to deal with this politically very important, originally pacifistic sect representing a mixture of Islamism and Hinduism, which later turned into a military order.

3. In his *Hinduism,* (London, 1911).

4. In *Indian Antiquary* (1912, 41, 76).

5. *Epigraphia Indica,* III, 171.

6. *India Antiqua,* IX, 272.

7. See, for instance, Shridar V. Ketkar, *An Essay in Hinduism,* (London, 1911).

8. This is to be found even in the ancient inscriptions. Thus a Maharaja 706 A.D. renewed a foundation of his ancestors and it is mentioned that one of them believed in Vishnu, another in Shiva; grand-children and great-grandchildren, however, worshipped the Bhagavati, hence were Durga or Lakshmi.

9. The specialists see in the *Purisha Sukta* of the *Rig-Veda* the "*Magna Charta* of the caste system." It is the latest product of the Vedic period. We shall discuss the *Atharva-Veda* later.

10. "Territorial economy" designates a stage in economic development. The term was coined by Gustav Schmoller, who distinguished between "village economy"—"city economy"—"territorial economy"—"national economy." (*Eds.*).

11. *Census of India,* 1911. Report, 1, 378.

12. *Census Report,* 1901, XIII, 1, 193.

13. Brihaspati, Tr. by Jolly, *Sacred Books of the East* 33, XIV, 28, 29.

14. *Ibid.,* XIV, 17.

15. In his *Indian Village Community* (1896). In details many of the conclusions of Baden-Powell are perhaps questionable.

The Main Grouping of the Castes

1. A. Weber, *Collektaneen, Indische Studien,* X.

2. G. Grant Duff, *History of the Mahrattas* (London, 1912).

3. See Caland in the *Zeitschrift far die Kunde des Morgenlands,* 1900, XIV, 114.

4. C. F. Bloomfield, *The Atharva Veda* in Bühler's *Grundriss.*

5. Pancav, 14, 6, 6 in A. Weber, *Collektaneen aber die Kastenverhältnisse der Brahmanen,* Indische Studien, X, pl. f.

6. Concerning the limits of, p. 620.

7. There is to be found a *purohita* of several princes according to A. Weber, *Collektaneen, Indische Studien,* X.

8. G. P. The reference of the German text is obviously erroneous, and should read p. 58, note 3. (*Eds.*)

9. Pulney Andy, *Journal of Indian Art and Industry,* cited by Coomaraswamy, *The Indian Craftsman,* 55. See also our later discussion.

10. The census reports give partly very detailed information.

11. Urban Rajputs are mentioned in inscriptions of the tenth century, *Epigraphia Indica,* III, 169.

12. Concerning the Dravidas see Hewitt, *J.R.A.S.* (April, 1890).

13. *Epigraphia Indica,* VIII, 229.

14. *Loc. cit.*, VI, 1953, (tenth century): The Indian name is interpreted thus.

15. *Ibid.*, 47.

16. *Ibid.*, 361.

17. The grant of Iba villages to the king's sons-in-law and their concomitant centralization into a political territory is described *loc. cit.*, IV, 185; Tamil region, eleventh century.

18. One may at least assume that the numerous land grants to vassals are not confined to relatives. The grants are mentioned after the destruction of the Chola realm in a documented date lined from the war camp of the victorious King Krishna (tenth century). *Ibid.*, 290.

19. Parts of a prince's domination are mentioned as a dowry, *Ibid.*, 350. The sale of a village plus its prerogatives by one vassal to another is mentioned *loc. cit.*, III, 307 ff.

20. For instance *loc. cit.*, IV, 180; V, 264.

21. See Rose in *Indian Antiquary,* (1907), 36.

22. Bühler, *loc. cit.*, (1896), 25, 261 f.

23. On the one hand, V. A. Smith, *Ashoka,* (Oxford, 1901), and especially Bühler, *Indian Antiquary,* 26, 334, maintain that scribes first under Ashoka began to execute certified royal edicts. S. Levy and others dispute this.

24. The parts important for us have been translated by R. Shamasastry in *Indian Antiquary,* (1905), 34.

25. Rose, *loc. cit.*, (1907), 36.

26. For Islam see C. H. Becker's works to be cited below.

27. R. Hoernle in the *J.R.A.S.* (1905), 1 ff.

28. See the excellent book of V. Kanakasabhai, *The Tamils 1800 Years Ago.* (Madras, 1904.)

29. *Epigraphia Indica.* V, 213.

30. Baden-Powell, *The Land Systems of India,* (Oxford, 1892), 3 vols., and the shorter compendium on the village community which was quoted earlier.

31. *Raiyatvari* is derived from *Raiyat,* the subject, the protégé (the client).

32. Cf. Caroline Rhys Davids, "Notes on the Early Economic conditions in North India," *J.R.A.S.* (1901), 859 ff.

33. Tamil inscription from the eighth century *Epigraphia Indica,* III, 142ff.

34. *Loc. cit.,* IX, 91; ninth-century inscription.

35. This is described, for example, in the great, first century B.C. inscription, *loc. cit.,* II, 87f.

36. Baden-Powell treats this extensively in his larger work.

37. They are so listed in a ninth-century inscription (*Epigraphia Indica,* I, 184); in addition to the king and the *thakurs* (feudal overlords), the *janapads* whom the translator rendered as "provincials." The inscriptions take only occasional note of a *Rayat* and obviously reference is made to him as a free man.

38. A royal grant of the twelfth century from Udeypur still is addressed to the *Rashtrakutra* (knights) and *Kuntunbi* as the two classes of local inhabitants, *loc. cit.,* IV, 627.

39. See Baden-Powell, *Land System,* II, 162ff.

40. *Epigraphia Indica,* IX, 277.

41. *"Pisang"* is derived from *paysan, paysan* from *paganus* which in Latin meant peasant, later also civilian, and among Christians heathen. Compare also the Hebrew *am hasrez.*

42. The *Mahabharata,* XIII, 60, 23, and *Manu,* IX, 327, still despise trade and money-lending.

43. Pischel and Geldner, *Vedische Studien,* III, 72 f.

44. *Artharva Veda,* III, 15.

45. *Rigveda,* VIII, 13, 5.

46. Thus for instance in Chanaukya's version of the *Arthasastra* of the *Kautaliya.*

47. Kennedy in the *J.R.A.S.,* (1898), 281. A short sketch of Indian monetary history is contained in the Imperial *Gazeteer, The Indian Empire,* Vol. II, Chapter IV, p. 137 f.

48. V. Kanaskasabhai, *The Tamils 1800 years ago,* (Madras, 1904).

49. *Indian Antiqua,* 1890, XIX, 231 f.

50. *Loc. cit.,* III, 249, 16; XII, 54, 20. See W. Hopkins, "The Social and Military Position of the Ruling Castes in India," *Journal of the American Oriental Society,* XIII, 57 ff.

51. A guild is in control of an administrative district; *India Antiqua,* XIX, 145; seventh-century inscription. The Maharaja of a

village and a delegated committee imposed a tax on a village for the construction of a cistern (*Ibid.*, 165).

52. The story of the *Vellala Charita* is told by Chaudre Dus, *The Vaishya Caste,* I, *The Gandhavarniks of Bengal,* (Calcutta, 1903). The book is a typical product of the literature called forth by the attempt of the Census of 1901 to determine the rank order of the castes.

53. See Lassen, *J.A.* III, 727, 786.

54. For the following see Hopkins in the *Journal of the American Oriental Society,* (1890), XIII, 57 ff.

55. Vol. XII, 67, 4 ff.

56. Vol. V, 35, 38.

57. *Ibid.*, 2, 7.

58. Vol. I, pp. 221, 31.

59. Vol. III, pp. 200, 92.

60. Vol. XII, pp. 88, 6-9; 118 ff.

61. *Imperial Gazeteer,* V, 101 for Ahmadabad.

62. *Epigraphia Indica,* III, 67; and IV, 298 f.

63. See the excellent essay of W. Hopkins on the guilds in his *India Old and New.*

64. For the following see the small publication of Ananda K. Coomarasnamy (D.Sc.), *The Indian Craftsman,* Prosthain Series (London, 1909). It cites good material not available to the author.

65. Coomarawamy (*ibid.*, 4) cites such a case from Weddeburn, *The Indian Raiyat as Member of the Village Community,* (London, 1883), a book not available to the author.

66. In Bengal the Nabasakha in 1901 amounted to 16.4 per cent of the population and originally comprised the following castes which today still constitute 84 per cent of its members: three peasant castes (the Baruis, Malakan, and Sadgop); the blacksmiths and related metal workers (the Kamar); potters (Kumhar); barbers (Napit); confectionaries (Mayra); weavers (Tanti); oil pressers (Teli). Usually the weavers and oil pressers and often the potters rate far lower.

67. For the division between old and new classes of village servants which is also connected with this development see p. 58.

68. *Kautaliya Arthasastra,* edited by Shamasastry, *Indian Antiquary* 1905, 54.

69. *Manu,* VIII, 413; X, 99-100.

70. The great inscription *Epigraphic Indica,* V, 23f, describes the foundation of a Chalukya king and clearly presupposes that the weaver's guild mentioned, appearing with its *gouda* (village head), lives in a special weavers' village. Besides this guild there are mentioned guilds of grain importers, palm juice distillers, and oil pressers of the place of the foundation besides its *gouda* and his sib; the king

imposes certain taxes upon all of them for the benefit of *Mahadeva* (*Shiva*) and his wife.

71. In the epics they were called *Panchkhalsi.* For a long time they retained commensalism and occupational mobility.

72. For the Kammalars see Coomarasvamy, *op. cit.*, 55, 56. In Bombay Province the same five crafts united as *panchals,* blacksmiths, carpenters, coppersmiths, stone masons, goldsmiths. As they employ priests of their own but adhere to all Vedic rites (vegetarianism, teetotalling) and pretended to be Brahmans, they often were persecuted under the Mahratta Peshwas.

73. The Greek reports and native sources (*Kautaliya, Arthasastra*) concerning such royal "boards of trade" may essentially compare to institutions which Robert Knox in 1662 reported of Ceylon (*A Historical Relation of the Island Ceilon*). This was unavailable to the author; excerpts are to be found in Coomarasvamy, *op. cit.*, 34 ff.

74. The liturgies of the royal goldsmiths, blacksmiths, potters, etc., could be commuted into a fixed payment of gold. (Coomarasvamy, *ibid.*, 38, 39.)

75. When, after the abolition of the monopolies and trade taxes, the competition of British factory products crashed down upon the artisans they opined that the abolition of the tax had undermined their existence. (Coomarasvamy, *ibid.*)

76. Knox describes the organization of such *ergasteria;* excerpts of Coomarasvamy, *ibid.*, p. 33 f. Obviously they were quite similar to the Pharaonic, late Hellenist, Byzantine, and Islamite *ergasteria.*

77. See for instance *Epigraphia Indica,* III, 295 f (eleventh century) and many other references.

78. Cf. Coomarasvamy's quotations from Col. Hendley, *Indian Jewelry,* p. 153; *op. cit.*, 56.

Caste Forms and Schisms

1. For all these questions see Gait's superb General Report of the 1911 Census, I, 377 ff.

2. Census Report, 1901, III; Report of Blackwood, IV.

3. The figures will be discussed later.

4. Blunt in the Census Report of 1911 reports for the United Provinces and Oudh (Ancient classical soil of Hinduism!), pp. 233 whence the above experts.

5. For example, by McGregor in the Census Report of 1911 for Bombay, VII, 200.

6. The existence of village committees suggesting the *panchayat* and deciding legal questions seems sufficiently substantiated for classical times; Cf. *Manu Samh.* XII, 1087.

7. Budhayana's *Sacred Books of the East,* 1, 5, 9, 1.

8. Budhayana, 1, 5, 9, 3. Mines and all workshops except distilleries of alcohol are ritually clean.

9. The relations of the Indian sects and salvation religions to the banking and commercial circles of India will be discussed later.

10. Cf. Census Report for Bengal (1911) concerning the training for commerce among the Baniyas.

11. These figures are from the 1911 Census.

12. V. Delden, *Die Indische Jute-Industrie,* (1915), p. 96.

13. V. Delden, *Ibid.,* 114-25.

14. *Ibid.,* 86.

15. *Ibid.,* 179.

16. See S. Boyer, *Journal Asiatique,* (1901) Serie 18. Concerning "repeated deaths" see especially H. Oldenberg, *Die Lehre der Upanishaden und die Anfange des Buddhismus.* (Gottingen, 1915.)

17. V. Delden, *Ibid.,* 1915.

18. As late as the twelfth century the ethnic boundary between Arians and Dravids at the Intravati is expressed in the different languages of the inscriptions. The administration retained the division. Yet, a place for people "who came from everywhere," hence represented an ethnic mixture was granted for a temple, *Epigraphia Indica,* Vol. IX, p. 313.

19. See the Census Report for Bengal, (1911), Part I, par. 958, p. 495.

Anti-orgiastic and Ritualistic Character of Brahmanical Religiosity

1. *Mysterium und Mimus in Rigveda* (1908). See also his observations on Oldenberg's *Religion des Veda,* in the *Wiener Zeitschr. z. Kunde des Morgenl, IX.*

2. To prove this is a main purpose of the cited work of V. Schröder's with which, however, some of the following is to be generally compared.

3. V. Schröder, *op. cit.,* 53.

4. In India this position is old. Oldenberg (*Aus Indien und Iran,* 1899, p. 67), refers with justice to the contrast with the Deborah song (which celebrates the victorious struggle of the Hebrew peasant comrades over the urban knighthood) in which Jahwe as confederation God draws near, unlike the victory song of King Sudas (Rigveda VII, -0) in which the magic of the priests does everything.

5. This compares with parallel phenomena in all territories repeatedly referred to by living Indologists, particularly H. Oldenberg's *Verienst,* (also V. Schröder does not disdain it). Arguments have been raised against it, namely, by E. W. Hopkins. Concerning the details

only the specialist can rightly decide. For understanding such comparisons are quite indispensable. The general psychological orientation of the intellectuals in China, India, and Hellas is, in the first place, in no way fundamentally different. As mysticism flowered in ancient China so Pythagorean esoterics and Orphism did in Hellas. The devaluation of the world as a place of suffering and transitoriness is familiar to Hellenic pessimism from Homer to Bakchylides, its capacity for establishing liabilities was conceived by Heraclitus, the "salvation" from the "wheel" of rebirth was found in the epitaph of Sybaris, the morality of the gods by Empedocles, the "memory" of an earlier birth and the redemption through knowledge as the privilege of wisdom was formulated by Plato. These are representations appropriate to any cultivated intellectual strata. The differences of development were located in interests and those established by political circumstances.

6. *Cathapatha Brahmana* II, 2, 2, 6.

7. Indeed, there are many duties of both other "twice-born" castes which in many ways can be construed as weakening the duties of the Brahman caste.

8. Traces of the concept of "natural law" were indeed often found, namely, in the epic literature, which indeed also in other respects was often in tension with the Brahmanical stream of the times which contained the salvation religions; so, namely, in the complaint of Draupadi in the *Maharabharata*. The source of "eternal law," *cacvata dharma*, it is said is dried up and therefore no longer distinguishable. Positive law is always doubtful (see I, 195, 29) and changeable (XII, 260, 6ff.) Power reigns on earth and there is no heavenly justice. Concern is here expressed at the cynical breaking of old customs in the narrow circle of the sib.

In general the need for a teaching concerning origins came to expression in orthodox teaching in time computation. According to the doctrine of epics, there were four time periods which were carried through in the world between destruction and reconstruction through the *pralaya* (twilight of the gods): first and highest was the Krita age, the last and lowest the Kali age. The caste distinctions indeed were established in the Krita age, when each caste does its duty willingly without expectation of pay or gain to itself. There was neither buying nor selling. Therefore salvation of all was possible and a god (*eka deva*) was common to all castes. In the Kali age the reverse holds, and the caste order is now in decay. Self-interest predominates—until *pralaya* comes and Brahma falls asleep. In this form the teaching was influenced by the later to be discussed *Bhagavata*-ethic.

9. The dialogue between the Athenians and Milesians by Thucydides is the famous example.

10. The classical formulation of this "Macchiavellianism," outside the *Kautaliya Arthasastra* cited earlier, is especially found in the *Yatra des Varahamichira* (translated by H. Kern in Weber's *Indischen Studien*). *Yatra* or *Yogayatra* signifies above all the consideration of omens which the prince entering battle has to consider. This art concerns itself with the science of "political administration" according to (*op. cit.*, I. 3) fixed in consequence of the *karma* doctrine, that the horoscope was not determined through *karma*, also having no independent meaning.

11. Founded by Gotama.

12. Founded by Kanada, (translated by von Röer, Z.D.M. (G. 21/2).

13. The atomists denied the dualistic Samkhya philosophy not because it would be impossible from the unextended to create the extended. Rather they objected because—as will be indicated later—it conceived of spiritual events as materialistic. For the Vedanta school, on the other hand, the empirical world was conceived as cosmic illusion (*maya*). This was found to be quite uninteresting. Decisive, however, was the fact that the philosophic position taken on all problems, showing itself ever and again, was decisively dominated by salvation interests.

14. Richard Schmidt has studied the respective literature in detail. One can readily see the sophistication of this eroticism and find conformation of H. Oldenberg's judgment.

15. Namely, the typical age classification.

16. The practical purpose of the rules was a compromise of social requirements with the duty enjoined upon one seeking salvation from the world through ascetic living. First it was necessary to procreate as a household. The reverse was advanced by *Vanaprastha* life. The distinction centered in the question as to whether one could be permitted to move immediately from the novitiate to the life of the ascetic.

17. Also it was in strict interrelation with ascetic life. The student of an alchemist who had once committed a sexual sin was at once repudiated, for magical charisma adhered to a correct life.

18. The obedient servant found only a limit to the teacher's power if the teacher demanded a performance of deadly sin or taught something which was not in the Veda. Generally, the teacher was venerated in prostrate position. In his presence, another teacher may not be honored. The *bramacharin* was forbidden: meat, honey, perfume, liquor, travel by wagon, shelter from the rain, combing the hair and brushing the teeth. He was commanded to regular baths, periodic breath control (corresponding to the later Yoga technique and reverence for the syllable, *"Om."* The old expression for "study" was to "practice chastity." The *Upanayana* ceremony with the reception of

the novice corresponded to the conclusion to the *Samavartana* sacrament. Vgl K. Glaser, *Z.D.M.*, (1912) Ges. 66, 16 ff.

19. The idea has increasingly been accepted that these steps were first established in competition with Buddhistic monasticism. This may be held to be unconditionally valid for the official order. That the practices were first created by Buddhism must, in terms of the original legends of Buddhism, appear improbable.

20. Grünwedel, *Die Buddhist. Kunst in Indien,* (1900) 2 Aufl. 138. (Mahapurscha is the God Vishnu.)

21. *Vishnu Purana,* III, 12 a.e.

22. Similarly the law books, (*Gautama* X, 67).

23. III, 12.

24. The Indian dancers, *Deva-Dasa* (Portugese *balladeirs,* French *bayaderes*) of medieval times were developed out of the *Hierodulen,* the hieratic–homeopathic, mimitic, or apotropaic–*sakti* and temple prostitutes by the priests (and the phenomena bound therewith of prostitution of wandering merchants) and are still today primarily bound up with the Shiva cult. They were obligated to temple service through song and dance and had to be literate–until most recent times the only literate women of India. For the numerous temple festivals, however; also, as in classical Hellenic times for all eminent society, they were indispensable, forming a special caste with its own *dharma* and, especially, inheritance and adoption rights, and were permitted table-community with the men of all castes given access to writing skills in contrast to (in the manner universal in antiquity) high-born women, for whom, writing and literary art were excluded, because they belonged to the *dharma* of temple wench and were held as shameful and likewise not valid. The dedication of girls to the temple followed by virtue of a votive offering, or by virtue of a universal sect duty as in the case of many Shiva sects), also as a caste duty (as by a weaver caste located in the Madras Province), while in all of South India today at least this practice is held to be dishonorable. Engagement and also white slavery appeared. The usual *Dasi* in contrast to the *Deva-Dasi* was a wandering prostitute of the lower castes without relation to temple service. The transition from there to the highly cultivated women of the type of *Aspasia,* corresponding to the *hetoiral* of classical drama (*vasantasena*), was naturally fluid throughout. The last-named type belonged quite as much as the quite well-educated inner-society of female scholars and female propagandists among the Buddhist philosophers (in the manner of the femine Pythagoreans), of the old distinguished intellectual culture of the pre-Buddhistic and early Buddhistic times which disappeared with the domination of the *guru*-monk.

25. Almost at the same time as the beginning of the first flowering

of Hellenic and Chinese philosophy and the Israelite prophecy. Any particular "borrowing" is not to be conceived (quite contrary to occasional references of Ed. Meyer concerning the common cosmic-biological conditionality of the temporal coincidence of these developmental stages). Concerning possible Babylonian influence see below.

26. Vgl. Oldenberg, *Aus Indien und Iran, op. cit.*

27. As a very general name for the holy man and ascetic this today is a designation for a tiny sect of North India somewhat comparable to the Quakers.

28. Today this name is often used quite without differentiation for all Indian mendicants, especially the Shivaists.

29. Still today Brahmans teach only the higher castes, only "twice-born" scholars or even only Brahmans.

30. In the epics the students of a Brahman go on strike when he wishes to take on more students (XII, 328, 41).

31. Some of such subcastes, namely, those which serve impure castes, are held to be impure.

32. The later and until today typical name of the monk (including Brahman monk) is *"bhikshu."*

33. *"Gosain"* means "his reason dominates." The hereditary *gurus* of many sects bear this title. Today it is hereditary in certain great Brahman families. See later.

34. So, explicitly *Manu,* II, 233.

35. This is already indicated by the inscriptions for example, *Ep. Ind.* III, 263, (tenth century).

36. Purely externally, one can best compare them with the Cynics.

37. So still today the *Sannyasi* cenobites in Bengal, however, it is usually the case.

38. On the other hand, there were monasteries in the Middle Ages with ruthlessly strict discipline. For example, from a South Indian inscription we learn that the Superior had the power of life and death over the inmates. However, in general, the old Hindu monks were wanderers who only temporarily during the rainy season or in old age resided in the *math.* The *mathanat* was the oldest resident *chelas* ("scholar") elected or hereditary. Sometimes the honor of headship was rotated. The *Mathanat* of the oldest cloister of a filiation was head of the whole. The characters of the founders of cloisters at times show striving for strict discipline. At the same time, they show that monastic establishment here as in Byzantium and the *"Vakufs"* in the Islamic Orient were characteristically motivated by purposes lying outside the religious sphere—that is, the seizure by political power of established monastic lands—the circumvention of confiscation or overloading with taxes which would constitute a sacrilege—also to

secure rents, which the founder attempted to reserve, for all times, for himself and his family by the foundation. Also the entailed establishment. Such is the case named by Campbell Oman, *The Mystics, Ascetics and Saints of India* (1903) which was intended to secure "administration" of surplus products, above all, also, the eventual rents from land ownership and the earnings from begging expeditions—in secret also trade proceeds—by monastic or temple establishment. The founder had a division of the spoils. The right of management is hereditary but indivisible; the right of inheritance established through statute. The means were typically those of the patrimonial bureaucracy and at times, theocratic, state orders, with insufficient formal private guarantees; the monastic land (usually not extensive for a hundred rupees a year was already a good rent in India) was tax free. In the course of further development there appeared in numerous Hinduistic (orthodox and heterodox) monasteries (also the Buddhistic) a typical prebendalization process. A monk married and made his place hereditary. For example, in the case of the (distinguished) Deschaschth Brahmans today both a *Bhikkshu*-(monkish) and a lay caste appear. They are distinguished only by the fact that only the monks proper had priestly qualification.

39. On this see the law books, for example, it is especially clear in *Baudhayana* II, 6, 11ff.

40. Costliness was not the reason for this as E. W. Hopkins indicates. This already appears quite untenable because precisely the lower classes also later retained the meat orgy.

41. This basic supposition came to expression in what is for us a grotesque form, especially in ancient Buddhism—but not only in it. An inscription tells that after his victory the king had freed his elephants and that then "with tears in their eyes" they hurried to join their companions in the woods. The account of the Chinese pilgrim Hiuen Tsang (seventh century) mentions elephants in Kashmir "which practice the law." (In St. Julien's translation.)

42. They are *Inanakanda:* "gnosis" in opposition to *karmakanda*, the "ritualistic knowledge."

43. One can be led astray by designating the *Smarta* literature as "profane." Its rules, too, are holy and unbreakable. However, they pertain not to the special schooling of the priests as such but to the training of the householder and jurist.

44. However not—as may be taken—in an artistically reconstructed "bardic speech," but in the idiom of ancient priestly families of the origin-territory of the literature. In Vedic times Sanskrit was the speech of the educated. In the Rigveda a prince is motivated by the desire to be educated to read Sanskrit. Rayson, *J.R.A.S.* (1904), 435; Thomas, *ibid.*, 747.

45. *Atharva Veda,* II, 27 (apparently the legal opponent is intended).

46. Echoes of the method, especially in the *Sankhya Aphorisms,* are ascribed to Kapila.

47. The first Indian historians were Buddhist, and Buddha appears to have been an "historical" fact.

48. Concerning Indian medicine, most convenient is Jolly in Bühler's *Grundriss* (1901).

49. A safe expression is required by the non-Indologists. Such is the *Sudhindranatha Vasu* in the *Sacred Books of the Hindu,* Band XII and Band XVII translated under the title: *"The Positive Background of Hindu Sociology"* (till now Book 1) commentaries with an Appendix by Brajendra Nath Seal *Sukranti.* "Sukranti" was quite characteristically conceived as "organic social science," somewhat in the way Comte comprehended the steps of social-science knowledge. And in fact this, of course, completely unscientific "organismic" systematics of the so-called "positivism" is congenial to Indian thinkers. Note the following: in mechanics all remained on a pre-Galilean level. In minerology Indian science remained essentially at the seven-metal doctrine which was also known in the Occident. In Chemistry three special inventions are ascribed to India: (1) the fixing of vegetable dyes with alum; (2) Indigo extract; (3) steel making out of which Damask swords were made (Seal, *The Chemical Theories of the Ancient Hindu*). In general, the *tantra* literature here alchemistically touched the territory of medicine, however, particularly anatomy and especially nerve anatomy. It also developed assimilation (not of the blood but lung assimilation) theories. It advanced knowledge of aspects of the nerve channels. Meditation over these paths, according to *tantristic* magic gave power. The brain (as for Galen) and not (as for Aristotle and even by significant Indian natural researchers Charke and Susrutu) the heart, was treated as the central organ already on the basis of considerable significant osteological knowledge. Fertilization and hereditary transmission (based on very financially significant horse and elephant lore) were also theoretically discussed (palingenetically, not epigenetically). Life which the materialists (Carvaka) interpreted in terms of spontaneous generation, the Samkhya through reflexive activity and the result of single energies, and the Vedanta in terms of a special "living power," provided the occasion for the acceptance of *"adrisa,"* "unseen," that is to say, "unknown" causes such as magnetism. And while a special science of breeding fastened on the confirmed "unknowability" of original causes the later Nyaya and Vaiseska schools thrust the ethical *karma* determinism of Indian theodicy into this gap in knowledge, as for us the "limits" of science provided the space for theological construction. Concerning their

medicine see Thakore Sahib of Gondal, *History of Aryan Medical Science* (London, 1896) and now Hoernle, *Studies in the Medicine of ancient India* (Oxford, 1907). (Neither was accessible to me.) Botany was essentially pharmacology. Concerning the significant grammatical work of the Indians, above all see vgl. Liebich's *Panini* (Leipzig, 1891).

On their mathematics and astronomy see the presentation in Bühler's *Grundriss* (Thibaut, 1899): all decisive (except in arithmetic and in algebra) elements were continued in Greek development (the degree and time of course were very much contended). On pure Indian earth only empiricism was possible without rational *"proof"* (that was decisive). The proof was obtained through appeal to contemplation somewhat in the manner of extreme modern adherents of "contemplation instruction." The formal logical schooling of thought was excluded, when it is victorious.

Concerning the financial-political writings (particularly *Kautalya Arthasastra*) see Narendranath Law, *Studies in Ancient Hindu Policy* (London, 1914), also not available to me. The rationalism of administrative technique could not offer any refinements. This was in itself not yet rational. The writings teach this.

Orthodox Hinduism

1. The literary fixing as "school doctrine" by Patanjali is relatively recent. The fact itself is at least older than the establishment of Buddhism. It is known by name of old in the teaching of the late *Upanishads*. Vgl. for all particulars: Garbe, *Sankhya and Yoga,* in Bühler's *Grundrisz,* (1896).

2. The upper castes in Bengal do not accept water from them; however, they wear the holy girdle. In part they are magical physicians, in part, however, also resident instrument makers.

3. Originally indeed it was a community response, somewhat corresponding to our "Amen," later it was mystically interpreted.

4. In order to dogmatically fix this point the *Mahabharatha* employed the means that for the time of the sojourn in heaven the web of *karma* is inoperative. For the new rebirth only the earlier relation on the earth was determinative.

5. *Atmapurana* XIV, 91-95 by Gough, *The Philosophy of the Upanishads.*

6. Whoever would trust himself with Indian philosophy must consult the somewhat formless but most talentedly written work of Deussen. His great service is not to be contested. Better for the considerations important to our purpose, of course, are the cited writings of Garbe and Oldenberg. Also the (missionary) writing of Dilger (*Die Erlösung nach Christentum und Hinduismus*) is not unusable.

7. See Garbe, *Samkhya-Philosophie* p. 192-93 translated passages.

8. In this case, the *Samkhya-Philosophy.*

9. On the whole question recently see: Schrader in the Z. D. Morg. G. 64 pp. 333f. He seeks to prove that *Yajnavalkya* is not, *samsara* as is assumed, counterposed to *karma* and salvation. It stands between the *Brahmanas* and the *Upanishads.* He holds that the soul wandering is an "anti-clerical concept" directed against the *Brahmana* teaching. It is doubtful that ritual has protective force whether lasting or temporary for the beyond. However, it must, indeed, be noted that the teaching of the Upanishads, according to the emphasis, actually represents the result of contemplations of the *Vanaprastha*-ascetic. These were removed from ritual service and could indeed very well be bearers of a (relatively) ritually alien teaching.

10. His spies watch over men and his commandments are inviolable. He knows everything (*Atharva-Veda* IV, 16, 2) and punishes sin. Vg. v. Schröder, *Reden und Aufsätze,* 17.

11. II, 2.

12. I, 1, 10.

13. VI, 34, 3.

14. In the Occident Christian mysticism and later certain manifestations of pietism were bearers of similar intellectual refinement of the spiritual elements in conscious "experience."

15. Or if one tries to establish its genesis in the peculiar interrelations which later joined together with its forerunners, practically the same emerges.

16. In Samkhya philosophy the finiteness of the organs mediating the material world and the spirit restricts consciousness, which still plays a role in Buddhism (as clarification therefore, the all-knowing Buddha still had need for meditation).

17. It was a general Indian supposition that darkness was somehow material as was light.

18. *Vasischtha* 16, 36.

19. *Apastamba* 23 v. 8 ff. To this, as the other passage here cited, Hopkins *op. cit.,* 252 ff. had referred. The law books are now in the translations of the *Sacred Books of the East.*

20. *Apastamba* 10, v. 14-15. This law book which contains the most negative formulas of this sort against contemplation technique is of course as Bühler (*S.B. of the East, Introduction to the Work*) indicates, South Indian, the home of the old Upanishad-Philosophy, also of foreign origin.

21. *Vasischtha.* 10, 4.

22. Namely, by Baudhayana, a condition to which Hopkins has already referred.

23. The oldest retained work of the school, the *Samkhya-Karika*

des Isvarakrishna, is found in Bechanarama Tripathi in the *Benares Sanskrit Series* (Nr. 9), (Benares, 1883) translated into German by Deussen, *Gesch. d. Philos* I, 3. The aphorisms (presumably) of Kapila were translated into English by Beal.

24. Officially the founder of the school was "Vyasa" (equals creator of the disposition), a collective name, also used for the editor of the *Mahabharata* and the collector of the *Vedas.*

25. *Maitrayana Up.* I., 2-4 ff is customarily cited in this connection.

26. *Brihadaranyka* Up., V, 2. a passage to which Winternitz *Gesch. der Indischen Literature* has called attention, which also indicates the lack of ethical content in the *Upanishad* and its bases.

27. In the usual enumeration: Jaimini's Mimamsa, Kapila's Samkhya, Vyasa's Vedanta, Gotama's Nyaya, Kanada's Vaiceska, Patanjali's Yoga. Vedant was the old Mimamsa which ritually displaced the Veda's "Purva (early) Mimamsa" also posed against the "Uttara (later) Mimamsa" (mimamsa signifies school research at least). For at very least classically valid in the highest sense only Mimsa (Purva Mimamsa) and Vedanta qualify.

28. In opposition to the *Loka Yata* was the school, seen as heterodox, of "materialism" which Carvaka (sometime in the third century B.C.) established. It denied all metaphysics and thus the authority of the *Vedas.* On it see Hertel, *Das penchatantra* (1914) and Hilltbrandt, "Zur Kenntnis der indischen Materialisten" (Festschrit für Kühn, 1916).

29. On this see Oldenberg *op. cit.*

30. So, for example, in the *Mahabharata* (VI, 30, 49). The *Bhagavadgita* knows the condition in this sense.

31. Quite naturally a metaphysics which fastens on the negation of behavior and feeling as the main indications of freedom from the earthly, necessarily must take dreamless sleep as the condition standing closest to its conceptualization. All animism is treated as the wandering of the soul during sleep. The *Upanishads* treats dreamless sleep and ecstasy in this respect as of equal value (see Gough, *Philosophy of the Upanishads* 36).

32. Vgl. for example *Maitr. Brahm. Up.* VI, 34, 9. The fate of the soul which in this meditation is washed pure of all impurity and lost in itself is indescribable. Das. 10. "Water is water, fire is fire, ether is ether—one can not individually distinguish therein; so it is what is taken up into the self." In the epic the portrait of the Brahman as a pre-blessed state of feeling does not preponderate, but appears more as an intellectual light. It is somewhat like the source of Plato's gnosis in the *Republic.* Otherwise it is comparable simply to a deep sleep.

33. The expression itself first belongs to the new speech, the fact is ancient.

34. Patricide and matricide itself. Only it can, that is to say, be of such kind as not quite to be in position to traverse.

35. On this see Gough, *Philosophy of the Upanishads,* p. 66 ff.

36. Buddhistic influence is first found in the Epics in the quite late sections.

37. Precisely a part of the decisive tensions of the *Bhagavadgita* must stem from ancient knightly times, above all, from the "fatalistic-ethic" of the knighthood.

38. The idea that sin finally lies in men themselves is opposed to the idea that sin is an unavoidable fruit of deeds of previous life, as a fate hovering over men, that men are only the implements through which either a dark destiny or—more correctly—or the chain of *karma* executes itself. (*Mahabh.* XII, 22, 11 ff. as well as 59, 13 ff. further IV, 5 and other passages.)

39. III, 29, 38 ff. This is the circumstance held as valid of old in the epics.

40. See E. W. Hopkins, *Rel. of India,* 417.

41. Translated into almost all the languages of the earth. In German with an excellent introduction by Garbe (Leipzig, 1901).

42. For not the attitude of *bhakti* (or which more later) but the thought of godly grace (*prasada*) is apparently the old pre-Buddhistic element of the *Bhagavadgita* (So. also E. W. Hopkins).

43. On this see R. G. Bhandakar, *Vaisnavism, Saivism and Minor Religious Systems* in Bühler's *Grundrisz* (Strassburg, 1913).

44. Kennedy, *J.R.A.S.* (1908) still holds this view. Likewise Grierson, *Ind. Ant.* (1908), 37. What he calls "Krischna Vasudeva" and takes to be the old Bhagavata-God, Vasudeva, was later identified with Vishnu. Macnicol, *J.R.A.S.* (1913), 145 takes it that Krishna was an old vegetation deity (occasionally incarnated in animal form) and therefore originally had plant rather than animal sacrifice (origin of *ahimsa*?). He refers to the later Krishna pantomime in which Krishna and his adherents painted in red (Summer struggle against the white demons (of Winter) as corresponding to the struggle of "Xanthos" and "Malanthos" in Greece. The sect of the Bhagavata worshippers has verifably been placed in the fourth century B.C. Its establishment is misplaced by Garbe *op. cit.,* some centuries before Buddha.

45. XI, 32, 33.

46. XVIII, 59.

47. XIII, 23: Whoever knows spirits and matter will not be born again, for he has also always lived.

48. II, 31 ff.

49. This expression Krishna, as XVIII, 48 indicates means "congenital," also it means the obligations established through caste *dharma* which are made identical with the godly fate. (Vg. II, 8, XVIII, 7, 9, 23.)

50. Caste duties stand in full circumference. Caste mixing, for example, led (according to I, 41) to hell, also it may be surmised that there was no equality of qualification for the death sacrifice.

51. XVIII 47 takes the classical stand indicated in earlier passages: "In itself it is better to have the deficient fulfillment of one's duty than to have right practice of the duty of another. Whoever fulfills obligations established for him by nature, suffers no blame." The second sentence is the Bhagavat twist of the basic ethical dogma of Hinduism.

52. XVIII, 11.

53. XVIII, 5, 6. Otherwise *karma* operates.

54. IV, 20, 21.

55. II, 42.

56. V, 2.

57. XVII, 5. Bgl. VI, 16, 17.

58. VI, 46.

59. V, 27, 28.

60. XVI, 21.

61. XIII, 9.

62. XIV, 22.

63. XIII, 23.

64. XVIII, 66.

65. IX, 30.

66. XIII, 13.

67. According to Bhandakar, *Ind. Ant.* (1912), 41, 13. See now also the same in Bühler's *Grundrisz, Vishnavism Savism and minor Religions* (1913).

68. The reference there is to the cult of the Bhagavat Samkarshana also Vasudeva (the typical name for the Krishna God). Shortly thereafter it appears that a Greek, Heliodor, in Taxila is named in the Bhagavata (*J.R.A.S.* 1909, S., 1087 ff). The three Indian cardinal virtues: *dama* (self-discipline), *tyaya* (liberality), *apranada* (discretion) were taken from a monument of a half-Greek convert in an inscription glorifying Vasudeva (*Z.D.M.G.* 63, p. 587). Near Eastern Iranian influences were also not excluded by further religious establishments; however, its reception is not necessary.

69. Hopkins had chosen this passage for the motto of his often cited work (*Rel. of India*).

70. III, 26.

71. IX, 30.

72. XII, 3.

73. VII, 21, 23.

74. *Ind. Art.* 1890 XIX, 61 (in the eighth century A.D.)

75. The inscription does not in any way stand alone. Also in a

deed of foundation (*Ep. Ind.* I, 269 f.) through which the merchants and traders of a city founded a monastery for a Shiva ascetic, who "seeing the highest light of God, free from the darkness of passion, had not thrown away the gift of sinful joy" appears the comparison (V. 69-70 to the picture of a young beautiful woman, given from a bath of love to a prince.

The Heterodox Soteriologies of the Cultured Professional Monks

1. Among the recent rich literature worth treasuring is Mrs. Sinclair Stevenson's, *The Heart of Jainism.* The main inscriptural sources are offered in Guerinot's *Epigraphia* Jaina (*Publications de l' Ecole francais de l'Extreme Orient,* 1908, X). Some important Sutras appear translated in the *Sacred Books of the East* (*Gaina Sutras,* by Jacobi). Other literature is cited in the given place.

2. In the *Kapla Sutra* translated in the *Sacred Books of the East,* p. 17 ff.

3. According to the *Kapla Sutra* (p. 22) Mahavira's embryo was miraculously transferred out of the body of his Brahmanical mother into that of a Kshatriya mother.

4. The existence of the soul was demonstrated by scholastic-ontological means by the *Saptabhangi Nyaya;* the theory that each statement could have seven different meanings.

5. Later Jainism took over numerous deities of orthodox Hinduism —such as the child deities (*Ep. Ind.* II, 315-6).

6. Although holding the incarnation of orthodox gods to be specifically unclassical and barbarian, orthodoxy still in later times retained the exclusiveness of hero worship. "How can the arhat who only fortuitiously came to earth and experienced success through virtue be compared to Shiva?" states an inscription (*Ep. Ind.* V. 255 from the twelfth century) of a famous school head of the eleventh century in religious dispute against the Jains.

7. *Op. cit.,* 138 ff.

8. *Ibid.,* I, 5, 6.

9. *Acharanga Sutra,* II, 15.

10. Instances are inscripturally presented. *Ep. Ind.* III, 198 (Twelfth Cent.). A holy man had in the presence of the community starved himself to death. *Ep. Ind.* V, 152. A prince from the Ganges Valley, after great military campaigns against Jain ascetics did the same (Tenth Cent.).

11. *Ach. S.,* I, 4, 1.

12. *Ibid.,* I, 2, 2.

13. *Ibid.,* I, 2, 4.

14. *Ibid.,* I, 6, 2. Opposition to the *Tat tvam asi* of the *Upanishads.*

15. *Ibid.*, I, 7, 8.
16. *Ibid.*, II, 2, 13.
17. *Ibid.*, II, 16.
18. Also a symptom of the great age of the order.
19. How old this custom—typical for all Indian sects—is, is difficult to ascertain.
20. The schism also led to a complete separation of the canonical literature of both parts and to special councils.
21. Many single prescriptions appear in all Jaina Sutras. Not only must all good nourishment and lodging be avoided (*Ach. Sutra* I, 7, 2), but it is also necessary to avoid the possibility that either out of excessive zeal of the householder (I, 8, 1) or the reverse, because the monk is dirty and stinks (II, 2, 2), the household has something especially prepared for the begging monk, for *krama* consequences ensue. The "*Reg-ln fur Yatis*" (teachers) thus especially sharpens the restriction not to question the layman to whether he has this or that object for it could lead the lay person in his zeal on an incorrect path.
22. *Ache Sutra* I, 6, 5.
23. Also all confirmed wandering monks were, and apparently had been for a long time, assigned to a monastery which controlled them. The land investiture without which Jain monasteries too could not exist was here in the form of a revokable, periodically reconstituted loan, in the fixing of the absolute free will of the gift and properly to maintain propertylessness (as the instructors indicate, most were accomplished in the form of foundations). The founder builds a temple and the land is established for the teacher (*Ep. Ind.* X p. 57 from the ninth century). According to rank the single living *sadhu* was more highly treasured than the monastic monk. Also the *upadhaya* (teacher) ranked behind him. He was only able to read text; the *acharya* had the right to authenticate them.
24. A schism occurred in a Jain community because the designated successor of a *suri* demanded the students of the former before he had died by virtue of his charisma. However, the community had other ideas. (Hoernle, *Ind. Ant.* (1890) XIX, 235 f.)
25. An *acharya* who was the head of a *gachchha* (community) or *sakha* (school) was called *suri* when he had young people studying with him, *gani*. Lists of teachers of single *gachchhas* are retained in the inscriptions. See for example *Ep. Ind.*, II, 36 ff.; III, 198 ff.
26. A correct *acharya* was called *tyagi-acharya,* a lax *sithilacharya*. In a Jain chronicle (Hoernle *op. cit.*, 238) a female deity (*deva*) affects an *acharya* in a moment of customary laxity with an eye disease. Restored again to power, he threatened her and reduced her to a *upasaka* (lay-sister) whereupon she—after he had dispensed sweetness—freed him from his eye disease.

27. Which was possible after twelve years of asceticism.

28. One could be tempted from taunt of "fly-strainer" which was hurled against Jesus in Jewish literature to infer that knowledge was diffused in the Near East of this Indian practice. For a corresponding prescription, so far as is known, did not exist for the Jews.

29. The highest piety is to permit oneself to be stung by insects without shooing them away. The great animal hospitals of the Jains are famous; the most famous is the one (on the coasts of the city) in which 5,000 rats are maintained. (J.R.A. Soc. 1834, I, 96.)

30. The consequences of these ritual prescriptions presumably contributed to the downfall of Jainism. The Jainistic king Komarpal of Anhilvara lost his throne and life because he would not permit his army to march during the rainy season.

31. In this respect the situation of the Digambara (Gymnosophists) and Swetambaras is different. For the first monastic asceticism is essentially stronger; like the Buddhists, their claims on the laity are milder, while their form of salvation is not much different. Some of them pursued agriculture.

32. Among them are found, of course, as Nr. 20 of the general post, "the otherwise really necessary." Books can be proved only as the basis of these titles.

33. Whoever practises deception will be born again as a woman.

34. In general it is the duty, even unconditionally in the salon, to speak the truth. Later this was tempered to the effect that one may not say an untruth, but when the truth is unpleasant it need not be unconditionally spoken.

35. Balfours, *Encyclopedia of India,* s.v. "Jain," II, 403, right half, center. This is no longer the case.

36. It is that which is proscribed as *lobha* (avarice).

37. Mrs. Sinclair Stevenson (*Heart of Jainism*) mentions the votive offering of a Jain of the recent past to earn "no more than 45,000 rupees" and to give the surplus as a gift—whereby, apparently self-evidently, it was assumed that to earn this amount presented no difficulties.

38. In Jain Dogmatics (vgl. das von Jacobi in the Z.D.M.G. 60, 1902 translated compendium Umasvatis) conceived *karma* as a poisonous material stuff engendered by passion. It corresponds with the theory, here of no further interest, of great and fine bodies in which the soul is wrapped. The finest accompanies the soul in its wandering. All these somewhat archaic representations speak of the great-age of the sect.

39. The confessionalism of Jainism always bore strong imprint of this and stood in contrast to other Hindu conventions which tended to shower the holy ones with gifts without differentiation.

40. Vg. Mrs. Sinclair Stevenson, *op. cit.*, 292. "It would be a sin for a mother to pray for her child to save its life. For that would represent desire and awaken *karma*."

41. An essential part of the Buddhist hieratic need for construction and paraments was lacking for the Jains.

42. On this see Hörnle, *Presid. Address* 1898, Royal Asiatic Soc. of Bengal, and Mrs. Stevenson, *op cit.*

43 Namely, by Hopkins, *op cit.*

44. Naturally all temple Brahmans were of somewhat degraded rank.

45. According to discussions (J. Campbell Omans, *Mystics, Ascetics and Saints of India*, 1903), with Jain merchants.

46. Gautama is the name of the Brahman *rischi* from which the Sakya sib claimed to stem, a sib apparently alien to the Brahmans of old.

47. The designation "Buddha," the enlightened, was ancient. "*Pratibuddha*" was a Brahmanical monk who through meditation achieved or seeks enlightenment.

48. As in the hands of such workers, as H. Oldenberg and Rhys Davids.

49. A phenomenon, here neglected because of lack of space very important for all Indian intellectual philosophy is relation to magic. A great number of apparently soteriological-rational presuppositions are customarily, at least originally, conditioned by magical significance. On the other hand, we can discern as well numerous important details determined purely by the power of tradition. Such is the holiness of the cow, especially the expiation-giving effect of cow urine. This has apparently been operative in Buddhist monastic rules since ancient times.

50. In addition to the old work (by Köppen, Kern, and others) so valued for the Buddhistic ethic, through study of the Pali canon and the others, namely, the inscriptural sources which establish the historical nature of the person of Buddha. In general, the work is important and particularly valuable on source materials. Alongside the old foundation work by H. Oldenberg (*Buddha*) is the work of Mr. and Mrs. Rhys Davids. It is the most readable and at the same time constructive synthesis of the standpoints developed by them. Besides this, are the short presentations in the writings of Pischel and by Edv. Lehmann which are available to wide circles. Also popular is the work by Roussel, *Le Bouddhisme primitif* (Paris, 1911) (Bd. I of the work published by theologians of Dominikaner-Universität of Frieburg the *Religions Orientales*). A scientific characterization is Kern's in Bühler's *Grundrisz*. Also there is a presentation in the collected works of the comparative science of religion. Single citations

will appear in the respective place. On Buddhistic dogma, de la Valle-Poussin, *Bouddhism* (Paris, 1909). Also there is the old work by Senart, *Origines Bouddhiques*. As to source material of ancient Buddhism, the Pali canon (*Tripithaka*) is translated into English in the *Sacred Books of the East*. The addresses and sermons of Buddha (those which according to tradition are ascribed to him) Neumann has translated into German in salient manner. A direct treatment of the peculiarity of ancient Buddhistic thought is perhaps best contained in the lecture of the "Questions of King Milinda" and (already interpreted Mahayanaistically) Acvagoschas *Budda Tscharita*, both in the *Sacred Books of the East*. Single citations are in the corresponding place. An introduction very much required is the popular and quite personal viewpoint of H. Hackmann in *Religion geschichtlichen Volksbückern* (*Der Buddhismus* I, II, and III. *Part II Reihe*, Heft 4, 5, 7 Tubingen, 1906).

51. The redeemer-quality of Buddha himself was only a secondary developmental product. His, indeed, super-human but not godly quality (only exemplary) is without the slightest doubt established in the earliest period of the order.

52. In the already mentioned "Questions of King Milinda" (IV, 1, 12).

53. *Quest. of King Milinda*. IV, 4, 16. When a Buddhist has "full love" no one can do him evil. Not even physically. For this love is all compelling. At least in its primary conception, one can do justice to this representation by conceiving it not in the sense of Dostoyevski's Starjez Sossima or Tolstoy's Platonic Karatajew, although certainly it could be sublimated thereto, but in the first place simply magically. The possession of ecstatic a-cosmic love is a magical quality. It also follows that through use of the sword or poison one spoils it and in this moment no longer has this charisma.

54. Concerning the nature of *maitri* which also plays a role in Yoga a discussion arose between Pischel and H. Oldenberg (*Aus dem alten Indien*, 1910) in which, it seems to me the latter is right. Its nature is "peaceful benevolence." Also in the rank order of lay virtues, good deeds, as Oldenberg shows, are occasionally represented. For the monks, however, they are only mentioned incidentally. Moreover, their lyrics do not seem, even in the most remotely similar sense, to be drenched with it, as is the case with the pietistic lyrics. "Wisdom" is and remains precisely the way to salvation.

55. It is to be found in Neuman's cited collection of the *"Reden des Gautama Buddha."*

56. Menander, an anterior-Indian (Indo-Sythian) ruler of early Buddhistic times. The dialogue collection is found in the *Sacred Books of the East* ("The Questions of King Milinda," Vol. 35, 36.) How far

the Aristotelian entelechy doctrine has been interworked with it is questionable. Yet one can generally assume an extensive originality of Buddhistic thought; precisely on this point great emphasis is laid.

57. "Skandhas." Also later Buddhistic inscriptions speak of the soul as an "aggregate" of circumstances. (*Ep. Ind.*, IV, 134.)

58. It seems to me that modern Buddhism seeks to make this teaching "scientifically" acceptable. Vg. *Ananda Maitreya* (*Animism and Law*) in the Public. of the *Buddhasasana Samagana* (Rangoon 2446, p. 16) Newton retained an animistic methodology in his mechanics. Faraday in a corresponding manner (phlogiston) advanced judgments in chemistry. In the theory of spiritual events Buddha put aside a lawful sequence (*karma*-conditioned). Naturally, however, it was not a physical condition or disposition inherited from the forefathers but only a special mental agency (the "thirst") which constituted the facts of the new establishment of mental life itself. The old Buddhist formulation is that the "I," "Vijnanasamtana," is a complex or a series of conscious events, while according to orthodox teaching, *Vijnana,* thought constitutes the seat of Ego-individuality as a valid unity (Vgl. de al Vallee-Poussin, *Journal Asiat.* 1902, 20.)

59. This consequence was taught in the "Questions of King Milinda" (III, 5, 7). *Karma* acquired in consequence of behavior and action led to the establishment of individuality anew, which had nothing in common with the old negation beyond the fact that it was from the failure to extinguish "thirst" that each further existence was forced. The construction was offered because the *karma* doctrine as the foundation of all suffering and of existence itself stood quite outside the question and only appears here in the frame of a free construction. Salvation problems as to the new nature acquired after death were not raised. As all the documents show, the massive fruits of a belief in soul sojourning of India in general were not as strong for Buddhism. That the enlightened before entrance in *nirvana* is omniscient and looks backward over the entire series of his rebirths was a somewhat early Buddhistic teaching (and not only Buddhistic). Above all, however, in literary and monumental sources also of the old (Hinayana) Buddhism, soul-sojourning is handled quite in Hinduistic manner. What the *karma* teaching implies later causes trouble in the "Questions of King Milinda," that is, its fatalistic consequences. Corresponding to the basic proposition that the discussion faced inextricably metaphysical problems and also was dangerous to the holy, it was taught that no one knows how far the influence of *karma* reaches. Likewise not every misfortune—somewhat of a splinter in the foot of Buddha—is a consequence of *karma.* For externally nature has its own lawfulness—*karma* also appears essentially to be related to

the soteriological interests of the soul: to life and spiritual suffering.

60. His behavior follows as consequence not of *karma* but only *kiriya* which does not lead to rebirth.

61. The description of the psychological qualities of the state of grace in the address ascribed to Buddha himself (Neumann, *Reden des Gautama Buddha*) Buddha speaks (I, Teil, 2 Rede) of "thoughtfulness," "serenity," "gentleness," "cordiality," "equanimity" of Insight, and of the error of arrogance, however, also, of dull fatigue (I, Part 8 Rede) of "inner dead calm" and "unity of mind" in a holy serenity born of self-deepening." (III, Part 6 Rede) and a form of consciousness (I, Part 2 Rede) achieved by self discipline. "This is the last life and never permits a recurrence."

62. Relatively old sources such as the *Tschullavagga* have among other things required of the master himself the unconditional denial of women. His aunt and foster-mother Mahapyapati have this to be grateful for—that they, in general, in subaltern manner were permitted holy seeking. Meanwhile, this position is difficult to reconcile with other sources. For a monastic order it is probable that the (relative) intersexual freedom of the old distinguished Kshatriya "salon" was later treated as quite the reverse.

63. "Seek not a refuge for any but yourself," it says in *Mahaparinibhana Sutra* (II, 31-35, *Sacred Books of the East*, XI, 35 ff; also in Germany by Schulze, *Das Rollende Rad*, p. 96 ff, especially p. 97). The contrast of Buddhism to Christendom is, outside of numerous passages in Oldenberg's writing, already worked out in v. Schröder's *Reden und Aufsätzen* (p. 109).

64. The expression is technical and appears in official inscriptions (for example, J.R.A.S. (1912), p. 119 and often).

65. For ancient Buddhism at least *nirvana* after death was actually equivalent to "blowing out," "extinction" of the flame and not like a dreamless sleep as was mostly the case in Hinduism, or like a circumstance of unknowable and unspeakable holiness, therefore pronouncing an adequate omen. Still in the Malinda questions (IV, 8, 69) *nirvana* is ambiguously described as a kind of cooling of the life thirst, a medicine boundless as the ocean which brings an end to age and death, a source of beauty and holiness, eternal, resplendent. The fulfillment of all wishes was still stressed (IV, 1, 12 f.). The honoring of the relics of Buddha did not change this. He is obliterated without trace, worshiping his relics serves rather to enhance one's zeal. Of course, the bridge from nonexistence to transition into complete mysticism was easily made.

66. "Questions of King Milinda," Book VI. The order, it was answered, required virtue. And all, since Buddha has extended salvation to the laity, are required to be monks, at least in an early life.

67. Minayeff, H. Oldenberg, de la Vallée Poussin. On this, see the last named in *Ind. Ant.* (1908), 37 1 ff.

68. See on this "Questions of King Milinda," IV, 1, 2 ff.

69. That this at least at times was the case is also indicated from the "Questions of King Milinda" (IV, 4, 6, Vgl. IV, 3, 4). That it was not originally the case is shown by the fact that in Ceylon the laity reads also the *Vinaya* text. All reckoning of the classes which were not able to receive insight even when they correctly included: (IV, 8, 54): animals, children under seven years, heretics, patricides and matricides, murderers of *arhats,* schismatics, apostates, eunuchs, hermaphrodites, unrehabilitated committers of deadly sins, etc. Finally, and particularly only to monks is salvation accessible.

70. "Questions of King Milinda," IV, 128 makes it plain that it could only be a schismatic monk, because only such would know the doctrine completely.

71. "Question of King Milinda," *op. cit.* (Eventually without its having been in an earlier life). A layman who has achieved the dignity of *arhat* can (according to IV, 3, 4) either die on the same day or become a monk. Also the most unworthy monk must receive reverence from the most worthy lay person because only the monk is bearer of the tradition of ruled order. In the beginning in the capital the Kshatriya were extolled. All this signifies a transformation of an original lay community into a monastic order.

72. A four-fold life-conduct was taught by the master. The first prepares for present well-being and leads to future woe: sensual chastisement. The second leads from present woe to future woe. These two, like irrational asceticism, lead "downward" even after death. Present woe, future well-being forms the third. It is typical of one so constituted in his natural situation that a holy life is led "with difficulty." He achieves heaven. Present and future well-being is offered by the fourth way of life. It is available to one who is not inclined to violent emotions and who easily attains "inner calm." He wins *nirvana.* (5 part, r. Rede by Neumann, *Reden des Gautama Buddha*). The rejection of irrational chastity is motivated quite in Jesuitical manner in Acvagoshas *Buddha Tscharita* (*Sacred Books of the East* 49) VII, 98-99. It destroys the possibility of self-control and weakens the bodily powers by which one may work for salvation.

73. Allan MacGregor as a convert and monk named Ananda Maitreya *The Four Noble Truths,* Public. of the *Buddhasana Samayana* Nr. 3 (Rangoon 2446 der Buddh. Aera, 1903). It is not as interesting that the primitive form of Buddhism is here historically quite correctly reproduced as that the Hinayana teaching today holds as orthodox and valid these interpretations of the old writings, which in itself is possible.

74. The modernization of meditational technique (*kammasthana*) consists in the displacement of—measured by the standards of modern medicine—the still strong, "pathological" character of the decisive holy circumstances in ancient Buddhism. The vision technique of the ten *kasinas* rest on the phenomena of the after-image of closed eyes and the four stages of peculiar ecstasy already lead in the second step to an ingeniously engendered "torpor," and then with the cessation of ecstasy to a "consummated serenity," experienced euporhia, and as the highest stage an absolute feeling of indifference.

75. *Vatthuwijja* corresponding to the Chinese *Fungschui.*

76. Great teachers of later orthodox Buddhism, according to tradition, have even repeatedly been overpowered by the power of "lust." They left the community and after passion was satisfied again joined the community. An example appears in J-Tsing's travel description 34, No. 7. This laxness was, among other things, doubtless a product of decadence and foreign to ancient Buddhism.

77. This is proven by the literary sources and legends. It was to the membership, especially of eminent people, of considerable importance. However, Buddhism was never socially exclusive insofar as the laity come into consideration. In later times there is to be found in Buddhist inscriptions (for example, those of Bühler in the *Ep. Ind.* II, 91 ff, the cited *Sanci Inscription*) representation from all status groups: nobles and peasants of a village; guild merchants (*sheth*); simple traders (*vani*); kingly scribes; professional writers; royal workshop foremen (*avesani*); soldiers (*asavarika*); laborers (*kamika*). However, merchants and traders predominate. In an ancient inscription of the 1st century B.C. (*Ind. Antiq.*, 1890, p. 227) one finds: one soldier, one stone mason, one householder (*Grihaspati*) and numerous spiritual persons as donors.

The Transformation of Ancient Buddhism

1. Such a genteel soteriology was precisely the basis of all its differences from Christianity. *Opposition* to genteel soteriology was fundamentally important to the latter.

2. Outside of the great collections, the most important may be found in V. A. Smith's *Ashoka* (Oxford, 1901).

3. This describes the usual manner as expressly explained in the "Small Stone Edict I." The king was a lay scholar for two and one-half years and now is in his sixth year in the order.

4. In the Columnar-Edict I decree.

5. In the decree recorded as *Great Stone Edict*. No. XIII.

6. *Great Stone Edict*, No. VIII.

7. *Ibid.*, No. VI.

8. *Ibid.*, No. IV; instead of the drum of war the drum of piety shall be beaten.

9. *Ibid.*, No. VIII.
10. *Ibid.*, No. I.
11. *Ibid.*, No. II.
12. Columnar Edict No. VII.
13. *Kalinga-Stone* Edict.
14. *Great Stone Edict*, No. IX.
15. *Ibid.*
16. *Ibid.*, No. XII.
17. Columnar Edict No. VI and VII.
18. Great Stone Edict, No. XII.
19. This is in the *Columnar Edict* No. VII and in the *Great Stone Edict* No. V.
20. *Great Stone Edict*, No. III.
21. *Ibid.*, No. VII.
22. *Ibid.*, No. IX.
23. *Ibid.*, No. V.
24. *Kalinga Stone Edict.*
25. *Great Stone Edict*, No. V and XII.
26. So it appears *"parisa"* must be translated.
27. *Columnar Edict*, No. IV.
28. *Small Stone Edict*, No. I. It is questionable whether here is meant men or gods and the Rupnath version could well be translated "the Gods, who he (the king) had taken to be true prove themselves to be false." Meanwhile, the opposition of the king to the ruling stratum is presupposed in the nature of the case.
29. *Great Stone Edict*, No. X.
30. *Small Stone Edict*, No. I, Rupnath version.
31. Two hundred fifty-six years after the renunciation of the world.
32. *Kalinga Stone Edict.*
33. The title in *Siam* means "Teacher of Kings."
34. There was, in general, beyond the basic commandments not to kill, steal, commit adultery, lie, drink alcohol, still the avoidance of dance, song, theatre, and certain scents and perfumes, and definite subsistence regulation. Especially serviceable was voluntary chastity. The earlier cited lay-decalogue could have been the source of this lay ethic.
35. *Tehullavaggha*, XII.
36. Much is to be said for the reasons which L. de Milloué (*Annals du Musée* Guimet, *Bibl. de Vulgarisation*, Conference v. 18, XII, 1904) adduces to prove that the inscription and also otherwise untraceable King Kalashoka (the Black Ashoka) is identical with the known Buddhistic monarch, and that the council of Pataliputra (242 B.C.) called during the reign of this king was identical with the

council of Vaicali. The difficulties rest in the tradition. According to Mahayana tradition, the course of the council of Vaicali differed from Hinayana accounts. This would not be strange. But the questions which were before the council of Pataliputra under Ashoka have been transmitted and are not simply disciplinary in nature.

37. Namely, whether in the dioceses more Upasatha collections be permitted.

38. Not permanently, however, e.g., apparently not in the time of J-tsing's travels to India (seventh century).

39. The name was derived therefrom by Hiuen Tsang (By S. Julien, *Hist: de Hiuen-Tsang*, p. 159.

40. Ch. 34 of the translation of Takakusu, No. 9.

41. The *Lalita Vistara*, taught that a Bodhisattva can not be born of a barbarian or border person (but only on the holy earth of India), but only in an eminent caste (Brahman or Kshatriya). The older *Mahayan-Sutras* (translated in volume 49 of the *Sacred Books of the East*) expressly accepts as self-evident that only a "son from a good family" can achieve salvation.

42. Published by S. Beal, *Travels of Fah Hien and Sung Yun*, translated from the Chinese, London, 1869.

43. In Kingdom "Kie-che" *op. cit.*, Ch. V. p. 15.

44. Sung Yun by St. Julien *op. cit.*, p. 188.

45. *Op. cit.*, (Beal) p. 537.

46. *Op. Cit.*, p. 67.

47. *Op. cit.*, p. 103 f.

48. *Op. cit.*, p. 197.

49. By St. Julien, p. 109.

50. *Ibid.*, p. 111.

51. *Libres vulares*, translated by St. Julien.

52. *Ibid.*, p. 185.

53. *Ibid.*, p. 205.

54. By St. Julien, *Hiuen-Tsang*, p. 230 f.

55. It would be absolutely impossible within the frame of this description to undertake an analysis of the theology of (in J-tsing's times) at least eighteen Buddhistic schools and their branches. Hence, after much reflection the approach has been chosen which also "modernistic" Asiatic Buddhists choose: namely, to present in as rational a form as possible a theological school which is midway between the extremes. As anyone familiar with the literature can determine we have often allowed, in the form of presentation, for the book by "Suzuki" although it is adjusted to "Western" needs. *Outlines of Mahayana Buddhism*, (London, 1907).

56. In Christianity its nature may most easily be conceived in terms of the impersonal conception of the "Holy Ghost" which is similar.

57. This is greatly emphasized by Suzuki, *op. cit.*, p. 344.

58. Suzuki's citations of sources would at least seem to indicate this, however questionable the degree of diffusion of such conceptions in ancient times.

59. As by Suzuki.

60. Somewhat like gnostic love-heart.

61. Namely, between the ancient classical doctrine of *sarvastavida*, which maintained the reality of the external world (in the manner of the Saykhya school) and Vedantic influenced schools, which came close to the doctrine of cosmic illusion.

62. The first two, indeed, were never eliminated, but they played no role in the interests of ancient Buddhism.

63. These were still dominant in the lowest heavens where, for example, Vedic deities live and souls who through *karma* have been temporarily moved to heaven.

64. These prevail still in higher heavens where Buddhistic saints dwell.

65. Mahayanaistic literature is characterized by its luxuriantly indulgent agglomeration of delights, wonders, and saints. This is the case even in the somewhat old Mahayanaistic Buddha—Legend of *Lalita Vistara* (translated into German by Lefmann) wherein and against the still relatively simple description by Ashvagosha—in the conceivable unartistic, but specifically mystical—magical manner—wonders are piled up and jewels, light beams, lotus blossoms, and all kinds of plants and perfumes are employed in a way suggesting the literature of decadence of the type of Wilde (*Dorian Grey*) and Huysmans. In truth, a mystical crypto—eroticism is present. The description of the beauty of Theotokos in *Lalita Vistara* and the prescriptions of the Amithapa—mediation in the *Amitayur-Dhyana-Sutra* give opportunities for glowing erotical fervor, always with references to trinkets, flowers, and sultry beauties of all kinds.

66. Probably this doctrine has not been without influence in the origin of certain important conceptions in Lamaism (the doctrine of the *Khubligahs*). More on this point later.

67. The ethical demands which works such as the *Amitayur-Dhyana-Sutra* (*Sacred Books of the East*, Vol. 49)—important for the mission of Mahayana in China and Japan—were moderate and graduated to need. Indeed, whoever does evil and is stupid falls at worst into the hell from which the imploration of Buddha Amitayur may save him. Whoever does evil, but at least does not malign Mahayana teaching, is already better off. Whoever is good to his family and practices benevolence fares still better. Still better is he who observes the ritual prohibitions and is discreet at the proper times. Greater bliss is attained by whoever believes the right doctrine (*karma* determinism), does not malign the Mahayana doctrine, and strives for

the highest qualities. Still more favorable is the fate of one who knows the meaning of Mahayana teaching by heart and does not speak ill of it. The pure land—the western paradise of late Buddhistic religion—will be reached by whoever either practices meditation or studies the Sutras of the Mahayana school or finally possesses the "loving heart" of the pure. (S., The steps of perfection, *op. cit.*, par. 22-30.)

68. The schools of the bordering lands of Northern India in the time of the Chinese pilgrimages, the Samatya and Mahasthavira, were held to be founded by Shudras. Both were subdivisions of the Vaibachia, which represented the ancient church. (Outside these there were not only the Madhyamika school of Nargarjuna, but also the Sutrantika [ritualists] and Yogachara.)

The Missions

1. The basic work on Ceylon by Trennant (5th Edition, 1860) was unfortunately not available to me. In Kern's *Geschicte des Buddhismus* may be found an account of the monastic history. Very instructive concerning the organization of monasteries is the official report by Bowles Daly (*Final Report on the Buddhist Temporalities Ordinance,* 1894). For the rest, Spencer Hardy's *Eastern Monarchism* is basic.

2. Unfortunately, the translations of Gregory were unavailable to me.

3. Especially the Mahavamsa.

4. As in Tibet, so also in Ceylon, apotropaic and exorcistic speech was systematically taught.

5. For both inscriptions see Furneau, *Le Siam ancien* (*Annales du Musée Guimet*, 27, 129, 187.)

6. See the inscription still to be discussed. *Op. cit.*, p. 233 (thirteenth century).

7. *Op. cit.*, p. 14.

8. *Op. cit.*, p. 144 (fifteenth century); inscriptural mention is made of a *mahasangharaya* (head of a congregation), p. 153, (sixteenth century) of the correct *Tri ratna*: *Buddha, dharma, sangha.*

9. *Op. cit.*, p. 171. This, too, is later than the great inscription of the thirteenth century which reports the introduction of writing and correct Buddhism.

10. Another king who bore the title of saint (*Shri*) (p. 21 f. *op. cit.*) had wished to be reborn as a *bhodisattva* in compensation for his merits. If this was denied him, then he wished to be reborn as a perfect and pious man and free from bodily illness.

11. See the great inscriptions of King Rama-Komhengs from the end of the thirteenth century. Furneau, *op. cit.*, 133 f. v. 85, 109.

12. *Ibid.*, verse 78.

13. *Ibid.*, verse 106.

14. See the opening of the inscription named; concerning the conquest of the king, its ending.

15. *Op. cit.*, verse 32.

16. *Ibid.*, p. 26. One should go directly to the king, not to the notables.

17. Cf. L. Furneau, *op. cit.*, p. 57.

18. Vgl. the inscriptions which Aymonier has published in *Journal Asia,* (1899) 9, Ser. 14, 493 ff and especially *ibid.*, (1900) 15, 146 ff (from the fifteenth to the seventeenth century). Some examples were used above.

19. *Op. cit.*, p. 16 f.

20. *Op. cit.*, p. 164.

21. *Op. cit.*, p. 153.

22. *Op. cit.*, p. 154.

23. *Op. cit.*, p. 170.

24. *Op. cit.*, p. 150.

25. *Op. cit.*, p. 151.

26. It is quite inaccurate to view Mahayanaism as the single representative of the missionary tendency in East Asia. China learned the holy writings of Buddhism first in the form known as it appears in the school of Sarvastivadas, a sect of the ancient Hinayanistic Vaibachika-doctrine, and the oldest students, partially the seafaring pilgrims, made little distinction between Mahayana and Hinayana. However, the fact that North India increasingly became Mahayanistic, the imported works to China and written in Sanskrit established Mahayana doctrine in the usual position. China was just in the process of developing into a pure continental state. On the other hand, there was no original dominion of the Hinayana school in Hinter India. Here, by contrast, most of the Mahayana missions were older. Later revivals in the traditions of the orthodox and neighboring church, the Ceylonese, were decisive.

27. The court of the emperor in Kyoto was correctly Shintoist. The purely secular Shogun in Yedo, however, could never take the place of a *tshakravati,* like Ashoka for he expressly recognized the emperor as a socially superior power.

28. The discussions and arguments were gathered from the annals of the Sung Dynasty by Edkins. With great conscientiousness the Confucian annalists listed every indulgence of Buddhism as suspicious and as a sign of weakness and a fruit of death. This was also done by the Manchu emperor Kuangti in the history of the Ming Dynasty.

29. Vgl., on this also, R. F. Johnston, *Buddhist China* (London, 1913).

30. It appears that the pilgrim Fa-Hien (around 400) in a time of distress at sea called on Kwan-yin.

31. Translated in the *Sacred Books of the East,* Vol. XXI by Kern (*The Lotus of the True Law*).

32. Running around a table with a cult object at a given sign with increasing speed and eventually driven with a whip.

33. According to Hackmann, *op. cit.,* p. 23. Based on personal observation against de Groat *op. cit.,* p. 227.

34. Concerning Korea, in addition to the current literature see the travel descriptions of Chaille-Long-Bey in the *Annales du Musée Guimet,* Vol. 26.

35. Both German authors, who have, out of personal intuition and exact knowledge of the Japanese language, provided the most reliable descriptions of the spiritual and material development of Japanese culture are (for the first) K. Florenz and (more for the second) K. Rathgen. The very serviceable book of Nachod resting on translations, namely, the old Kojiki and Nihongi "Annals" (first translated by Chamberlain into English, later by Florenz into German), which is basic for Japanese cultural history, however, is not essential for our special purpose. Some individual citations will be given later. Among legal sources Otto Rudorff in the supplementary Volume V of *Mitteil, der D. Ges. F. Natur-und Völkerkunde Ostasiens* (1889) published the very famous *Tokugava-Edikte.*

36. There is a very lovely sketch by Florenz in *"Kultur der Gegenwart."* Also valuable, because it rests on personal observation, is the popular representation by Hackmann in *Religionsgeschicte. Volksbuchern* (III, Reihe 7, Heft).

37. Apart from the decisive factual circumstances mentioned in the text, the epigraphic material which is always decisive for judgment was not available to me in translation. Also, unfortunately, the Transactions of the Asiatic Society of Japan were not available to me.

38. On this is the good collective representation of M. Courant (*Les Clans japonais sous les Tokugava* in the *Annales du Musés, Bibliotheque de Vulgarisation.* 1904, T. XV).

39. Cf. Haas in the *Zeitschrift fuer Missionskunde und Religionswissenschaft,* 1905.

40. *Sacred Books of the East,* Vol. 49.

41. *Ibid.*

42. *Ibid,* 41.

43. See the Census Report on Bengal, 1901.

44. Concerning Lamaism, Köppens *Religion des Buddha,* (Berlin, 1857-58) is always worth reading. The contemporary, most widely significant authority is Grünwedel. (See his material in *Kultur der Gegenwart* I, 3, 1 and writings to be cited later. In general, the Rus-

sian literature is basic, but it was not available to me.)

45. The name of this "great teacher" who was "born from the lotus" (*padmasambhava*), as he was called officially, is not known.

46. Grünwedel, *Mythologie des Buddhismus in Tibet und der Mongolei* (Führe durch die Lamaistische Sammlung des Fursten Uchtomski) Leipzig, 1900. The book gives by far the best developmental history of Lamaism and is generally used here.

47. The following is essential according to *Posdnjejews Otscherki byta buddijstkich monastyriei budijstkawo duchowenstwaw Mongolii* (it was not available to me). The decisive points, however, are contained in numerous translated citations by Grünwedel, *op. cit.*

48. In practice, this duty of the Dali Lama has fallen into disuse so far as the very simple procedure was employed: the Dali Lama hardly comes of age before he is poisoned as, for example, occurred in 1874.

49. Concerning the Potala von Lhasa, the great work of Percival Landon, *Lhasa* (London, 1905) comes into consideration; it was written on the basis of findings of the English expedition. Good descriptive material on the normal monastery appears in the travel description of Filchner's concerning the monastery Kumbum on the upper Huang ho (*Wissenschafliche Ergebnissase der Expedition*, Filchner I, 1906).

50. Filchner maintains that every third son must become a Lama.

51. Hackmann relates that the reception of too important novitiates by the monks is occasionally resisted for they feel their power position would be threatened.

52. Namely, the so-called "holy trade" of the Lama is known, a continual trade corresponding to the obedience of the laity; each time a valuable object is exchanged somewhat as follows: for a silk veil, a sheep, for this a horse, and so forth. A kind of reverse "Hans in Glück" (Vgl. Filchner *op. cit.*).

53. The instruction was guided by a Hutuktu. The faculty officials were all changed in one to three years. Each faculty had three.

54. Filchner found fifteen students so engaged in Kumbum.

55. Filchner found 300 students for this in Kumbum; the business is very profitable.

56. The themes were often of more than "talmudic" scurrility (Filchner *op. cit.*).

57. By far the best introduction among German works is Grünwedel's much quoted work.

58. Filchner himself did not believe this was done by the Lamas themselves, that the individual only believed in his own particular magical power.

59. Filchner, *op. cit.*

The Orthodox Restoration in India

1. Of new work on the Indian religious sects see particularly E. W. Hopkins, *The Religions of India* (Boston and London, 1895). Of modern Hindu works see particularly Jogendra Nath *Bhattacharya* (presiding pandit), *Hindu Castes and Sects.* (Calcutta, 1896)—extremely anti-sect. For a short sketch see M. Philipps, *The Evolution of Hinduism,* (O. Madras, 1903). Of older works Barth *op. cit.*, and the serviceable writing by Wilson.

2. On this see O. Franke, *Pali und Sanskrit* (Straszburg, 1902). Pali is the speech of ancient Buddhism, of the Singalese canons, the edicts of Ashoka in the third century B.C. apparently in general of educated "Aryans" of North India. According to Franke, the speech stems from Vedic Sanskrit and has its origin in Ujjain, the territory where Ashoka was located as princely state holder and the birthplace of his wife. Franke seeks to prove that the Kashmir and the Himalaya region was the origin of the secondary and literary speech of figured Sanskrit. In these areas it was first employed in kingly inscriptions and in the literary and monumental memorials of the Mahayanists, Jains and Brahmans, in the neighborhood of Mathura (the land on the Ganges and Jamuna). Since the 1st century B.C. penetrating them further South and East for political reasons with the importation of Brahmanhood. Sylvian Levy (*Journal As.* 1902, 1, 96 ff) translated commentary by Burgess (Ind. Antiq. 33, 163 ff) indicates that the penetrating barbarian dynasties—particularly the (religiously indifferent) Kshatrapas, in contrast, for example, to the orthodox Brahman Satakarnis (which composed and edicted in Prakrit)—employed Sanskrit until, under the (confessionally tolerant, through praying to Brahmanical deities) Gupta Dynasty in the fourth century, Sanskrit became the universal literary speech in North India. Be that as it may, it remains highly probable that the magical significance of the old holy speech, which occasionally also appears with the Buddhists, played an important role in its reception. This Levy also assumes.

3. It appears too that Hindu princes extol themselves for never having killed "outside war," in their calling. The orthodox Indian dualism, thus, is not between "political" and "private" ethic but only an instance of the specialization of *dharma,* indeed according to the spheres of behavior.

4. The confirmation of a king's son (Mahadagaputra) as a member of the Vishnu sect was conceived to be the occasion for a foundation. *Ep. Ind.* IV, 96 f.

5. The bitter struggle in the course of these events will not be described here and in general, the available documentary material can be described only incompletely. The events left numerous traces

in the monuments. The struggle took place not only between Buddhistic and Jainistic orthodox sects but between single Brahman schools as well. An example must suffice. The destruction by Shivaists of a Jain Temple in whose place the *lingam* was erected is mentioned *Ep. Ind.* V. p. 285.

The merchants and traders of a city founded (*Ep. Ind.* I, p. 269) a monastery for Shiva ascetics, and a school with a land endowment for the diffusion of Brahmanical knowledge is mentioned. The respective Brahman is "strikingly equipped in Samkhya doctrine" and an "independent thinker in tantristic doctrine," he "knows the Vedas," is trained in mechanics, art, music, and poetry and in the Vaiseska system. The great revival of Shivaism under the Western Chalukya Dynasty was especially described in an inscription for the twelfth and thirteenth century (*Ep. Ind.* V. p. 213 ff). It is said of one of the grandfathers of the hereditary Shiva priests, *Smasavara* that he understood self-control, meditation, immovable acstasy, silence, prayer formula, deep contemplation, and was of good character with deep devotion for Paramesvara (Shiva). While most people understand logic, or rhetoric, or dramatics or poetry or grammar alone, Samasvara had mastered them all. He had mastered the Nyaya and Smakhya systems. He was learned in the monastic schools: Nayaya, Vaiseska, Mimasta, Samkhya and—astonishingly, Buddha or Buddhistic philosophy, even the *Puranas*. Also a universal "interconfessional" educational form, *Ibid.*, p. 227. Disputations with enemies is mentioned. Moreover, there appears a founder of a Shiva sect of whom it is said that he was "an underwater fire in the sea of Buddhism," a "thunderbolt in the mountains of Mimamsa." He cut down the great tree of Lokayatas. He slew the great snake of Samkhya. He laid an axe on the roots of the tree of Advaita (Vedanta) philosophy. He destroyed the Jains. Against the Nayagikas he provided protection. He was himself a Vishnuist in discernment, a Shivaist in clarity as to things. *Ibid.*, p. 255 mentions a hot disputation with the Jains, out of this, however, emerged the founder of the *lingam* sect Basava, (*Ep. Ind.* V, 23 and *op. cit.*, 23) raising his sect in strong opposition to all others, especially the Jains.

Ep. Ind. IV, 12 the Vishnu Sect founder Ramanuga is named as the representative of "true Dravida-teaching" and "he taught against those representing the doctrine of illusion" (Vedantists).

Indications of a princely established religious speech are found also in numerous inscriptions. An important means of propaganda were the beautiful holy hymns of *bakti* religiosity developing, in great numbers according to expert judgment, around the seventh century in South-Indian Tamil literature. The holy signers and teachers who visited the court were almost always bearers of the reaction. Under kingly auspices Buddhism was broken. However, so too, in short order, was the community organization of Jainism as well. This has occurred in South India almost everywhere since about the ninth century. Both were, at their roots, intellectual soteriologies.

6. See Winternitz, p. 448.

7. This, of course, may be said only with qualifications. The intellectuals remained predominantly either of the view that behind these highest gods there was an impersonal spiritual foundation or they were themselves turned into semi-depersonalized powers.

8. The Buddhists and Jains of ancient times not rarely have Shivaistic or Vishnuistic names, hence, Bühler with justice concluded that the cult of these gods is ancient.

9. Concerning the scientific influence of *tantra literature,* see references above.

10. "Wine and women are the five-fold *mukara* and take all sins away" is a saying of the orgiastics.

11. The unfortunate thing about British accounts is that the authors almost always perorate about this "abominable practice" in the usual, puritanically prudish manner instead of giving an accurate account of the actual events, permitting one to obtain an accurate picture of its meaning, (or they simply deny its existence as, for example, does the *Encyclopedia of India* in many of its articles and as, in general, do cultivated Hindus.

12. The castes of the "left hand" include particularly the earlier mentioned *parschsala* (five trades) of king's craftsmen: smiths, carpenters, coppersmiths, stone masons, goldsmiths; then the Beri-Sethi, apparently old guild merchants; further the Devangada: weavers, Gnaigar; oil pressers, Gollnur; potters, Palayan (Pariah); the earlier weavers but now landlords, Beda; fowlers and Madiga; tanners and shoemakers.

The Brahmanical castes of the "right hand" include, outside the members of the Bankjar (wholesale merchants), apparently immigrants from North India, Komati (shopkeepers), Gujarati (bankers from Gujarat), Kumhar (potters), Rnagajeva (color and calico printers), Naindu (barbers), Jotiphana (oil pressers with oxen) and the Okhalaya (a landlord class) also the lower class of the Kurubar (shepherds), Agasa (washers), Besta (fishermen and umbrella porters), Padma Sharagava (weavers) Upparava (dam builders), Chitragara (painters), and part of the Palayan caste called Wallia. In the last case the rift also goes through the middle of the caste (Paria). Those adhering to Buddhism (to which presumably the castes of the left hand belong) present no grounds for fusion. The castes of the left hand simply have not accepted Brahmans for priests (rather than their own shamans) and have not given up their old orgiastic cult practices or had not at least at the time of the schism; today they are suppressed.

13. The union of the phallic fertility cult with rites for overpowering the originally predominant sickness demons serving Rudra seems already have been accomplished before the Mahabaratha.

14. In Brahmanical ritual, calling on the sun is retained (Surya in the *Rigveda*), though indeed, pure sun worshipers (*Saura*) first make their appearance under the influence of immigrant Mithra priests at about the beginning of our era.

15. There may still be at least eighty million Hindus who are only *lingam* worshipers.

16. Mazumdar (J.R.A.S. 1907, 337) among other things takes issue with Rhys Davids because all passages of the *Mahabaratha* which mention the cult are interpolations.

17. Concerning him, see Kshinath Trimbuk Telang in *Ind. Antiquity*, Vol. 5.

18. *Vishnu Purana*, III, 9 f.

19. According to an immense number of inscriptural documents, this was the established rule by all monasteries and schools of higher education.

20. For example, (for a temple) an inscription, from about the eighth century, which is published in *Ind. Antiq.*, (1891, XX, 289) wherein a (*Vishnuistic*) Tamil king confirmed an "agreement" with a "patron" (founder) of a temple and thereby decreed that at the threat of punishment of confiscation of his wealth each founder must remain in the service of the god and may serve no other. Also a forceful union into parishes was decreed. Educated priests could be formed into an order only by force.

21. In the oldest example (for a Buddhistic temple) in the inscription *Ep. Ind.* II, 87 f., out of about the third century B.C., a committee (*bodhagothi*) was created for administration of the Buddha cult. For a Hindu temple in the ninth century A.D., *Ep. Ind.* I, 184, horse handlers from different areas came together and imposed an assessment on themselves, the proceeds of which were to be distributed by quotas to different holy establishments. The administration choose a *panchayat* of *goshthikas* from esteemed members and of whom the most important (*desi*) served as representative of the association to the outside.

22. So in the Shivaist inscription of a Kanaug king of the tenth century, *Ep. Ind.* III, 263.

23. Modern Buddhism.

24. In this, as in general so many of the preceeding observations, see R. G. Bhandakar, *Vaishnavism, Saivism and minor Religious Systems*, in Bühler's Grundrisz (Straszburg, 1913).

25. To the Shivaists also belong (so far as they were Hindu) the robber sects which to Kali, a female deity of Shiva, brought a division of the booty and made human sacrifice. Among them were some which—like the Thugs—do not let blood on ritual ground and sacrifice always by strangulation (Hopkins, *op cit.*, p. 493, Amm. I, p. 294 Amm. 2) according to the letter of a British officer of the 30 years. Concerning the sadistic Durga-orgies see p. 491 Amm. 2 and p. 492 Anm. 2). The usual form of the representation of Shiva and the Shivaistic goddess, a mixture of obscenity and wild bloodiness, hangs together with this form of orgiasticism.

26. The *Basava Purana*, the fundamental writing for this, is not translated. Unfortunately, the special literature of the sect was also unavailable to me.

27. The opposition of the sect to the Brahmans was so sharp that one village community denied the digging of a village stream because there a Brahman would be able to make his dwelling (and would be able to have ritualistically pure water at his disposal).

28. The upper caste called itself Vira-Shiva-Brahmana. The priests and traders (out of the Baniya caste) constituted the first stratum, handworkers and oil pressers followed, finally, the impure caste. Intermarriage between the castes no longer occurred; rather the lower castes had become endogamous.

29. This indentification was apparently already complete in the time of Megasthenes (third century B.C.).

30. Grierson, *I.R. As. Soc.* 1907, 311. The view that something of the sort was established secondarily, possibly under the influence of the Nestorians (as has been maintained), permits no denial.

31. In the Chaitanya sects the steps of serviceability were: (1) *santi* (meditation), (2) *dasya* (active service of God), e. *sakhya* (feelings as for a father), finally, (5) *madhurya* (feeling as that of a girl for her beloved)—a specifically feminine habitus as well.

32. Christianity is ascertainable without any doubt in the sixth century in South India, in the 7th century in North India.

33. On this see Grierson, *I.R.A.S.* 1908, 337 f. Grierson has also translated the modern theological work of Pratapa Simha (of 1866) (I.R.A.S. 1908). Grierson's contention (I.R.A.S. 1911, 800) that *bhakti* was first preached in South India is disputed and hardly acceptable.

34. The comparison employed is that of a hired laborer (who works for pay) who has to make good the damage if he destroys anything. On the other hand, when a house slave destroys anything the master must stand the damage. (The Evangelists had a similar comparison in mind when they said, concerning the work claims: "They had their pay therein.")

35. The same may be seen, for example, in the *Aphorisms of Sandilyas, I.R.A.S.* 1907, 330.

36. A Viaschnawa inscription from the thirteenth century (*Ep. Ind.* VII, 198) states "I have no need for gain nor the accumulation of riches, and none whatsoever for sensual lusts. What will come, O God, let it correspond to the foregoing behavior. This alone I ask; also in the future let me worship undiminished at your holy lotus feet"; also the possession of a worshipful godliness as a personal goal. At the same time, the inscription represents that inactive life-attitude, typical of a pure belief-religiosity (also including Lutheranism).

37. Also at least in South India Shivaism intensively practiced *bhakti.* It was the main seat of a strong asceticism partly resting on this foundation. Here Shiva constituted a God to whom one had access only through grace, not through service. Not Vedantic means but only his acceptance made salvation possible. Thus the competition with Vishnu was especially sharp. (See Senathi Raga from the 8th Oriental Congress, 1883, Bd. II, p. 291.)

38. Vishnu temple frescoes are less gruesomely fantastic; however, they are as plain and occasionally as crassly obscene as the Shivaistic frescoes.

39. An example of such work is provided by the *Vishnu Purana* (English translation by Wilson, 1864).

40. The name (that is, in the form of Baishnab) is partially that of small castes which developed through prebendalizations and secular rationalization, somewhat like those of the Yogins. In general, the strictness of the asceticism was less for the Vishnu monks than for the Shivaists—quite corresponding to the character of the religiosity. The Bairagi monks (Bairagi equals "free from the world") of Ramananda, gave the holy girdle at confirmation to all castes without differentiation. Later they tolerated nunconcubines and lived in their often large rice-monasteries in a somewhat secular manner.

41. Yet in South Indian Bhakti-Shivaism priestly power had few limits. (*Senathi Raja, op. cit.*)

42. In fact, its religion soon became essentially a belief in demons and *bhakti* became a magical means. Its holy books were compiled out of the *Puranas.*

43. In pronounced measure the Nager, which included the mass of Shudra peoples from Malabar, soldiers of thinking—by virtue of a furlough system—were peasants. Their cultural station was relatively high. They were mostly vegetarians and worshipers of Krishna and Rama.

44. The *gosains* of these merchant sects distinguished themselves through reliability insofar as they had a fixed tariff for their services; for example, for permission for the drinking of the bath water of the

guru, seventeen rupees, for the privilege of "being closeted with him in the same room," 50-100 rupees, (Jogendra Nath Battacharya, *op. cit.,* p. 457).

45. In principle admission was open to all castes, outside the cobblers, tailors, washers and some of the lower barber castes; actually, only rich persons, essentially Banya.

46. Especially the Gujarati and Rastogi Banya.

47. *Rel. Sects of the Hindus* (London, 1861). The sources were not available to me for examination.

48. On him see Balfour's *Encyclopedia of India,* II, 766.

49. It may also be mentioned, that the Vishnuists were diffused geographically in an interesting manner in relation to the universally diffused Shivaists. This was in such manner that the followers of the Ramanujas and Madhavas were especially in Decan; the others, indeed, the Vallabhas, were found in India proper, especially in the West; the Chaitanyas in Bengal; the "Ramas" proper, the Ramandi-sect also were generally diffused in North India. This geographic diffusion was, so far as may be determined, essentially conditioned by political circumstances. The relatively weak representation of the Vishnuists in the South had its foundation in the fact that the Peschwar (s.o. I. p. 66s.) in Mahrattas empire was a Shivaist.

50. The decisive facts may be found most conveniently in Jogendea Nath Bhattacharya, *op. cit.*

51. The extreme limit for the Brahmans may be seen in the not completely degraded "Sat-Shudra" caste, whose gifts under some circumstances may be taken—in Bengal if they are sufficiently large! However, there are always the "Ashudra pratigahi" from whom nothing may be accepted, the most outstanding and scorned of the "Shudra yajaka."

52. So the generally rich priests of certain famous pilgrimage places in Benares.

53. So a Srimukh of the abby of Shringeri decided as to the membership of a particular group of Mysore Brahmans of the caste.

54. Shringerie, for example, took into consideration all orthodox Shivaists in South India, for whom the monastery had power of excommunication.

55. So the members of the Sapta Sati, an immigrant sib in Bengal in the seventh century before King Adisaur, or the "panch gaur" the five, most distinguished North Indian sibs.

56. For the high noble Kulin Brahmans in Orissa for example, stemming from the sixteen shashan villages (old king's foundations) composed exclusively of Vaidika, Sanskrit education was held to be indifferent.

57. Against this it is possible that these "Niyogin" are to be distinguished from the Vaidika Brahman priests.

58. In North India "secular" Brahmans can often receive *dakshina* as *gurus;* this always refers to Brahmans of lower rank.

59. The old Bengal brewer caste (now mostly merchants) was abstinent and chaste.

60. The resentment over this may be seen plainly enough in the cited book by J. N. Bhattacharyas, an upper pandit, loyal adherent of the English dominion and the caste order, and hater of plebeian *gurus.*

61. On this point see J. S. Speyer, Z.D.M.Z. (1913) 67 p. 347 concerning the edition of the Sang Hyang Kamehayanikam by I. Katz (Kon. Inst. V. D. Taal-, Land-en Volkenkunde v. Ned. Indie 1910). The Buddhistic ethic has been reduced to rudiments. (Instead of monastic chastity, for example, procreation is prohibited in the neighborhood of holy objects.) Whoever has achieved *prajna* (the highest wisdom) through *puja* (worship of Buddha), *Yoga,* meditation over the *mantra,* and unconditional obedience of the *guru,* is forbidden no sort of enjoyment (Strophe 37 of the poem).

62. Evidence of the strong belief in fate appears not only in the detailed legends which have as a theme the irreversability of events, but also in folkwisdom (by Liebich, *Sanskrit-Lehrbuch* (Leipzig, 1905) for example, p. 274-75. No. 87, 80, 93). *Karma* alone, the deeds of a previous life establishes indubitably the fate of men as well as gods (*Ibid.,* Nr. 88, 93, 96, 101) is throughout in accord with proverbial wisdom.

63. Among sources made accessible by Liebich, *op. cit.* in translation occasionally the words appear: p. 281, Nr. 14 either love or the woods (asceticism). One has wasted his life who has neither thought of Shiva nor has experienced love (p. 229, Nr. 11) who has neither wisdom nor riches, nor piety, nor eroticism (p. 305, Nr. 4x) who has possessed neither knowledge nor military fame, nor has possessed beautiful girls (p. 313, Nr. those with especially beautiful figures) and thereby (p. 319 concluding verse of the collection and other passages) coordinated these different values into the best possible whole. Also the gods Shiva, Brahma, and Vischnu appear as "slaves" of the god of love (p. 278, Nr. 1). On the other hand Shiva appears as the enemy of wives (p. 283, Nr. 83) and the god of love (p. 301, Nr. 29) or as chastiser of these (p. 313, Nr. 90). This all corresponds to the organic relativism of all Indian ethics mentioned earlier and illustrated from some of the monuments.

64. So according to the meritorious indologist Grierson. See on this, and against it, the introduction by Blunt in the Census Report (United Provinces) of 1911.

65. Perchavel: Ram, Ram Satya Rama (Vishnuist).

66. Generally in such cases, a "highest" God is venerated, then the old Parmesvara.

67. See the passages by Liebich *op. cit.*, p. 265, No. 40, 41.

68. *Ibid.*, No. 43.

69. The special Indian form of the accumulation of great wealth is best illustrated by the good fortune of Vaidika who in the thirteenth century was called to Kotalihapur by a Raja on whose house roof a dead goose had fallen. He was wanted to avoid the negative consequences of this bad omen. In addition to immense fees for expensive ceremonies, he received in thanks gifts of land and the position of Zamindar—all to such extent that the family until recently was reckoned as the richest in Bengal.

Occasionally a business was made of Panchatantra (see the passages by Liebich, *op. cit.*, p. 99) and other forms of gaining wealth were practiced (namely, begging, king's service, agriculture, wisdom, usury). As forms of trade there were, in addition grocery trade, deposits and receiving deposits, community management, trading with strangers, and the transport of goods. Gain through the quoting of false prices and through the use of false weights and measures and equivalent forms was subject to strong opposition by Jain ethic as was the case for the Puritans.

The General Character of Asiatic Religion

1. See the already cited *Mahasutasomajataka* in the translation by Grünwedel, *Buddhist. Studien.* V. D. Kgl. M. f. Völkerk, Berlin V. S. 37 f.

2. Only in this sense can one accept Percival Lowell's spirited development of the thesis of "Impersonality" as the foundation of the East Asian mind (*The Soul of the Far East,* Boston and New York, 1888). His dogma of the "monotony" of Asiatic life rests on the mentality of an American and certainly would be a source of astonishment to all East Asiatics. Concerning the peculiar kernel of the "monotony," a citizen of the United States could well consult James Bryce as the valid classical witness.

3. In India, April was the time for the assumption of a life of wandering mendicancy as a ritual duty for the members of the lower castes.

4. Namely, for our consideration the hereditary neurology of the presumably strong tendency toward hysteria and auto-hypnosis of the Indian would be relevant. It is questionable as to how far differences of disposition are in fact basic to an art of technical neuropathic ecstasy.

5. It is not the case, as Percival Lowell opines, that it is char-

acteristic that Chinese invention (indeed not all) is in service of art and not economically attuned. Also for us, experiment was born in art and belongs to it. Also in Asia military technique and therapeutic purposes were important for most "inventions." However the rationalization of experimentation by art and its diffusion from art to science was decisive for occidental development. Not "impersonality" but, rationally evaluated, the "lack of causality" was the thing, which in the East restricted, thc so-called "progress" to professional rationality.

INDEX

(Since the bibliographical references are not contemporary the footnotes have not been indexed. They are valuable primarily for reference to Max Weber's source materials.)